A Concise History of Australian Wine

John Beeston

A Rathdowne Book
ALLEN & UNWIN

First published in 1994

A Rathdowne Book
Allen & Unwin Pty Ltd
9 Atchison Street
St Leonards NSW 2065, Australia

National Library of Australia
cataloguing-in-publication data

Beeston, John
A concise history of Australian wine.

Includes index.
ISBN 1 86373 621 2

1. Wine and wine making—Australia—History. 2. Wine industry—Australia—History. I. Title.

641.220994

Designed by Guy Mirabella
Set in Berkeley Old Style
Printed by SRM Production Services SDN BHD, Malaysia

10 9 8 7 6 5 4 3 2

Contents

Introduction

Australia's awareness of wine has grown tremendously in the past thirty years so it seems only fitting, a few years after the bicentenary, that Australia should be more conscious of its wine history.

This book is an introduction to the history of Australian wine and of necessity deals with its pioneers—some of whom were proselytes of wine as a measure of temperance in the ongoing 19th century battle against 'ardent spirits', while others came upon wine simply as an alternative crop and prospered in their endeavours. It deals also with some of the political and economic events which created the Australian society we know today and the effect of those events on our wines and winemakers.

A Concise History of Australian Wine is not intended to be exhaustive or encyclopaedic in any way, but a readable and common-sense account of what to me is a subject of enduring interest.

John Beeston

ONE

A climate so favourable

> In a climate so favourable the cultivation of the vine may doubtless be carried to any degree of perfection, and should no other articles of commerce divert the attention of the settlers from this part, the wines of New South Wales may perhaps here after be sought with civility and become an indispensible [sic] part of the luxury of European tables . . .

So wrote Captain Arthur Phillip RN, first governor of the infant colony of New South Wales in an early letter to the colonial secretary, Lord Sydney.

Scarcely two and a half years after settlement at Sydney Cove, the colony's first chaplain, the Reverend Richard Johnson, was hardly less optimistic when he wrote to his friend Mr Henry Fricker in August 1790.

> Vines, I think will do in time, better if the climate were hotter, but as they do not require the most rich soil, we are in hopes of seeing these turn to some account, and I promise you, if ever wine be made here and not prohibited from being exported, I will send you a specimen and perhaps may drink your health in a Bumper of New Holland Wine.

Amongst the many shrubs and plants carried by the eleven ships of the First Fleet were the seeds of the 'claret' grape and several rooted vines, which were planted within a few days of arrival in a makeshift garden next to the Governor's tent in a spot thought to be a few metres from the eastern end of what is now Bridge Street in the business heart of Sydney. Life in Sydney Cove, though hard by any standards of the time, was not to be without its expectations. By September 1788, Governor Phillip was growing optimistic about his garden.

> I have some oranges, figs and vines, pomme roses, apples, pears, sugar cane and strawberrys *[sic]*that I brought from Rio de Janeiro and the Cape in fine order so that I hope a few years will give the luxurys *[sic]* as well as the necessarys *[sic]* of life . . .

Phillip's optimism was to prove unfounded; the vines, whatever variety they may have been, did not do particularly well in Sydney Cove. Despite Richard Johnson's forecast, the climate was too warm and humid in summer for *Vitis vinifera* ever to thrive on those harbour banks.

Rose Hill, later known as Parramatta, was the colony's first inland farming settlement, twenty-four kilometres west of Sydney Cove and, importantly, accessible by water. Because of its produce, it was a godsend for a semi-starving population and a chance for Phillip to bolster his earlier rosy assessment of the colony's prospects. Here, away from the humid coastal belt, the soil was richer and the climate drier, 'the most promising spot yet seen in our neighbourhood . . .' and 'the only hope of raising grain'. On 2 November 1788 the settlement party arrived. By December 1790 the Governor reported that 'the corn was exceeding good. About two hundred bushels of wheat and sixty of barley . . .' And the vine? In July 1790 Phillip had

> about a thousand cutting of Vines now in the ground and have had a few grapes . . . It is surprising to me how the Vines thrive and I am in hopes next year of having a Vineyard of five or six acres.

Which ground? He does not say whether it was his garden at Sydney Cove or the new settlement at Rose Hill, for though the first few berries would probably have come from his Sydney Cove garden, his proposal for a substantial vineyard of five or six acres (about two hectares) must surely have been intended for Rose Hill.

His vineyard visions were quickly reduced. Only a month later, in writing to Sir Joseph Banks to thank him for the promise of more vines he goes on

> the few [vines] that I brought from the Brazil and the Cape have increased so as to have put it in my power to send five hundred cuttings to Norfolk Island and I suppose we have two thousand in the ground here and at Rose Hill, where a Vineyard of two acres will be planted next year. Last year produced two good bunches of Grapes which may be mentioned as being the first this Country has produced, tho' being neglected they decayed on the Vine.

The vintage of 1791—'two bunches of grapes were cut in the Governor's garden from cuttings of vines brought three years before from the Cape of Good Hope'—though sparse was nevertheless handsome according to Captain Watkin Tench, the colony's first grape correspondent. He described the fruit 'of a moderate size, but well filled out; and the flavour high and delicious.'

That opinion of the colony's grapes was confirmed by no less a person than the young Elizabeth Macarthur, newly arrived in the colony. Her controversial husband John and sons James and William would, some twenty-five years later, become the colony's first visitors to the famous European vineyards. In March 1791, in a letter to her mother, Elizabeth noted that

> the Grape thrives remarkably well. The Governor sent me some bunches this season as fine as any I ever tasted and there is little doubt but in a very few years there will be plenty.

Vines were starting to impress the colony's small number of private settlers as well. Its first vigneron was most likely Phillip Schaffer, a German from Rheinhessen, 'never', according to Tench, 'professionally a farmer', but the son of an owner of 'a small estate on the banks of the Rhine, on which he resided' and where he assisted his father in his labours particularly in the vineyard. Schaffer took up his grant of 140 acres (fifty-six hectares) on 17 April 1791 at Rose Hill, now renamed Parramatta. Schaffer was indeed a man of industry, for barely eight months later, with the assistance of four convicts, he was cultivating over twelve acres (five hectares), the greater part sown to maize, a small part to wheat and 'one [acre] in vines and tobacco'. As the ever-observant Tench noted in his diary,

> his vines, nine hundred in number, are flourishing and will, he supposes, bear fruit next year. His tobacco plants are not very luxuriant. To these last two articles he means principally to direct his exertions. He says (and truly) that they will always be saleable, and profitable.

Even in 1791 in convict Parramatta, there were expectations of a bottle of wine and a good cigar.

The optimism of Tench and the persistence of Schaffer, or 'old Chiffer' as Captain William Paterson later called him, were to be rewarded; in 1795 he made, in all probability, the colony's first wine. As Paterson records in a letter of March that year to Sir Joseph Banks,

> old Chiffer has made this year from a small vineyard 30 rod [0.08 hectares] ninety gallons [10 litres] of wine in about two more I think we will not want to purchase either wine or brandy for common use, the vines I think produce better than at the Cape.

And its quality? If we may link Schaffer's wine with T. F. Palmer, one of the Scottish Martyrs, and an early brewer of maize beer, he commented six months later that 'the grape thrives, with the untmost luxuriance & wine tolerably good is already produced. This will be the staple article of commerce'.

The Vineyard, Rose Hill, c. 1798, where in all likelihood the first Australian wine was made in 1795. Artist unknown.

'Tolerably good' though it may have been, Schaffer produced little more wine, for two years later he sold 'The Vineyard' to Captain Henry Waterhouse RN for £140 ($280) and moved to Pittwater, married later and, according to Dr John Dunmore Lang, died a drunkard. 'The Vineyard' endured rather longer, later passing to Hannibal Macarthur, nephew of John, and later still to the Roman Catholic Church, in whose pastoral care it remained until 1958, as a convent, producing altar wine until it finally succumbed to the march of industry in the 1960s.

But what of Governor Phillip's public vineyard on his most favoured 'Crescent' site? The assiduous Tench remarked,

> Went round the cresent *[sic]*, at the bottom of the garden, which certainly in beauty of form and in situation is unrivalled in New South Wales. Here are eight thousand vines planted all of which in another season are expected to bear grapes.

Vintage 1792 produced three hundredweights (153 kilograms) of 'very fine grapes', the quantity 'next year' promising to be 'very considerable'. But Governor Phillip was not to report upon the ensuing vintage, leaving the colony an invalid on 11 December 1792, his health hourly growing worse and 'hoping that a change of air might contribute to his recovery'. His colony was still grasping for self-sufficiency, but more confident now in its agricultural endeavours.

When he left, not a drop of local wine had yet been made but, importantly, he had shown that grapes could flourish even in the hands of an invalid, botanically ignorant as he himself admitted, with the assistance of only a 'tollerably' good gardener. The climate had certainly justified his optimism. All that was needed was the will to succeed, the very persistence that Phillip Schaffer showed a little more than two years later.

TWO The Macarthur years

Though Captain Phillip had left Port Jackson weary of responsibilities and broken in health, in 1792 Lieutenant John Macarthur was just reaching his prime. Aged twenty-six, he settled near Parramatta on Elizabeth Farm, named in honour of his wife, and by 1793 had built a 'most excellent brick house with three acres [1.2 hectares] given to grapes and other fruit'. Macarthur thus became the colony's second recorded private vigneron.

What of the public domain? During the last years of the eighteenth century, the Crescent vineyard was apparently neglected. Understandably in a colony still only on the threshold of survival, wheat, meat and Indian corn were given priority. These years also saw the increasing use of spirits not only to slake thirsts but often as currency. This public intemperance was quite alarming to Governor King, who in the name of temperance encouraged the production of beer from local barley and ordered the replanting of the Crescent. In 1801 two French prisoners of war, encouraged by a salary of £60 a year, renewed the Crescent vineyard at Parramatta by planting 7000 vine cuttings. A further 5000 followed in 1802. In 1803 the Frenchmen made their first wine from the Parramatta vineyard, so poor according to contemporary accounts that local authorities decided not to ship samples to London. It was certainly not to the taste of Governor King who considered that his French prisoners 'knew very little of the business'. Nonetheless King persisted. Thirty acres (twelve hectares) near Castle Hill were prepared for planting in August 1803. Unfortunately the young vines or cuttings were blight-afflicted and did not flourish. Nothing more was done at Castle Hill.

In all likelihood there were many other Parramatta settlers with a few vines on their grants, but the only other record of a local farmer planting a vineyard in that area was of George Suttor in 1801. It failed. He was later to have much greater success with oranges and other fruit trees.

By 1803 the name 'Australia' was increasingly used for the continent Flinders had circumnavigated, and on 5 March the *Sydney Gazette* published (undoubtedly at the request of the Governor) the first Australian article on viticulture, offering practical advice on establishing a vineyard and making wine and brandy. It was obviously translated direct from the French without any regard for conditions in the southern hemisphere, for in it advice is given to prune the vines in January and February (midsummer!).

But who was taking notice? Perhaps a few emancipists, free settlers and retirees from the New South Wales Corps, interested in fresh fruit. Certainly not the mass of the population . . . the convicts and the soldiers who guarded them. Not only did the colonists not know how to make wine, very few of them knew how to drink it or how to appreciate it except for its alcoholic strength. For a vast majority—soldier, sailor, convict and trader—the vital victual was rum and it was that liquor that caused the whole structure of government in the colony to totter on its foundations in the first decade of the nineteenth century. For the time being, the colony ran on rum, lacking a group or social stratum that could not only afford but actually preferred to produce and drink wine.

The events of this first decade of the new century tell us little about wine, but they speak volumes about the character of John Macarthur. If there were a political or social pot to be stirred, Macarthur was ever ready with a vigorous ladle and always the first to be served. In 1801 he wounded Lieutenant Colonel Paterson—his commanding officer and the same Paterson who had reported on 'Old Chiffer'—in a duel and was sent to England for court martial. He avoided punishment, but did resign from the New South Wales Corps, at the same time persuading the British government, then faced with Napoleonic Blockade, that New South Wales was an ideal place for wool production. Having bought a flock of Spanish merinos from the Royal Stud and obtained a grant of five thousand acres and the promise of more land if he were successful in wool production, he selected land at Cowpastures, much to Governor King's displeasure. Needless to say, he was so successful with his sheep breeding that his estate, Camden Park, was to be the centre of wool growing and of tremendous importance to the economy of New South Wales for the next generation. It would also be the site of one of the first vineyards of importance in the colony, but not before Macarthur's political ardour had perforce been cooled.

By 1808 the 'rum' economy of New South Wales was vigorously fermenting. 'Rum', the common colonial name for any spirits, had become the currency of the colony, illegal tender for most goods and services at highly inflated prices and especially as payment for convict labour. The new governor, William Bligh, of the infamous *Bounty*, was determined to put a stop to it. Macarthur, his ladle deep in the 'rum' barrel, was arrested by Bligh and charged with sedition. Released by Major George Johnston, Commander of the New South Wales Corps and a former brother officer, Macarthur in turn persuaded Johnston to arrest Bligh, who thus suffered the indignity of his second mutiny and was held for over a year. Johnston immediately took the reins of government of the colony until replaced by the same Paterson who had been wounded by Macarthur eight years previously. Macquarie, the colony's fifth governor, arrived in late 1809 to replace Bligh who, now released and suitably aggrieved, journeyed to London to seek justice. Johnston, recalled and court-martialled, was cashiered, despite the testimony of Macarthur, who himself was warned not to meddle further in New South Wales politics. This 'warning', in effect an official exile from New South Wales, and the need to educate his sons, was to hold Macarthur in Europe until 1817.

Never one to let opportunity slip by, he put his enforced absence to good use, travelling widely in Europe during 1815 and 1816 with his teenage sons, James and William, 'for the express purpose', as William later wrote, 'of collecting vines and of obtaining information respecting their culture'. As he further relates,

> about thirty of the best varieties of vine (from six to twelve cuttings or plants of each) were entrusted to a nurseryman near London. In April 1817, this collection, or what was said to be this collection, was embarked with us.

When in October 1817 John Macarthur, an unlikely apostle of wine temperance if ever there was one (at this time, wine, as opposed to 'spirits', was widely regarded as a temperance beverage and Macarthur as an entrepreneur of 'rum' (spirits) was an unlikely apostle of wine), reached Sydney, the collection appeared to be thriving, but then the Macarthur luck evaporated, for in William's own words,

> after several years careful cultivation, the only sorts which we obtained were those now known as the Gouais (Folle Blanche), Muscat Noir, Black Hamburgh, Little Black Cluster, Miller's Burgundy and Sweet Water, of which all but the first three had been previously introduced to New South Wales.

So by the carelessness or 'knavery' of a nurseryman, as Dr Alexander Kelly was later to put it, Macarthur's diligence (or was it opportunism) had been thwarted and with it the first conscious effort to collect 'the best varieties of vine' for the colony of New South Wales. Those unfortunate vines, which Macarthur had planted at Camden Park, were table grapes—black muscat and black hamburgh; red wine grapes already in the colony, little black cluster (most likely a clone of pinot noir) and miller burgundy (pinot meunier); an unexciting white wine variety, gouais; and an all-purpose white variety, sweetwater (chasselas), suitable for wine or table but indifferent for both. Lesser men than the Macarthurs might have given up, but they persevered with their second-rate varieties, planted them in two vineyards in 1820, one at Camden Park and one at Penrith, and built a winery quite substantial for its day at Camden Park, where merino wool was certainly not intended to be a monoculture. Indeed the Camden Park winery under the tutelage of Macarthur's son, Sir William, was a leader amongst New South Wales wineries during the next fifty years. As for John Macarthur, he again became a leading political figure, being appointed to the New South Wales Legislative Council in 1825 and serving for seven years before his removal by Governor Bourke in 1832 for unsoundness of mind. He died in April 1834, wool not wine being his legacy. But his son's pragmatic interest in wine and vines was to be of inestimable worth to the infant wine industry of New South Wales.

THREE

Australia's wine explorers

If John Macarthur was one of the compelling personalities of the early years of Sydney Cove, so indeed was Gregory Blaxland, whose friend, Sir Joseph Banks, had reputedly influenced his emigration to Sydney in 1805. Like Macarthur, Blaxland rarely wasted an opportunity, so much so that during his voyage he stayed for a while in Madeira and also at the Cape, familiarising himself with vines and winemaking and indeed buying some vine cuttings at the Cape. On his arrival, he bought 'Brush Farm', near present-day Ermington to the north-west of Sydney, but like most of his contemporaries he was fascinated by commerce and, one suspects, by the rum trade, especially as one of his early mercantile activities was listed as distilling. Nonetheless his other major interest was cattle grazing and his quest for pastures new was one of his reasons for crossing the Blue Mountains in 1813 with Wentworth and Lawson. He was also a meticulous observer, identifying two 'blights' in his own vines, the first affecting young leaves and shoots by causing a burn or scald (perhaps modern blister mite) and the second appearing as a black spot on the grapes and preventing them from ripening (black spot or anthracnose).

In 1816 he enlarged his vineyard, which is commemorated to this day in the name 'Vineyard Creek' on Sydney's Victoria Road. There he reputedly raised the 'claret' grape from seed, but by the mid-1820s he was certainly growing and indeed vinifying only two varieties—'burgundy' (most likely pinot noir) and 'miller burgundy' (pinot meunier). In Busby's second book, *A Manual of Plain Directions for Planting and Cultivating Vineyards and for Making Wine* (p. 37), he states that the 'burgundy' grape was improperly called the 'claret' grape in Sydney at that time. Busby describes what must have been pinot noir as 'a small grape and the berries closely set on the bunch'. He further mentions that 'these two grapes are the only ones which Mr Gregory Blaxland has cultivated for several years in his vineyard at Brush Farm near Parramatta'.

In 1822, by shipping to London a quarter-cask of red wine (almost certainly a blend of pinot noir and meunier) containing a ten per cent brandy stiffener for the six-month voyage to London, Blaxland took up the challenge of the Royal Society of Arts, which had some years before offered a medal for the 'finest wine of not less than 20 gallons [ninety litres] of good marketable quality made from the produce of vineyards in New South Wales'.

It was received by the judges with modified rapture, being awarded a silver medal and adjudged to be

> a light but sound wine with much the odour and flavour of ordinary claret . . . The general opinion seemed to be that although the present sample from the inexpertness of the manufacturer and the youth of the wine, is by no means of superior quality, yet it affords a reasonable ground of expectation that by care and time it may become a valuable article of export.

With such faint encouragement, Blaxland again tempted the palates of the Royal Society of Arts in 1827. The following year they awarded him a gold medal for a wine 'decidedly better' than that of 1823 and 'wholly free from the earthy flavour which unhappily characterises most of the Cape wines'. Though Blaxland could scarcely be called a winemaker of commercial size by any modern standards, he was certainly the man who, according to Sir John Jamison, had 'the merit of being the first who cultivated the vine to the extent of making a few casks annually' and thus may be called the first commercial winemaker of New South Wales.

Though Brush Farm wine was to disappear into history, Camden Park and William Macarthur, vigneron, were just hitting their straps. In 1830, when his vines were 'five and six years old' (perhaps as old as ten, if the first had been planted in 1820), Macarthur made 250 gallons (1137 litres) of wine from one acre (0.4 hectares) of vines, though many of the grapes had been destroyed by a hail storm. That we know what wine was now being produced on a small commercial scale is due to James Busby, the meteor of Sydney's wine firmament during the 1820s.

Arriving in Sydney early in 1824 with his father John, a civil engineer and surveyor who later was to provide Sydney with its first permanent water supply, James had journeyed for some months before his arrival in 'the best wine districts of France, residing' for some time in the neighbourhood of Cadillac, a small town on the right bank of the Garonne not far from Bordeaux and immediately across the river from the more famous regions of Barsac and Sauternes. As he says in his *Treatise on the Culture of the Vine* (Sydney, 1825, p. xviii), he was 'under a strong impression of the importance to the colony of any increase of its exportable commodities' and had undertaken the trip 'with a view of acquainting himself with the cultivation of the vine for the making of wine' and '. . . to ascertain to what extent it might be profitably cultivated in New South Wales'. Upon his arrival he found a thriving and boisterous town of about ten thousand inhabitants, with 'many individuals and families of a different description from that of which the bulk of the colony formerly consisted' including 'men of enterprise and industry', the very stratum of society non-existent a generation before, settlers who could perhaps be persuaded to produce and consume wine in what Busby considered to be its proper social environment. It certainly was, in his opinion, a society in which 'ardent spirits' and 'muddling ale' had little part to play, but it remained an Anglo-

Celtic society, dependent upon wool as its chief export and little used to wine as a staple beverage. Busby seemed to feel that his mission in life was to change the drinking habits of colonial New South Wales.

Within months of his arrival, he had received a grant of 2000 acres (810 hectares) near Singleton in the Hunter Valley, at that time on the extremity of civilisation in New South Wales. He named his property 'Kirkton', though it is doubtful whether he ever saw it. Instead, he took up an appointment as principal of the Male Orphan School to establish an agricultural institute on 12 300 acres (nearly 5000 hectares) at Bull's Hill near Liverpool, then a small settlement to the south-west of Sydney, established by Governor Macquarie some thirteen years before. There he naturally specialised in viticulture and spent the next few years putting the theories expounded in his treatise into practice as he supervised the planting of the Orphan School vines. Whether due to stringent economic conditions or to his own proselytising personality, he lost his position at the school in 1827, but the vineyard came to fruition under the care of his successor, Richard Sadleir, ten gallons (forty-five litres) of whose 1830 vintage was taken to London by Busby in February 1831 when scarcely a year old. In an experiment obviously designed to see how the wine travelled, Busby had half of it put into pint (500 millilitre) bottles and the remainder into a small cask. On arrival, he found that some of the bottles had spoiled owing, he believed, to insufficient care in washing the bottles, but the wine in cask still on lees 'was perfectly sound', being pronounced by a 'very eminent Oporto wine merchant and a very respectable Bordeaux wine merchant to be a very promising wine'. The wine, obviously robust, stirred much interest, for the Bordeaux merchant showed it to some dinner-party guests, who felt it resembled port without brandy or at best burgundy, but certainly not Bordeaux. The port merchant offered the comment that though the wine was sound, it would soon turn sour, unless fortified with brandy. On his return to Sydney, Busby was obviously delighted to report that

> the writer has this day [25 October 1832] opened a bottle . . . brought back with him to Sydney, and has found it perfectly sound; and, in his opinion, a well flavoured and strong-bodied wine.

So Australia's second wine exporter had proved by his round trip of over 40 000 kilometres that Australian wine could certainly travel.

There is no doubt that his treatment by the Orphan School authorities rankled with Busby and though between 1827 and 1830 he occupied several government positions of middling importance, he always felt that he had a grievance to redress.

Despite this chip on his shoulder, on his return to Europe in 1831 he was to make arguably the greatest contribution to Australian viticulture in the nineteenth century. Before that journey, he wrote the first book on Australian viticulture and winemaking based on conditions in Australia. His second book, *A Manual of Plain Directions for Planting and Cultivating Vineyards and for Making Wine in New South Wales*, diplomatically dedicated to the Governor, Lieutenant General Ralph Darling, and distributed at the Governor's behest to each of the District Constables of the Interior, was an immediate success despite its solid mouth-filling title. Its practicality must have pleased its colonial readers as much as the untried theories of the first—*A Treatise on the Culture of the Vine and the Art of Making Wine*—had displeased them. Who could fail to be moved by what is the epitome of an Arcadian philosophy which reads as appealingly today as it did 160 years ago.

> The man who could sit under the shade of his own vine, with his wife and children about him and the ripe clusters hanging within their reach, in such a climate as this and not feel the highest enjoyment, is incapable of happiness and does not know what the word means.

Between September and December 1831, having interviewed his masters at the Colonial Office, Busby made an extensive tour of Spain and France, disembarking at Cadiz and immediately 'hiring a passage-boat to cross the Bay of Cadiz'. Landing at Port St Mary's, the port of Jerez de la Frontera, he tasted the local manzanilla, the *vin de pays*,

> a light pleasant beverage, having at the same time a mellowness and flavour, which . . . would after a little habit, procure for it the preference even of those who would find it insipid at the first trial.

Little escaped his notice. From the dimensions of the cellars, the solera system of sherry maturation, the 'amotillado *[sic]*' sherry abounding 'in the peculiar nutty flavour' and the albariza soils containing 'about 70 per cent carbonate of lime', every detail of Spain's Mediterranean viticulture and winemaking was absorbed. And not only viticulture; the olive trees were also scrutinised. In fact one feels that everything was minutely examined with a view to its usefulness in New South Wales. It is a scrutiny not entirely without flaw for Busby observes how 'the settler of New South Wales could adopt with advantage . . . the hedge of prickly pear' so prevalent there. He was never to see how much more prevalent it would become when introduced to Australia.

He also met all the right people, not, one suspects, because he was any kind of social climber but because they were aware of the problems that might be encountered in commercial agriculture and winemaking. Thus he hobnobbed with Don Jacobo Gordon and Don Pedro Dumeque, whose families are famous sherry makers to this day. But it was the varieties of grape and methods of viticulture and winemaking that provided the obvious inspiration for his travels. Thus he stresses the importance of pedro ximinez in the sweet wines of the district, palomina in the making of amontillado sherry, and how fashionable a new variety, uva de rey, was becoming.

Nor were the rough highroads of southern Spain any more secure than those of New South Wales from the ministrations of brigands. As Busby explained,

> it would be madness to attempt travelling . . . as the roads are so much infested with robbers that every person who attempts to travel, unless under the protection of the Ordinario, is sure to be stripped. The latter personage purchases immunity for himself and his passengers by paying a sort of Blackmail every journey.

Nor even then were they ever entirely sure they were safe. There was obviously a surge of adrenalin a few days later. As Busby relates,

> About eight miles before reaching the former town [Antequera], a party of horsemen came in sight to the evident consternation of every one. It was said they belonged to the party of Jose Maria, a famous brigand, who has 35 men well-mounted and equipped and levies contributions on all the roads throughout the province. They did not however approach nearer than half a mile . . .

Thus ended a close encounter.

Another Busby encounter was his introduction to the 'large white Muscatel', muscat gordo blanco, which was in 1988 Australia's most commonly used white wine grape. According to Busby, 'this grape, my companion informed me, does not succeed in the interior [of Malaga] and therefore all the Muscatel raisins are raised within two leagues of the coast'. Busby also tasted the wine of the gordo blended with pedro ximinez. Due to the value of gordo as a drying grape, winemaking was merely a secondary use, perhaps as it should be in Australia today.

> We tasted some wine made two months before from the Pedro Ximenes grape and also some from that grape mixed with the Muscatel: both were as sweet and luscious as possible. The grapes, when dried, are worth double what they would yield when made into wine and therefore they are never made into wine unless spoiled by the rain.

After six weeks in Spain, Busby crossed into France and proceeded to Perpignan, where again local cultivation was dominated by the olive and the vine. Roussillon, the local red, was made of 'three varieties of vine, the Grenache, which gives sweetness, the Carignan, which gives colour and the Mataro, which gives quantity'. He was impressed by local oxen, 'as fine almost as any I have ever seen', but not by the wool, 'not of a quality that would be reckoned fine in New South Wales'. Once more he espouses the cause of the olive, even stressing what he saw as its health benefits.

> There are, perhaps, few prejudices stronger than that of the English against the general use of oil, which they are accustomed to consider as a very gross kind of condiment; and perhaps there is no prejudice more unfounded. For surely the pure vegetable juice of the olive is far from being inferior, in delicacy, to butter, the animal fat of the cow; and there can be no doubt, that oil is also more wholesome and congenial to the human constitution, in a hot climate, than the latter.

As he progressed through France, so more and more did he fulfil the purpose of his mission. Thus at Perpignan on 21 November 1831,

> I found the Messrs Durand had sent to my hotel 9 bundles, containing 50 each, of nine distinct varieties of vines . . . The kindness and attention of these gentlemen to me, a perfect stranger, without the slightest claim to their notice, is worthy of remark.

And so he journeyed on to Montpellier, where he was welcomed enthusiastically at the Botanic Gardens.

> I was not long in discovering this collection, which was numbered up to 560 varieties (of vines) . . . Finally Professor Delisle told me that I was not only welcome to cuttings of all the vines he had, but he offered me his correspondence for anything he could in future supply.

Busby could only make up 437 (of these varieties), 'the remainder being either wanting in the original or marked as identical with some previous number'. But there was no doubt that Montpellier impressed Busby. 'The Botanic Gardens of Montpelier *[sic]* is only second in France to that of Paris. It appeared to me to be kept in very high order.'

From Montpellier Busby proceeded via Marseilles to the valley of the Rhone, where at Tain, below the hill of Hermitage, the pre-appellation controllé winemaking practices of France were elucidated.

> The greatest part of the finest growth [of Hermitage] are sent to Bourdeaux to mix with the first growths of Claret . . . The finest Clarets of Bourdeaux are mixed with a portion of the finest red wine of Hermitage, and four-fifths of the quantity of the latter which is produced, are thus employed.

Who said that cabernet shiraz was a uniquely Australian blend? It seems that it was quite common in Bordeaux in 1831, especially in the most famous vineyards.

Busby was also a keen student of soils, noting throughout his Journal how the occurrence of limestone in the soil usually indicated the presence of superior wine.

> It is probably to this peculiarity that the wine of Hermitage owes its superiority, for to all appearance many of the neighbouring hills on

James Busby: apostle of the vine in New South Wales and, in his later life, first British resident in New Zealand. Artist unknown.

> both sides of the Rhone present situations equally favourable, although the wine produced even upon the best of them never rises to above half the value of the former and in general not to the fourth of their value.

In Burgundy, he encountered his beloved limestone once again.

> Nearest the top [of the vineyard slopes of the Côte d'Or], the soil contains the largest proportion of lime, and this in general yields the dryest and best wine. On descending, the clay begins to predominate, and the wine gradually falls off in quality till it becomes the vin ordinaire of the country.

He also noticed how very much 'subdivided' the vineyard of Chambertin had become, with five or six proprietors dividing amongst them 'a piece of ground not exceeding one acre[0.4 hectare] in extent'. It is very much worse today. One hundred and sixty years of inheritance have sometimes reduced the area of land under single ownership of many *grand cru* vineyards to a few square metres, with the consequence that standards of viticulture and winemaking are sometimes poor and the wines of a *grand cru* which should, theoretically, be of excellent quality are often very variable.

Busby was fortunate also to see Clos Vougeot operating as one estate of forty-eight hectares, very large by present-day Burgundian standards. The methods of Burgundian wine-making that he describes are interesting also. About a third of the stalks were fermented with the must. 'If the whole of the stalks were taken out, the quality of the wine, as has been repeatedly proved, would be inferior'. The same argument, stalks or no stalks, continues in Burgundy today. And as for cool fermentation of pinot noir, 'the fermentation is sometimes over in 30 hours, at other times it continues 10, 12 and even 15 days. The best wine is always produced from the most rapid fermentation'. Though Clos Vougeot now has more than seventy-five proprietors (the French laws of inheritance having frittered away its economic viability and rendered its wine variable to say the least), the debate about the fermentation temperature of pinot noir goes on. He also described the white winemaking techniques at the Clos, commenting on the confusion of 'white pineau' (pinot blanc) and 'chaudenay' (chardonnay), 'which resembles it so much' and how these varieties are for as long as twenty days in 'small casks'. Fermentation of chardonnay in new small oak is a recent development in Australia—*plus ça change, plus c'est la même chose.*

Busby was also well aware that in viticulture as in all else, silk purses cannot be made from sows' ears. He realised then (and such foresight is even more important today) that great wines come only from fine grape varieties grown in great vineyards, which in turn require great labour and great expense. As he explained at the end of *Journal of a Tour* (Sydney 1833),

> in all those districts which produce wines of high reputation some few individuals have the advantage of selecting a particular variety of grape and managing its culture so as to bring it to the highest state of perfection of which it is capable. The same care has been extended to the making and subsequent management of their wine, by seizing the most favourable moment for the vintage by the rapidity with which the grapes are gathered and pressed, so that the whole contents of each vat may be exactly in the same state, and a simultaneous and equal

> fermentation be secured throughout—by exercising equal discrimination and care in the time of drawing off the wine, and in its subsequent treatment in the vats or casks where it is kept—and lastly by not selling the wine till it should have acquired all the perfection which it could acquire from age, and by selling, as the produce of their own vineyards, only such vintages as were calculated to acquire or maintain its celebrity. By these means have the vineyards of a few individuals acquired a reputation which has enabled the proprietors to command almost their own prices for their wines; and it was evidently the interest of such persons, that the excellence of their wines should be imputed to a peculiarity in the soil rather than to a system of management which others might imitate. It is evident however that for all this a command of capital is required which is not often found among proprietors of vineyards; and to this cause more than any other, it is undoubtedly to be traced, that a few celebrated properties have acquired and maintained almost a monopoly in the production of fine wines.

What did Busby's tour achieve? A collection of 543 vine varieties (437 collected at Montpellier, the others collected at other places in France and Spain), of which 362 reached New South Wales, 'alive and, for the most part, healthy'. Included in the collection were all the classic French varieties that we are accustomed to seeing on labels, with the possible exception of merlot and gewurztraminer, unless they arrived incognito as either 'melarot' 'merlé d'Espagne' or 'épicier'. There were also some of the Spanish sherry varieties, pedro ximines, palomino (called 'temprana' by Busby) and, as mentioned previously, the ancestors of our bulk wine and all-purpose cultivars, gordo blanco and doradillo as well as red table grapes such as black muscat and cornichon and whites such as muscat of alexandria and other drying varieties.

The collection was planted in Sydney's Botanical Gardens, intended in Busby words as 'a national collection of vines'. Certainly it was not perfect. Doubtless some varieties perished before they could be replaced; most assuredly some were mislabelled (William Macarthur, for one, pointed to a confusion in the catalogue between cabernet sauvignon and pinot gris). but the truth of Busby's words ('national collection') holds to this day.

Busby left New South Wales within months of his return: he

had obtained his colonial preferment. From 1833 to 1840, he was the first (and last) British Resident in New Zealand making the first New Zealand wine to very good effect at the Residence at Waitangi. It was, as the French explorer Dumont d'Urville tells us, 'a light white wine, very sparkling, and delicious to taste, which I enjoyed very much'.

Busby was never to see his collection again. It was ultimately neglected, left to the mercy of the Sydney climate and uprooted twenty years later. Fortunately Busby's foresight had seen to it that a duplicate collection had been established on his property at Kirkton in the Hunter Valley and cuttings had also been sent to Macarthur at Camden Park, to Melbourne and to a new colony that was to be overwhelmed by wine—South Australia.

Busby seemed to believe his duty was to propagate the vine, to crusade for temperance against the 'ardent spirits', 'to promote the morality of the lower classes of the Colony, and more especially of the native-born youth'. In this modern era, such moral rectitude is seen as tub-thumping and elitist, if not a little ridiculous, but examined in its proper period, in a colony still substantially penal yet with an increasing number of native-born Australians, his cries for moderation and self-control are those of a social reformer with a good deal of common sense. Indeed they are echoed by the wine industry today.

Busby was very much a man of his times. Though he himself felt slighted in his later years and may never have made a drop of wine in New South Wales, in whatever way one measures achievement, his contribution to Australian viticulture can only be assessed as vast. He had shown others the foresight and application so necessary to found a new vineland. He was indeed the apostle of the vine.

During his latter years in the colony and immediately after his departure, interest in viticulture grew apace. Though few wanted to risk an entire livelihood on it, 'men of property' were often willing to try a few vines. Some went even further. Thus Sir John Jamison employed the 'Rhenish vigneron' F. A. Meyer to plant a terraced vineyard of 7 acres (2.8 hectares) at Regentville on the Nepean River. By 1835 the vineyard had been expanded to six hectares, including 'upwards of 200 varieties'. He made his own wine, brandy, cheese (resembling 'Chester') and also produced tobacco. John

Manning, the Registrar of the Supreme Court, started a vineyard at Rushcutters Bay in 1833. Indeed, in that year, fascination with the vine ran so high that the Rhenish vigneron himself advertised his services 'for winter pruning on moderate charges' in the *Sydney Herald* and, with the death in 1835 of Thomas Shepherd, an early nurseryman (whose name was commemorated by 'Shepherd's riesling', an early misnomer for semillon), the *Sydney Herald* was most fulsome in its praise of him.

> To Mr Shepherd is chiefly to be ascribed the extended cultivation of the vine in this colony . . . which has also been greatly promoted by the zeal of Mr James Busby . . . of whose exertions Mr Shepherd was a warm admirer.

Although the vineyard outposts in what is now Sydney suburbia and on the Hawkesbury plain thrived for most of the nineteenth century (one such, Minchinbury, was later to become even more famous in the twentieth), settlement began to march beyond the County of Cumberland, taking the vine with it. To the south-west of Sydney, Camden Park was a whole microcosm of agriculture. There were not only merinos, but also wheat, olives, silkworms and vines. All were tried; most were successful, especially the merinos. It must be said in all honesty that William Macarthur's vinous pursuits were carried on the sheep's back, but certainly by 1830, as mentioned above, he was producing wine of a quality that would later bring overseas acclaim. By 1838, he was confident enough in the future of the vine in Australia to import and successfully acclimatise rhine riesling, though whatever happened to the 'rischling', a variety from the Department of Bas Rhin imported by Busby, remains a mystery.

In 1842 he exchanged his pruner's knife for the pen, writing an extremely lucid and intelligent account of his winemaking experiences in a series of articles for the *Australian* under the name of Maro. Though they were by no means Roman bucolic poetry, despite the pseudonym, they were exceedingly practical and intended to be of assistance to any aspiring viticulturalist of his time. Thus he revealed methods of grafting vines, frost prevention, pruning, trellising, terracing and sloping a vineyard, everything in fact that would be useful to a beginner. By 1844 his articles were embodied in a book, *Letters on the Culture of the Vine*, and it is to Sir William Macarthur that we owe our knowledge of the performance of the vine varieties in common use at that time. Macarthur could write of riesling that, though acclimatised, it 'has not been sufficiently long introduced to estimate the quality or quantity of its produce in the Colony'; hardly surprising since he had introduced it himself only six years before. The fruit did, however, 'have a peculiar spicy flavour'. Of verdelho, he is more positive.

> Imported in 1825 by the Australian Agricultural Company. Small oblong or oval white grape. This, all its qualities considered, is the most valuable grape for wine we have hitherto proved in the Colony. It produces with tolerable certainty . . . from 300 to 500 gallons and sometimes even 700 gallons to the acre [3334 to 7780 litres to the hectare]. The wine, rich and generous, evidently capable of being kept for a great number of years. It does not appear to become fit for use until past its fourth year, and even then, it improves greatly with age . . .

It obviously suited Camden Park and, made as it was with a warm fermentation, as we make reds today, it needed some time to mature and allow all its elements to come into balance. It was verdelho which caused Macarthur to have his famous quarrel with the equally important winemaker James King of Irrawang in the Hunter Valley, for Macarthur had noticed that it appeared to suffer from 'stuck' fermentation, leaving unresolved sugar in the wine, then, as now, a grave worry to a winemaker. King, never one to refuse to give advice, suggested that he try adding to the ferment the must of gouais, a little-regarded wine variety, which, though 'light, thin and spirituous', did assist verdelho to ferment to dryness and stability. Macarthur apparently never acknowledged King's assistance and even, so King alleged, pretended that the solution was his own. Macarthur responded by saying that he was quite 'unconscious of having made use of any information which Mr King imparted to him'. Such was King's fiery temper that these bitter recriminations separated the two most eminent winemakers in New South Wales until King's untimely death in 1857 (King will be dealt with in the following chapter).

Macarthur also classified the known grape varieties usefully into early-, mid- and late-season ripeners, listing among early ripeners the pinot, 'pineau' gris, 'pineau' blanc—had Busby's 'chaudeny' (chardonnay) already been confused with pinot blanc?—'burgundy' or 'small black cluster' (surely pinot noir, cultivated by both Busby and Blaxland) and 'Miller's burgundy' (pinot meunier), noting that the latter varieties were often deficient in colour. They remain so to this day.

For mid-season Macarthur specified amongst others riesling, tokay (there was as much confusion concerning this variety then as there is now), the muscat family, the intriguingly named 'epicier' (was it gewurztraminer?) verdelho (or madeira), scyras (shiraz) and the Bordeaux brotherhood: cabernet sauvignon, malbec, verdot and sauvignon blanc (strange, this last one, as it usually ripens very early indeed). As late ripeners, he prescribed Busby's introductions from the south of France, carignan, mataro and blanquette, good practical advice in a land where the next vineyard might be several days' journey away. (Pioneering vignerons often in ignorance planted mixed vineyards, so they would be perplexed when some varieties appeared to be ripe and others were not. No other advice, such as a chat with a neighbouring vigneron, was available.)

Macarthur was not only a writer and vigneron. Like his father, he was a political lobbyist, but for wine. Lamenting the inexperience of winegrowers in the colony, he pressed increasingly for the import of skilled labour for New South Wales vineyards. Despite the opposition of the Colonial Office to European (as opposed to Anglo-Celtic) labour, he ultimately succeeded, securing permission for six German families to come to Camden Park in 1837 and then, a decade later, having the ban lifted altogether.

In the 1850s Macarthur was at the peak of his powers, organising the formation of the New South Wales Vineyard Association and, ever concerned with the overseas reputation of New South Wales wine, representing the colonial government at the Paris Universal Exhibition of 1855, an exposition of enduring vinous interest not only because it classified the leading growths of the Haut Médoc and Sauternes, but because it placed Australian wine before the eyes of the world for the first time and in particular before the nose of Napoleon III. By securing a place of honour on that presentation table, the wines of Macarthur and James King (for he had travelled to Paris also) proved not only that New South Wales existed but that it could produce wines of a quality much greater than mere 'local' beverages (common beverages of a locality anywhere). History does not record what that particular Napoleon did with them. Perhaps like his famous ancestor he drank them with water.

The story of the Camden Park vineyard is really the story of Sir William Macarthur. When he declined, so did his vineyard. Within three years of his death at eighty-two in 1882, the vineyard, decimated by phylloxera, was grubbed out and never replanted.

FOUR

Hunter Valley beginnings

Though settlement had spread to the Hunter Valley by the early 1820s there were only 15 acres (six hectares) of vines scattered about the Valley in 1832. They were shared among ten growers, most of whom had substantial grants favourably located close to the rivers of the region—a logical choice of site when farming unknown country, not only because of the proximity of water, but also because alluvial soil, mostly rich and fertile, has usually been chosen for agriculture since man first farmed.

With one exception, Dalwood, now renamed Wyndham Estate, none of those vineyards exists today. One of those growers was William Kelman, who managed the Busby property, Kirkton. Despite the flying start in vine varieties given him by his brother-in-law, he proceeded cautiously, having only one acre (0.4 hectares) in a property of 2000 (800 hectares). In 1834 Kelman decided, however, that the vines showed such promise in the area that the vineyard should be increased to ten acres (four hectares), a choice that caused even the vine-enthused Busby to arch his eyebrows:

> before he has even proved the capabilities of the soil, I think it unlikely that his wine will be above the Vin Ordinaire and it is very doubtful whether that, even if managed with more skill and convenience than he can hope for many years, will meet a market at any price in Sydney.

To Busby, the management of ten acres was 'no joke' and in letters from New Zealand to his brother, Alexander, he worried mightily about market prospects.

> Tell him from me, that he had better let distillation alone, and drink his wine new—there are many places (the majority of those in France) where the wine will not keep over twelve months and they of course drink it before it spoils . . . [then just in case he was thought too damning, he added] tell him that I should not object to a sample of it myself.

Busby had misjudged Kelman's winemaking skill, for in 1839 he wrote to his brother to find out the valuation that Kelman had placed on the wine, as it was obviously quite good.

> Habit has made us both like it better than almost any other wine, and I intend to engage a couple of quarter casks [about 300 litres] annually for which I thought of offering fifteen pounds [$30 or ten cents per litre] . . . Do you think he would consider it too low? If not, it might be of use in fixing the price of any more he might have to dispose of. I think there would be little chance of any one giving him more—and few persons would I think drink it at all except those who have been accustomed to natural wine in France . . .

The price offered by Busby was by the standards of the time very high (beef and pork were four cents a kilo and milk about one cent per litre). Even a decade later, the price of Hunter wine was only eleven cents a litre, but then there were few who could afford to drink wine. Busby was perhaps attempting to set a top market price for what he thought was a quality product in a market where it would be offered only to a few rich and discriminating buyers, and after all the money was going to the family anyway.

Those were times of trial and error. There was little skilled labour in the vineyard and even less in the winery. Obvious markets were small and distant and means of distribution slow and primitive—bullock dray and an excessively priced steam packet service controlled by a monopoly were the principal means of transport from the early Hunter Valley. The wonder is that they persevered; that they did speaks volumes for the fascination of converting grapes into wine.

Kelman's experiments were plainly fruitful in every sense, for by 1843 the Kirkton vineyard had extended to fifteen acres (six hectares) and he was having great success with the 'white hermitage' grape. Most probably that was the marsanne, one of the two white varieties personally collected by Busby from the Hill of Hermitage (the other was roussanne) and propagated by Kelman, who in addition to his winemaking and managerial role at Kirkton was also chief nurseryman.

Another who was very willing to experiment with the vine in the Hunter Valley was George Wyndham. Reaching Sydney in 1827, he bought 1100 acres (445 hectares) in the following year, close to the Hunter River, north-east of present-day Branxton, naming his property 'Dalwood' after a family estate in England. By 1832 he had two acres (0.8 hectare) of vines. It had not been an easy enterprise. In June 1830 he had received 600 vines from Busby. 'They were dead, before I got them', recalled Wyndham laconically. Undeterred, in August of the following year he planted again and by January 1832 had 1400 vines. In July that year he obtained cuttings of 'Muscatel, Black Hamburgh, Red Portugal, Green Malaga, Constantia and Black Cluster' (pinot noir). Two years later, his vineyard had grown to five acres (two hectares), consisting of both table grapes and red and white wine varieties.

It was apparent that most of these new recruits to Hunter Valley farming were treading cautiously. Food was to be their first priority—or so they thought—as rust plagued their wheat and the local insects enthusiastically devoured a totally new order of vegetables. Yet they persisted on this new agricultural frontier.

In 1836 Wyndham made over 7000 litres of wine, his first vintage the previous year 'promising to make good vinegar'. Adversity was never a total stranger to Wyndham. As late as 1845, the Dalwood vineyard was little more than five acres (two hectares) and when in the early 1840s a dispiriting depression brought the embryonic New South Wales economy to a halt, Wyndham was obliged to offer Dalwood for rental and to move to another property, 'Bukkula', near Inverell.

Others began just as carefully. James King, who arrived in the colony the same year as Wyndham, traded profitably as a merchant for several years before planting his property 'Irrawang' near Raymond Terrace in 1832 and again in 1834 'with a greater variety of sorts, many of which had shortly before been imported into this country from France by Mr Busby'. Making his first vintage in 1836, King acknowledged his own lack of experience and was keen to learn as well as to promote the wines of his adopted land. Thus in the 1840s he started a correspondence with von Liebig, the German chemist. It obviously developed his winemaking skills enormously, for his 1844 Shepherd's riesling (semillon) became quite renowned, drawing praise from as far away as Germany. Herr Vollpracht, a senior official of the Duchy of Nassau, writing on the Duke's behalf in 1857 (the year of King's death), observed enthusiastically that

> the white wine, both for flavour and strength, rivals the best sorts of ours. It was only found to be 'firmer' what we render in English by the word 'riper' than our wines usually are at such an early period [the wine was then only thirteen years old]. You see, dear Sir, that your endeavours to grow a wine which might be worthy to be introduced into the chorus of Steinberg and Rüdesheim and Marcobrunner, have been crowned with the fullest success.

For tributes such as that, even allowing for the fulsome phraseology of nineteenth-century correspondence, the Hunter Valley of King's day owed him a huge debt of gratitude.

King, like his verbal antagonist, William Macarthur, was also an ardent proselytiser of the vine. As a founder and first chairman of the Hunter River Vineyard Association, a 'society for the purpose of promoting the culture of the vine and turning its products to the most profitable account', he organised comparative tastings of members' wines, ensuring that every detail of the vine growth and winemaking was disclosed. Like Macarthur, he roamed the corridors of power, petitioning the Legislative Council in 1849 to request the imperial government to reduce import duty on Australian wines. At a time when the Hunter Valley was producing 275 000 litres of wine, King obviously believed that the future of the industry lay in export. In all of this King and the Association had the enthusiastic backing of the local press—the Maitland *Mercury* reporting the meetings in detail and giving most of the objectives strong editorial support. Yet King was a prudent man, despite his fiery temper. Even three years before his death in 1857, his vineyard was still only fifteen acres (six hectares) in extent, though with plans for a further nine acres (3.6 hectares). When King died overseas at the comparatively early age of fifty-seven, he had already gained significant successes (his was the other New South Wales wine placed on the table of honour before the Emperor Napoleon in 1855). Who knows what he might have achieved for Irrawang, the Hunter Valley and indeed for Australia, given another decade of life?

King's Irrawang vineyard was virtually to fall with him, but there was one other famous name in the Hunter Valley at this time—William Charles Wentworth, who owned the Windemere and Luskintyre vineyards on the banks of the Hunter east of Dalwood. Even for Wentworth, times were adverse, for in 1848 his vineyards were advertised to let—thirty acres (twelve hectares) with twelve acres (nearly five hectares) in full bearing.

Despite the hard times of the 1840s, there was a growing, almost glowing pride in Hunter River wine. In 1848, there was a celebrated tasting at the Hunter River Vineyard Association. An 1843 red made at Alexander Warren's Brandon vineyard and an 1846 red of James King (perhaps a blend of 'pineau noire' and 'pineau gris') were put up against a Chambertin of unknown vintage. The Brandon red of unknown variety was certainly preferred by the Association, perhaps justifiably, for even Chambertin was, as Busby had noted seventeen years earlier, becoming quite subdivided with a consequential variation in winemaking standards.

Another enduring identity, whose name is seen to this day on some of Australia's best bottles, reached Sydney Town in September 1840. Dr Henry John Lindeman, himself the son of a doctor, became a surgeon in 1834. The traditional story has it that he joined the Royal Navy and that after six years of service in London, Madras and the China Station, he decided to emigrate to New South Wales, then portrayed as a colonial Xanadu by the idealistic prose of Edward Gibbon Wakefield. But no record apparently exists of his naval service or of his ship, *The Marquis of Camden*, ever travelling to China. Be that as it may, after his arrival in Australia he paused but momentarily in Sydney and settled in Gresford, then a frontier of civilisation on the banks of the Paterson River, where he set up practice.

In 1842 he purchased 'Cawarra' and, no doubt because of the success of men such as King and Kelman, in 1843 planted vines. Cawarra, destined to be one of the most famous Australian vineyards of the nineteenth century, thrived with pinot noir, cabernet sauvignon and shiraz central amongst its reds and semillon, verdelho and white pinot (in all likelihood chardonnay) the cynosures of its whites. By 1850 his wines were stated to be 'akin to the Bordeaux' and known to be of the highest quality.

Though Lindeman was not then a name of renown in colonial New South Wales, he was to become a man of influence in Australia's infant wine industry. Joining the Hunter River Vineyard Association in 1850, he became its president twice, in 1863 and 1870, all the while supporting Busby's thesis of moderation—that the drinking of light table wines with meals would prove an antidote to the spread of alcoholism caused by 'ardent spirits'. Like Busby, Lindeman too had ultimate faith in the future of Australian wine.

> When our connoisseurs sip, taste and purchase, there will no longer be any doubt that New South Wales can produce a wine of superior quality, and that the days are fast approaching when a few indefatigable wine growers, having swept from their path prejudice, doubt and the innumerable difficulties, will reap their reward in having the honour of pioneering their adopted country as one of the great wine producing countries of the world . . .

He suffered his own share of adversity, losing his first winery, cellars and wine, valued at £1500 in a deliberately lit fire in September 1851. The fire is a fact, but what Lindeman then did to retrieve his fortune is less certain. Allegedly he overcame this crushing blow by taking himself to the north-east Victorian goldfields where he used his time profitably in the oddly associated pursuits of medicine and gold mining.

In due course, his fortunes restored, he returned to the Hunter Valley, having acquired during his Victorian sojourn extensive knowledge of and an admiration for the rich fortified wines of its north-east region, an insight he put to profitable account not only by buying the wines for sale with his own, but also later buying a vineyard at Corowa in New South Wales where similar wine could be made free of intercolonial customs duty.

Recent research however throws considerable doubt upon his movements after the fire. Perhaps he never left the Gresford area. If he did leave, and went to the goldfields, there were of course goldfields much nearer to the Hunter Valley, those of Hill End, north of Bathurst for example. The most likely explanation is that he continued his medical practice and his farming at Cawarra, rebuilding his cellar some 18 months later with the proceeds of the sale of cattle.[1]

His business acumen was widely recognised, George Wyndham in 1873 attributing his own success to a joint wine sales operation with Lindeman set up in Sydney in 1861. Lindeman went further in 1870. Realising that his business had outgrown its Cawarra home and in all probability that a wine business should be close to its main market, he moved it to Sydney, establishing headquarters, storage and bottling facilities at the Exchange Cellars in Pitt Street, Sydney. In 1879, two years before he died at Cawarra, he took his sons, Charles Frederick, Arthur Henry and Herbert, into the partnership.

By 1850 there were 570 acres (230 hectares) of vines in the Hunter Valley and 1070 acres (433 hectares) in the colony as a whole. All the modern varieties of quality—semillon, chardonnay, verdelho, pinot noir, shiraz and cabernet sauvignon were present and acclimatised. The growers had successfully lobbied both the colonial and imperial governments for lower licence fees and tariff equality with Cape wines on the British market and at last there was a sufficient supply of expert labour for vine dressing and cooperage.

To what extent had New South Wales table wine penetrated the Sydney market of the 1840s? An honest answer must be, hardly at all! Sydney in 1840 was a roistering seaport of about thirty thousand souls where, with an ounce of good luck, one could make a small fortune or, with an equal amount of bad, have one's throat cut almost on the same day. The colony had maintained its thirst for 'ardent spirits': its liquor import bill for 1840 was £500 000—£25 ($50) for every man, woman and child in the colony. As an example, the trade list of the colony published 'by Authority' and dated 1 August that year contained, amongst other liquors, '30 quarter casks 5 hogsheads 300 cases of gin, 20 quarter casks 3 hogsheads brandy, 50 octaves 47 quarter casks 10 cases wine, 105 tierces bottled beer . . . 3 puncheons rum'. This is just one shipment by one liquor merchant in Sydney at that time. In 1838 it is estimated that there were more than 200 licensed public houses in Sydney alone and more than three times as many illegal dispensers of sly grog. No doubt the time would arrive for New South Wales wine but in 1840 it was a droplet in a sea of alcohol.

[1] Norrie, *Lindeman*, 1993

FIVE

The vine outside New South Wales

The colonisation of Australia spread slowly by land, but rather more expeditiously by sea. By 1803 there was a permanent settlement at Hobart Town, three years later at Launceston, and with those often reluctant communities came the vine. In 1823 one Bartholomew Broughton planted a vineyard at Prospect Farm, New Town. By 1827 he had obviously prospered, for in that year he advertised over 1300 litres of his 1826 vintage for sale. Contemporary testimonials complimented the wine on its quality. By 1828, however, Broughton was dead. His property was purchased by a Captain Swanston, who plainly felt that Tasmanian wine promised much for the future, as he increased production five-fold over the next twenty years.

In 1850 Swanston himself died, ruined by one of those periodic bank crashes so endemic in the nineteenth century. The vine, which had flourished in those early years in Van Diemen's Land (vineyards were planted at Windemere on the Tamar, Falmouth and Breadalbane) came to a full stop in the middle of the century.

Who knows why? Those cool area cultivars, pinot noir and sweetwater (chasselas) would have reached Hobart at an early stage. Indeed a generation later in the 1840s, all the classic varieties were available, including sauvignon blanc, shiraz and cabernet sauvignon. Why did the infant Tasmanian industry die? The three most likely reasons were lack of a big enough market, lack of skilled labour, and one peculiarly Tasmanian cause, the climate, for then, as now, vine exposure and aspect were factors critical for the success or failure of the Tasmanian vine.

As the Blue Mountains proved impenetrable during the first quarter century of the settlement of New South Wales, so the need to find suitable agricultural land pressed hard upon early colonial governors. An early colonisation of southern 'New South Wales', undertaken at Port Phillip (so called after the first governor of the colony) was abandoned by Lieutenant-Governor David Collins in 1804 in favour of Hobart. A similar official attempt failed in 1828. In 1835 an early colonial entre-preneur called John Batman made those initial colonising posturings that left the New South Wales government no choice but to intervene two years later: in a transaction repugnant to social consciences today he exchanged blankets, axes, knives and handkerchiefs for nearly a quarter of a million hectares of Aboriginal land. Beads, another customary object of barter, were inexplicably missing on this occasion. Even in the early nineteenth century, the Crown had considerable qualms about this 'purchase', not so much because it expropriated Aboriginal land but rather more because it ignored the Crown. Nonetheless the colonists arrived in numbers, found their rural fertility and an equable climate and stayed. In 1839 Charles La Trobe, an Englishman of French extraction, arrived to be superintendent of the town of Melbourne, as the Governor, Sir Richard Bourke, had dutifully called it after a leading English politician of his day. He found a population of more than two thousand inhabitants. For the vine, the choice of La Trobe was auspicious. Not only had he lived for some years in Neuchâtel in Switzerland, he had married a Swiss, Sophie de

Montmollin, and the connections arising from this marriage were later to encourage a steady stream of Swiss emigrants, younger sons of noble rank such as the de Castellas and, importantly, skilled agricultural workers, whose first-hand knowledge of the vine would prove invaluable. La Trobe himself planted a vineyard in the grounds of 'Jolimont', the government residence of the time, but he was probably not the first 'Victorian' to plant grapes. Pride of place in that respect is disputed between Edward Henty, who in 1834 travelled from Tasmania to his property in Portland carrying with him 'a cask of grape cuttings' (nothing further being ever heard of the vineyard) and William Ryrie, who in 1837 over-landed from the Monaro Plains in southern New South Wales, squatted at Yering in the Yarra Valley and most certainly had planted an acre (0.4 hectares) of vines by 1840.

Within ten years of its foundation there were not only numerous small vineyards in Melbourne and nearby areas, but also in Geelong and the Yarra Valley. There was a vineyard in what is now Collins Street (the business heart of the city) owned by Skene Craig, La Trobe's Commissary Officer, another in the centre of Melbourne owned by Pelet, husband of La Trobe's housekeeper. Yet another was established above the banks of the Yarra. In 1840 one of the pioneers of Victoria, John Pascoe Fawkner, a man of many pursuits, convict, inn-keeper and newspaper editor, planted ten acres (4 hectares) at his property, 'Pascoe Vale', near present-day Flemington. Soon South Yarra, Toorak and other parts of Melbourne's nascent suburbia were dotted with vineyards.

The Swiss connection seemed to strengthen every year: the Deschamps family were of winegrowing stock in Neuchâtel; Paul de Castella, arriving in 1848, bought part of Ryrie's Yarra Yering station, including Ryrie's small vineyard. It must have been producing some impressive wine, for in 1854 de Castella purchased 20 000 cabernet sauvignon cuttings from Chateau Lafite. By 1857 the Yering vineyard covered nearly 100 acres (40 hectares). With such an impressive pedigree, how could his wine avoid almost immediate fame? Indeed it could not, for in 1861 a cabernet wine from Yering won a gold cup offered for the best Victorian wine by the Melbourne *Argus*, the newspaper founded by the wineloving J. P. Fawkner. By 1860 the vine was firmly established in the Yarra Valley.

Geelong also had its Swiss (and German) vignerons. In 1842

David Louis Pettavell and Frederick Brequet settled at Pollock's Ford, nostalgically planting 'Neufchâtel', in soil of a 'red porous loam, sparsely intermixed with limestone'. Prominent amongst their vines was pinot noir, brought from Dijon.

Southern 'New South Wales' or Port Phillip was independently minded from the start. By 1840 its population had doubled to 4000, settlers pouring in from Van Diemen's Land and across the Murray. It had thirty hotels and three newspapers and firmly resisted attempts from Sydney to turn it into a penal colony. It protested also against what it considered to be a disproportionate share of taxation levied from Sydney, and even when it was allowed representation in the New South Wales Legislative Council, the demands for independence persisted. That movement, supported by men such as Fawkner, now turned politician, ultimately gained the reluctant support of La Trobe, who became the colony's first lieutenant-governor on independence in 1851. Quite appropriately when a celebratory toast at a ball in honour of the occasion was proposed by La Trobe late in 1850, it was drunk in wine made at Pelet's vineyard in the centre of Melbourne.

By the eve of its separation from New South Wales, the Victorian vineyard area, small though it was in extent at 164 acres (sixty-six hectares), was flourishing and would in the next half-century outgrow the vineyards of the mother colony and threaten those of South Australia.

In stark contrast to the *de facto* origins of Victoria, South Australia was most certainly *de jure*. There was no bartering here. Inspired by that colonising idealist, Edward Gibbon Wakefield, the South Australian Company presented a Bill to the British Parliament in 1833 to authorise settlement. From the outset all Crown lands were sold and convict labour was most certainly not welcome.

The region was tolerably well known. Flinders had mapped the coastline in 1802; Sturt had navigated the Murray River to its outlet into Lake Alexandrina in 1830; Captain Barker climbed Mount Lofty in 1831 and sealers and escaped convicts had subsisted on Kangaroo Island for twenty years.

From its first selection as a site in 1836, despite the opposition of its first governor, John Hindmarsh, who preferred present-day Port Lincoln, Adelaide was to be a model city. That this is so today was due to the determination of Colonel William Light, a Peninsular

War veteran and the colony's first surveyor-general, who chose the port, the site of the city five miles (eight kilometres) inland and, by the end of March 1837, had completed the survey of the first 1000 acres (405 hectares) of the city.

Vines were planted within months of the foundation of the settlement and when Governor Hindmarsh arrived in December 1836, there were already 300 'citizens' to greet him. By 1837 there were vineyards at Chichester Gardens, North Adelaide, planted by John Barton Hack, George Stevenson planting in the same area in the ensuing year. To the west of Adelaide at Underdale, H. H. Davis, obtaining a large quantity of cuttings from the Busby collection, planted the colony's first commercial vineyard betweeen 1837 and 1840.

But who made the first wine? The traditional rivals were John Reynell and Richard Hamilton, though the names of Hack and Walter Duffield have now been added to the lists. Hamilton took up his land near Glenelg in June 1838 and, if he planted immediately, could well have made an 1841 vintage, though scarcely an 1840, unless he bought grapes. Argument has raged over dates of registration of titles and taking possession but if John Reynell did settle in the area south of Adelaide that bears his name in July 1839, unless he had bought grapes or earlier planted land without title, there is absolutely no justification for any Reynell wine before 1842. In neither case are the winemaking claims supported by satisfactory document-ary evidence recorded at the time or soon after. Records of plantings by both men there certainly are, but no contemporary records of winemaking.

The other challengers, John Barton Hack and Walter Duffield, have better documented though later claims. Hack subdivided his North Adelaide property in 1839 and moved to 'Echunga Springs' in the Adelaide Hills where he planted 500 vines that year and a further 3000 in 1842, making his first wine in 1843, according to the South Australian Register. Later that year, however, Hack fell into the hands of a major creditor, who took possession of the vineyard and leased it to Walter Duffield, who made his first wine in 1844.

Duffield is reported by the Register in June 1845 to have made six hogsheads of wine, presumably of 1845 vintage—Hack's further plantings of 1842 might just have been coming into bearing. The journal went on to congratulate him on the 'commercial' scale of his operation—about 180 cases of wine, quite large for a city of a few thousand inhabitants, very few of whom would have had the wherewithal to drink wine, unless they had grown and made it themselves, as many were later to do.

In 1844 he had also made wine, a hogshead of 'Echunga Hock' (presumably from Hack's 1839 plantings, then in their second year of production), and, obviously possessed of a keen marketing flair, promptly sent a case of that wine to Queen Victoria.

It is at this point that accounts of Duffield's gesture differ. One version[1] states that the shipment was certainly sent through the proper channels, through a London importer and the Colonial Office, for there is a letter to the Queen from Lord Stanley, then Secretary of State for Colonies, disclaiming any knowledge of the quality of the wine, but suggesting that the gift be accepted, because to do otherwise might be considered a slight to the colonists. Whether the Queen was amused or not is not recorded.

The other account[2] opines that the Queen's South Australian government was most certainly not amused and prosecuted Duffield for illicit winemaking. Either way, Duffield stands as South Australia's first known exporter of wine.

Though we have no knowledge of Duffield's grapes except that they were white, we do of Reynell's. From Camden Park, William Macarthur sent 'pineau' (whether 'gris' or 'noir' has not been firmly established), proffering the advice that only vines of classic table-wine heritage should be planted. When the cuttings failed, so did the counsel and Reynell turned his attention to those Spanish stalwarts, pedro ximinez and palomino, then newly arrived from Spain.

Other famous names appeared on the Adelaide vinescape soon after. Dr Christopher Rawson Penfold arrived at Largs Bay in 1844, having already bought sight unseen (not an unusual migrant practice), 'a truly valuable estate at Makill (Magill) for £1200 [$2400]', a princely sum in those days. He began his medical practice immediately at his property, which he called 'The Grange'. Like most of our early free settlers, he did not travel lightly, bringing with him his own collection of vine cuttings from the best areas of the south of France and planting them in the first year of his arrival. At first the sweet produce of those grenache vines, for that was what he had mostly propagated, was only for private medical prescript-ion, never for public consumption. Like himself, his patients were mostly immigrants, who if they were not pale and under-nourished in the old country, soon became so on steerage rations during an often rough and perilous four-to-five-month voyage. Thus for anaemia Penfold prescribed his grenache wine, strong in iron and certainly not deficient in alcohol. Even today, 150 years later, wine is useful in restoring iron to the human body. Thus in the 1840s 'Grange' Grenache was available only by prescription, but this was later to change.

Settlement in South Australia also proceeded rapidly to the north-east. In the early 1840s in the Barossa Valley, so called by Colonel Light after the site of one of Wellington's victories in his Peninsular campaign, there appeared at first a trickle and then a flood of non-conformist Silesian Lutherans who had refused to integrate their church with King Frederick's established state religion. Their emigration was actively encouraged by the London banker and merchant George Fife Angas, owner of a vast tract of the Valley (11 300 hectares) and chairman of the South Australian Company, who sought as settlers solid god-fearing folk, prepared to pass the weekday hours in honest toil and the sabbath in worship of their creator.

In 1847 Johann Gramp, of Bavarian farming stock, who had already been in the colony for ten years working as a labourer and a baker, arrived in the Barossa, bringing with him not only the sweat of his brow (that was expected!) but also according to family tradition, a vine variety ordered from Germany that was to prove eminently suitable for the area, rhine riesling. Those first riesling cuttings were planted at Gramp's small property on Jacob's Creek. In 1850 Johann's son, Gustav, was born and the first vintage produced an octave (fourteen gallons or sixty-four litres) of white hock-style wine.

The Barossa was not to be entirely populated by German stock. In 1849 a Dorset brewer, Samuel Smith, came to work as a gardener, spending each available moment on his small block of thirty acres (12 hectares), which he named 'Yalumba'. This was a classic example of Edward Gibbon Wakefield's theory that all colonial land should be paid for (and not granted freely) so as to encourage the investment of capital by large and small settlers alike. This in turn would provide the funds to finance the emigration of free labourers, who would eventually save enough either to expand existing smallholdings or buy new holdings further out, an evolutionary process which would see both settlement and the local production increase due to a greater number of local consumers.

In the hills high above the Valley in 1847, Joseph Gilbert was also planting a vineyard as part of his substantial Pewsey Vale station. His wines, made of riesling, verdelho, shiraz and cabernet sauvignon, would make his name famous in his lifetime. Henry Evans of 'Evansdale' near Keyneton was another hill vigneron who became renowned in the 1850s for his shiraz and riesling wines. But there would be other famous names in the Valley and its hills, some destined to make a more lasting impression. Seppelt is one, but of that name and others, more later.

On the Gawler plains north of Adelaide Dr Richard Schomburgk, later director of the Adelaide Botanic Gardens, established 'Buchsfelde' in 1849 and by 1853 was acclimatising over ninety varieties of vine. To the west of Adelaide, Richard Hamilton continued with his Ewell estate at Glenelg, while to the south John Reynell steadily increased his vineyard area, building in about 1845 the renowned 'Cave' cellar, preserved to this day and now part of the handsomely restored Thomas Hardy & Sons headquarters.

About this time Dr Alexander Kelly, one of South Australia's first wine authors, planted his 'Trinity' vineyard near Morphett Vale. He was later to found the Tintara vineyard and winery, a venture that was to go disastrously wrong.

The vine also followed the northern road taken by the explorer Eyre in 1839, though it was a hesitant trail in the first ten years. A few vines were grown here and there on large pastoral runs to provide fresh fruit or simple beverage wine for the labourers. Edward Gleeson, the first mayor of the town of Clare, which he named after his Irish birthplace, correctly divined the future, subscribing to a public fund for the import of vines from the Cape. Over five hundred vines, his share, were planted on his property 'Inchiquin' in the late 1840s.

Although relatively little wine was being produced in South Australia by 1850 (Dr Kelly recorded only 282 acres (114 hectares) of vineyard in Adelaide in that year), certainly the settlers were prepared to persist for, as Kelly also remarked in the proper spirit of Edward Gibbon Wakefield when commenting on the lack of labour caused by the gold rushes in the ensuing decade,

> the Adelaide vine grower . . . depended on his vines, either partially or solely, for his subsistence and could not afford to let his property go to ruin for want of a little care and extra labour.

They also had justifiable confidence in the future, George McEwin, an early horticulturalist, having no doubt that wine 'would become a source of great wealth to the colony, the climate and soil being ideal'. During the next 150 years, those prophetic words would ring true, but they would also at times prove false.

Rule number one in the Colonial Handbook for the Settlement of Australia (surely there must have been one!) was obvious: find water. Rule number two, of almost equal importance to any coastal settlement: establish a port. Rule number three, in any temperate colony, seemed to follow automatically: plant vines. Indeed the settlement at Swan River Colony seemed assured of 'success' before its foundation, as a ship of that name, commanded by Captain James Stirling, later the first lieutenant-governor of the colony, explored the area in 1827. Two years later, Captain Charles Fremantle, commanding HMS *Challenger*, took formal possession of the western third of Australia on behalf of the British government.

Captain Stirling and his settlers arrived later aboard the transport *Parmelia*, which was accompanied, appropriately enough for the future of the wine industry, by HMS *Sulphur*. A passenger on *Parmelia* was Thomas Waters, a botanist turned viticulturalist turned winemaker with practical experience in South Africa. Although Waters did not plant the first vine in Western Australia (this honour went to a Mr Charles McFaull, whose vineyard at Hamilton Hill lasted only a very short time before it was moved elsewhere), he was certainly the colony's first winemaker. Within a few months of his arrival, Waters was granted fifty acres (twenty hectares) of land near present-day Guildford on the Swan River, where he planted his vines and olives. The following year (1830), he dug the first wine cellar in the colony. Olive Farm, as it came to be called, still produces some of the best Swan River wines today and is thus the oldest continuously existing winery in Australia. By 1842 Waters was producing enough wine for public sale.

Government House also assisted the cause; a plant nursery, including vines, was established in its garden, just as Captain Phillip had done over forty years before in Sydney.

One of Waters's companions on board *Parmelia* was Captain John Roe, who was the colony's first surveyor-general. In 1840, at his property, Sandalford, Roe planted a vineyard primarily of table grapes, but with a few varieties for domestic wine.

By contrast, Western Australia's biggest present-day producer came on the scene later. Houghton was named after one Colonel Houghton, an officer in the Indian army, who with two others purchased a property at Middle Swan, most likely as a nest egg for their retirement. As at Sandalford a small vineyard was probably planted early on for fresh fruit and domestic wine. Indeed Colonel Houghton must be counted as the most famous absentee vigneron in Perth's history, as he is reported never to have set eyes upon his property and yet the wine company bearing his name is today the largest in the state.

But all this was in the future, for by 1850 there was only one commerical vinter in the colony, Waters, producing a mere trickle of wine.

How was Australia's infant wine industry placed by the turn of the half-century? The Australian colonies, the most senior of them over sixty years old, were just recovering from the severe economic recession of the 1840s, yet there was no doubt that they were still thirsty. The manifests of cargo vessels of the time are full of references to puncheons of rum, hogsheads of brandy and cases of gin. Though the writings of Busby and Macarthur spurred on the cause of temperance and wine, the general populace of Sydney seemed not yet to have heard of it. Proud as its makers were of the quality of New South Wales wine, it would remain an extremely small industry in need of a greater market.

In the environs of Adelaide, there was enthusiasm but as yet no great skill, while in the proudly independent townships of Melbourne and Geelong, the Swiss connection ensured some expertise in a craft that was as yet of minute importance. Elsewhere the vine was moribund or a matter only of domestic concern. Viewed as a whole, our infant wine industry needed continued drive, European expertise and above all willing markets, if it were to survive, and those markets, in a most unexpected way, it was about to obtain.

[1] Ilbery, 'First off the rank', an historical monograph published in the *Australian Wine Browser*, 1979.

[2] Halliday, *Australian Wine Compendium*, 1985.

SIX

Gold and the road to market

'Put it away, Mr Clarke, or we shall all have our throats cut!' Such was the atypically nervous reaction of Governor Sir George Gipps in 1846 to an early discovery of gold. An able and courageous governor, Gipps was in office at the time not only of the Myall Creek revenge murders, when he ordered the trials of local station hands who had slaughtered twenty-eight Aboriginal men, women and children, but was also the man responsible for curing the worst economic recession in the colony's history to that time. In 1846 Gipps, a broken man, resigned his commission and returned to London.

His successor, Sir Charles Fitzroy, was more sanguine. Hearing of the Californian rush of 1849 and the subsequent economic boom, he authorised a reward for a successful discovery, sat back and waited. The results were not long in coming. One restless prospector, Edward Hargraves, returning empty-handed from the goldfields of California, recognised the familiar signs of gold in the hills and creeks north of Bathurst in New South Wales. He instructed John Lister and the Tom Brothers in the art of gold-fossicking and on 12 February 1851 they took the first gold from Summer Hill Creek. Within weeks of the find, of which Hargraves made no secret for he was more than interested in the reward of £10 000 offered by the New South Wales government, hundreds of diggers stricken by goldfever wended their way to the canvas town of Ophir. They came from all classes and all places; in fact so alarming was the exodus caused by the epidemic that the new Victorian government, anxious to preserve its straying population, itself offered a reward to anybody finding payable deposits of gold within 200 miles (320 kilometres) of Melbourne, a distance which reached the Murray River border with New South Wales and most inhabited places of the colony.

This was perhaps an unnecessary gesture, as Victorian gold was discovered in June of the same year, and when substantial finds were made in Ballarat still later that year, the Victorians would go nowhere else. Within three years of these finds the population of Victoria, then scarcely fifteen years old, quadrupled to 300 000 and by 1856 the population of Australia as a whole exceeded one million. Not surprisingly the population was mostly concentrated in the gold-bearing colonies, Victoria having the largest numbers with 450 000 and New South Wales 350 000. By contrast South Australia, where no gold had been found but which had begun colonisation about the same time as Victoria, could scarcely muster 100 000 souls, while Tasmania and Western Australia (where a great deal of gold awaited discovery) were well behind.

What did gold do for wine in this era? In more established wine-producing areas, its immediate effect was disastrous. Labour, both unskilled and skilled (which was scarce anyway), became extremely hard to find. Those vineyard owners who did not depend upon their wine for their existence abandoned their vines. Those who did, carried on as best they could. Gold, like the bubonic plague in the fourteenth century, caused an immediate agricultural decline. Fewer labourers meant higher pay, which in turn meant higher costs and more expensive wine.

Unlike the plague, gold would enrich some of its addicts, elevating them to a level of society to which they may previously have been totally unaccustomed. Yet in those regions of gold, even during the rush itself, the winemakers and purveyors of food and drink never had it so good, for miners have ever been a thirsty lot and whether in parching heat or even the ice cold of a Ballarat winter, wine was an accommodating companion. So at this time the Victorian vine followed the mine—from Melbourne to Ballarat, Ararat, Bendigo and other regions and back again—to slake the thirsts not only of the miners but also of that thriving capital not far away.

Those seekers came from everywhere. They sought not merely gold but a new life. Thus from France to the Great Western goldfields via Beechworth came Jean and Anne Marie Trouette, together with Anne Marie's brother, Emile, arriving there in 1858. The Great Western gold had diminished by 1863, so Jean and Emile purchased an estate near Great Western which they called St Peters. Jean had had experience of winemaking in Gers, a *département* better known for its armagnacs that for its table wines. By 1867 they had 50 000 vines and 2000 fruit trees in bearing. That year they produced a quantity of a least 500 gallons (2275 litres) of red and white wine of good quality. That we know this is due to the Gold Medal for White Wine and the First Class Certificate for red awarded to the entries at the Intercolonial Exhibition held in 1883. The Trouette name was not to be long at Great Western. By 1885 Jean was dead and his son Nicholas, twenty-six, was tragically asphyxiated the following year by carbon dioxide fumes while trying to rescue a cellar hand who was similarly overcome. By 1897 the remaining Trouette family, mother Anne Marie and daughter Marie, plagued by a series of bad seasons, sold out to an English family named Merton.

Joseph and Henry Best, who also were to contribute much to the wine development of the Great Western area, were purveyors of food. Arriving as infants in Launceston in 1833, they reached Melbourne in 1838. When in 1857 the Victorian gold rush was at its height, Joseph and Henry, then aged twenty-seven and twenty-five decided to go west to the diggings, but not with picks, gold pans and cradles. Their capital was invested in cattle yards and a slaughterhouse in Great Western. Building their butcher's business on the hunger of the miners in Ararat, Stawell and Great Western in the space of eight years, they made sufficient money to become men of property.

Joseph bought his 'Great Western' property in 1865, cleared, fenced and cultivated it, planting his vine cuttings the following year. He was apparently a man of some discrimination, for though the first cuttings planted were obtained from the nearby Trouette vineyard, the rest came from an undisclosed source 200 miles (320 kilometres) away. As it was unlikely that they would have come from anywhere west, north or south of Great Western, it is most likely that their source was the Yarra Valley and perhaps the de Castella brothers. Making his first vintage of 38 gallons (172 litres) in 1868, he had extended his vineyard to fifty acres (twenty hectares) by 1876. The following year saw a vintage of 7000 gallons (31 850 litres) of wine. The establishment was also growing, there being in 1870, according to the *Ararat Advertiser*,

> a fine winepress; adjoining the wine press house is the cellar, a large building lately put up, and it has two lofty stories *[sic]* sunk beneath the surface where the temperature cannot be but cool. The cellar will hold 20,000 gallons which Mr Best estimates about two years' produce.

Eight years later, there were many large casks and

> a decline leads to a main storage cellar. This portion comprises 4 drives 7 feet [2.14 metres] by 4 feet [1.22 metres] crossed and recrossed by other drives of equal length. The entrance drive is 90 feet [27.5 metres] long . . .

Thus between 1870 and 1878 the famous Great Western 'drives' had been begun, no doubt by miners down on their luck who needed the money. Excellent though these tunnels were for the maturation of table wine, there was no doubt that they would be of even greater worth for the bottle maturation of sparkling wine.

Joseph Best died a bachelor in 1887 aged fifty-seven years and obviously was a winemaker of great talent (as witness the number of gold medals and first prizes awarded to his wines at international exhibitions in the 1870s and 1880s), yet there is no evidence that he ever attempted to make sparkling wine, an oversight that would most certainly be set right by his successor, Hans Irvine.

The younger Best brother, Henry, also trod the wine path, setting up in 1866 the 'Concongella' winery virtually opposite his brother's vineyard. With the hindsight of history, his has been the 'Best' name to survive in Great Western to this day.

In some places in western Victoria the vine (in very small numbers) even preceded the mullock heaps. One such was Avoca, where there were a few vines as early as 1848.

In Bendigo the vine may also have anticipated the rush, though certainly if it was not there before, it most assuredly was afterwards, there being over forty vineyards in the surrounding countryside by 1861. There were even vines close to chilly Ballarat at Dead Horse Gully, hopefully not the effect of the local wine.

The lure of gold sent trekkers to the north-east of the colony; there, around Rutherglen, substantial finds were made. Some lucky individuals even picked up nuggets in what was to be the high street of the town, while others stayed to plant vines, noticing the flourishing vineyards at nearby Gooramadda, planted by James Lindsay Brown, the owner of the run, in 1851. By 1870 a carpet of vines had spread over Rutherglen. It had become the largest vineyard area in the colony.

Many of the names of those early Rutherglen vignerons have faded into history, but others have been more durable. Readily recognisable is the name of Morris. George Francis Morris, a Liverpool bank clerk, arrived in Melbourne aged eighteen in 1852 at the height of the gold fever. Like many others he immediately set off for the most recent discovery. In his case it was the Ovens River in the north-east. Obviously imbued with more than a modicum of commercial sense, Morris soon realised that the path to gold was not littered with nuggets, but might more steadily be pursued by supplying the miners. After several years as a merchant both at Buckland and Beechworth, he returned to England very much a man of substance in 1858, taking his young wife Sarah to meet his family. The following year his son Charles Hughes Morris was born.

Returning to Australia later that year he bought 220 acres (89 hectares) on the Gooramadda run, which he named 'Fairfield'.

Though he was surrounded by a sea of vines, Morris, cautious as ever, did not immediately take the plunge, restricting 'Fairfield' initially to an experimental vineyard of ten acres (4 hectares) planted about 1864. Now that the alluvial gold had been virtually worked out and the ensuing gold fever had somewhat abated, there were fewer miners and consequently fewer local opportunities for advantageous wine sales. So Morris devoted 'Fairfield' primarily to wheat, oats and grazing.

The Morris caution was perhaps justified, for the Rutherglen vintages of the late 1860s and early 1870s were neither easy to sell nor to get to market. Yet the district within a decade was to boom. The reason was the usual admixture of economics and wine tastes. The regional reds were rich, ripe and alcoholic (they still can be made so); they had been seen in London where the *goût anglais* (at least of the man on the Clapham horse bus) favoured such wines and, importantly, by the end of the 1870s they could be transported to Melbourne directly by the new Rutherglen extension of the North Eastern Railway. Others in the district began to show the way. The first George Sutherland Smith had gained 'honourable mention' for one of his wines at the 1873 Vienna Exhibition. In 1874 the Caughey brothers, a pair of eminently successful Melbourne wine merchants, bought their Mount Prior property close to 'Fairfield' and began to plant vines immediately.

Even without export, the economic prospects appeared bright, for in 1874 'imported' wines (and for 'imported' read wines from anywhere outside Victoria) were taxed at four shillings per gallon[1] (by comparison a gallon of Rutherglen wine sold for one shilling (ten cents). With Melbourne being the leading wine market in Australia, any Victorian winemaker could justify virtually any expenditure on vineyards and wine-making equipment. Thus it is quite surprising that Melbourne did not become a Venice of the south, a city whose streets were flooded with cheap red wine of abundant strength.

In a viticultural scene of such economic promise, George Morris expanded and expanded. By 1876 there were sixty acres (twenty-four hectares) under vine at 'Fairfield'; by 1884, 200 acres (eighty hectares). He had the largest winery in the largest Victorian wine-producing area—3500 acres (1418 hectares) by 1885.

And when all of this was sustained from 1886 onwards by a resurgence of the gold boom due to a new mining technique that enabled the working of deep alluvial 'leads', the horizon appeared limitless. But nature is a leveller and within twenty years George

Morris, then a wine potentate, and 'Fairfield', the palace amongst wine estates, would be reduced to the ranks.

Though George Morris was the leading vigneron of the Rutherglen region, other pioneers of that era were no less ambitious. One such was the Scottish carpenter, George Sutherland Smith, who accomplished a very successful transition from river trader to vigneron. Arriving in Australia in the 1850s, he first traded by boat along the Murray River in partnership with his brother-in-law, John Banks. By 1864 sufficient capital was accumulated to buy what real estate agents might today describe as a desirable river frontage. Sutherland Smith quickly developed a winemaking talent (his success at the 1873 Vienna Exhibition bears testament to this) and quickly profited by it, for in 1880 he started to build at All Saints the castellated cellars that stand today not only as a symbol of Victorian permanence but also as an indication of his origins. He was a member of a family that had been for generations carpenters engaged in the maintenance of the Castle of Mey in Caithness.

Another Scot, who did in fact mine in the area, was John Campbell, who reached Rutherglen in 1858. When the gold petered out, he settled next to his mine on a thirty-two hectare block, named after the mine 'Bobbie Burns'. Among his plantings of shiraz, pedro ximinez and riesling were a few brown muscat vines, which were to make the reputation of the district in the years to come.

The siren song of gold attracted all manner of men. Not only bank tellers and butchers but doctors and lawyers were entranced by the seductive melody. (Witness the story of Dr Lindeman.) George Harry Brown was a youthful law clerk before his arrival in Melbourne in 1852, but city practice held no fascination. He immediately set out for Bendigo with his pick and his gold pan. Unfortunately for him, but luckily for the vine, he was one of the many who laboured virtually in vain. He saved just enough to buy a property at Hurdle Creek close to Milawa in partnership with four others. The venture obviously prospered, for George Brown was able to buy out his partners.

In 1857 a migrant Scot named John Graham arrived in the region with his schoolteacher daughter and bought 125 acres (fifty hectares) of the Oxley Plains, close to the future village of Milawa. Marrying Graham's daughter, George Brown joined Graham in his farming activities, expanding Graham's table-grape vineyard by planting wine varieties. On Graham's death, the couple moved the short distance from Hurdle Creek to Milawa, taking with them their son, John Francis Brown, who had been born in 1867. Twenty-two years later, in 1889, he was to make the first Brown wine.

In the 1840s the imperial government, after frequent petitions from New South Wales, allowed the immigration of indentured German labourers to increase the working skills of the colony in many crafts. Viticulture in particular benefited. When their indentured term was complete most of them settled on their own smallholdings. One such, Anthony Ruche, found his way to the Rutherglen region in the late 1850s (another such family, the Gehrigs, established themselves at nearby Barnawartha) and there established a small winery and vineyard of about one hectare. Ruche was a man of few needs or excellent credit, for he did not part with the wine he made for over twenty years. When at last he did (or was obliged to), 7000 gallons (31 850 litres) of old vintages were sold to a prominent Melbourne wine merchant for £1680 ($3360), an average price of 10.69 cents per litre. The merchant reportedly doubled his money in a single day. Such apparently was the burgeoning popularity of the Rutherglen area in 1880. The Ruche property soon after passed into the hands of the Chambers family, whose name is today identified with the sumptuous liqueur muscats and tokays of the region.

Bailey is also a name familiar to all lovers of that quintessence of the north-east—liqueur muscat. Richard Bailey was one of the first settlers of the new township of Melbourne, establishing a cartage business there in the late 1830s. A few years later he set up a general store in the tiny township of Glenrowan, about to be the gateway to the golden north-east, and later still the native heath of the indomitable Kelly clan. Richard Bailey was obviously one of those fortunate individuals destined to be in the right place at the right time, for in Glenrowan at the height of the gold fever, no merchant ever had to pan for it. It was there in every transaction, so persistent were its addicts in its pursuit. In 1870 when the gold boom had become a distant echo, Bailey bought the rich red granite country lying a few kilometres to the west of the township and planted vines in the ensuing decade. The reds that the Bailey family would produce would be as uncompromising as the Kelly armour and require almost as long to soften, but their muscats, long flavoured and liquorous, would, in that memorable Burgundian phrase, slide down the throat 'like the infant Jesus in velvet trousers'.

By 1860 popular confidence in Victoria Felix knew no bounds; horizons only existed to expand and so rapidly had the Victorian economy grown that there were wine enthusiasts who felt that the days of subsistence farming before the gold rush, in which a small vineyard played but a minor part, were now over and wine might become an attractive economic unit in its own right. The age of the entrepreneur had arrived.

Thus in 1860 the prospectus of the Goulburn Vineyard Proprietary made the following confident pronouncement.

> That Victoria is a country eminently adapted by nature for the cultivation of Vines is a fact that has long been generally known. The means we possess here of making wines of the most delicious quality and better suited to the inhabitants of these colonies as a healthy beverage than most of the light wines which are imported, has also been equally well known to those who are conversant with the subject. The wines of the Rhine and the Moselle can certainly be equalled, but in some cases will probably be surpassed by the vintages of the Goulburn, the Loddon, the Campaspe and in fact the whole valley of the Murray . . . Besides the commercial benefits, the best sanitary and moral results may be anticipated because a wine-drinking population is never a drunken population . . .

It was the type of exhortative prose that might well have been written by Busby a generation before, but it was in fact the work of the gentleman, scholar and poet, Richard Heingist 'Orion' Horne, a multifaceted personality who reached Melbourne in 1852, attracted by the lure of gold. His career in Victoria is worth closer examination.

Despite his distinctly literary background, his first appointment was the command of the gold escort from Ballarat to Melbourne. In 1853 he became gold commissioner on the Goulburn River, 'a wide sprawling district of empty graves, recently golden gullies, quartz hills, lush savage forests, mournful lagoons and miserable swamps', but the position was not to his liking, for he obtained leave of absence in 1854 and returned to Melbourne. There he continued his employment as the Australian correspondent for the London magazines of Charles Dickens, his former London editor and

Richard 'Orion' Horne: a man of letters and a most unlikely entrepreneur.

confidant (Thackeray was another friend), seeking Dickens's intercession in support of his appointment to the Chair of English literature at the recently established University of Melbourne (he was unsuccessful). He was also an amateur actor and a keen guitarist who, presumably as the climax to his musical career, composed a cantata in honour of HRH Prince Alfred Duke of Edinburgh on his arrival in Victoria in 1868. He was a student of electricity and, forty years before its time, interested in human flight, prophesying that 'the time shall come when men shall . . . use the air as a great highway for travel to any part of the globe . . .' He proposed also the construction of a railway to Seymour, the opening of the Goulburn River to navigation, the cultivation of the mulberry tree (for silk production), the cactus (for the cochineal insect) and the commercial slaughter of the kangaroo for human consumption. There were a few pies in which Horne did not have a finger. In short, he became a man of opinion in the bustling Melbourne of his day, at dinner parties and soirées, upon committees and inquiries.

One of his committees was that set up to establish 'a company for the cultivation of the vine and for the making of wines on the banks of the Goulburn River'. Horne was obviously determined that there should be such a vineyard, for the events that were about to unfold would have deterred many men from proceeding.

The proposed company was to have been established to buy a tract of land from one Andrew Sinclair, in need of extra cash from his property, Noorilim Station, abutting the Goulburn. Sinclair was obviously a hard-drinking 'bush gentleman', who cared little for wine and whose chief tipple was rough 'brandy'. Perhaps wine would have turned out better for him, but what happened to Sinclair is best left to Horne.

> Mr Sinclair came down to Melbourne to arrange terms with the proposed Company . . . On the first day of his arrival, being at dinner at Bignel's hotel, some colonial wine was recommended to him as being very fine. It was one of the pale golden Kaludahs [a Hunter white]. He drank the first glass, and looked thoughtful, then a second glass and looked round, as though he fancied we were all laughing at him. Somebody asked what he thought of it, for it really was a beautiful and delicate wine. 'Well', he said, 'I think that a glass of sherry in a bucket of water, would represent all its qualities—so far as my taste is concerned'. A day or two afterwards Mr Sinclair was missing. Nobody knew what had become of him. 'Off on the spree', it was said. At the end of two or three weeks, the unfortunate gentleman's body, disfigured by insects, reptiles and the native cat and dissolving in the sun, was discovered in the scrub of the seashore near St Kilda, where it appeared he had wandered after having been hocussed by some brandy he had drunk in one of the evil villas of the suburbs.

Sinclair's death focussed Horne's mind sharply. The Noorilim purchase would have to be abandoned as the vendor had died and there would be great delays before any purchases could be completed. So a further meeting of the shareholders was called and it was proposed that the vineyard be relocated on the neighbouring Tabilk run, in which the prominent landowner Hugh Glass was interested. Importantly also for the future of the project, two new shareholders were enrolled, the brothers John Pinney Bear and William Huchins Bear, both mature and widely experienced men of the land.

The meeting, held in Melbourne on 6 June 1860 'for the purpose of forming the company to be entitled the Tabilk Vineyard

Proprietary', successfully completed the relocation and Horne's dream of a vineyard on the Goulburn River became reality. With a capital of £25 000 ($50 000) the new company bought 640 acres (259 hectares) of the Tabilk run for £5/10/- ($11) per acre. Progress thereafter was swift, for the Burgundian manager of the project, Ludovic Marie, had already been appointed and advertisements for one million vine cuttings placed in the leading colonial newspapers of the day. By the end of 1860, sixty-five acres (twenty-six hectares) had been planted with the enthusiastic assistance of Horne, then aged fifty-seven, and two dozen labourers. By 1861, 200 acres (eighty-one hectares) were under vine, 'all of them healthy and free from blight', according to a contemporary report.

When Ludovic Marie left in 1862, this change precipitated others. Horne,[2] secretary pro tem, was replaced and the vineyard was leased for a time to J. E. Blake (a member of the company). Yet by 1870 the huge 'Old Cellars', 300 feet (ninety-one metres) long, had been completed, the vineyard fully planted and a new manager of Swiss ancestry, Leopold de Soyres, had been appointed.

De Soyres did not last long, resigning in 1872 to run a general store at Dookie and later to plant a vineyard there as well. A succession of resident part-owners and managers followed, including a Melbourne chemist, William Ford, who bought the shares of Hugh Glass, who had died in 1870.

The rock upon which the managerial foundations of Tabilk rested at this time must have been John Pinney Bear. Indeed it may have been Bear who decided that after fifteen years of existence, during which there were several corporate reorganisations, it was also time for a name-change. 'Chateau Tahbilk' was first mentioned in 1879. Was it Bear's idea or that of the manager appointed in 1877, Francois de Coueslant?

By 1873 the Tabilk vineyard was producing a substantial quantity of wine (112 000 litres in that year) and so a 'new' cellar was planned in 1875 to hold nearly 900 000 litres of maturing wine. During the construction of this cellar there were two events of note: the first was an odd coincidence of name—the excavation contractor was one James Purbrick of Seymour, though no relation to the Purbrick family which was to buy the estate fifty years later; the second was the placement of a time capsule in the new wall of the cellar containing 'the daily and local journals and a scroll recording the event together with two bottles of Tabilk wine'. Though there were grave fears to the contrary, the cellar was completed in time for the 1876 vintage, shortly after which Bear's fellow shareholder, Ford, died. Bear was now on his own, though with the able assistance of de Coueslant from 1877.

What grapes were cultivated at Tabilk at this time? The list of available wines is illuminating as most were obviously what we would today call 'varietals': riesling, verdelho, pedro ximinez, muscat, malbec, cabernet and shiraz. There were also varieties much less fashionable and even unknown today such as aucerot and gouais.

By 1877 Tabilk was firmly on its feet, producing between 30 000 and 35 000 gallons of wine (136 000–159 000 litres) per vintage. Due to Bear's energy and vigour and de Coueslant's skill it was to double its production and then to face, with most of the other vineyards of southern and central Victoria, the greatest trial of vinegrowing in the nineteenth century, phylloxera.

In 1861, despite the decline of the gold boom, the original vineyards of the Melbourne suburbs as well as those of Geelong and the Yarra Valley were flourishing. In that year there were 340 acres (137 hectares) of vines in the County of Bourke, or what might now be called the Melbourne metropolitan area. This was to grow to 850 acres (344 hectares) by 1871. Immediately to the north-west of the city at Sunbury, Craiglee was planted in 1864 by James Johnston, one of the founders of the Melbourne *Argus*, and quickly gained a reputation for quality reds[3].

John Fawkner, another early press baron and legislator, was by 1850 producing 9000 litres of wine at Pascoe Vale. For the times it was an impressive quantity and must have brought with it its own marketing problems. Still more does it typify the enthusiasm and industry of those wine pioneers.

In fact unlike the climate of Sydney, that of Melbourne so suited the vine that virtually all the early suburbs had a vineyard or two. Nineteenth century Hawthorn in particular built a reputation in wine to rival that of its football team a century later. So too were there a number of vineyards in fashionable Toorak, one as large as thirty acres (twelve hectares) owned by a Swiss.

To the east in the Yarra Valley, Paul de Castella was well established at Yering. By 1857 an important part of the new estate had been planted with the cabernet cuttings got from Chateau Lafite. Its vineyard was evidently thriving, as a correspondent of the *Illustrated Australian News* reported in April 1866.

> The large illustration of this month gives the busy and joyous scene of gathering in the vintage. The sketch was taken at Yering, the property of Mr [Paul de] Castella on the Yarra flats. 100 acres are there under vine cultivation, while fresh ground is being occupied yearly. Some of the vines are now of 20 years standing, and their healthy and luxuriant aspect testify *[sic]* the suitablility of the soil for vine culture, as well as admirable management. About one-half of the 100 acres are in bearing, and the yield is about 400 gallons per acre.
>
> The soil is a loamy clay, with a gravelly sub-stratum. The grape varieties are Pineau, Hermitage, Burgundy, White Chasselas, Gouais and Tokay. [Strangely, no mention is made of cabernet sauvignon, which must have been a dominant part of the vineyard.] . . . the wines of this district are becoming very popular in Melbourne and enterprising colonists are fast filling up the valley with similar establishments, three being already in good working order and ardently competing for superiority.

These competitors would not yet have included Paul's brother, Hubert, who reached the colony in 1854 and began to plant his vineyard, St Hubert's, a decade later. His vines would have been too young to compete with his brother's at that time. Nor would they have included, in all probability, Guilaume de Pury, who began to plant Yeringberg in the same year as Hubert. They may have included the Deschamps Brothers, who had established vineyards near Lilydale in the late 1850s, and Samuel de Pury, owner of Cooring Yering, set up about the same time and grubbed out in 1870.

However fierce the competition for what little table wine there was, the Yarra Valley was obviously an idyllic place. Let Hubert de Castella describe its elysian fields in the 1880s.

> About thirty miles from Melbourne, a basin of some 20 000 acres lies, surrounded by the Dividing ranges on the north and east, by the Plenty ranges to the west and by the Dandenong mountain and its spurs to the south. Hills after hills seem as if they had tumbled down from this last mountain, invaded the valley from the open end, and stopped just

> sufficiently far away from the winding Yarra to display a succession of most romantic landscapes.
>
> On the border of the rich meadows through which the river meanders, three of these rounded hills, two miles from each other, stand, each crowned with one of the above-named vineyards [Yering, Yeringberg and St Hubert's].
>
> Nature has intended them for the cultivation of the grape. The soil is perfection, abundantly productive, but light and of gray color on heavy clay subsoil. Every acre planted with vines is on the incline, facing the rising, the midday or the evening sun. As to climate, the moisture supplied by the broad plains, which cools down the nights during the hot season and frees the locality from frost in spring, renders it particularly favorable.
>
> . . . St Hubert's is just in the centre of the basin I described. The hill it occupies slopes down on all sides from the habitations and other buildings, which, like a small village, stand on a plateau of forty acres dotted with grass plots and clumps of pines. The vineyard, one mile in length by nearly a half a mile in breadth, covers all the ground between the houses and the plain.

De Castella then describes how dense fog rising at night from the plain usually protected these hillside vines from the dangers of frost and 'insures to the must the lightness so peculiar to the Yarra wines' and how (here echoing Busby's words 60 years earlier)

> had not the wines of these vineyards reminded the three foreign friends who planted them (his brother Paul, Guillaume de Pury and himself) of the good wines of France they had met with in their younger days, they would not have fought so long—some of them to their sorrow—the hard battle of the pure light wines against a population of beer and spirit drinkers.

They fought so well that the Yarra's wine reputation owed its all to the de Castellas and de Purys. The vineyards of Yering, Yeringberg and St Hubert's would establish such a reputation for quality, that, despite their disappearance in the 1920s, their fond memory would linger as a kind of vinous Camelot and would lead in no small part to the restoration of the vine to its rightful place in the Valley in the 1970s. But all lay nearly a century ahead.

At Geelong in the time of gold, the vine's progress was no less spectacular. By 1861 it had the largest vineyard area in the colony—560 acres (226 hectares), far outstripping Melbourne, Rutherglen and the Yarra. It was an extremely busy port and of course the entry to the western goldfields. Its pre-eminence as a port would, in fact, later lead to its extinction as a vineyard area, but this anticipates our story.

As vignerons, the Swiss were again to the fore, although there was a substantial German proprietorship also. By 1861 there were more than fifty vineyards in the region and, though grapes would have sold well to the miners as fresh fruit, there were also many wineries.[4] Yet what Geelong seemed to lack was a regular distribution system. As the numbers of hogsheads mounted, there were periodic wine auctions. In one of these in 1863, over 26 000 litres of wine were sold at prices ranging from nine cents to fifteen cents a litre (shades of Busby's offer to his brother-in-law over twenty years earlier). Though the region did not know it, by 1875, Geelong had reached the summit of its success. The vignoble (vineyard area), consisting chiefly of pinot noir, chardonnay, meunier, shiraz and roussette and spreading in a westward arc from the north to the south of the town, was renowned in its day, but its rapid downhill slide was due to a cause that still sends shudders through vintners even today. (See chapter 8, 'The scourge of the vine'.)

Some contemporary authorities such as Ebenezer Ward believed that vineyards had existed at Bendigo from the time of first settlement of the region some fifteen years before, but by 1861 there were more than forty vineyards around Bendigo stretching from the Campaspe River in the east to the Loddon in the west.

The Bendigo vineyards showed the typical growth spurt of the times: from 125 acres (fifty hectares) producing a mere 1500 gallons (6825 litres) of wine in 1861 to 490 acres (198 hectares) and 53 000 gallons (241 000 litres) by 1869. Growth was slower at Bendigo during the 1870s, the vineyard area reaching its peak about 1880 when there were about 540 acres (218 hectares) yielding 60 500 gallons (275 000 litres), the production of an estimated one hundred wineries.

Certainly at this time the wines of Bendigo made their presence felt on the world stage, for at the Vienna Exhibition of 1873 a furore erupted when the French judges, having highly praised some hermitage entries, then withdrew in protest when they discovered the wines were from Bendigo, because 'wines of this quality must clearly be French'.

By 1861 one result of the gold rush was the burgeoning popularity of Australian wine. We have seen Horne's description of the Kaludah white and Sinclair's reaction (both of which would probably have been the same to any wine). One of the subscribers for ten shares in 'Australian Vineyards Pty Limited', a reorganisation of the Tabilk Proprietary which took place about 1866, was one J. E. Blake, gentleman.

John Elliott Blake was an experienced Hunter Valley hand, having an involvement (perhaps as manager) in the Kaludah vineyard of the Scottish and Australian Development Company in the late 1840s, as well as being an original member of the Hunter Valley Vineyard Association and lessee of Irrawang after King's death in 1857. Whether Blake was the Melbourne agent for the sale of Kaludah and Irrawang wines or a lover of Hunter wines in general is hard to ascertain but as another important Victorian wine personality of the 1860s and 1870s, the Reverend Dr John Ignatius Bleasdale, put it, 'in an incredibly short time [Blake] made us thoroughly acquainted with Irrewang *[sic]* and Kaludah, white, red and rosy'.[5]

Bleasdale also was a character of the Busby mould, preaching (who knows perhaps literally from time to time, as his area of pastoral concern included Geelong) the propagation of temperance by moderate wine drinking. As he said when, soon after his arrival in 1851 he was offered a 'half pint of rum and water, by the smell about half and half' by some 'more or less drunk' bushmen in a city street, 'from that time, I turned my attention and all the knowledge I possessed then to forwarding winegrowing and drinking as the one efficient cure for spirit drinking and drunkenness'.

Bleasdale was a man of keen insight as well as considerable influence, early on appreciating the limestone subsoils and cool climate of the Geelong district as being important to the production of fine table wine. Like Horne, he too was a man of worth on committees and commissions, being appointed in 1865 to a royal commission responsible for the organisation of the intercolonial exhibition. He himself was chairman of the wine committee. A few years later in 1873 he made a report for the Victorian Department of Agriculture, classifying Victorian wines from region to region, and when he at last wearied of Victoria, it was not to return to England or to Rome, but to travel once more to a New World wine land, California.

How did the Melbourne press view the development of vineyard Victoria in the age of gold? It was nothing if not bullish and chauvinistic. In April 1866 the *Illustrated Australian News*, showing its artist's impression of a vintage at Paul de Castella's Yering estate prophesied thus,

> the vineyard interest in Victoria, should it progress in the future as it has done in the last decade, will be entitled to rank as the fourth great producing interest of the Colony . . .
>
> The odd acres [of the early days] have swelled to thousands; at Sunbury, Tabilk, Yering and in the Albury district may now be found vineyards, each comprising from fifty to one hundred and thirty acres of land, whilst on every side the traveller cannot fail to meet with plots of the life-giving plant, of dimensions according with the objects of the owner, be they growing wine for sale or simply for family use.

The piece fulsomely praised the beneficial effect of such vineyards upon 'the health and morals of the people' and observed that

> already in the western districts [presumably Geelong and environs] in which vine culture is longest established, many hotels [obviously vendors of 'ardent spirits'] have been closed in consequence solely of the facilities for obtaining native wines from the numerous growers.

Wine was also cheap, varying from 'three to five shillings a gallon [seven to eleven cents per litre], at which a well-managed vineyard will yield a very respectable income and at which, too, the working man of Victoria can well afford to make a liberal use of it'.

Thus in what would become the 'Garden State' the vine was health-giving, morally suitable and cheap. What is more, it could be grown virtually anywhere.

> The southern half of the continent of Australia would appear to be peculiarly adapted for the vine . . . but in Victoria, more especially, the whole country seems adapted for growing the vine to perfection. Excepting only on the very highest portions of our mountain ranges,

> the vine thrives and produces wines of the most delicate quality, for which at some future date when we produce them in excess of our own wants, a demand will doubtless arise in Great Britain
> (*Illustrated Australian News*, April 1866).

This prophecy would be fulfilled but not by those delicate wines of southern Victoria.

Though the newly truncated colony of New South Wales lost its Port Phillip district in 1851, the gold rush but briefly stunted the growth of its vineyards and the enthusiasm of its vintners not at all.

In 1850 Sydney held its first wine show at which James King duly exhibited. He received a first prize and the gold medal of the Australian Botanic and Horticultural Society for a white wine of 1846 vintage 'considered . . . to be a dry, pleasant wine and perfectly sound'. The Hunter River Vineyard Association had been formed on 19 May 1847 under the dedicated chairmanship of James King of Irrawang, near present-day Raymond Terrace. The other moving spirit in its creation was Henry Carmichael of Prophyry, a property some kilometres to the north of Irrawang. It had been formed after a somewhat heated controversy amongst the members of the Hunter River Agricultural Society about the relative worth and profitability of vines and wool, a discussion which, like that of chalk and cheese, can never be satisfactorily resolved.

The activities of the first few years of the Society were published in 1854 and contain what today might be termed its 'mission statement'.

> We happen to have emigrants from a country which does not produce wine; our knowledge of its growth and manufacture, therefore, is only the result of our reading and limited experience in this. We may be said, then, to be merely groping our way singly in the dark. To make the most of our position—to make known to each other such favourable points and circumstances as we may notice in our operations—to exhibit the result of our individual doings—and to meet, periodically, for that purpose, is the object of the present proposed association.

Though its members, like inexperienced winemakers anywhere, were of varied talent, the Society certainly fulfilled its mission, by all contemporary accounts raising the standards of local winemaking and proving an effective lobby group in such matters as the reduction of imperial tariffs and the import of skilled German labour. Importantly, the exchange of information thus engendered began to show the suitability of certain wine varieties such as semillon and shiraz for the region. Typical of the comments about the better wines produced at its tastings must have been those of the Maitland *Mercury*'s correspondent who covered its 1860 meeting. 'A pale clear light wine possessing bouquet and a very delicate flavour. A delicious wine. I could drink any amount of this: it must be Dr Lindeman's wine.'

To what extent then had the wine of New South Wales penetrated the market by 1860? We have already seen how popular it was in Melbourne. It was even more so in its own localities. In the words of the Maitland *Mercury* once more,

> the greater proportion of the wine of this colony is consumed in neighbourhoods where it is grown. Its cheapness, and the facilities for obtaining it, as well as its intrinsic recommendations, have long brought it into very general use in the winegrowing district . . . it is the almost exclusive beverage of the labouring people; and the large and increasing demand that has there sprung up operates to prevent many of the growers consigning to the Sydney market.

Yet for some reason it was not sought in the larger urban centres of the time.

> Strange to say however, the wines are but little appreciated by the large urban population living in the immediate centre of the winegrowing districts, probably owing to there being no hotelkeeper in Maitland sufficiently enterprising to introduce and recommend them at his bar as a common beverage.

Hotel-keepers were not the only problem. Transport to market also presented vast difficulties, freight by bullock dray being slow and dangerous while carriage by sea from the Hunter Valley was expensive until the monopoly of the Australian Steam Navigation Co. was broken in the mid-1850s.

By 1860 Hunter wine production had surpassed 60 000 gallons

(273 000 litres). Far-sighted winemakers such as Dr Lindeman and George Wyndham were certain that local markets would never absorb their increasing production, so in 1861 they employed a youthful salesman, J. D. Lankester, to sell their production of 'about 40 000 gallons [182 000 litres] the greater proportion of which will, in course of time, be forwarded to Sydney'.

It was about this time also that some of the ancestors of the present day Hunter winemakers began to settle the Pokolbin area of the Valley.

Edward Tyrrell was a youth of fifteen when he arrived in the colony in 1850. A nephew of William, the newly installed Bishop of Newcastle and initially under his tutelage, Edward at first tried dairying near Singleton. The venture failed. Fortunately in 1858 he heard of land selections available near the Brokenback Range and applied in time to secure a forested block of 330 acres (134 hectares) of mostly basaltic loam on a limestone subsoil. He set to work immediately building a slab hut (which still stands) and planted a few acres of wine grapes. In 1864 he constructed the 'old' winery, long since surrounded by accretions of galvanised iron and timber, very much in harmony with the original. By 1870 there were thirty acres (twelve hectares) planted to semillon and shiraz with a little ugni blanc and perhaps aucerot. Hesitancy concerning aucerot is perhaps necessary as twenty-eight years later in an interview given to the Maitland *Mercury*, Edward Tyrrell was at that time making preparations to plant more of 'a new grape of which Mr Tyrrell possesses a small area named Aucerot, given by Mr Lindeman and described as the king of white grapes'. At that time,

> the estate, which went by the name of Ashman's, comprised 500 acres [200 hectares] of splendid soil . . . [having] 29 acres [twelve hectares] of Hermitage [shiraz], Madeira [verdelho], Shiraz [ugni blanc] and Riesling [semillon], the former (Hermitage) being especially good.

Edward had not enjoyed robust health, and may also have been feeling his years (he was then sixty-three), for the reporter adds, 'his sons are now old enough to relieve him of many cares and appear quite able and ready to do it'.

Another of the present-day winemaking families is Drayton, whose forebear Joseph reached Sydney in 1853. It had been a voyage of personal tragedy for Joseph, as his two-year-old son Charles died on board ship. It was tragedy redoubled when his wife and newly born daughter died at Sydney's quarantine station within weeks of their arrival. Nonetheless, Joseph and his surviving son, Frederick, continued to Lochinvar where Joseph soon remarried.

By the late 1850s he had settled in Pokolbin at 'Bellevue', the site of the present winery. His first crop, however, was wheat not wine, but about 1860, clearly cognisant of develop-ments in the district, he planted vines. Sometime later, William, a son by his second marriage, acquired the forty acre (sixteen hectare) block adjoining Bellevue. More vines followed, as did prosperity, for close to the turn of the century William was able to outbid a rival for a property previously owned by his wife's family by reputedly paying £1000 ($2000) an acre, a princely sum comparable only to city land prices of his day. One would have thought that the price for the land alone would have made any wine produced from the Lambkin estate instantly world famous, yet the land waited seventy years longer for its first vines.

John McDonald came to Pokolbin in 1870, building a house and winery and planting every vine on his 'Ben Ean' property with his own hands. Though his winery stands today as Lindeman's Hunter Valley headquarters and the brand 'Ben Ean' sells many bottles of Lindeman's, the region's only memory of McDonald, who sold his winery to Lindeman's in 1912, is the name of the road leading from Pokolbin to Rothbury.

There were other names, too, renowned at that time but long since submerged by history and illustrious now only in the silence of country churchyards. Munro of 'Bebeah', whose wines once challenged de Castella's at the Melbourne Exhibition of 1881, the Wilkinsons of 'Coolalta', (long a brand name and vineyard of Lindeman's) and 'Oakdale', still a working vineyard, and Brecht of the original 'Rosemount', one of those German labourers brought to Australia as a result of the successful labour lobbying by William Macarthur.

Far more than the Paris Exhibition of 1855, where the wines of the Antipodes were regarded as something of an oddity, the Bordeaux International Exhibition of 1882 focussed the spotlight of quality on Hunter wines. As well as Brecht, James Kelman (son of William) of Kirkton won gold for an 1876 Hermitage, Philobert

Terrier being equally successful with an 1875. Others to strike gold were Munro of Bebeah and John Wyndham of Dalwood.

Yet the Bordeaux jury was not overgenerous in its praise. As Henry Bonnard, manager of the New South Wales stand at the Exhibition stated in his report to the New South Wales Legislative Assembly,

> the general opinion of [the jury] has most positively been expressed that, of all the foreign countries which have lately inaugurated the cultivation of the vine, Australia has done it the most successfully and in the shortest time. The best Australian red wines were not judged to have the same merits as the best or even ordinary good wines of France . . .

So after general praise, a general let-down. Bonnard proceeds.

> The results of the several first tastings, which . . . were made by . . . highly qualified experts, who rank first amongst the winebrokers and tasters of Bordeaux, were given very reservedly and measuredly; their remarks were quite in favour of the wines, so far as being raw material, which could easily be transformed or ameliorated by successive treatment; but it should be taken into account that these wine experts were of those who deal in nothing but the best and most select quantities of the wines of the Medoc, wines with which no other, so far, stand by comparison.

Good raw material, then, but obviously in need of more winemaking refinement. But even with all the winemaking polish in the world, the wines would never resemble Bordeaux. *Vive la différence!*

West of the Great Divide, the lure of gold had also peopled the Mudgee region; in 1851 the diggers flocked to Hill End. Within weeks the tent town had a population of 800 and further discoveries at Home Rule and Gulgong ensured permanent settlement in the area.

To Mudgee in 1858 came Adam Roth, one of those German vine dressers, brought to Camden by William Macarthur and recently free of his indentures. With goldfields all around there was tremendous demand for provisions of all kinds, especially for fruit, vegetables, meat and wine. Roth, on his fertile thirty-seven hectares by the banks of the Eurunderee Creek, was certainly the right man in the right place at the right time. Other Germans came also, and with names like Roth, Kurtz and Buchholz, the Cudgegong Valley became a German wine settlement, with 160 hectares under vine by 1880, rivalled only by the Barossa.

McWilliam is a family name that looms large today in the Murrumbidgee Irrigation Area and the Hunter Valley yet Samuel McWilliam was barely acquainted with either of those areas. An Irish immigrant, he settled first near Sale in Victoria in 1860, moving north to the Corowa district of New South Wales ten years later with his wife and their infant son, John James McWilliam or JJ as he came to be called. In 1877 the first McWilliam vines were planted at Corowa and later the wine was sold from a wineshop in the town. Later still the McWilliam family would outgrow Corowa and become a dominant wine family in New South Wales, but this would await the arrival of the twentieth century.

Wine production was indeed growing throughout New South Wales. By 1865, according to the New South Wales Statistical Register, there were 1243 acres (503 hectares) of vineyard in wine production throughout the colony, yielding 168 123 gallons (764 960 litres). The Hunter Valley provided the lion's share of 583 acres (236 hectares), about forty-seven per cent of the total area, and with 90 535 gallons (411 930 litres), nearly fifty-four per cent of the total of that vintage.

Eleven years later in 1876, wine production in New South Wales had risen ninefold to 831 749 gallons (3.78 million litres) from 3163 acres (1280 hectares), the share of the Hunter Valley (though still the colony's largest production area) having fallen slightly in percentage to thirty-eight per cent in area (1200 acres) and in yield to 47.6 per cent (396 201 gallons—1.8 million litres).

What were the other chief wine-producing areas of New South Wales at this time? Though the suburban vineyards of Sydney still existed, production was minimal, only 340 gallons (1547 litres) yielded from 3.75 acres (1.5 hectares). Further west, the thriving country town of Parramatta vintaged 5320 gallons (24 200 litres) from 51 acres (twenty-one hectares), while in the neighbouring Hawkesbury plain country, Penrith had a vineyard area occupying 128 acres (fifty-two hectares), which produced in that year 24 960 gallons (113 570 litres). Further south, close to the Nepean River, the vineyards of Camden, Narellan, Picton and Campbelltown were over one hundred acres (forty hectares) in extent.

As well the north-coast regions of the colony produced surprisingly large amounts of wine. Grafton, the Macleay River, the Manning River, the Richmond River and Port Macquarie combined in 1876 to yield 40 520 gallons (184 360 litres) from 133.5 acres (fifty-four hectares).

Inland, what are today called the Southern Highlands and the South-West Slopes (the latter area now reborn as the Hilltops region) were also quite productive, Wagga having seventy-three acres (thirty hectares) yielding 13 500 gallons (61 425 litres) in that vintage. Yet by far the largest single wine-producing district in New South Wales was Albury, with vineyards of 993.5 acres (402 hectares) and an 1876 vintage in excess of 237 500 gallons (1.08 million litres). The area may have been popular because of the similarity of its wines to the heavy reds of Rutherglen across the border.

Vintage 1876 represented the high point of New South Wales production for the next twenty years, not to be surpassed until 1895 when 885 673 gallons (4.03 million litres) poured from the winepresses. By that time there was another wine power in Australia to be reckoned with, a colony whose wine had not ridden on the back of the gold boom, whose wines had been severely penalised by exorbitant intercolonial tariffs and which had learnt by bitter experience the many trials and the rare triumphs of export sales. That colony was South Australia.

---

[1] In 1879, it would be increased to six shillings (sixty cents) per gallon.

[2] Horne's role in the creation of Tabilk remains a mystery. He held no equity in the company, yet worked prodigiously in what proved to be a temporary position. Why?

[3] Craiglee Hermitage 1872 is the oldest Australian red I have ever tasted. In 1974, though then a centenarian, it certainly could be drunk and there is no doubt that forty years earlier it would have been in prime condition.

[4] So well did the grapes sell that winegrowers often sold them as fresh fruit, leaving wine to be made from 'over-ripe and rotten grapes' (Bellperroud, *Essay*, 1859).

[5] In 1860 the *Sydney Morning Herald* reported that '3000 dozen of the Irrawang and Kaludah wines have been sold in Melbourne'.

SEVEN

The surge of South Australia

In 1850 there were 282 acres (114 hectares) of vines in South Australia, the vast majority in what are now the city and suburbs of Adelaide. That same year on 18 August, appropriately aboard the *British Empire*, the twenty-year-old Thomas Hardy arrived, bringing with him a month's clothes, a knife, a fork, two spoons, a plate and his fiddle. After seeking employment 'in the grocery line', he succeeded five days later in securing a place 'keeping cattle among the hills for some time, then bullock driving and work in the vineyard for seven shillings [seventy cents] a week with a prospect of a rise in a short time'. His employer was John Reynell. Hardy got his rise (two shillings a week) on 6 October, worked for Reynell till Christmas and never looked back.

Barely had he left Reynell when gold was discovered in New South Wales and a few months later in Victoria. Hardy was but one of the multitude lured to the fields and one of many who 'forgot' to obtain a licence. Fined one pound (two dollars), a large sum in 1851, for that indiscretion, he decided that mining should be better left to the miners who, after all, had to eat. Drawing on his cattle-droving experience, he herded stock to the goldfields, sold them to butchers and made sufficient money in two years to marry his cousin, Johanna, and buy a property of fifteen acres (six hectares) on the banks of the Torrens three miles (five kilometres) downstream from Adelaide. By 1854 he had planted 'Bankside' with a little over a quarter of a hectare of shiraz and grenache, good varieties to fortify, as he was later to find out.

In 1857 he sent two hogsheads of his first vintage to England, returning himself two years later as the emigrant made good—a successful son of the South Australian soil. Hardy, however, had hardly begun to thrive. Olives, oranges, lemons, dried fruit—they all had flourished, but wine above all. By 1862 he was making nearly 7000 litres of wine.

The South Australian vintage was growing apace, 312 000 gallons (1.42 million litres) from 4000 acres (1620 hectares) in that same year. Virtually every landholder with a hectare to spare planted grapes, mostly of heavy-yielding varieties, As a result, with vastly more enthusiasm than skill, South Australia's novice winemakers flooded the colony with rough red wine. Though there was quantity, there was little quality and even less foresight. The jeremiahs forecast doom. As the *Observer* commented caustically, 'there were prospects that failure would teach them [the vintners] to produce an article which would be prized in the markets of the world'. As in New South Wales a generation earlier, but on a regrettably larger scale, there was an almost total lack of expertise. Crude methods produced cruder wines. By 1868 nearly four million litres of wine lapped the banks of the South Australian wine lake. As Ebenezer Ward, the colony's first wine commentator, remarked, 'the greatest bugbear of the wine industry is to contend with the large quantities of young immature wines annually forced into the market'.

What markets? Markets were virtually non-existent. In the words of Dr Alexander Kelly, another noted writer of the time,

> the sale for colonial consumption must be a limited one, in Adelaide more especially, where every cottage with a few roods [a rood is roughly equivalent to 1000 square meters] of ground is able to grow wine enough for the use of its inmates; while seeking a foreign market implies making a good, ripe, keeping wine, which will stand the hardships and trials of travel by sea and land.

Australian wine as an imported article first appeared in British customs records in 1854, when 1384 gallons (6297 litres) were received. Though nearly 25 000 gallons (113 750 litres) were recorded the following year, the totality of shipments to Britain for the ensuing eight years (until 1864) amounted only to about 44 000 gallons (200 200 litres). At that time only wines with a solid reputation were acceptable in London. Unknown wines shipped on spec, and many were, often found their way back to the maker untasted with shipping to his account. Prices for such wines, even when purchased, were as low as three cents a litre. It was a highly precarious business. Nevertheless, in Kelly's opinion, London was the only way to go.

> The time has now arrived when the winegrowers of this Colony must bestir themselves, and boldly face the difficulties before them. They must be prepared to take their stand on ground already occupied by the experienced winegrowers of Europe, who have a name and a prestige of centuries in their favour, and it will require no ordinary amount of application and care to produce wines which will find acceptance in England and elsewhere . . . The unsuccessful experiments hitherto made in shipping our native wines to the London market need be no discouragement to our efforts; the combination of unfavourable circumstances under which the attempts were made could not but lead to failure. In the first place, the wines were, many of them, raw and new, and unfit for so long a voyage. That they reached their destination without being utterly spoiled speaks well for their soundness and keeping quality, for many of them were not fortified with spirit; but no wine, even the best, could endure such a voyage without being very much out of sorts; and it would require time, rest and attention in the cellar to restore it to a healthy condition.
>
> That our wines received the necessary care after their long voyage is extremely doubtful . . .

Kelly was of course correct. London dockers were not wine experts, nor should they have been expected to be, nor indeed should unsolicited wine have been entitled to any 'necessary care'. The fault lay in the inexperience of the South Australian winemaker.

If London was of little assistance at this time, neither were the intercolonial markets of Victoria and New South Wales, for each, keen to protect its own growers, had erected impen-etrable tariff barriers. So the first South Australian romance with the vine faded rapidly during the late 1860s. Between 1865 and 1885 the area under vine fell by a third from 2685 hectares to 1758 hectares. Nevertheless the romance of the vine springs eternal. It would certainly not be forgotten.

During this era of extremely difficult marketing, Thomas Hardy remained firm as a rock. By 1863 his vineyard area covered 35 acres (fourteen hectares). In 1865 he produced 14 000 gallons (63 700 litres). Not only was he able to use the whole of his own crop, he was financially stable enough to buy in grapes from growers who would otherwise have gone to the wall.

Into the wine-marketing morass that was South Australia in the 1860s now stepped Dr Alexander Kelly, a man of vision as we have seen, if not ultimate wisdom, yet another of the legion of medical men consumed by a passion for the Australian vine. Kelly, the author of *The Vine in Australia* and *Winegrowing in Australia*, I have already quoted. Well-versed in oenology and armed with seventeen years' practical experience of viticulture and winemaking in his own vineyard, 'Trinity', he was fascinated by the potential of McLaren Vale as a winegrowing area. Kelly the doctor, a man of influence, respected by the South Australian establishment, incorporated the Tintara Vineyard Company on 20 November 1862. Kelly the investor contributed half the company's capital, £1500 ($3000); while notable businessmen of the day such as Sir Samuel Davenport, Sir Walter Hughes, Sir Thomas Elder and others subscribed for lesser amounts. Eighty-five hectares were bought from the Crown in December 1862 and planting began the following year. No record survives of the first planting but the second in 1864 was eight hectares of mataro, shiraz, grenache and a little carignan, all varieties of moderate to good bearing capacity, which likewise would produce moderate to good wines. Kelly the manager was paid £200 ($400) a year and required to devote the whole of his time to the business of the company. By June 1866 nearly twenty-four hectares were under vine and another eight ready for planting. By 1867, the year of publication of *Winegrowing in Australia*, Tintara's first wines were in the cellar. Kelly the winemaker made both table and dessert wines with the greatest care and skill. But what of Kelly the marketer?

By 1871 the cellar at Tintara was beginning to fill. As local sales were but a trickle, it was decided to send him to London on an urgent sales mission. There he met Peter Bond Burgoyne who agreed to act as agent. In addition, the Tintara Vineyards Association was set up in Old Bond Street to act as a marketing organisation. The export outlet had been put in place. It failed. Tintara wines could not, according to Burgoyne, be sold at a profit. Why? Was it Burgoyne's lavish expenditure, reported at nearly £2600 ($5200), a small fortune in those days? Was it his incompetence? It seems unlikely: he made a fortune from the sales of Australian wine in the next thirty years. Yet perhaps in a resistant London market, he got his experience at Tintara's expense. Was it the quality of the wine? Two hogs-heads of wine were returned from London in 1873, rejected as being unsound. Perhaps it was no wonder, as Kelly himself had earlier written of the vagaries of the London docks.

Whatever the reason, the Tintara project collapsed. By 1874 there were mutual recriminations. London alleged poor quality; Adelaide replied with accusations of slipshod accounting and unjustified expenditure. There were further injections of capital into the London operation by Sir Walter Hughes, a merchant adventurer, one of Australia's first mining magnates and owner of Spring Vale vineyard (later to be called 'Quelltaler') at Water-vale north of Adelaide, but by 1876 Tintara's road to disaster was inescapable.

On 8 September 1877 the South Australian Register announced the purchase by Thomas Hardy of 'Tintara Vineyard, the well-known property of Dr Kelly . . . together with 27,000 gallons [122 850 litres] of wine comprising portions of the vintages of the preceding seven years, not including the last'. Kelly died a month later.

Where Kelly had failed, Hardy succeeded. In one year he had financed the whole of his purchase by the sale of all those seemingly surplus gallons.

Yet, Hardy's erstwhile employer, John Reynell, had found the road to prosperity full of potholes. After setting himself up with a mixed farm, as was the custom in those day, he decided in the early 1850s to concentrate on vines. He had built a cellar in 1845, now famous as the 'Old Cave' and part of Thomas Hardy's present headquarters. He had also bought more cuttings from William Macarthur at Camden Park, this time riesling, cabernet sauvignon, malbec, gouais, dolcetto, constantia, verdelho and tokay. Whether he had difficulties with his wine sales (a common problem in those days) we do not know, but certainly by 1854 he was in financial trouble to such an extent that he was obliged to become a property developer and subdivide part of his extensive holdings to form the present town of Reynella. Now a man of capital, as well as property, Reynell could afford to concentrate on his vineyard.

Reynell and Kelly were not the only early names of import-ance in the Southern Vales. George Pitches Manning planted Hope Farm vineyard during the 1850s (possibly in 1850 or 1855). It is said to have so impressed Dr Kelly by the quality and vigour of its vines that it became the inspiration for Kelly's ill-fated Tintara scheme and indeed supplied it with some of its early planting material.

In the isolated vastness that was South Australia in the mid-nineteenth century, versatility was the one virtue above all amongst early settlers that could ensure triumph over adversity. Arriving on board the *Buffalo* in 1836, Frank Potts was such a man. In 1850, at the age of thirty-five, he settled at Langhorne Creek on the banks of the Bremer River, later naming his winery 'Bleasdale' after his clerical friend the Reverend J. I. Bleasdale, whose substantial contributions to Victorian viti-culture at this time have already been mentioned. Though Potts' selection was evidently fertile, as evidenced by the tall stands of red gums, the rainfall was too marginal for sustained agriculture. So Potts arranged his own irrigation scheme. After clearing sufficient country to plant thirty acres (twelve hectares) of vineyard with shiraz and verdelho, he dug water channels and diverted the river, using the excavated clay for bricks for his cellar and the felled red gums as timber. In the fashion of the time, the early wine produced was probably fortified and sold locally. Potts's enthusiasm for wine spread to his sons, three of whom (there were eight) planted their own vineyards; one, Edward, building his own winery. Potts however was too adventurous a spirit to be totally entwined in the vine, for, as an older man, he took to boat-building, again using local materials and often dragging his yachts overland to race off Adelaide.

Potts died in 1890, the same year as another Langhorne Creek vigneron, Arthur Formby, planted thirty acres (twelve hectares) of cabernet sauvignon and shiraz on his Metala vineyard, which was to become renowned in the 1960s as the source of Metala Cabernet-Shiraz, a rich claret style made by Stonyfell.

That other pioneer of South Australian viticulture, Richard Hamilton, continued the development of his five acre (two hectare) Ewell vineyard at Glenelg, twelve kilometres to the south-west of Adelaide. Aged sixty, Hamilton died in 1852 to be succeeded by his son Henry, who considerably expanded the vineyard in 1860 at the time of the first grape boom in South Australia. Like the Reynells and the Hardys, the Hamiltons would become one of the patriarchal wine families of South Australia.

By 1850 Dr Penfold's fame as a medical practitioner was rapidly spreading. His success in the treatment of anaemia, a common disease amongst early immigrants, by the prescription of his own fortified wine has already been noted. Whether this was because of the restorative power of the wine or the warm colonial climate is a matter for debate, but nonetheless his name was becoming widely known.

As the diary of his wife, Mary, tells us, the Penfold wine style at this time was mostly fortified. An entry in that diary made during 1864 lists a white wine, blended from sweetwater (chasselas) and frontignac; a red wine (of no given varietal definition); a frontignac and a muscat. In 1870 he died aged fifty-nine, leaving his business to be carried on by his widow and his son-in-law, Thomas Hyland.

The nineteenth century wine industry, though not a usual female occupation (few occupations were), produced some remarkable women. The widow Penfold, like the Widow Clicquot two generations before, was determined to press on. And press on she did. By 1880 there were 485 000 litres in the Magill cellars, mostly of fortified wine. In 1881 she acquired the neighbouring vineyards and cellars of Joseph Gillard, whom she immediately appointed manager of the Magill cellars. By 1885 there was a thriving intercolonial and trans-Tasman trade and the vineyard area had grown to 404 hectares. The growing reputation of the Penfold name would far outstrip the hopes and anticipations of a country doctor or his widow.

There were other important vineyards in what are now the eastern suburbs of Adelaide. One was Auldana, the property of Patrick Auld, planted in 1854 close to Dr Penfold's Magill estate with all the popular grape varieties of the time, verdelho, tokay, muscat, gouais, grenache and a little 'carbonet'. It was a substantial area—ninety-three hectares and Auld soon realised that it would require greater human and capital resources than his own and in addition that it would yield more than enough wine for local markets.

As a result, by 1861 Auld had floated a company—the South Auldana Vineyard Association—to exploit it. The next year, with a vintage of 13 500 litres of red and white wine, he decided that London promised so well as a market that, in concert with a Mr Burton, he formed a London company, Auld, Burton & Co., to promote exports.

Yet another vineyard founded in the shadow of the Mount Lofty Ranges in present-day suburbia was Stonyfell. This 'stone mountain' was initially planted with one and a half acres (0.6 hectares) of mataro in 1858 by one Henry Clark. By the early 1860s, Stonyfell had mushroomed to 32 acres (13 hectares) of 'black portugal', muscat, sercial and doradillo and, upon Clark's death in 1864, passed into the ownership of his brother, Algernon and brother-in-law Joseph Crompton. By 1873 Crompton was in sole control, a situation which continued until 1888 when Crompton's severe financial difficulties led to a sale of Stonyfell to Henry Dunstan, a contractor far more interested in its stone than its vineyard. In time the vineyard and quarry would be separated but this awaited the arrival of one Henry Martin.

If Thomas Hardy had arrived as a single man, unfettered by family responsibility except for his cousin and future wife, Johanna, Joseph Ernst Seppelt enjoyed no such freedom, reaching Adelaide early in January 1850, not only with his wife and three children, but also accompanied by thirteen families of neighbours and a group of young men from his tobacco and snuff factory. The population of his Silesian village, Wustewaltersdorf, must have been severely depleted.

Before his departure he had bought a town acre (0.4 hectares) in the city of Adelaide and also an eighty-acre (thirty-two hectares) country selection at Golden Grove. He therefore arrived as a man of property. Regrettably, like many emigrants, he had little cash;

SSL: M: B10612

Auldana, 1872: the estate of Patrick Auld, who recognised the need to export South Australian wine.

the story has it that he exchanged his town acre for a good horse and a fair harness. His sight-unseen choice of property at Golden Grove also proved unlucky as it was found to be quite unsuitable for tobacco. A year later, undaunted, he continued like some latter day Moses with his entourage to the near wilderness of the newly settled Barossa Valley, buying 164 acres (77 hectares) of land at Tanunda. Again he tried tobacco. Though it grew prolifically, its leaf was much too rank for use in cigars or snuff; so as other Germans were finding that the vine flourished, he followed their example. While awaiting the maturity of his vineyard, he also tried wheat as a cash crop. He was immediately successful, for by 1853 the demand from the Victorian gold-fields was so great that he received one pound (two dollars) a bushel (twenty-seven kilograms).

But gold was a difficult ally. Though he sold his wheat, he lost his labourers. His young tobacconists, like snuff thrown to the winds, scattered to the goldfields. But his wines pros-pered and his bullock drays regularly carried casks to the auction at Gawler. His drays also went east to the Murray to catch the paddle-steamers plying as far upstream as Wentworth, Albury and even Bourke. To Adelaide he sent liqueurs and cordials.

In 1867 the grand design of what is now Seppeltsfield was started, when the first part of these substantial cellars was erected. Solid blocks of Barossa bluestone and thick hardwood timbers still attest to Joseph Seppelt's determination to build for permanence. In an age of patriarchy, Joseph Seppelt had decided his family's future. It was to be wine.

When the cellars were completed, Joseph retired from the business. His twenty-one-year-old son Benno, keenly interested in science, succeeded him in 1868. It was not to be a long retirement, for a few months later, Joseph was caught by a cold change while strolling in a light summer suit. Within twenty-four hours, pneumonia had claimed him.

It was doubly unfortunate for Benno, losing at one stroke a father and a valued advisor, for at this time South Australia was suffering a vast overproduction of wine coupled with an almost total absence of market.

Benno Seppelt somehow struggled through, making two important decisions—extending in 1875 the stone cellar which he had helped his father build eight years before and opening a new distillery in 1877. The distillery marked the dawn of an epoch of unparalleled expansion. In 1878 the capacity of the building, extended only three years before, was quadrupled. A new laboratory, vinegar plant and further land purchases soon followed.

Seppeltsfield was also successful in those gigantic phen-omena of the nineteenth century and triumphs of the industrial revolution—the universal expositions. At Sydney in 1880, seventy-five of its ninety-five exhibits secured prizes. More important even than Sydney for the future of the South Australian grape at that time was the London Colonial and Indian Exhibition of 1886 where.

> the absolute purity of the wine was established . . . The most exhaustive tests were applied, and every sample came out exactly what it professed to be—the pure juice of the grape . . . The general testimony was that Australian wines compared favourably with the best German Hocks and the best French Sauternes and Clarets.[1]

London was also decidely bullish, one of the judges declaring that he had 'the greatest expectation that in the near future a great proportion of the wine consumed in this country will not come from the Continent, but from our own colonies'.

For Benno Seppelt, the London market was obviously one of quality. In that age when sherry was gaining in popularity, his sherries were much sought after (especially in the Albert Hall where deliveries of fifty cases were the order of the day), and his lighter table wines were also noticed. The London correspondent of an Adelaide journal, wrote, 'Of the red wines, the Claret is decidedly the best. In whites, the best of his samples is the Blanquette, a delicate wine of pleasing character . . .'

At home, the Seppelt expansion continued. By 1888 even the 'new' winery was inadequate, so he designed another one, which he built in a rather isolated position across the creek from the original stone cellars, allowing, as was his wont, adequate room for growth. In the same year, production topped 1.2 million litres, though only 135 000 litres came from Seppelt's own vineyards.

The few riesling vines that Johann Gramp had planted at Jacob's Creek in the late 1840s yielded their first vintage in 1850. Little did Gramp realise that he was one of the pioneers of a grape variety that many South Australians still regard as the premier white grape, despite a general Australian fad for chardonnay.

By 1859 Johann, in common with many other South Australian settlers (too many, in the wisdom of hindsight) had decided that the colony's future lay in viticulture. Few places were more favourable than the Barossa Valley and so in that year he confidently expanded the Jacob's Creek vineyard. An obvious admirer of rhine riesling, he planted sixteen acres (6.5 hectares) of that vine with five acres (two hectares) of frontignac and smaller areas of shiraz (3.75 acres) and cabernet sauvignon (1.5 acres). After this expansion, Johann moved cautiously but successfully through the troubled times of the 1860s and 1870s. In 1874, Gustav married and, on a forty-acre (sixteen hectare) block given him as a wedding present by his father, planted a vineyard which he called 'Orlando'. Three years later, no doubt on the vines coming into bearing and being given control of the family enterprise by his father, he transferred the business from Jacob's Creek to his home block at Rowland Flat, though Johann continued to make wine at Jacob's Creek, which was transported to Rowland Flat when a year old.

Like early colonists in the Hunter Valley, the first settlers of the Barossa came prepared, in modern terminology, to diversify. Thus William Salter grazed cattle and sheep on his Barossa holdings from 1844, posting his ten-year-old son Edward as both shepherd and sentry from time to time. In the mid-1850s he opened a copper mine on his property, 'Mamre Brook', and in 1859, in obvious imitation of the prevailing fashion, planted a four-acre (1.6 hectares) vineyard to shiraz vines. So during the decade of the 1860s, those three primary industries—mining, grazing and viticulture—proceeded side by side.

Copper prices failed in the late 1860s and wine was a disaster, especially in the hands of those lacking skill or experience. Yet the Salter family pressed on with its unsophisticated winemaking. From the notes in Edward Salter's *Vigneron's Journal*, it was all very impromptu. To lower the temperature of the ferment, as Edward records, 'take out a quantity in a tub from the vat when it rises to the tumultuous fermentation and then add it as the wine in the vat gets hot'. It was both practically and commercially hazardous, too. The Salters, gaining tunnelling skill from their mining experience, had excavated their first wine cellar in the side of a hill. To their dismay, during one particularly wet winter their cattle, cropping grass on the hillside, added weight enough to the earth roof to cause a landslide. What happened to the wine, the casks, or for that matter the cattle is not recorded, but it can be imagined that the cellar design was later much improved.

At that time wine commerce was also at best speculative and at worst financially disastrous. As we learnt from Alexander Kelly, 'trial' shipments were very common. One such Salter shipment to London produced, two years later, a demand for fifty pounds (one hundred dollars) from the warehouseman and no account of the wine or the casks. Similar consignments to Calcutta, Mauritius and Brisbane brought the same results.

Yet the Salter pragmatism, as the *Vignerons's Journal* informs us, certainly produced improved wine, or at the very least wine more to the maker's liking. From the first vintage in 1862, foot-trodden as was the way in those days, 1800 gallons (8200 litres) of rich, tannic shiraz red were made. Certainly fermented dry, it was unfortunately not to the vintner's taste. The next year a small amount of fortifying spirit was added after fermentation. Again he was dissatisfied, so he increased the amount of spirit after fermentation. Still the wine remained 'tart'. Was Edward's palate not attuned to dry reds or was volatile acidity his problem? By 1866, when seven per cent fortifying spirit was added during fermentation, Edward was better pleased, reporting in the *Journal* that the usual tartness which had typified previous vintages had disappeared. By 1869 sufficient spirit was added during ferment to produce a wine of nineteen per cent alcohol. Edward Salter had grown to like his shiraz 'port'.

William Salter died in 1871 and thereafter Edward took over the management of the estate as well as the vineyard. Now the vineyard was expanded. By 1873 there were forty acres (sixteen hectares), thirty (twelve hectares) of shiraz and ten (four hectares) of albillo (a sherry variety). About 9000 gallons (41 000 litres) of wine were vintaged in that year. Sales were made in Sydney and New Zealand by Salter's travelling salesman, Alfred Birks, who himself was later to become a vigneron in Clare. Markets were growing. They had to. But they were also recognising the quality of Salter wines. As Edward wrote at the time,

> you will no doubt have noticed that we obtained a first prize and four second prizes at your Sydney Exhibition and this with only five exhibits. The price for our Constantia is four shillings [forty cents] a gallon [4.5 litres] f.o.b.

During the 1870s the wine styles remained fortified, as a glance at the Salter list shows: 'Port, Sherry, Shiraz and Constantia'. Persuaded by overseas market trends, the Salter styles would change slowly as the century wore on.

In the promised land that was South Australia in the mid-nineteenth century, George Angas was not only a sponsor of hard-working, God-fearing Germans. He also saw to it that hard-working, God-fearing Anglo-Saxons were there in equal numbers. As I have mentioned, one of these, Samuel Smith, reached Adelaide with his wife Mary, his son Sidney, and his daughters Martha, Elizabeth and Mary Jane, early in 1848. For a time he stayed at Klemzig, a German settlement near Adelaide, but soon accepted a position as an orchardist in Angas's orchard in the Barossa Valley. Hard work and his own capital soon enabled Smith to buy thirty acres (twelve hectares) of the Angas Estate. The following year, 1849, he planted vines on his property 'Yalumba', an Aboriginal word meaning 'all the country around'. Though proud of his estate which, in his wife's words, was 'a green carpet all around us' and 'the prettiest place for miles around', he soon became restless. Though pretty, his property was very small and Samuel was nothing if not ambitious.

Long on labour but short on resources, Smith soon realised the need for more capital. It was this exigency that took him and two companions with a six-oxen team to the Bendigo goldfields in 1852. After sinking sixteen shafts without luck, Smith might have been forgiven for trying some other occupation, but on his seventeenth attempt he struck it rich—within reason.

The three hundred pounds realised by his gold bought him another eighty acres (thirty-two hectares) of land at one pound an acre, farm equipment, including a plough, two horses and a harness, with sufficient change for additions to the homestead and the erection of the first wine cellars. By 1862 his vineyard, planted at this time wholly to shiraz, extended over fourteen acres (5.7 hectares), half of which was fully bearing. His brewing experience (which gave him practical knowledge of ferment-ation and other basic skills) held him in good stead, for in 1863, those impulsive days of the first South Australian wine boom, he produced 3000 gallons (13 650 litres) of wine which was, importantly, sound. For a man who could have thrived equally well on brewing beer, for which there was an obvious market, Smith's decision for wine was remarkable, but perhaps new days demanded new ways and wine it was to be!

By 1866 the wine boom had bust. Overproduction, uneven quality and lack of markets, any one of which was an adequate reason for the bust, had united to deal the infant industry a knock-out blow from which it would not recover for twenty years. Yet Samuel Smith exhibited his wine in that year at the London International Exhibition where it was awarded a bronze plaque. It was obvious that his wine 'travelled', but how good that wine was, indeed how good any colonial wine was, is very difficult to assess in present-day terms. Certainly if it was good enough to be bought by a London merchant, it was at least sound, and depending on the ethics of that merchant could either appear under its own colours or disappear into a mass blend of boarding-house 'burgundy'.

By 1887, the year of the South Australian silver jubilee, S. Smith & Son, Samuel and Sidney, could stand shoulder to shoulder with the other emerging giants of the South Australian wine industry, Hardy, Seppelt and Penfold, to celebrate that first half-century in which they had all played so prominent a part. At this time the Yalumba vineyard had increased to seventy-six acres (thirty-one hectares) planted to shiraz, sherry (identified in the 1970s as chenin blanc), frontignac, dolcetto, tokay, mataro and muscatel.

One of the vehicles of that display of patriotic pride was the Adelaide International Exhibition at which S. Smith & Son presented, obviously to an admiring public, the bounty of Angaston, which included 'canned fruits and tomatoes, a trophy of wines consisting of port [for which Yalumba in this age of full-bodied dry red had built up quite a reputation], sherry, claret, reisling *[sic]*, frontignac, constantia and muscatel, medals and diplomas and a silver cup'. Fifteen of their com-petition wines were also on display, including 1870 sherry, 1886 'ruschette', 1884 'peyan' and 1881 dolcetto. The Exhibit-ion handbook paid due tribute to its native wines, noting that they were 'gaining in favour here everyday; persons who had never before kept any but foreign wine in their cellars are now using South Australian wines in preference to the imported'. It was evident that any cultural cringe was now beginning to disappear from the colonial palate.

In the hills above the Seppelts, Gramps, Smiths and Salters, Joseph Gilbert pressed on with the development of Pewsey Vale, 'a rugged site in a mountain vastness', when Ebenezer Ward visited it in 1862. By that year the vineyard had grown from the initial one acre planted in 1847 to sixteen acres (6.5 hectares), despite devastation by a severe frost in 1855, as a consequence of which, according to Ward, 'the head [of the vines] had to be taken off with saws'. Gilbert obviously found that shiraz, cabernet sauvignon, riesling and verdelho were well suited to the site for, in Ward's words, he 'has almost every year increased the extent of his vineyard, planting Verdeilho *[sic]* and Riesling for the white wines, and Shiraz and Carbonet *[sic]* for the red'. To a twentieth-century observer, this vineyard would have appeared quite modern, being mostly

SSL: M: B19003

Gilbert's Pewsey Vale Cellars, c. 1877:
substantial, solid and famous in their day.

planted in wire-trellised rows eight feet (2.4 metres) apart with four feet (1.2 metres) between vines and cane-pruned.

As for the wines, according to Ward

> it is Mr Gilbert's custom not to sell his wines until they have attained three or four years' age and we cannot help remarking that it would be extremely fortunate for the reputation of South Australian wines if the majority of our vignerons were in a position to follow such a judicious course. Here . . . we considered the choicest wine to be the Riesling, thoroughly matured, fragrant, delicate and pure. Mr Gilbert has some of this of the vintage of 1852, and some of every vintage since. There are some persons, however, who would probably prefer Mr Gilbert's red wines, made from the Shiraz and Carbonet *[sic]*, especially that of his earlier vintages, a wine that would fairly rival if not outvie the finest Burgundy. To return to the Riesling for a moment [Ward was obviously enchanted by riesling from the Barossa hills, as many have been since], we may mention that a short time since a number of gentlemen—all experienced connoisseurs—met together in Adelaide for the purpose of testing the relative merits of this same Riesling [of the vintage of

1854, we think], and some choice hock, considered to be the best wine of its class ever imported to this colony. The decision was in favour of the colonial product.
(Ebenezer Ward, *The Vineyards and Orchards of South Australia*)

Ebenezer Ward was not the only person to pay tributes to the surpassing quality of Gilbert's wines. The *Medical Times* of London a few years later called his 1864 Claret, 'a fine mature wine, grapey and potent, fit to rank with Hermitage', while Thomas Hardy described Pewsey Vale Riesling as being 'fine, light and delicate . . . and nearer in type to the Rhine wine than any produced in the colony'. In 1867, a high point for Gilbert, his wines (the shiraz and riesling) received praise from the French at the Paris Exposition, and he personally was the recipient of a medal at the Melbourne Intercolonial Wine Exhibition in recognition of his services and success as a vigneron and for the general excellence of his wines.

Joseph Gilbert died in 1881, being succeeded by his son, William, himself already a pastoralist and winemaker at the nearby property 'Wongalere', which he had inherited from his mother. At Wongalere, cabernet saugivnon, shiraz and malbec were grown on a vineyard which by 1893 was eighteen acres (seven hectares) in extent. During this time, Pewsey Vale maintained a production of about 10 000 gallons (45 500 litres), but had extended its vineyard area to twenty-nine acres by 1893.

However, the increase in area saw no diminution in quality for, upholding the family tradition of excellence, the Gilbert wines achieved success in Bordeaux in 1882 and 1895, as well as at the colonial wine shows of Sydney, Melbourne and Adelaide. By 1903, the combined production of Pewsey Vale and Wongalere, all sold under the Pewsey Vale label, was 17 000 gallons (77 350 litres).

In those same hills about twenty kilometres to the north-east of Pewsey Vale, Johann Christian Henschke, a builder and stonemason, set up a small farm near Keyneton, then called North Rhine, in 1862. As was common practice in those days, the farm included a small vineyard, from which the family wine was to be made. The first vintage was in the mid-1860s, the first cellars being erected about that time to contain a wine yield of about 300 gallons (1365 litres). First sales were made in 1868. Johann's son, Paul

Gotthard Henschke, born in 1847, continued wine production and sales for the rest of the century, finally turning to fortified winemaking in the first decade of this century.

By 1850 Clare had it own mining boom. For once copper had anticipated gold. Though more menial, it still brought solid prosperity to the mid-north of South Australia. The mines at Burra, about thirty-five kilometres to the north-east of Clare Village, as it had come to be known, required food, and as the mines boomed so did the farms and villages of nearby areas. Vineyards soon followed and after modest beginnings in the 1850s there was, as elsewhere in the colony, a surge of vinegrowing in the 1860s. Though mining declined, the boom continued, this time in wheat: the fields were positively Texan in size, one reputedly five kilometres long.

As in the Hunter Valley in the same period, agricultural workers were paid partly in kind—wine, beer and flour featuring sometimes more prominently than cash. Thus large properties often had small vineyards, while those that did not, purchased wine for that very purpose from nearby vintners. The markets were quite local and when the wheat fields turned to dust, as they often did in times of drought and disease, there were troubles aplenty for the area's winegrowers.

In 1862 there were seventy-one acres (twenty-nine hectares0 of vines in the Clare region, producing about 6800 gallons (30 950 litres) of wine. By 1870 the area had more than quadrupled to 320 acres (130 hectares). In typical fashion did Francis Treloar advertise his Prospect Farm wine—he had over 3000 gallons (13 650 litres)—for sale by auction, a cust-omary and often the only method of sale in country regions in those days. 'Sound and in good order, and being the pure unadulterated juice of the grape, is especially suited for the coming hay and wheat harvests. Terms—cash, or credit until harvest as may be agreed.'

Francis Treloar was a restless soul; after visiting three Australian colonies (Tasmania, New South Wales and South Australia), South Africa (where he joined the army), and returning to his native Cornwall, he finally resolved to return to South Australia in the late 1840s. After further peregrinations to the Burra copper fields, he was one of the many hopefuls who travelled to the Victorian goldfields in 1851.

One of the few to strike it lucky, he found sufficient pay dirt to buy 117 acres (forty-seven hectares) of land near Watervale in 1852. The following year he planted vines on his property, 'Spring Vale', then sold it in 1861 to Walter Hughes, that same mining magnate and co-venturer in Alexander Kelly's ill-fated Tintara Vineyard. Treloar, the soldier, wanderer and miner, was also a farmer competent enough to win the trust of Hughes, who appointed him manager of his old property. In the meantime Treloar had bought an adjoining property which he named 'Prospect Farm'. Again he planted vines, establishing five acres (two hectares) of cuttings in 1862. Treloar continued his previous winemaking practices, offering part of his crop for sale by auction as harvest wine each spring. Yet for its times, Prospect Farm remained of moderate size. According to a contemporary report (1895) in the *Adelaide Observer*,

> Mr W. G. Treloar (the son of Francis), Prospect Vineyard, has 10 acres in full bearing and 15 acres under young vines . . . A very good crop (2½ tons to the acre) was showing at the time of my visit and this I learnt was the case throughout the district. There are small cellars on the property and Mr Treloar says they expect to make between 2000 and 3000 gallons of wine. It will not be possible to handle the whole of the yield and the surplus grapes will be sold to Messrs Sobels and Buring.

Indeed the whole property was sold shortly afterwards to those gentlemen, who would make Spring Vale (or Quellthaler as they had germanicised it) into the most prominent Clare producer.

In 1868 Walter Hughes, reputedly on the recommendation of his retiring manager, John Treloar, had appointed the twenty-nine-year-old Carl Sobels as winemaker-manager of Spring Vale. Though a coppersmith by trade, Sobels had also learnt the winemaking art from his father, who had been winemaker for William Jacob, assistant surveyor to Colonel Light and one of the pioneers of the Barossa Valley; Jacob's name is locally commemorated by a Barossa creek and nationally by a popular Orlando red.

Upon his appointment, Sobels found the property already planted to thirty-five acres (fourteen hectares) of vines. Almost immediately he began the erection of the first stage of the imposing bluestone cellars, which are a major attraction of the Watervale district today. By 1882, according to J. M. Richman, Hughes's nephew and heir, the vineyard had been extended to seventy-five acres (thirty hectares) and included amongst its varieties what might almost be a modern complement of cultivars, cabernet, shiraz, malbec and riesling, as well as mataro and the mysteriously named red and white Spanish. We also learn from Richman that 1882 was a year of sparse quantity, the normal vintage of 10 000 gallons (45 000 litres) being reduced to 7000 (13 850 litres) because of drought.

Hermann Buring arrived in South Australia in 1849 aged three. After an early career as a country shopkeeper, doubtless where he learnt a good deal about merchandising, he was employed at Seppeltsfield between the years 1866 and 1869. Here was his introduction to the wine industry, an entrée that he apparently found so inviting that upon his departure from Seppeltsfield he returned to Adelaide where he immediately set up as sole agent for Spring Vale wines, an appointment not quite as fortuitous as may be imagined as he was Carl Sobels's brother-in-law. By 1890 Buring and Sobels, in partnership, had purchased Spring Vale from Richman who had inherited it from Sir Walter Hughes in 1887. The new firm would grow quickly; for Quelltaler, as the estate soon came to be known, the prospects were bright indeed.

Late in 1848, the year before the infant Hermann Buring reached Australia, a wealthy German farmer named Weikert arrived in Adelaide with a party of emigrants he had organised in a very similar way to Joseph Seppelt. Accompanying Weikert, obviously a devout man, were two Jesuit priests, one of whom was Father Alois Kranewitter.

Unlike Seppelt's party, the Weikert group broke up on arrival due either to sickness or dissension amongst them. Weikert together with Fr Kranewitter pressed on to Clare, where he had decided to settle. The story also goes that they or another Austrian priest, Brother John Schreiner, who arrived slightly later and was to be first winemaker of that ecclesiastical group, brought with them a mystery grape (which came to be called Clare riesling), only recently identified as an obscure southern French variety named crouchen. The import of vinestocks by emigrants was a common enough practice, but why a group of Germans and two Austrian priests would import an unknown French grape variety and not one more familiar to Austrian viticulture defies logic. Perhaps the variety was obtained as the group journeyed to its port of embarkation or at the Cape or even on arrival in Adelaide.

Whatever the source of that 'Clare riesling', it was established in 1851 on a parcel of land bought by Fr Kranewitter three kilometres to the south of Clare, called by the brothers Sevenhill in the belief that it would become an important centre of Catholic faith, perhaps even the Rome of Australia. Even a small creek, which runs through the property in times of heavy rain, was called the Tiber.

The small seven-acre vineyard (2.8 hectares) of 1858, thrived. It had been planted for the purpose of producing sacramental wine, and in 1851 rudimentary cellars had been excavated. By 1858 the grounds of what was to be the Sevenhill Jesuit College had grown to over 400 hectares and the winery had been extended to include a still. Winery operations of that year yielded 4500 litres of wine and 270 litres of spirit all, according to the correspondent of the *Chronicle*, from one acre (0.4 hectares) of bearing vineyard. What superprolific grape variety was used is not recorded, but for this report to be accurate, its yield must have been at least twenty-three tonnes to the hectare. In addition to quantity the vineyard must also have produced quality, for the College wines won first prize at the Auburn Horticultural Exhibition in the same year.

By the early 1860s the brothers were so confident in their viticultural endeavours that the marvellously solid stone cellars that are still in use today were erected. Shortly after, in 1864, the College church was begun, a construction which, due to lack of funds (in the time-honoured ecclesiastical tradition), was a decade in the making. By 1884 the vineyard had grown to twenty-seven acres (eleven hectares) and in that year produced 4000 gallons (18 200 litres) of mataro, shiraz, madeira and verdelho. By 1890 Sevenhill had become one of the leading vineyards of the Clare region supplying not only sacramental wine which was unfermented, but also red and white wines of the more usual kind.

In 1890 the wine industry in Clare was about to boom. Though it was at that time but a drop in the wine production lake of South Australia, it was to profit greatly by export to London during the last decade of the nineteenth century and, in common with other South Australian areas, to exploit in the first decade of the twentieth the more lucrative markets of the eastern states newly prised open by the Federation compact.

[1] Hodder, *History of South Australia* 1893

EIGHT

The scourge of the vine

By 1874 Geelong, unbeknown to its vintners, had reached the summit of its viticultural success. Thereafter the downward plunge was swift.

Phylloxera, the minute vine vampire that destroys by sucking the life-giving sap, *Vitis vinifera*, was first noticed at Fyansford to the west of the town in 1875 (though some say it was 1877). In response to this epidemic, for which there is still no cure, only prevention, and to the mounting concern of Victorian vignerons, the colonial government decided upon the ultimate solution, putting into effect a comprehensive 'vine-pull' scheme and paying in the process the considerable sum of £50 000 ($100 000) in compensation to affected growers. Though by the early 1880s the technique of grafting vinifera canes on to resistant American rootstock (still the only sure defence against the louse) had become generally known, the panic-stricken government, determined to localise the invader to Geelong, took not a scrap of notice. By 1881, 210 hectares had been uprooted in the Geelong district and, with a further seven ordered to be destroyed, the resultant vineyard area was a mere ninety hectares.

Eradication of course was completely ineffective. By 1893 the louse had reached Bendigo. Yet the government took exactly the same measures and spent the same amount of money as it had over ten years before. The public subsidy of vine grafting as a protective measure was again ignored.

In its approach to the wine industry the Victorian govern-ment was not totally devoted to eradication. The colony's agricultural base needed to be extended and, as a result of the boom in South Australian wine exports (especially in heavy alcoholic reds), the government determined that Victoria should have a share of this prosperity. The result was a vine-planting scheme of ten dollars per hectare for vines planted after mid-1889, which in practice favoured those Victorian areas which specialised in heavy reds, as they were the wines which were selling well at the time. As a consequence, in the six-year period from mid-1889 to mid-1895, the area of vines in Victoria more than doubled from 5154 hectares to 12 122 hectares, Rutherglen in particular growing spectacularly. As a result, though the depredation of phylloxera went largely unnoticed in production statistics, the market became glutted with heavy, often ill-made reds optimistically destined for export. When political and economic factors such as temperance-inclined politicians and the bank crashes of the early 1890s were added to this recipe for disaster, a whole menu of political and financial discontent confronted the government of the day. In fairness to that government, it must be stated that its table was laid with the best of intentions, with second-stage bonuses planned for the production, maturation and export of the resulting wine and the advice of government experts. This part of the scheme never came to fruition.

In its misguided way, the bonus scheme was of great assistance to the vine louse, by encouraging the rapid spread of vine propagation material without regard to even the most basic of quarantine conditions or the cleaning of boots, cartwheels or vineyard implements and then paying the vinegrower for his negligence. The fact that it coincided with the spread of phylloxera in Victoria in the late 1890s is patently obvious when one considers that phylloxera in its winged form needs readily available hosts such as wild vines (which do not exist in Australia) to travel any distance. For it to spread in any other way it needs to hitchhike and this it can only do through human agency, via farm animals, vehicles and implements.

In 1899 phylloxera attacked Rutherglen. The first skirmishes were light and caused little damage, but by 1906, whole vineyards had been laid waste as the insect steadily sucked its way underground through the district. Too late had the government reversed its policy of eradication and quarantine in favour of replanting of resistant rootstocks, for supplies of rootstocks were minimal and many growers in fact believed that such stocks actually encouraged the pest. The consequence was a general devastation of the Rutherglen region, a result devoutly welcomed by some such as the then extremely active temperance lobbies; even the royal commission, set up to inquire into the bounty scheme, offered the unsympathetic advice that the vineyard area of Victoria might then be reduced to a more viable economic level.

Phylloxera continued its scourge of north-eastern Victoria, crossing the River Murray into the Albury-Corowa region of New South Wales in 1906 and decimating the substantial vineyards of that district, which for a time had rivalled the Hunter Valley in production. Most were never replanted, although one did survive. John Delappe Lankester had managed Dr Lindeman's Sydney sales office forty years before and was, in 1906 at the time of phylloxera, managing J. T. Fallon's Albury vineyard at the age of nearly seventy; when it was destroyed by the louse, never to be replanted, Lankester left to manage his own vineyard at nearby Ettamogah. Lankester, born in England in 1837, lived on to achieve his century, dying a few months later after a lifetime in the service of wine.

As for phylloxera, it too soldiered on, destroying the Milawa district of north-east Victoria in 1915 and then, with few other vineyard worlds to conquer, retired from the fray as vignerons became increasingly aware of the importance of grafting in phylloxera-affected regions and of quarantine in those that were not. Its list of Victorian victims had been impressive: Geelong (1875), Bendigo (1893), Goulburn Valley (1895), the North East (1899) and Milawa

(1915). No less so were its conquests in New South Wales: Camden (1888), the outer Sydney metropolitan area (1890s) and Albury-Corowa (1906).

Phylloxera was but one factor in the decline of vineyard Victoria. Additionally there was in the 1890s a severe economic depression gripping the whole of eastern Australia and also, though observed by few at the time, a growing change in public taste both at home and abroad in favour of stronger red and fortified wines, which experts such as Hubert de Castella lamented, ascribing it to lack of education. Writing in 1886 about wines recently tasted at the Rutherglen Wine Show, he deplored the trend:

> this state of things—a preponderant production of wines too strong for ordinary consumption—is due in a great measure to the influence of certain commerce, which asks for a high degree of alcoholic strength in wine at a minimum of price, in order to affect manipulations afterwards. Alcohol is the virtue, or rather the vice, which the growers are advised to secure.
>
> Thus influenced, even in their local exhibitions, the vignerons who organised them, forgetful of past lessons and indulging in self-glorification, instead of favouring clean, dry wines, as light as their climate can produce, adjudicate the greatest number of prizes to what their list of awards calls sweet full-bodied red, and sweet full-bodied white—abomination of desolation.
>
> What will it serve them to fill their cellars with undrinkable wines, even if for a short time? Wine sellers and grocers are ready to give a larger price for sweet and strong, which the prosperous Australian middle classes only prefer until they are educated to lighter wines—that consumption is limited and that market soon glutted.

De Castella went on to predict that such wines would disappear from the market within ten years, but he was quite wrong. What vanished were the vineyards of southern and central Victoria, in no small part because of market forces and phylloxera, but in the case of his own beloved Yarra Valley, due to sheer economics—and ultimately the dairy cow! But this would not happen for another generation and in the mean time there were other moves abroad to spread the vine.

Who knows whether that up-and-coming young politician Alfred

Deakin had ever known or cared about phylloxera? He had certainly learnt about irrigation, however, in the early years of the 1880s as a fledgling legislator on a fact-finding tour of California. The flowering of deserts has long been a fancy of prophets and politicians. Deakin was just such a mixture. Later to become one of the fathers of Federation and three times prime minister, he entered the Victorian parliament in 1880 as a bright young lawyer-journalist aged twenty-four. In 1886, as a result of his Californian sojourn, he invited George Chaffey, a pioneer of irrigation in the Golden State, to come to that other golden state, Victoria, with his brother, William, for that very purpose—to make a desert flower. Upon their arrival, they immediately recognised the suitability of the red plains of Mildura for irrigation. Though the plains were red, the carpet most certainly was not. Suddenly the whole project became fraught with difficulty. What was previously thought to be an arid wasteland suddenly bloomed with dollar signs. For the bureaucrats, it had the potential to be a financial paradise. Things had to be done correctly. The delaying skills of Victorian bureaucracy were never more effective. Tenders had to be called; perhaps even legislation was necessary. In 1887, throttled by Victorian red tape, the Chaffeys turned in utter frustration to the neighbouring colony, South Australia. At Renmark they were made extremely welcome and within a year their irrigation scheme had begun.

The Victorian government had in the meantime called its tenders and received none. No doubt disconsolate and somewhat chastened, it turned again to the Chaffeys, offering them the same land on virtually the same terms sought in the first place. Remarkably the Chaffeys did return, developed their irrigation settlement, sold the land in four-hectare lots and charged for the water. By 1890 Mildura, previously a small riverboat village, had a population of three thousand. Alfred Deakin doubtless took the credit, though the Chaffeys did the work.

By 1895 the desert had indeed blossomed, but so had the problems. Two years earlier one of those bank crashes, endemic in the nineteenth-century Australian economy, had produced disastrous results for those dependent on credit. Chateau Mildura, the Chaffeys' winery, built in 1892, was steadily filling with unsold wine, a not uncommon situation at the time. Indeed portions of the 1892 and 1893 vintages had been distilled (a harbinger for the future course of Mildura if ever there was one), for the River Murray, due to a freakish drought, had become a series of muddy puddles and much of the fruit bound for market from this latter-day Eden had rotted on its drought-shackled wharves. The wine produced was fortified where possible and sold locally, and suitable vineyards were grafted from wine grapes to table grapes; the locals thought the River Murray would flow long before the wine market improved. Some indeed felt that the wrath of God had been visited upon them for meddling with nature. Perhaps deserts were not meant to bloom anyway. By 1900 the Mildura horizon was gloomy indeed. It would darken yet more.

Between the total disaster that was phylloxera and the blessing that irrigation was thought to be, wine export was the ultimate lottery. The opportunistic shipments made by those early Barossa vignerons have already been mentioned. By 1880 wine export was becoming more organised, though it had not been without its tribulations.

As we have seen, in 1862 Patrick Auld had incorporated in London together with one Burton, a customs agent, a company to sell not only his own Auldana wine but more importantly (from a nationalistic point of view) all Australian wines. Though initially called, prosaically enough, Auld, Burton & Co., its name was soon changed to the more impressive 'Australian Wine Co.'.

Almost immediately there were problems with officialdom, for the duty imposed on wines entering the United Kingdom was then ten cents per gallon (4.5 litres) where its alcohol content was 26° proof spirit or less, but twenty-five cents per gallon if this alcohol content were exceeded. Such alcohol taxation rates had obviously been decided by reference to the natural table wines of France, where wines rarely reach this limit without fortification, and to those of Spain and Portugal whose better-known wines at that time were always fortified. To the British it was a limit that separated black from white. The wines of Australia, however, bred under a much stronger sun, seemed to defy this particular aspect of specific gravity, occasionally finishing fermentation around 26° proof; some were, as we have seen, fortified.

For each side of the argument, experts were hastily enlisted. For the British, the eminent Dr Thudicum (a Trollopian name if ever there was one) dogmatically asserted that it would 'upset the scientific facts hitherto established throughout the world' if table wine could be naturally fermented at a higher level than 26° proof spirit (14.86° alcohol). Another British expert, Mr J. S. Keene, reported to Her Majesty's Customs as follows,

> no one with any pretension to a knowledge of the subject could admit that wines, by any natural process, ever attain to such strength as many of these stand at, while even in some instances where the strength is less than may naturally be reached in special cases, there are strong evidences of added spirit which would have been better omitted.

In other words, skulduggery was suspected. At best it was thought that, like the stuffed platypus sent to London nearly a century earlier, Australian wine was some sort of freak; at worst someone was perpetrating outright fraud. However, just like that platypus, Australian wine refused to conform to the scientific norms of the day.

In support of the Australians, importers such as the young Peter Burgoyne (in 1872 at the beginning of a long and successful career of shipping Australian wines to London), experts like Dr Bleasdale and winemakers such as J. T. Fallon of Albury leapt to the defence of the new export, asserting that naturally fermented wines could indeed reach 26° proof and more without a hint of fortification. A royal commission (the usual Australian way of divining eternal truth), set up to investigate the problem in South Australia, Victoria and New South Wales, found that 26° was often exceeded and in 1874 a report advised Her Majesty's Customs in London that the average proof spirit of fifty-nine wines shown at the International Exhibition of that year was 26.39°. Dr Thudicum had been effectively debunked.

In the mean time (1872), the findings of the Australian royal commission had been published in the British medical journal, the *Lancet*, in a highly favourable manner, finding those Australian wines to be pure and healthful beverages well-adapted for chilly northern climes. The day of the tonic 'burgundy' had arrived and a substantial export industry was to develop by the turn of the century.

The earliest officially recorded figure for the export of Australian wine is 155 000 litres for the year 1880-1, although from 1864 to 1885 United Kingdom import statistics show an average annual import of Australian wine of 147 000 litres, a period during which such imports caught up with and surpassed those of the Cape. This was a consequence of Gladstone's budget of 1860, which abolished the preferential duty on Cape wine and caused a considerable boom in Australian plantings, especially in South Australia. By 1890 exports had increased to 1.877 million litres and a decade later (1900) had doubled to 3.778 million litres. Not surprisingly, Britain was the chief market and here the prime mover of Australian wine soon became P. B. Burgoyne and Co., after a promising start by Auld, Burton & Co. (The Australian Wine Co.), whose brand name 'Emu' was to prove very successful. Despite this the Australian Wine Co. encountered financial difficulty, going into liquidation in 1885; two years later Walter Pownall bought the company, presumably for the 'Emu' brand.

It is estimated that in the last thirty years of the nineteenth century, Peter Bond Burgoyne imported more Australian wine and paid more British customs duty than all his rivals put together. Certainly, as we have seen in his dealings with Dr Alexander Kelly, he was a controversial figure and not only a mover but a shaker as well. In the late 1880s, when on a business visit to Adelaide, he caused a furore when he reproached some South Australian winemakers for 'making inferior grapes into poor, vapid, characterless liquids'. Never-theless on that same journey he still managed to buy substantial quantities of wine and always forecast a promising future for the Australian industry.

Perhaps it was just that confrontationist approach of Burgoyne that caused the South Australian Winegrowers' Association to approach the South Australian Premier, Sir John Downer, late in 1892, seeking the establishment of a government warehouse in London where South Australian wines could recuperate after their long voyage from Adelaide. After all, as the Association's representatives pointed out, though wine shipments had grown in volume, they had not increased in value and this was probably because the prices paid depended on the state of the wine at the time of arrival (often out of condition because of malolactic fermentation). Though the South Australians were not necessarily to know this, another factor accounting for the indifferent prices paid may well have been the ultimate purpose to which the buyers intended to put their Australian purchases. Such young wines were often blended with lighter more fragile European wines to give them greater body and alcoholic strength ('bonesetters', as they are called in the trade, were within the bounds of legality then, though illegal in the European Commission now).

It was not a proposal that received unanimous South Australian support. 'Free-market' winemakers such as Benno Seppelt were opposed to it; others like Thomas Hardy were ambivalent, supplying both their own agent (the ubiquitous Burgoyne in Hardy's case) and the London Wine Depot, as it was to be known.

On 2 February 1894 the *Times* reported,

> The Government of South Australia has resolved upon establishing in London at a cost not exceeding £3000 per annum for five years, a depot for wines and produce from that colony . . . It was originally proposed to have only a store to which South Australian wines could be consigned for the purpose of restoring them to condition after the long voyage, opportunities being at the same time afforded to wine merchants and others to test the wines and make their purchases through the shippers' agents.

As the *Times* further informed its readers, that scheme had been substantially changed (most regrettably in the view of the London agents) to allow the manager of the Depot (Edward Burney Young) to act as agent for the consignors in disposing of the consignments at their expense as to freight, insurance and storage.

Young responded enthusiastically to his enlarged commission, as we again learn from the columns of the *Times* about a year later.

> Messrs Southard & Co., under the instructions of Mr E. Burney Young . . . offered yesterday at the London Commercial Sale Rooms, a quantity of good quality wine including hock, muscadine, claret and burgundy. This was the first attempt to dispose of any quantity of colonial wine by public sale, and the trade showed great interest at the experiment, attending in large numbers, buyers from the country as well as London being present, while representatives from some of the continental shippers watched the results of the sale.

In this report of 1 February 1895, the *Times* mentions some whites being sold under the 'Orion' brand, registered on behalf of the Depot by Young and possibly inspired by the success a decade before of 'Emu'. But it was

> Australian claret that created most interest and the prices obtained for it compare most favourably with the Bordeaux wines . . . Practically the whole of the offerings were disposed of and were generally taken by buyers who have not hitherto been known as distributors of colonial wines. Many provincial firms made good purchases . . .

The London agents were horrified. What had promised to be a convenient warehouse for tasting colonial wine at one's leisure now threatened to be a dangerous competitor, especially as by 1900 the Depot was selling nearly 452 000 litres of wine a year. Naturally Burgoyne and Pownall did what they could to white-ant the Depot, suggesting that its wines were second-rate and that only their wines were of top quality. Though this response was predictable and to a certain extent quite true, for they represented the larger South Australian firms who by that time had most to lose by shipping inferior wines, what was not so easily prophesied was the hostile reaction from sectors of the South Australian industry, especially the newly established Stanley Wine Co., whose founder, J. H. Christison, was especially critical.

By 1901 the whole matter had become a political football and was referred (as usual) to a royal commission. The complainants laid two chief complaints. The first was financial: the Depot simply took too long to sell their wine and then was tardy in paying, continuing to debit charges for storage, treatments such as racking and interest on the basic advance payment of one shilling a gallon made on the shipment of the wine to London. The second was secrecy. The depot would not disclose the names of the buyers to the winemaker nor the winemaker to the buyer. This infuriated Christison, who could see quite clearly the conflict between his 'Stanley' brand and 'Orion' owned by the Depot. In his evidence he complained,

> Mr Young is selling Stanley wine in London, but he will not tell who is the maker of the wine. I have letters to prove that he will not give the brands of the wines . . . I do not think that is fair. The depot was started to assist the winemaker here. I do not see why they should keep

> anything secret. I will give you an instance: 8,000 gallons [36 400 litres] of our wine were sold to one man, and sold at a big price. If I could get the name of the merchant or if he could get ours, we could do business, and we would gladly pay a commission . . . Mr Gilbey is a large merchant and I think it was his people who bought our wine.

As the moving spirit of the Depot, Young defended his position valiantly against this attack from a somewhat unexpected quarter. It was necessary, he alleged, for producer and purchaser to remain unknown to one another so as not to bring any wine into disrepute and so compromise the government's (Depot's?) position and as for payment to the winemaker, this was the treasury's responsibility not the Depot's. And what of the 'Orion' brand? Well it was much easier to sell wine under one unknown brand in a new market than under sixty or seventy. And finally, as for those disgruntled London agents, it was essential to sell retail rather than wholesale because they had firstly refused to stock the wines and had only complained when they saw the retail demand that Young had created.

Though there was merit on both sides and the suggestion made that wine payments be accelerated, the commission was evidently not in favour of government enterprise, finding against the Depot and recommending that it be sold at a proper valuation to a private concern. The commission's findings met with no immediate response from the government and it was not until Burgoyne, who was responsible for two-thirds of all South Australian wine exports, announced in February 1903 that he would buy only from the Depot, 'as every little merchant or grocer now has the right to do' or from other London agents dealing in Australian wine, that major South Australian winemakers, fearing the loss of a major export market, beseeched the government to dispose of the Depot, which in April 1904 was sold to the Commonwealth of Australia Wine & Produce Co. It had lasted barely ten years.

The decade of wine and roses that was Edwardian England must have been difficult for London importers of Australian wine, for though the total level of Australian wine exports remained reasonably consistent (for example 1900-1—3.778 million litres, 1910-11—4.303 million litres) there were threats from Burgoyne to discontinue direct purchases and a complaint from W. A. Gilbey in a letter to the *Times* that notwithstanding a thirty-five per cent increase in population in the previous thirty years, wine consumption was actually less. Whether this was a conspiracy to keep prices down is anybody's guess, but major Australian winemakers such as Seppelt and Hardy were unwilling to take any risks with Burgoyne and Pownall who were by that time importing ninety per cent of the wine, not a drop of which at that time originated in Coonawarra.

NINE

The birth of Coonawarra

People with preconceptions about how great wine regions should appear on first acquaintance are certain to be sorely disappointed when they view Coonawarra for the first time. There are no golden slopes or classic chateaux with turreted roofs, just flat eucalyptus-dotted countryside. In 1840, except for the swampy lowlands, it would have been very similar in its general aspect, as the Austin brothers, the area's first permanent white settlers, approached with a mob of merinos to graze on the 280 square kilometre Yallum run. After eleven years, the Austins sold Yallum to the Wells who in turn disposed of it in 1861 to John and George Riddoch.

Like the wisest of those who rushed to the Victorian goldfields in the 1850s, the canny Scots-born Riddochs made their original fortune by providing the necessaries of life to hungry and thirsty miners. John Riddoch also struck rural 'gold' in the soils of Yallum, for by 1880 the run extended from Coonawarra in the north fifty kilometres south almost to Mount Gambier, encompassed nearly 700 square kilometres of grazing country and carried over 160 000 sheep. In that year also he completed the construction of a twenty-room mansion at a cost of £14 000 ($28 000), an expense which was severely to strain a previously close relationship with his son. Every bit the local grandee, Riddoch in the very next year (1881) entertained royalty, the young princes George (later to become King George V) and Albert, both midshipmen on HMS *Bacchante*. Contemporary illustrations of parts of their tour show them riding, playing tennis, planting trees but not of course sampling the local wine. That was still over a decade away.

At this point, another Scot became an essential part of the Coonawarra story. He was William Wilson, who had arrived in Australia as a shepherd but was a man of much greater agricultural expertise, having worked for some years in the Mediterranean vineyards of France and Spain. Like most immigrants of his time, Wilson tried his luck on the Victorian goldfields, was modestly successful and bought a hectare of terra rossa soil in the town of Penola. Putting his Mediterranean experience to good use, he rapidly gained a growing reputation for the quality of his small orchard and garden, attracting at the same time the attention of Riddoch, as that same red loam also extended north through Riddoch's Katnook property which adjoined Yallum Park. What was more, it had also been noticed how well this red loam drained in comparison to the spongy black soil next to it, so much so that in those days before permanent road surfaces, the red soil with its free drainage was the only reliable location for the main north road.

Exactly why John Riddoch decided to subdivide 1147 acres (465 hectares) of that terra rossa country is unknown. Perhaps cash flow was at a low ebb, as the South Australian government was forcing more and more graziers to buy instead of lease their holdings. Perhaps wool was undergoing one of its periodic downturns. But in 1890 subdivide he did, into ten acre (four hectare) blocks, selling the land subject to strict planting conditions for £10 ($20) per acre over a term of ten years at five per cent per annum interest. Later a further parcel of 812 acres (329 hectares) was added to the subdivision. In so far as any smallholdings in rural Australia at that time had 'modern conveniences', the Penola Fruit Colony as it was at first officially called, was as well off as any other, possessing a school, a co-operative store, a post office and a railway station little more than a kilometre away.

There were twenty-six original 'colonists', who started planting in 1891. According to the widely-travelled W. Catton Grasby, a former headmaster of Roseworthy Agricultural College who was witness to the first decade of its development, during that first season 95 000 vines and 10 000 fruit trees were planted. By 1897, 220 acres (eighty-nine hectares) of vines were being cultivated by the Coonawarra colonists, while Riddoch had, in Grasby's own words, 'shown his own faith in the future of the colony' by planting 128 acres (fifty-two hectares) of vines with the result that the vineyard composition of Coonawarra at that time was 181 acres (seventy-three hectares) of shiraz, 110 acres (forty-five hectares) of cabernet sauvignon, twenty-seven acres (eleven hectares) of malbec and thirty acres (twelve hectares) of pinot noir.

In addition Riddoch had honoured his undertaking given at the time of subdivision by erecting a substantial winery. Let Grasby describe it.

> The cellars are an imposing structure, situated on a slight rise near the township, and about half a mile from the Coonawarra Railway Station. They are built of limestone and comprise a basement and main floor with a loft floor above. The climate is so good that the nights are always cool, so that the difficulties met with in other places owing to the rise in temperature do not arise here. In addition the water supply . . . is so good and cool that the operation of fermenting wine is a comparatively simple one.
> (W. Catton Grasby, *Coonawarra Fruit Colony,* 1899)

The cellar was also well equipped for its time. Grasby continues.

> The crusher is driven by a portable steam engine. The must is run into fermenting tanks by means of chutes. The fermenting tanks are of masonry, cemented, and cooling coils are available if necessary. Adjoining the fermenting room is the laboratory and two offices. The

> cellars contain a few oak casks of 1000 gallons [4550 litres] capacity, but the standard size is 500 gallons [2275 litres] and the fittings leave nothing to be desired; indeed the equipment is one of the best in South Australia . . . A feature of the Coonawarra fruit colony has been that the promoter has had ample capital at his disposal so that the money trouble so frequent in connection with such schemes has been entirely absent. A new settler going to Coonawarra has the experience of earlier settlers to advise him, he has the planted blocks as object lessons to guide him, and in addition he has the right to the help and instruction of the practical men working Mr Riddoch's blocks. If a novice can go into fruit and vine growing with safety anywhere, he can do so at Coonawarra.

Indeed Riddoch had secured the services of one of the best viticulturalists and winemakers of his time, Ewen McBain, Roseworthy gold medallist and former Assistant Government Viticulturalist under Professor Perkins, of Roseworthy College founded in 1883.

With such equipment, capital and personnel, the prospects of Coonawarra seemed limitless. Let Grasby gaze further into the crystal ball.

> It is generally agreed there is a period of prosperity ahead for grapegrowers and winemakers; and if this be so, everything seems favorable for a great development at Coonawarra. Under specially favorable circumstances a vineyard in South Australia will produce a crop in three years, and the average vineyard will give a fair and regular yield when five years old, but no one should go into vine planting who is not prepared to wait from five to seven years. Anyone who can do this and is able and willing to work, and has intelligence and power of adaptability, should find Coonawarra almost an ideal rural home. He will enjoy one of the best climates in the world, a healthy outdoor life, pleasant associations and the prospects of a safe and regular income.

After eulogising this rural Utopia, Grasby now becomes more cautious.

> But he must not be misled into expecting anything more than a reasonable profit on investment, and a reward for labor done. Nature is

a just dealer, and one must not expect fortunes and the comforts and health of rural life to be combined.

One cannot emphasise the statements made in this paragraph too strongly. It is necessary that men should be hopeful or they will never progress. A doubter misses his chances from too great caution. The optimistic individual often gets himself into difficulties from lack of caution . . . I am particularly desirous that it shall not be said in years to come that I misled anyone, however unintentionally; but I am equally anxious not to err from over-caution. There may be conditions of which I am not aware that may affect the judgment, but all evidence at Coonawarra seems to point to success for those who have the necessary qualifications to claim it. Unless my judgment is at fault, the conditions for successful cultivation are favorable; then there remains the consideration of the marketing of produce . . . My belief is that the future of Coonawarra will depend mainly on its wine and apples . . .

It seems fair to say there is room for several thousands of acres. it is proved that the best varieties of wine grapes grow well and that the quality of wine made from them will probably be hardly surpassed in the colony, and only equalled in localities equally favored by climate. It is fair, I think, to say that there is little or no doubt about there being a market for wine of such excellence. Mr Riddoch has ample capital, and stands pledged to use it for the purchase of grapes and the making of wine. This is a most important fact, for, although I look forward to some of the settlers, with special facilities, establishing individual wineries, it would not be generally desirable. Mr Riddoch has, however, co-ordinate interests as the founder of the Colony, and it seems to me that, even if he were willing to do so, he cannot take advantage of his position as sole buyer of grapes, without damaging his interests to a far greater extent in other respects. It is therefore reasonable to say that unless the conviction that there is a future market for the wine is wrong, the conclusion that there is a splendid opening for grape growers is correct. So far I have only considered the prospects of the British market, but with the realisation of the Australian Commonwealth and the consequent inter-colonial free trade, there will be a vastly extended Australian market.

Just how correct was Grasby, the contemporary pundit? In his forecasts of the quality of Coonawarra wine he was a prophet of unerring accuracy.

> Coonawarra claret promises to have a very high and wide reputation—indeed there is no doubt but that it will be a beautiful wine of good body, fine color, delicate bouquet and low alcoholic strength.

This was a prediction that has more than fulfilled its truth in the intervening century. On marketing, however, events were to prove that he was very wide of the mark.

But Coonawarra was at the end of the earth and the rest of South Australia cared not a skerrick for its marketing possibilities. Thomas Hardy was finding McLaren Vale to be of increasing importance. By 1886 his vineyard plantings there had grown to nearly 1500 acres (607 hectares) and were capably managed by his nephew, Thomas Nottage, and John Kelly, son of Alexander. His total vintage was approaching half a million litres and in addition he had erected a still, being certain that he would 'produce a pure brandy, equal to the best brands of cognac . . . '

The following year (1887) Hardy, now aged fifty-seven, decided to take his sons James, Thomas Nathaniel and Robert into the business, incorporating a family company which became known as Thomas Hardy & Sons Limited. The filial duties were allotted as follows: to his eldest son James, aged thirty-two, responsibility for sales and distribution; to Thomas Nathaniel, twenty-five, plant and maintenance; and to his youngest son Robert, winemaking. Hardy himself remained firmly in control. During the 1880s he had placed the emphasis directly on wine quality and urged the rest of the South Australian winemaking fraternity to do likewise. The wine writers of the time echoed this trend: 'in place of the vile trash that used to be termed colonial wine, there is gradually being introduced an article which compares favourable with some of the best products of the old wine countries'. (*Observer* 1884) This was also the age of local, national, imperial, intercolonial and international exhibitions. Hardy not only entered these enthusiastically, but also took part in their organisation. He was chairman of the wine committee at the Adelaide exposition of 1887, which had 487 wine entries and fifty-three spirits, while at Bordeaux in 1882 a Hardy entry won a gold medal 'first class' and at the Paris International Exhibition in 1889 another gained a gold medal 'against the world'. As Hardy told his audience in one of the many speeches he made to the wine community in the colony,

> to increase the English trade, which is now so promising, we must keep up the quality of our wines, and that may only be done by planting good kinds in the soil to which they are suited. That is the greatest part of the business. That of the winemaker is to handle the grapes in the best possible way and to mature wines and to produce uniform samples of as few types as possible.

In the McLaren Vale of the late 1880s and 1890s, Hardy's enthusiasm certainly proved contagious. In 1887 his former manager, John Kelly, following his own father Alexander's example, established Tatachilla, planting in its first two seasons 124 acres (fifty hectares). He later went on to establish 300 acres (122 hectares), becoming the largest individual vineyard owner in South Australia. In 1890 the Kay brothers, Herbert and Frederick Walter, planted 'Amery' and built substantial stone cellars in accordance with a model devised by Dr Kelly some years before. In 1891 A. C. Johnston bought 'Pirramimma', making a first vintage in 1900. 'Wirra Wirra' also made its first vintage in that year. In 1891 the Hope Farm vineyard, which had been established about forty-one years previously by George Manning, was bought by W. H. Craven, who made substantial extensions to the cellars. In fact by 1903 there were nineteen wineries in the district, which produced in total over three million litres of wine.

Thomas Hardy & Sons Limited remained by far the largest producer in the district, indeed they became the largest producer in the colony in 1894, when they made over 1.4 million litres of wine, surpassing this figure in 1896 with over 1.75 million litres. The vast majority of the wine was red, 'claret', though a little chablis was also made. A popular fivepenny lunch in Adelaide in 1881 was a ham or tongue sandwich accompanied by an iced claret at Hardy's Bankside Wine Bar in Grenfell Street. In the same year Hardy built a substantial bluestone building in Currie Street as his new city cellars and headquarters. A decade later it had been outgrown and Hardy moved headquarters in 1893 to Mile End just west of the city, where a two-storey building with a fifty-seven metre frontage had been erected in chateau style on 0.7 hectares of land at a cost of £2500. It contained a modern laboratory, blending vats and storage capacity for 360 000 litres of wine, as well as stables for Hardy's horse teams and their carts. It was from Mile End that the many millions of litres of Hardy red destined for London started their long journey, including the quaintly named Hardy's Ferruginous. It is said that Hardy never tired of pointing out the ironstone in the soils around Tintara and the tonic qualities allegedly given to his red by this ferruginous soil, so much so that on one occasion when he was escorting a young Cuthbert Burgoyne, sent by his father, Peter, to learn the trade, around McLaren Vale, they came upon a simple cottage built of the reddest of ironstone. Upon sight of this the young Burgoyne, obviously quite weary of the 'ferruginous' countryside, exclaimed, 'Look, a ferruginous house!' It is not recorded whether Thomas Hardy, then aged sixty-three and one of the patriarchs of the South Australian wine industry, smiled.

The decades of the 1880s and 1890s raised Thomas Hardy to the height of his power and influence in South Australia. If there were a committee or inquiry concerning fruit or vines without Hardy's membership at least, it was hard to find. More often he was chairman or deputy. He was vigorously involved in the fight against phylloxera, travelling to the affected colonies to examine the situation first-hand. Ultimately in 1899 he became a member of the Board to administer the South Australian legislation which brought a strict quarantine into effect. He was an active federationist, being a member of the executive of the South Australian Federation League throughout the 1890s. He was President of the Winegrowers' Association and the Chamber of Manufactures and chairman of several boards concerned with activities as far removed from each other as education and bottle manufacture.

Though never formally trained in winemaking or wine sciences, Hardy was always concerned with the quality of South Australian wine. As he said in a speech reported by the South Australian Register in July 1875, 'as long as sweet wines are required, this [acid degeneration] will continue to be the dread of winemakers, unless some of our scientific men take up the question and show us the cause and nature of this unfortunate deterioration'.

One of the 'scientific men' to take up challenges such as this was Arthur James Perkins, an oenology graduate of the University of Montpellier, who took up the position of Government Viticulturalist at Roseworthy College in 1892, later becoming Professor of Viticulture in 1895 and Principal of Roseworthy in 1904. In 1900 in a paper entitled 'The Diseases of Wine' published in the *Journal of the*

Department of Agriculture Vol 4, 1900-01, he listed four chief causes of disease in wine. Simply stated, they were: poor hygiene, poor handling, poor fermentation and poor wine composition.

If the rules of simple hygiene were ignored, 'a dirty, untidy cellar' became 'a veritable hotbed of disease'. He stressed the need to disinfect walls and floors. 'Carelessness, in this respect, I believe to be at the root of nine-tenths of the troubles in our cellars'.

As for poor handling, he ascribed failure to top up casks and to rack young wines of their lees as two primary causes of disease and off-flavours.

Poor fermentation Perkins put down to excessive temperatures arising in the fermentation of musts of high sugar content. He believed that must-cooling was essential and actively advocated a type of water cooler designed in California.

A combination of all the problems mentioned above would of course lead to poor wine composition, for healthy wines needed proper levels of ethyl alcohol, tannins and acidity. He suggested that suitable alcohol levels were 12-15% alc/vol for dry wines and 15-20% for sweet.

The work initiated by Perkins was to be much further advanced in the 1930s as the infant science of microbiology came to greater maturity.

How far did Australian winemaking methods, plant and technology advance during the nineteenth century? For an outline of the basic methods employed in the first thirty years of that century, we can do little better as a starting point than refer (perhaps it should be 'defer') to James Busby. In his 1830 book, *Manual for Vineyards and for Making Wine*, he summarises what can essentially be called the 'cottage industry' approach to winemaking, at that time perfectly appropriate for an Anglo-Celtic settler with an acre or two of vines in a new land virtually ignorant of wine and its making.

Let Busby outline his methods:

> a review of the process with grapes that have attained all that perfection which our grapes will undoubtedly attain, when we have more experience of the best kinds to cultivate, and the stocks shall be no longer young, will shew how very simple it is—amounting only to this—That the grapes should first be freed from the stalks and from any rotten and unripe berries—That they should then be broken and

> crushed by treading them in a tub—That the whole contents of the tub-juice, skins, seeds and all should then be emptied into a vat - That when the heat of the fermentation in the vat is over, the wine should be drawn off into properly cleaned casks—That these casks should be left open at the bung-hole, to allow the wine to throw off the yeast which will work to the surface—That when the wine has ceased to throw off any yeast, the cask should be bunged up, and left to stand till winter—When, the wine, after being drawn off into clean casks, should be sulphured, and so the whole process be concluded, and the wine left fit for use.

What equipment did that budding winemaker need? For fermentation, he suggests a large cask with one end knocked out such as 'those brought out as ship's water casks' of a capacity of 200 gallons (910 litres) with a hole bored in its side about six to eight inches (fifteen to twenty centimetres) from its base.

For destemming the bunches, which should then 'be pressed [crushed] with all possible speed', a forked stick with three prongs will suffice. 'Fixing one of the outside prongs in the centre of the . . . tub, keep turning the others around till all the grapes are detached'.

For crushing, a large cask was cut into two tubs, which were to be supplied with false bottoms, about three to four inches (eight to ten centimetres) from their base, strongly supported by that base. Again holes were to be drilled in the false bottom and in the sides of the tub between the bottoms to allow the grape juice to escape into three or four buckets. Both tubs and fermenter were to rest on strong stands, obviously higher than the bucket. A funnel was also required.

In addition, Busby suggests three or four 'pipes' (a cask of 520 litres in volume) or six to eight hogsheads (half the volume of a pipe and when empty easier for one man to handle), as well as some smaller casks to allow bigger casks to be broken down into smaller quantities of wine.

Busby found little else required. Sulphur candles for burning in casks, sulphite of potash (potassium metabisulphite) in minute quantities for stabilising the wine after racking, salt and hot water for cleaning out casks, and eggwhites for fining were then the only other assistants in the winemaking process. Perhaps though, if one were rich, like Mr Gregory Blaxland of Brush Farm, one could have 'a very complete winepress' made by a carpenter in Sydney named Flood. Yet 'those in possession of a cheese press will find no great difficulty in applying it for this purpose. But a beam of wood to act as a simple lever will answer very well, and it will cost nothing.'

And the motive power for this equipment? The winemaker, suitably shod for treading the grapes and pressing the must, if a wine press had not been built, in 'a pair of strong wooden shoes'. Such was Busby's method. Its equipment was simple and its main requirement was cleanliness.

Thirty years later there were few changes. Ebenezer Ward in 1862 visited Henry Evans at Evandale.

> Mr Evans adopts a simple process in the manufacture of his wine, and its chief characteristics appear to be care and cleanliness. To the absence of cleanliness with regard to casks and utensils, and of care in keeping the casks full during fermentation, he attributes in a great measure the disappointments which overtake many wine producers . . .
>
> He uses a mill for crushing red grapes for dark wine [not mentioned by Busby], but in treating white grapes for white wines, he adheres to the primitive system of pressing with bare feet [no change here]. He believes that the best constructed mill crushes some of the seeds and gives thereby a harsh and unpleasant flavour to the wine.
>
> He removes the rough stem from both red and white grapes by rubbing them through a box with a grating at the bottom [where is the three-pronged stick?] . . .
>
> Mr Evans does not prolong the fermentation in vats in accordance with the ordinary custom [Busby felt no need for haste in taking the wine from the fermenting vat, even after primary fermentation had subsided and malolactic fermentation was going on provided it was 'still sweetish'], but draws the wine off into store casks before the sweetness is quite gone. To save the trouble of filling up the casks several times a day, which would otherwise be necessary, he inserts in each cask a thin tube made in the shape of a syphon, the longer leg in the cask and the shorter one in a vessel of water, and by this means the carbonic acid gas [CO_2] is allowed to escape, but the atmospheric air is excluded. The secondary [malolactic] fermentation is continued thus in the store casks for a considerable time, and the result is found

> to be that the wine acquires clearness and maturity more quickly than when the fermentation is more fully completed in the vats.
> (E. Ward, *The Vineyards and Orchards of South Australia*, 1862)

At this time the more assiduous winemakers such as Dr Kelly were investigating the control of fermentation temperatures and recommending the use of 'worms' (hollow tin-plated copper coils through which cold water was pumped) to cool the must. The industrial revolution was beginning to reach Australian wine cellars.

By 1890 it had arrived. A Seppelt promotional booklet, *Views of Seppeltsfield*, published early in the twentieth century, describes the Seppeltsfield winery of 1890.

> The winery is a structure 120 feet [36.5 metres] by 90 feet [27.5 metres] and was built in 1890 according to Mr [Benno] Seppelt's own design. This building is placed upon a hillside, and at the higher end under a broad verandah, are placed two crushing mills, each capable of treating 100 tons of grapes daily. Within the building are 60 tanks, each of a capacity of 2000 gallons [9100 litres], the tanks being in terraces, so that all the racking is accomplished by gravitation. By experimenting, Mr Seppelt, over 20 years ago, found that during fermentation the 'must' had to be restrained below a certain temperature, and so adopted a cooling apparatus, consisting of coiled pipes, through which flows cold water. Limited space precludes an adequate description of this Winery, which by disinterested globe-trotters, is said to be equal to anything of its kind in the world.

Those disinterested globetrotters may have been equally impressed by the Seppeltsfield storage cellars, which at that time had a capacity of nearly one million gallons (4.5 million litres). Certainly Professor Arthur Perkins, Government Viticulturalist, was.

> I know of no cellars, either here or in Europe, so perfectly conceived, from the general plan down to the minutest detail, for handling economically enormous bulks of wine. It is said that imitation is the sincerest flattery. I cannot therefore be accused of insincerity since the cellars . . . now being erected at Roseworthy Agricultural College are mere copies, on a very reduced scale, of Mr Seppelt's splendid buildings.

The Seppelt copy proceeds:

> to convey an impression of the volumes of wines in these cellars, we may mention that were they put into quarter casks [135 litres in volume] and were these placed end to end, they would extend 13¼ miles [21.3 kilometres] . . .

Most of that long thin line of wooden casks would have been American oak, sweet and vanillan and just the thing for full-bodied dry Barossa shiraz or sweet red. The staves were imported in 20 000 lots and made by the 'six to ten coopers . . . constantly employed at Seppeltsfield'. There was also a laboratory, under the supervision of Mr Oscar Seppelt, Benno's eldest son, who had 'technical training and extended experience in European Viticultural Colleges'. By the early 1890s Oscar was using yeast cultures imported from Europe and by the turn of the century making his own.

Though winery equipment and techniques were becoming more sophisticated and steam power was used by the bigger wineries, by 1900 the sources of the motive power needed in winemaking remained as they had been during the previous century—manual labour and gravitation. James Busby, who had died in England in 1871, would have noted the arrival of the industrial revolution with approval, though perhaps he would have been relieved to see that treading shoes, made of leather, not wood, were still occasionally worn.

Though Benno Seppelt may not have been quite as active in public life as Hardy, he was certainly just as dynamic in his business ability and as far-sighted in his vision of the future. One writer, obviously impressed with the man, described him thus: 'Geniuses are seldom practical, but this gentleman is an engineer of singular powers, a student, a chemist and a merchant all in one . . . ' This tribute was paid after a visit in the late 1880s to Seppeltsfield, which was then 486 hectares in extent and described as

> one of the show places of the colony . . . quite a little town, and as one inspects in turn the laboratory, the winery, the cellars, the distillery, the vinegar works, the cooperage, the blacksmith's shop and piggery, he is impressed with the methodical way in which everything is conducted . . .

In 1888 'Seppeltsfield crushed 1800 tons of grapes, only about a tenth of which came from its own vineyards, and produced 270 000 gallons (1.23 million litres) of wine, a task of no great difficulty as the winery had sixty fermentation vats, each with a capacity of 2000 gallons (9100 litres) after which the grapes were pressed by one of the few hydraulic presses in the colony. Nor did Benno waste the skins, using them as pig feed and also a vineyard fertiliser. It is recorded that such grape-fed porkers produced very special bacon.

By the turn of the century, Seppeltsfield was producing over 400 000 gallons (1.8 million litres) and was the biggest winery in the biggest producing area (the Barossa Valley) in the colony. Fermentation capacity had doubled since 1888; there were now 120, 2000 gallon (9100 litre) tanks and two hydraulic presses which could handle 150 tons of must a day. Storage and maturation capacity approached five million litres in accordance with Benno's policy of holding reserve stocks for as long as ten years and when that stock required bottling, one bottling crew could achieve 500 dozen a day.

Samuel Smith, founder of Yalumba, died in 1889 and Sidney Smith, then aged fifty-one, took charge. Already Sidney's sons, Percival Sidney and Walter Grandy, were in their twenties. To Percival fell the tasks of production and winemaking, to Walter the responsibility for sales and promotion. And promote Walter did!

The age of the billboard had arrived and Walter was nothing if not media-minded. A passion for big-game hunting quickly gained him the nickname 'Tiger' and his sales tours were mostly made to countries where there was at least a prospect of a trophy or two. Thus Walter made extensive tours of India, Africa, Ceylon, Canada, Singapore and New Zealand, his sales orders being frequently received at Yalumba in the company of tiger skins or antlered heads. In all this Walter was very much in tune with the spirit of the times, for the cities of Asia and Africa that Walter visited were very much outposts of the British Empire and the Pax Britannica ruled the world.

So with Walter in charge of advertising, Yalumba's posters scaled the peaks of the age of imperialism, depicting in 1893 for example the Indian North West Frontier War with gruesome detail of severed arms, pools of blood and the battle cry 'Yalumba Wines to the Front!'

Others recalled what today would be regarded as shameful memories of the past such as the shooting of Aborigines with the caption 'Yalumba Wines are pure and wholesome'. Bizarre messages that today would be regarded as provocative at best all stressed the excitement of wine.

How good were those wines that were so spiritedly promoted? According to the *Observer*, by 1890 Yalumba was becoming quite famous for two port styles—Old Port, 'a strong, generous and very full-bodied wine . . . extremely pleasant . . . insidiously inviting—a wine so seductive that one needs to be careful as to the quantity [one drinks]' and Special Old Port—an older tawny style, reputedly aged for fourteen years and depicted as 'a wine . . . urgently required in the sick-room for invalids just picking up their strength, being bright and clean'. Indeed Yalumba, described at this time as the 'Oporto of Australia', was simply reflecting a growing trend among contemporary Australian wine-consumers—the change of taste to fortified wine.

With those raucous appeals to jingoism and quality products increasingly accepted in the market place, Yalumba bounded ahead. By the turn of the century, with its home vineyard then 110 acres (44.5 hectares) in extent and buying many more tonnes of grapes from local growers, Yalumba was set to storm into the new century. And storm it did, making a record 180 000 gallons (819 000 litres) vintage in 1903, that year the third largest in South Australia after Seppeltsfield and Chateau Tanunda. Though Sidney Smith died in 1908, in that same year there arose the classic blue marble facade and the imposing clock tower which still stand today as a memorial to Yalumba's nineteenth-century prosperity and as a bold announcement of its confidence in the twentieth century.

Equally confident in its future was Chateau Tanunda, built in 1889-90 by G. F. Cleland & Company Ltd, which shortly thereafter changed its name to the Adelaide Wine Company. Here was a living embodiment (the Stanley Wine Co. was another) of the investors' response to the growers' call for new companies to take up grape production which was often surplus to the requirements of established winemakers. For its age, the Chateau was big even by the standards of Seppeltsfield. In 1893 the *Australian Vigneron* described it thus:

> the principal building . . . built of stone with brick dressings . . . is 250 feet [76.2 metres] long by 110 feet [33.5 metres] wide and 40 feet [12.2 metres] high and capable of holding 1,000,000 gallons [4.5 million litres] of wine. The cellars are built on the face of a hill sloping towards the south. Owing to the fall of the ground, the grapes are delivered into the top storey direct from the wagons, and are taken by steam elevators to the strippers [destemmers] and crushers, which are capable of treating 100 tons of grapes per day. The crushed grapes fall into shoots [chutes], which carry the must into vats by gravitation. In addition to the wine cellars there are other buildings, including the distillery and bonded stores. The cellars and plant cost £27,000 [$54 000] . . .

Chateau Tanunda initially shared in this time of prosperity, rapidly gaining an excellent reputation for brandy and producing 325 000 gallons (1.48 million litres) of wine in 1903, the second largest maker in South Australia after Seppeltsfield. There seemed no limit to the ambitions of the Adelaide Wine Company. The corporate net was cast far and wide. In 1910 it bought the Riddoch cellars in Coonawarra, as well as building a new winery next to the railway station at Lyndoch, in the words of the *Wine and Spirit News*, 'to give a more central and convenient place of delivery to the growers'. In 1914 it was selling over 26 000 cases of brandy annually as well as holding 250 000 gallons (1.137 million litres) in bond. Popular belief had it that it controlled over half the brandy stocks then in Australia. It pressed on, erecting a winery and distillery at Renmark, but by 1916 was forced to confess that it had run out of cash. The Chateau and the Lyndoch winery were bought by the company's chief competitor, Seppelts.

The flood of grapes that periodically overwhelmed the existing winemaking facilities of the Barossa Valley in the late 1880s and 1890s caused not only the rise of new wineries such as Chateau Tanunda, whose later forte was to be distilling, but also attracted established distillers such as Tolley Scott & Tolley to invest in such potential profitability.

This company had its origins as the East Torrens Winemaking and Distilling Company in the inner Adelaide suburb of Stepney in 1858. After mixed fortunes in its first thirty years of existence it was purchased by the English distiller, Thomas Scott, and the Australian Tolley brothers, Ernest and Douglas, in 1888. In 1894, responding to an obvious regional need, they established the Angas Park Distillery at Nuriootpa. Its chief feature, according to the journalist Ernest Whitington, who visited it in 1903, was

> a double-barrelled Mabille Press, which is crusher and presser combined. All the juice is won from the grapes and the pressed skins are forced out in solid round cakes. This machine works beautifully and has given the greatest satisfaction.
> (Aeuckens & Ors, *Vineyard of the Empire*, p. 103)

In the previous year (1902), Tolley Scott & Tolley had bought the Nuriootpa winery of Messrs S. & W. Sage, 120 metres away across the main road, which they used as fermenting house and storage cellars. Total storage capacity at both buildings was 250 000 gallons (1.137 million litres). In 1903 the vintage of Tolley Scott & Tolley, or TST as it later came to be called, at Angas Park was 160 000 gallons (728 000 litres) the fourth largest in the Barossa Valley in that year.

In 1877 on his succession to the family business, Gustav Gramp transferred to his 'Orlando' property a kilometre away at Rowland Flat. There for the next nine years in what must have been rather cramped temporary accommodation, for the Jacob's Creek cellar seems not to have been expanded, he made increasing amounts of wine. Finally in 1886 he built substantial ironstone cellars. Though the Gramp production was (compared to Seppelt) quite small at this time, his reputation as a white-winemaker was growing apace, for a report of the *Australian Vigneron and Fruitgrowers' Journal* of 1895 noted the Adelaide visit of the Italian warship, *Christoforo Colombo*, and how much Prince Luigi of Savoy, a member of the Italian royal family, had appreciated the Gramp's Carte Blanche, a leading hock style of its day, so much so that by royal command, a quantity was bought for the ship's stores.

Gustav had also added a further string to his bow—that of nurseryman, for in a letter from Walter 'Tiger' Smith in 1890 to Gustav, an order is placed for 5000 cuttings of pedro ximines as well as a few hundred of any table varieties that he could spare.

Production in 1892 from his then twenty-three acre (9.3 hectare) vineyard, four acres not then bearing, was 3200 gallons (14 560 litres), increasing to 7500 gallons (34 125 litres) in 1903; Johann

Gramp in that same year (sadly his last vintage) produced 2500 gallons (11 375 litres) at Jacob's Creek, a combined production of 10 000 gallons, which is quite small compared to the total Barossa vintage of 1. 315 million gallons (5.98 million litres) in that year. The growth years of Orlando were yet to come.

The wine boom of the 1880s and 1890s in South Australia gave birth in Clare to all shapes and sizes of wineries. Wendouree, if it were to be established today, would be termed a 'boutique'. In Clare in the 1890s it was a medium-sized vineyard twenty acres (eight hectares) in extent, planted to shiraz, cabernet sauvignon, malbec and mataro. It had been established in 1892 by Alfred Percy Birks and his brother.

A. P. Birks had always been on the fringe of wine. As a young man he had sold wine in New Zealand on behalf of Salter's and so it was only natural that he would seek to build his own domain. An early mention of the vineyard occurred in the *Northern Argus* (still the newspaper of the district) on 7 February 1896 and though the mention is entirely favourable, there is a hint that the grape market was as usual unreliable.

> Messrs Birks . . . have a very nice vineyard and orchard . . . 20 acres planted of the shiraz, cabernet, malbec and mataro varieties. If the proprietors cannot find a market for the latter variety, they intend to graft with cabernet.

By 1903 a small winery had been erected, which produced in that vintage a quantity of 1000 gallons (4550 litres) which was sold to a lusty infant not then ten years old but already the local giant, the Stanley Wine Co.

That wine boom, spurred on by swelling export markets, enthused South Australian growers large and small to embrace once more the vine. It was a romance that had left many of their fathers lamenting thirty years before but which nevertheless the sons were prepared to renew. Like the Birks brothers, the other winegrowers of Clare proved no exception to this trend. In 1890 there were 234 acres (ninety-five hectares) of vines in the region. By 1897, 1431 acres (580 hectares). As we have seen in the case of Thomas Hardy, they were not without encouragement from the wine industry establishment, nor were government officials at all circumspect in their estimation of the prospects of success. During a visit to Clare early in 1892, a Victorian expert touring the region at the behest of the Central Agricultural Bureau was reported in the *Chronicle* (3 March 1892) as informing his audience that

> . . . they could not go wrong . . . in growing wine grapes, as they would find a suitable market for years to come. Six million sterling was expended annually in England in the import of wines, and, in this district wines of high character should be produced . . . The future was bright before them and they need not hesitate in planting vines . . .

Despite this exhortation, Clare as a winemaking region did suffer a fundamental problem. There were too few existing wineries. Where was this new flood of wine to be made? Was there to be a multiplicity of small wineries each serving its own vineyard? Professor Perkins of Roseworthy felt that this might be the solution. As he said in his annual report of 1895-6 to the government, 'Today the grower should be the winemaker; his perishable crop should not be under the whip-hand of the winemaker'. Thomas Hardy, always the apostle of professionalism in winemaking, felt that no grower with less than fifty acres (twenty hectares) of grapes should make his own wine. He doubtless remembered the bad old days of the 1860s and the rejected exports of South Australian wine, and in a paper of 1 April 1893 said as much to the South Australian Vigneron's Association. Others looked to some form of cooperative, provided they personally did not have to contribute much.

But Clare did possess its own solution to the problem. It had a disused jam factory of substantial size and at a meeting of anxious growers in February 1894, according to the *Observer*, 'it was suggested that this would be a suitable place'. Later that year, four of the town's most solid citizens, Dr Otto Wein-Smith; Mr Magnus Badger (a delightful name for a solicitor); John Christison, owner of the local Enterprise brewery and grapegrower; and J. H. Knappstein met to form the Stanley Wine Company. In 1895 under its winemaker-manager Alfred Basedow, another scion of German stock whose family was to be prominent in Barossa Valley winemaking in the twentieth century, Stanley made its first vintage of 4000 gallons (18 000 litres), a modest enough quantity in the light of what was to come, but obviously wine of quality, as the wines were prize winners at the Adelaide Show. The wines were a tribute not only to the Clare region, but also to Basedow, trained at Montpellier in France with subsequent experience in winemaking in Germany, Spain and Portugal and, according to Christison, who was admittedly biased, the best winemaker South Australia had ever seen.

The following vintage (1896) saw a yield 'between 11,000 and 12,000 gallons [50 050–54 600 litres]' of wine according to Christison who, though very happy with its quality, was rapidly finding out what a great deal of capital wineries required and was beginning to have doubts about the profitability of the project. As he said in a speech at the official opening of the cellars early in 1897,

> When we started we thought a few hundred pounds would send the whole thing going like blazes; it seemed no small matter to start making wine, and indeed we had no intention of spending much money. So after we had made the wine we thought we had better sell it to one of the big wineries which would be running around after us to buy it. But we found it was too young, no one wanted it, and we would have to keep it another year. So another year came around, and of course we had to have a manager. We had to buy more casks, and we had to extend the facilities. Last year (1896) we made between 11,000 and 12,000 gallons and I am happy to say we were very successful: our young claret took first, second and third prizes at the Adelaide Show and our young light wine was highly commended. But there was another year coming on and the vines were another year older, so we reckoned we would have to make double the quantity of wine this year. And when we came to sell last year's wine, still we were met with the answer No, we don't want that, we want matured wine. So there was two years money tied up, and we had to face a third year. The machinery cost considerably more than £200 to install and there are hundreds of pounds worth of casks in the cellar, the price of the big ones being £13/10/- [$27] each, and every cask, barring about 30 hogsheads, was made here. This new building will hold about 60,000 gallons [273 000 litres] of wine. The wine industry, it seems, is like pouring soapsuds down a sink.
>
> As to the growers, you must accept that the company has spent and risked a lot of money, and you must recognise that fact. This season has not been as good as last, there being less juice in the grapes, and

> you cannot expect the same price as last year. I sell my grapes to the company the same as everyone else, and I don't expect the same price for them this year. I also want the growers to indicate in advance how much fruit you have and not expect to bring it all in on one particular day. We want to provide as many casks as are necessary, and not leave you in the lurch. We are making wine here, and we are going to make the best wine in the colony, as we have the best winemaker South Australia has ever seen. But we do need co-operation from the growers.

Such were, and still are, the swings and roundabouts of winegrowing, the gluts and scarcities, the years of plenitude and paucity.

As those Clare vineyards matured, naturally the grape production increased, but Stanley kept its promise to accept all fruit offered. In 1899, 36 000 gallons (163 800 litres) of wine was made; in 1900, 40 000 gallons (182 000 litres). Still more was anticipated. As Basedow said in a report to the Company.

> I should say that this vintage [1900] was only about one third crop, the cause of the shortage being the late frosts, several vineyards being cut as much as four times. There are approximately 1,100 acres [446 hectares] under vines in this district, all the grapes of which are bought by the Stanley Wine Company.

Basedow was just as innovative as he was skilled. We tend to think of refrigeration in wineries as a creature of the last thirty years, but his report continues.

> My refrigerator works very well. I have had a blower fixed up to blow a big draught of air onto the pipes, and I reckon I can now cool 1,000 gallons [4550 litres] of wine 10 degrees [Fahrenheit] in a little over an hour with a thousand gallons of water.

Stanley grew and grew. Even though the surprisingly large vintage of 1901 delayed it, the Company still accepted every grape offered, the result being a yield of 80 000 gallons (364 000 litres), more than twice as big as the previous years, doubtless to the chagrin of Christison. Nevertheless, as the *Observer* reported, 'to avoid the possibility of a block in future, the Company is looking forward to further enlarging the cellarage and also the capacity for manufacture . . . ' Most of this wine was of course destined for the London cellars of Peter Burgoyne and it was at the Adelaide Show dinner late in 1902 that the fiery Christison made several remarks too many. As the Adelaide press rather gleefully reported,

> he [Christison] also remarked on that occasion [the opening of the Stanley cellars some five years before] that the winegrowers were under the thumb of one man, and that the Government had started in opposition to him— God bless the Government. Someone said to him [Christison] afterwards, 'You made a mistake in what you said; you will never sell a gallon of wine to Burgoyne' and he had replied, 'Burgoyne can go to Timbuctoo' . . . They [the winegrowers] were afraid of one man, and they all knew who that man was. There was not a man who had the pluck to come forward and speak a word against this man. A vigneron said 'If I say a word against that man I won't be able to sell my wine to him'. Did they think that sort of thing advanced the wine industry?

Nor was Burgoyne a man to accept a slight with equanimity. He was hardly pleased but one suspects that he rather enjoyed the stance of the injured innocent. Early in 1903 he replied through the columns of the *Adelaide Chronicle*.

> Even while Christison was speaking, a shipment from his vineyard was being sent to me, and perhaps it will scarcely be credited that the mail was simultaneously carrying an order to Mr Christison from this 'Burgoyne' for no less than 40,000 gallons [182 000 litres] of wine, which he had placed under offer to me. Those who were present seemed to have been pleased with Mr Christison's oration, the point of which appeared to be that the taxpayers must be squeezed as much as possible in the interests of the wine industry, and to oppose 'Burgoyne'. A more deplorable position to be taken by an intelligent man, anxious to advance the industry, it is impossible to conceive.

Biting the hand that fed the wine industry was definitely not to be encouraged.

Christison died eight years later, 'a bluff, hearty, honest, good-natured man', according to his obituary in the *Adelaide Observer*.

Solid virtues all, but subtle, discreet or diplomatic he was not.

Christison's widow sold his interest in Stanley to his erstwhile colleague, J. H. Knappstein who, born in Prussia, had arrived in Clare as an eighteen-year-old in 1877. Knappstein was nothing if not astute, for he rapidly built a considerable business selling local fruit to the wheat farmers and buying eggs which he then sold in Broken Hill. Nothing was wasted. Even the bran in which the eggs were packed was sold—to the miners as feed for their pit-ponies. Shortly thereafter he became a ship's chandler and provedore in Adelaide. Success once more saw him open a branch in Perth, where he took his large family (his first marriage had resulted in four sons, his second in seven sons and one daughter). In the mean time, Knappstein had also managed to become one of the largest vineyard owners in the Clare region—sixty-five acres (twenty-six hectares) about a kilometre west of the Clare-Sevenhill road, planted to shiraz, malbec, cabernet, mataro and grenache, and a second vineyard, fifty acres (twenty hectares) in extent, carrying all the above varieties except grenache and adding muscatel and frontignac. The *Northern Argus* of 14 February 1896 was most enthusiastic, 'without exception they look of splendid growth . . . the luxuriant growth of the vines must be an encouragement to the Manager of the property'.

Those vines continued their 'luxuriant growth' and by 1903 Knappstein was Stanley's principal grower, providing about 120 out of the 650 tons of that vintage. In that year Stanley,with its production of 100 000 gallons (455 000 litres) was by far the largest winemaker in Clare and was in fact equal sixth in production (with Penfolds) in the whole of South Australia. All the more reason then for Knappstein now to return from Perth and examine his Stanley investment, for his co-venturers, Wein-Smith and Badger, were distinctly jittery and anxious to sell, especially as the volatile Christison had just offended a major customer, and 'the best winemaker in South Australia', Alfred Basedow, was becoming more and more interested in greyhounds to the detriment of his winemaking duties. At this point Knappstein decided to test his own sales skill by taking 20 000 gallons (91 000 litres) of wine with him on a journey to London, a trip which apparently convinced him that despite the mutual dislike of Christison and Burgoyne, the English market was full of potential. On his return therefore he bought out Wein-Smith and Badger and also the minority interest of Basedow, who then left.

Thus by 1904 Knappstein held three-quarters of Stanley and seven years later would own the entirety.

By 1892 the vineyards of Springvale (not yet Quelltaler) under the astute management of Buring and Sobels had increased to 120 acres (forty-nine hectares), including fifty acres (twenty hectares) at Leasingham and forty acres (sixteen hectares) at Watervale both fully bearing, and another thirty acres (twelve hectares) in young vines still to come into bearing. Here too the export business was thriving, 18 000 gallons (81 900 litres) being shipped to London in 1891, and though 70 000 gallons (318 500 litres) were still held at Springvale, Carl Sobels was decidedly optimistic. As he told the *Observer*, 'any person holding land in a winegrowing district should pay his attention to vine cultivation, as there is a good market for the product'. In common with most other South Australian winemakers of his time, he foresaw an unlimited wine market.

It seemed he was right. By the mid-1890s, both the Springvale cellars and the Adelaide headquarters in Currie Street had been expanded, Springvale to a capacity of half a million gallons (2.28 million litres) with, in addition, 'steam crushers and other new appliances so as to be in a position to treat the much larger quantities of grapes' (*Observer*). Relations with London were excellent also. As the *Observer* went on,

> the proprietors of Springvale find no difficulty in disposing of all the wine they make. Messrs Burgoyne & Co of London, being so pleased with the sample that they have standing orders for any quantity of it to be shipped to them.

The second generation of Burings looked promising also. In 1896 young Leo Buring had been awarded the gold medal on his graduation from Roseworthy and had proceeded overseas to further his studies at Geisenheim and Montpellier. Now also the 'Quelltaler' brand began to make its appearance. Perhaps 'Springvale', its English translation, had ceased to have charisma enough for the late nineteenth century market, but nonetheless the new name became immediately effective and on an intercolonial (soon to be national) scale. By 1905 the *Australian Vigneron and Fruit Growers' Journal* could announce that

'Quelltaler Hock . . . which is the product of Messrs Buring and Sobels well-known Springvale vineyards, South Australia, is now well established on the Victorian market, and sales are increasing monthly'. Meanwhile technical innovations had continued. As the reporter of the *Observer* told his readers in 1903,

> one of the features of the establishment is the must pump, which was imported from France. Mr Sobels was the first to introduce this splendid machine. It pumps the crushed grapes, juice and skins to any part of the cellar, does away with wooden shoots [chutes], and is a great aid to cleanliness.

Though the Springvale vineyard had not increased in size, its winery production certainly had. The *Observer* goes on,

> There are 120 acres in bearing altogether [the same area as in 1892] but the firm purchases the yield from about 200 acres in the district. Messrs Buring and Sobels will make between 50,000 and 60,000 gallons [of wine this year] . . . After this vintage Messrs Buring and Sobels will have about 200,000 gallons of wine in stock.

What types of wines were being made? Obviously 'export burgundy' loomed large in the Quelltaler scheme of things but, exports aside, in white table wines there were of course hock and a chablis style, while in red, predominant in production for the local market as well as for export, there was a claret popularised under the San Carlo brand. In fortifieds, there were also port, sherry and frontignac. These were also wines of quality, which can be gauged by the successes in the 1904 Adelaide Show, in which a total of fourteen first, second and third prizes were won.

There were other major wineries established in the Clare region at this time. In 1892 as a result of the Clare wine boom, that same John Christison in partnership with one David Lyall established a vineyard on what had previously been a dairy farm and called it St Andrews. As a result of his increasing commitment to the Stanley Wine Co., in 1895 Christison sold his interest to Lyall, who made his first vintage of 3500 gallons (15 925 litres) in 1896, having built a substantial winery with a storage capacity, according to the *Australian Vigneron and Fruit Growers' Journal*, 'of over 60,000 gallons

(273 000 litres)' and cellars three storeys high. And the wine? . . . wines sampled by us proved, without doubt, that Mr Lyall is determined that the St Andrews wine will make a name for South Australia.' By 1903 St Andrews was the third-largest winery in Clare with a production of 25 000 gallons (113 750 litres), sold chiefly to London but with a substantial local trade. Others in the region to flash like meteors at this time and then to fade after a few decades were Wooroora and Koonowla.

Thus Clare had created its vineyard. Though small in contemporary comparison with the Barossa, it was by 1900 comfortably linked with 'export burgundy' and the London trade, but with the solitary exception of Quelltaler, the success of Clare would be mirrored by the success of the Stanley Wine Co. until well into the second half of the twentieth century.

Nor was the grape boom that had created Coonawarra and greatly enlarged the Barossa Valley, Southern Vales and Clare absent from areas closer to Adelaide.

At Magill Penfold's grew steadily under the guiding hands of Mary Penfold, her son-in-law Thomas Hyland and from 1881 Joseph Gillard. By 1892 it was time for the third generation of the Penfold family to join the business. Frank Penfold Hyland (who with his brother Herbert Leslie had adopted the Penfold name by deed poll) immediately proceeded to France where he studied winemaking for three years. Mary Penfold died in 1895, but by that time Penfold was a very important name in South Australian viticulture. In 1903 it was the largest maker in the Adelaide region, producing 100 000 gallons (454 600 litres), twice as much as its near neighbour Auldana and, with Stanley Wine Company, the sixth-biggest winery in the state.

To the north-east of the city of Adelaide there had been substantial vineyard development in the hilly terrain of Tea Tree Gully and Hope Valley. Dr William Angove arrived in Adelaide in 1886 and quickly took up practice in Tea Tree Gully. Three years later he leased a thirteen hectare block adjoining his home, partly for access to the Tea Tree Gully Creek, which would improve the water supply to his house and garden, but also to plant ten acres (four hectares) of vines. In 1891 he acquired two eighty-acre (thirty-two hectare) blocks in nearby Hope Valley, planted vines and called the property the Tregrehan vineyard after a family home in his native Cornwall.

Realising the need for a cellar, he arranged in 1894 to make his wine at Brightlands cellars, which were owned by an old family friend, Canon Farr. This informal arrangement continued until 1898, when Angove took a formal lease of Brightlands, and ended altogether in 1905 when Angove built the St Agnes cellars on his home vineyard block, which had been bought in 1896.

His first vintage of commercial size, in 1894, was made from shiraz and tinta amarella for his reds and riesling and gouais for whites.

As a new and untrained winemaker Angove's wines of the 1890s were of variable quality. Though he gained some success from year to year at the Adelaide Wine Shows, winning a special prize in 1896 in Class 3 for Best Red or White Wine and several Very Highly Commended and Highly Commended awards, he also earned the displeasure of Professor Perkins who, in February 1897, described one of his wines as 'absolutely worthless and spoilt beyond redemption'. Nonetheless Dr Angove pressed on, pragmatically acquiring winemaking knowledge from vintage to vintage. By 1903 his Tea Tree Gully vineyards were nearly one hundred acres in extent and his Brightlands winery was producing 10 000 gallons (45 500 litres) of wine.

In 1892 Douglas A. Tolley, one of the founders of Tolley Scott & Tolley, set up a separate vineyard venture, planting his vineyard close to the Tregrehan vineyards of Dr Angove. The purchase and planting of this thirty-two hectare estate was followed by the acquisition of a further 16.5 hectare block the next year. Initial red plantings were cabernet sauvignon, shiraz, mataro and malbec, accepted wisdom for the times, while only one white variety, madeira (was it verdelho or another of the Madeira varieties or perhaps even semillon?) was tried. In 1894 Douglas Tolley employed his first winemaker, John Ramsay, who was to hold the post for thirty-seven years. From his very first vintages Tolley also bought grapes from local growers in Highercombe, Golden Grove and Tea Tree Gully and by 1903 was producing 14 000 gallons (63 700 litres) of wine, chiefly of red table wine labelled claret and burgundy, though some white was also made and sold under the 'chablis' label. The Tolley name would grow steadily in the twentieth century.

Except for the vigour of Hans Irvine at Great Western and the export requirements of P. B. Burgoyne, who erected his Mount Ophir winery near Rutherglen in 1893, the final years of the nineteenth century brought an imperceptible decline in Victorian viticulture. The reasons were obvious enough: phylloxera was rampant; government policies against it were largely ineffective; and on top of all this markets were depressed due to the severe financial depression of the 1890s. In addition its winemakers seemed to be undergoing what today might be termed a mid-life crisis. As the vines grew older, so too did winemaking attitudes harden. The clear distinction between the delicacy of the southern wines and the strength of those of the north-east was never more noticeable. Unlike de Castella, his Swiss compatriot, Francois de Coueslant of Tabilk was not confident of changing the *goût anglais*.

> I have thought, myself, long ago, that our wines might be improved in delicacy by gathering earlier, but will that be a recommendation for an English palate? English people, accustomed to Port and Sherry, like strong wine. Although, probably, with time they will come to know better, but for the present they do not care for light stuff.

De Coueslant departed Tabilk in 1887. His employer, John Pinney Bear, died in 1889 and with Bear ended Tabilk's era of stability. There would now ensue a period of stagnation during which the wine fortunes of Tabilk, though exporting 50 hogsheads (11 800 litres) of wine a month in 1890, would suffer in common with the rest of cooler viticultural Victoria.

In north-east Victoria there was uncertainty also. Not only had phylloxera made its inevitable entry into Rutherglen in 1899 but there was a planting boom, as a result of which the destructive effects of the louse on grape production went almost unnoticed until 1906. By that time the era of George Francis Morris had also largely passed. Fairfield was in the management of his younger son, Robert, and Wilfred, a grandson. George Francis died on 8 January 1910, leaving Fairfield in the hands of his executors, who in accordance with their duty offered the property for sale in June 1911. It was, according to an advertisement, a 'magnificent property', having 'capacious cellars and building, winery, plant' and 'residence' offered 'at prices based only upon the market value of the land, plus a low valuation for buildings and plant'. Though 1220 acres (494 hectares) were for sale, the vineyard area had declined to

210 acres (eighty-four hectares), a far cry from a claimed 700 acres (283 hectares) in 1894. The wines, however, which included 'Hermitage, Shiraz, Mataro, Burgundy, Charignan [sic], Carbinet [sic], Brown Muscat and Malbec', would be familiar in style to all lovers of the area today. A contemporary journalist noted how shiraz made both dry and sweet reds, describing a port 'made from the Hermitage [shiraz] grape, gathered . . . fully ripe and contain(ing) an extra quantity of saccharine matter'. The dry shiraz was 'a rich red wine' and in addition there was pedro, 'a pure Sherry'.

The enthusiasm for the sale of the property, however, existed only in the minds of the trustees and it was not sold until 1917, presumably due to the slackening export markets caused by the First World War. Unlike South Australia, Fairfield and the Victorian wine industry as a whole did not revive at war's end. Though Fairfield would decline for another sixty years, the Morris name would not be lost to winemaking.

Charles Hughes Morris, the eldest son of George Francis, was born in 1859 and spent his early years managing his father's agricultural interests throughout north-east Victoria and south-western New South Wales. In 1887 he travelled to France to learn more of the winemaking craft. While there, Charles Morris, possessed of no French, met an elderly Louis Pasteur, the elucidator of the fermentation process, whose English was, unfortunately, similarly sparse. Fortunately for Morris, an interpreter was found immediately.

In 1897 Charles Morris purchased Mia Mia, a property with similar soil to Fairfield and about three kilometres to the east, planting ninety acres (26.5 hectares) of shiraz and brown muscat, a vineyard which in every sense presaged the next century of Rutherglen wine. Though seriously affected by phylloxera during the next decade, he pressed on with his winemaking, in 1910 buying another property on very sandy soil across the Murray River at Balldale in New South Wales. The vines planted there on their own rootstocks, brown muscat, shiraz, grenache, doradillo, pedro and others, survived the onslaughts of phylloxera and the poor markets of the times. Though the great days of Fairfield would never return, the name Morris would grow in winemaking fame as the exemplar of the brown muscats and rich shiraz reds of the Rutherglen region.

Though New South Wales produced nearly four million litres of wine in the 1896 vintage, it was not a time of buoyant optimism.

The bank crash of 1893 threw the colony into economic disarray. Wineries everywhere were in difficulty. In the Hunter Valley, after the early death of John Wyndham, son of George, in 1887, an era of prosperity that had made Dalwood (with Lindeman's) the leading producer of the colony had rapidly come to an end, the Commercial Banking Company of Sydney taking possession as mortgagee in the 1890s and selling to J. F. M. Wilkinson of Coolalta in 1901. Besides the everyday financial travail, oidium (powdery mildew) added to the air of gloom. In 1896 H. M. McKenzie, the correspondent of the *Maitland Mercury*, described the melancholic scene.

> The departed glory of Dalwood is a thing to be deplored. The place of recent times has undergone a vast change, and though the vineyard continues to flourish as of old, and the capacious cellars are stored with as much as 90,000 gallons [409 500 litres] of wine, there is an air of depression hanging over the place that is at once infectious . . . The last three years have shown a falling off in quality owing to the unfavourable seasons, beginning with 1892, which was satisfactory, followed by 1893, a shade worse, and finally 1894, which was distinctly bad. The vines, too, suffered a good deal from oidium.
>
> To see these cellars with only three men employed at the present time—no less than 20, I am informed, being the number in former times—is a sufficient proof how stagnant trade is.

Yet the ailing economy of this period, which brought disaster to some, introduced others to a distinctly changed way of life. One such was John Younie Tulloch, till 1893, or perhaps even 1895 a storekeeper in Branxton, who at that time took possession of 'Glen Elgin' in satisfaction of an overdue debt. By the turn of the century the grocer turned vigneron had restored an ailing vineyard and established a reputation for quality that would last still another century.

So too there came to Pokolbin in 1893 a Scottish coalminer named William Elliott, who bought a dairy farm called Oakvale, converting it to vines in the next few years. In the years after Federation and a great deal of hard work, the name 'Elliott' would stand honourably with 'Tyrrell' and 'Drayton' amongst the smaller Hunter makers.

The same decade saw the founding of the New South Wales Wine Co. in 1896. Its wine was to be sourced from vineyards to the south of Pokolbin in the Mount View foothills. Planted in 1880 by Charles King (no relation to James King of Irrawang), this vineyard would create two famous twentieth-century Australian reputations—Maurice O'Shea and Mount Pleasant.

Another famous Hunter vigneron of this time was Karl Brecht, of Rosemount, at first a shepherd, made his reputation by excellent winemaking during the 1870s and 1880s, a fame consummated by a gold medal at the 1882 Bordeaux Exhibition for what else but an 1880 Hermitage (Shiraz), to this day the classic red grape variety of the Hunter Valley. Though Brecht died in 1888, his family obviously continued to make wine of quality during the 1890s. To quote H. M. MacKenzie once more, 'I am informed Mr Brecht near Muswellbrook is turning out a class of Champagne so popular, he can hardly keep pace with the demand'. The Brecht reputation lingered on until 1916, when the vines were uprooted and the property returned to grazing. In that area, another fifty years would elapse before the flame of wine would be rekindled.

As the Hunter Valley approached the twentieth century, most of the old winemaking families, now well into their second generation, were still there—Kelman, Carmichael, Lindeman and Wyndham. Time had worked in a leavening of new faces from the old country such as Tyrrell, Drayton and more recently, Elliott and Tulloch, and also a smattering of new nationalities, Germans like Ekert, Brecht, Bouffier and the occasional Frenchman, like Philobert Terrier, all capable of excellent wine, as the results of local and international exhibitions frequently showed.

In Mudgee, trading difficulties similar to those of the Hunter Valley were being experienced. Unsold production and the bank crash had made winegrowing a most penurious occupation. By 1895 Fredericksburg, the Buchholz winery, was in dire financial straits and was sold in 1899. The golden days of Mudgee were past.

The McWilliam family, however, was just beginning to broaden its horizons. In 1895 a new wineshop was opened in Junee and, a little later, another in Goulburn. Yet Junee, with the dynamic JJ McWilliam now firmly in control of the family business, was to be the centre of activities for the next eighteen years. By 1902 two vineyards and the Markview winery had been established close to the town, but another epidemic was to infect the vignerons and orchardists of New South Wales and with them the McWilliam family.

This time it was not the calamity of phylloxera or the travail of oidium or even the lure of gold: it was the siren song of water.

In Western Australia in the 1850s and 1860s, Perth's suburban vineyards were also expanding. Dr John Ferguson, the colonial surgeon of the whole territory, had purchased a part of the Houghton Estate, the home block and its small vineyard, making thirty gallons (137 litres) of wine in 1859. This obviously acted as a spur to further vineyard development in the Swan Valley, though vineyards also sprang up at Baker's Hill to the east of the city and at Armadale to the south. Legend has it that it was in the old Houghton cellar in 1869 that Moondyne Joe, Western Australia's only bushranger, was captured very much the worse for wear after copious draughts of the cellar's best fortified wine.

In country areas, the vine followed in the footsteps of the first settlers. There were vineyards near Bunbury on the south coast and at Katanning, not very far to the north of present-day Mount Barker. In the 1890s when gold was discovered at Coolgardie and Kalgoorlie, so the demand increased for wine. Britain too with its liking for robust reds was a market for the Swan River vineyards. By 1905 the most reluctant member of the new Federation was producing close to a million litres of wine.

The sun-scorched earth of Western Queensland is as unlikely a place as any for the vine to exist, let alone flourish, but it was at Roma in 1863 that Samuel Bassett planted a few hundred vines. It was typical of the try-anything attitude of a new settler in a new land. Remarkably in a climate where the rainfall (560 millimetres) is hardly sufficient, those vines—solverino; syrian; red, white and black muscat; black cluster; red heritage; riesling and mataro—succeeded admirably. By 1874 there were sixty-two acres (twenty-five hectares) of vineyard, all producing fortified wine. By 1900 the Romavilla vineyard, 450 acres (182 hectares) in extent, was one of the largest in Australia.

Far to the south-east of Roma is the most temperate and, for the vine, the most favourable region of Queensland. High in the Great Divide, the Granite Belt near Stanthorpe in Southern Queensland is a natural orchard area. Not surprisingly in 1878 Father David, a local parish priest of Italian origin, planted vines near his presbytery and made wine, probably for altar use. However, for many years table grapes assumed a far greater importance than wine and it was not until the 1920s when Italian fruit-growers made wine from surplus table grapes for sale to their canecutting compatriots in the north that a rudimentary wine industry was established near Stanthorpe.

In Tasmania the vine seemed to die with Captain Swanston in 1850, but there was a brief flicker of interest a generation later when an engaging Italian silk merchant, Signor Diego Bernacchi, and several fellow countrymen attempted to recolonise Maria Island. The island, formerly a repository for hardened convicts and Maori recalcitrants, was planted with some acres of mulberry trees and vines, the latter being allegedly hung with artificial grapes, presumably to attract investors to the project, which may indeed have succeeded, were it not for the depression and the bank crashes of the early 1890s, which drove Bernacchi and his colonists to abandon the venture and return to Melbourne.

There were no serious attempts to make wine from Tasmanian grapes for a further seventy years.

Thus, for Australia's now well-established wine industry, the beginning of the new century saw a vineyard area of 26 134 hectares, a vintage in 1901 of 23.28 million litres and export shipments chiefly to London of 3.78 million litres. The preferred wine style was red, sturdily made and dry or fortified, whether for local or export consumption. Lighter wine styles were made and drunk at table by society's upper levels, but fashion and Anglo-Celtic heritage generally preferred sweetness and alcoholic strength. Another two generations and two world wars would be needed to educate Australians in the civilised use of wine.

Though the export future of Australian wine appeared extremely promising at the end of the nineteenth century, there seemed to have been little constructive thought given to its nomenclature. In the very earliest days of winemaking, the 1830s and 1840s, winemakers were probably pleased if their product was a sound saleable beverage. If their skill was such that the wine had a style recognisable to the palates of the few colonial winebuyers, then they were doubly content. But by 1850, growers' associations allowed comparisons to be made between local wines and those of other regions, both Australian and international. Though wine standards were rising, no attention was given to the problem of the identity of Australian wine. What did emerge was an echoing of European names, generics such as hock, white burgundy, claret, burgundy and later, when such styles became increasingly popular, port and sherry, side by side with varietal and estate names. Thus in New South Wales, William Macarthur's Camden Park label would proclaim a wine of varietal origin such as 'Reisling *[sic]* 1867' and, proudly 'Australian Wine'.

The London export lists of Australian wines rarely showed estate names. On such lists commoner and lower-priced offerings were generic Australian wines such as claret and burgundy (perhaps these were the multi-blended boarding-house burgundies of the time, higher-priced were varietally named wines which appeared on the Emu list in 1887 such as 'Carbinet *[sic]* Sauvignon' top-priced at thirty-two shillings a dozen. In those days (nearly a century before Britain joined the Common Market, London did not seem to care what they were called either, though occasionally London interests representing French Shippers took umbrage. One such confrontation was the Keystone Burgundy case in 1908, when French interests disputed the use of the term 'burgundy' for Australian wine. They lost, the court ruling that as long as there was no misleading description of the wine, the use of the term 'burgundy', preceded by the name of its country of origin, Australia, was quite permissible. In other words, the word 'burgundy' was a generic term.

This ruling sat ill with French interests at the time, as it has done during the rest of the twentieth century, and one contemporary Australian wine man even sought to defuse the issue by adding the suffix '-alia' to truncated versions of the more common generics of the time. Thus devised were such names as 'Claralia', 'Burgalia', etc.

Such a weird solution of course pleased no-one and the old system of generic, varietal and occasional estate labelling continued. The Keystone case discouraged further French litigation and when, after the Second World War, Australian wine exports declined as British palates demanded lighter table wines from France, the issue seemed to die.[1]

[1] It was not forgotten, however, and years later in 1992, as a price of easier access to the European Economic Community, of which Britain was a part, Australia agreed to phase out the use of such generic terms over several years as Britain had once more become an important export market.

TEN

Federation and the road to reality

The Belle Epoque, that last brilliant ember of the nineteenth century, was for Australia an era of both prophecy and profligacy. The population had reached 3.2 million; 10 million cattle and 100 million sheep grazed the countryside; 2 million hectares were sown to wheat; and gold production exceeded one million ounces a year. Wine yields nearing 12 million litres annually provided a flourishing though often difficult export market. Yet, unbeknown to most, a peak had been attained. At the time few saw that Australia's spectacular pastoral success rested on foundations of sand. Large areas of marginal pasture were turned into desert by over-grazing; the greed for wheat took everything from the soil, giving little in return, and periodic drought completed the desolation. Even in Australia's new Gardens of Eden—

the irrigation areas—the first signs of salination were appearing. But by 1893, Australia's pastoral profligates had never been wealthier. The bank crash of that year ruined the speculator both in town and country, and only in Western Australia did a gold boom salve the wounds of the economy.

The prophets, however, were not discouraged. Sir Henry Parkes in 1890 was campaigning openly for Federation. In 1891 there was a massive convention in Sydney to discuss the political unification of Australia. But colonial rivalries defeated Parkes, who never saw his dream come to reality. Popular enthusiasm for Federation was irresistible in the Eastern States, and in 1897 a second, this time successful, convention in Adelaide reached agreement on most points. In 1899 referenda held in the colonies gained approval from the five eastern colonies with only Western Australia abstaining. In July 1900, without a shot fired in anger, Queen Victoria gave her assent to the *Commonwealth of Australia Constitution Act*.

For the colonial wine industries, its most important provision was the abolition of tariffs between the states—as they were to be called from that time. Henceforth that first law of Darwinian economics would apply—only the financially fittest and the most commercially skilled would survive. By 1 January 1901, the date of Federation, it was obvious which state was the most adept at wine marketing. South Australia had viewed Federation with pleasurable anticipation for several years before the actual event. In 1899 a commentator in the *Adelaide Chronicle* expressed the prevalent opinion of South Australian winemakers at the time.

> I have not yet met a vigneron who does not . . . enthusiastically whoop for Federation. One and all they firmly believe that our wines are destined to become favourites, and have a large sale in the other provinces, especially New South Wales and West Australia, when the duties are taken off.

Indeed, barred for many years by the now abolished duties from major participation in the markets of Sydney and Melbourne, the South Australians leapt at their chance. Thomas Hardy & Sons established a Sydney office within the year; Penfold's opened its Sydney office in 1904 and Seppelt's branched into Fremantle and Brisbane.

Swept forward by a national change in taste in favour of fortified wines and local brandy, by their export expertise and not least by subsidies from their own government, the South Australians marched triumphantly into the eastern states. The New South Wales growers simply could not compete in price and style. The Victorians had never really recovered from phylloxera, though for a few years until it succumbed Rutherglen struggled on, serving its export markets with its full-bodied dry reds and its local ones with the obvious quality of its fortifieds. The political circumstances of the age favoured the creation of national wine companies and the South Australians were astute enough to realise it. At maximum revs, the South Australian industry accelerated, vintage 1903 producing in excess of 11 million litres and though the growers' enthusiasm as well as their crops were tempered a little by mildew in ensuing seasons, by 1906 yields were again growing. Such was the South Australian impetus that, by the outbreak of the First World War, interstate 'exports' utilised about 2 million litres of South Australian wine, compared to 100 000 litres in 1900.

Not only were interstate branches opened, interstate vineyards were bought also. Penfold's were particularly active, acquiring Dalwood in 1904 and Minchinbury eight years later, as well as expanding substantially in South Australia. Thus cellars at McLaren Vale were acquired in 1910 and a large winery erected in Nuriootpa in 1912 to be enlarged further by the addition of a distillery in the following year. In 1913 also, within months of the foundation of the Murrumbidgee Irrigation Area, Penfold's erected a substantial winery at Griffith.

Seppelt's, by far the largest wine producer of that time, also saw the need to expand. Its movements into Western Australia and Queensland have been mentioned, but soon after there followed branches at Broken Hill and in 1914 Melbourne. But its Victorian activities were not complete, for in that year as well it acquired the Clydeside vineyard and winery at Rutherglen, which was then recovering from the travail of phylloxera, due to the introduction of resistant rootstocks by Francois de Castella, a member of the famous Yarra Valley family of vignerons. In 1916 it took a further giant step by buying Chateau Tanunda, one of its chief Barossa rivals in production, from the liquidator of the Adelaide Wine Company. By this purchase the Seppelt company, for it had been incorporated in 1902, had the potential virtually to double its output and to secure the lion's share of the Australian brandy market.

But the flourishing house of Seppelt was not yet finished with its wartime acquisitions. Since 1888 Hans Irvine, a Ballarat businessman, had laboured long and hard to bring a dream to reality. That dream was to produce a fine sparkling wine as close to champagne as he could make it. He had bought the Great Western vineyard and winery of the late Joseph Best for the sum of £12 000 ($24 000), acquiring about 70 000 gallons (318 500 litres) of wine, fifty-five acres (twenty-two hectares) of vineyard and 450 acres (182 hectares) of grazing land. He soon engaged his 'champagne' maker, Charles Pierlot, a native of Reims and a former employee of the house of Pommery. Irvine was obviously a man of dedication and Pierlot a maker of quality, for the reputation of Great Western was quickly established. One of the more notable early visitors to the cellars was Samuel Langhorne Clements, better known as Mark Twain, who was also an admirer. In one of his travel sketches in the 1890s, he wrote,

> The Stawell region is not productive of gold only; it has great vineyards and produces exceptionally fine wines. One of these, the 'Great Western' owned by Mr Hans Irvine, is regarded as a model. Its produce has a reputation abroad. It yields a choice Champagne and a fine Claret, and its Hock took a prize in France two or three years ago. The Champagne is kept in a maze of passages underground, cut in the rock to secure it at an even temperature during the three year term required. In these vaults I saw 120,000 bottles of Champagne.

Before Irvine's venture, Australian 'champagne' style was generally undistinguished. As a French expert, Monsieur Simon, remarked in 1888, it was 'far distinct in body, bouquet and delicacy from the Champagne produced in France'. Irvine and Pierlot changed all that, so much so that by Federation, the governor-general, Lord Hopetoun, confidently predicted that Irvine's wine would 'satisfy the most exacting connoisseurs'. Indeed during the thirty years of Irvine's ownership, Great Western wines gained over one hundred gold and silver medals and trophies.

By 1910 the subterranean 'drives' originally excavated in Joseph

Hans Irvine popularised Australian sparkling wine.

Best's time extended 1.6 kilometres beneath Great Western; Irvine's vineyards spread over eighty hectares around the village and his 'champagne', already famous throughout Australia, was beginning to gain an international reputation.

The man himself had been a member of the Victorian legislature, the newly formed federal parliament and one of the leaders of the wine industry, but unfortunately his name would not survive him, as he had no children. So when the time came for him to retire, as it did in 1918, he sold his Great Western enterprise to B. Seppelt & Sons, with whose principal and great personal friend, Benno, he had apparently reached an understanding some years before.

In the first years of the new century the house of Hardy suffered several setbacks. In 1905 the Bankside cellars, its birthplace fifty years before, with all its casks and wines, were destroyed by fire, never to be rebuilt. What equipment could be saved was transferred to its substantial Mile End cellars a few kilometres away. Jack Stoward in his memoirs vividly described the hopeless battle against the flames.

> I had just reached home about half a mile away, when I heard the [factory] whistle. I observed the smoke and returned as quickly as possible. The fire had a big hold. I started the steam pump in the well to fill the tanks in the roof of the cellar, hoping to overflow them and flood the floors below. It was soon realised that this was hopeless. There was nothing available to fight the fire—no water—nothing we could do. A hot north wind was blowing and the wooden floors and other woodwork were old and dry. The heat was intense and caused the staves of the vats to open and from these thin streams of wine spurted. Spirit vapours from the heated wine caught fire and burnt with blue flames. All the afternoon, the fire raged, the top floors and burning casks crashed into the lower cellars, which were three to four feet [0.9 to 1.2 metres] deep with wine. Wine was also running down the roadways in streams.
>
> As there were no means of communication, a messenger had to be sent to Adelaide Fire Brigade, which arrived about an hour after the fire had started.The Brigade could do very little, for there were no water mains. The nearest main was on Holbrook's Road, but the brigade hose was too short. Subsequently the Hindmarsh Volunteer Brigade arrived, but met with little success. By using its hose it was able to get one pipe line through, but it was not of much use—it was too far through the canvas hose and there was no pressure. The City Fire Brigade had brought down its fire engine, driven by steam, and put hoses from this into the cellar and pumped out the burnt wine on to the fire to try to check it. By 5 pm there was very little left . . .
>
> (R.A. Burdon, *A Family Tradition in Fine Winemaking*)

The loss of cellars, wine and equipment was estimated at £25 000 [$50 000]. The cause was unknown and the only explanation Stoward offered was that

> the weekly practice of burning a sulphur match in all the empty casks and vats to keep them sound was carried out as usual. An employee would burn the sulphur match on the cask and knock the burnt residue into a bucket which he carried with him for that purpose. He

may have been careless and disregarded the fact that the weather was very hot.

Stoward also stresses the difference between the winery foreman, a position he occupied at Mile End and later at McLaren Vale, and winemaker, or 'wine expert'. The foreman certainly made the wine from day to day during vintage and ensured that all equipment was in working order and that the wine, of whatever quality, was kept sound by supervising everyday winery operations such as racking, topping up and sulphuring casks. The 'expert' was in charge overall, assessing wine quality and recommending the purchase of new equipment and the use of new systems.

Just how important the 'expert' was and how skilled he had to be, let Jack Stoward relate.

> Dubois [the 'expert'] supervised the winemaking at Mile End, Tintara and McLaren Vale during the 1908 vintage and in the 1909 vintage . . . The Professor [Dubois] was dissatisfied with the winemaking machinery and persuaded the firm to import two crushing and pressing plants from France. These were bought through his brother, in Paris, who was an engineer there. In due course the machinery arrived. It consisted of a vertical elevator, crusher and drainer and an Algerian Continuous [press] and was used at Mile End. (R. A. Burdon, *A Family Tradition in Fine Winemaking*)

Identical equipment was bought for McLaren Vale. Stoward continues.

> As these two plants had to be ready for the 1910 vintage, no time was lost in moving and re-arranging engines, shafting and drives, attending to steam piping, water connection, concreting foundations and tanks and much other preparatory work. The installation of the two plants gave me a very busy time.
>
> The 1910 vintage, with the new machinery, was not a success. The presses were no good . . . The screws of this press had one right hand and one left, driven at the same speed and pressing the marc into one core. The idea was that the two screws revolving inwards with the assistance of the stalks would prevent the core from slipping. But such was not the case. Some types of grapes went through fairly well. Shiraz

> was the best, of these we could press about 6 or 7 tons an hour. The more fleshy type (Doradilla and Muscatel) could only be pressed at the rate of 2 or 3 tons an hour. If one tried to push more through, the skins and juice would be forced back through the rollers.
>
> Thus the new method was a failure. Had we not had the side crusher and the single screw Mabile press at McLaren Vale we would never have put through the vintage. We had of course the same trouble at Mile End and had to work all hours to get the grapes through. The quality of the grapes was less than at McLaren Vale. Unfortunately, delays caused growers to take their grapes elsewhere. After the vintage, Dubois left. (R.A. Burdon, *A Family Tradition in Fine Winemaking*)

The departure of Dubois was predictable. He would probably have been dismissed anyway, but other losses of what today would be termed top management were less easy to bear. In 1901 James Hardy, the eldest son and first manager of the newly opened Sydney office, had died suddenly. Ten years later, Thomas Nathaniel, the second son in overall charge of the company at that time, died at the age of forty-nine. A few months later, on 10 January 1912, Thomas Hardy, the founder of the firm, also died, two days short of his eighty-second birthday. In his sixty-two years in South Australia he had actively created a nationally respected winemaking company from a small orchard. The *Adelaide Advertiser* in its obituary went further, praising him as 'the pioneer of the wine industry in South Australia'. The first-generation Hardy had perished. Now it was the turn of the second and third.

In far-off Coonawarra it was the grimmest of times for producers of table wine.Young Bill Redman knew it only too well. At fourteen years of age he had arrived in Coonawarra, just before vintage in 1901, the year of John Riddoch's death. Even before that vintage the Riddoch cellars held over 800 000 litres of unsold wine. In the face of a negligible market for table wine, Riddoch's executors took the only alternative, distillation.

During his five-year sojourn at the Riddoch cellars, Redman had risen to the position of head cellarman, learning the basics of winemaking from winemaker-manager Ewen McBain. Soon he was to learn the 'economics' of wine selling: two cents a litre wholesale for Coonawarra red in 1905 and two dollars' wages for a sixty-six hour week when he left in 1906. No wonder then that he took a brief 'holiday' farm-labouring in Pinnaroo to the north. Upon his return he joined his family working at their sixteen hectare dairy for two years.

In 1908 the executors of the Riddoch Estate, by then desperate to dispose of assets, persuaded him to buy a sixteen hectare block in full bearing for $1800, $300 down and the balance over ten years at four per cent per annum interest, with the first vintage to be picked at the vendor's expense. So with his father John and his brother Robert, the firm of John Redman & Sons began.

The 1908 vintage went to the Riddoch cellars for distillation and with an $800 income from their first vintage, the Redmans were off to a fair start. As it was a return, however, of little more than one cent a litre of juice sold, Bill Redman soon realised that grape growers rarely become rich and that, as his own winemaker, he could hope for much better. Hope, indeed, was the operative word, there was little other encouragement for new winemakers. But in 1909 his hope was rewarded in the form of a commercial contact with Douglas Tolley, the owner of the Hope Valley winery and vineyard to the north-east of Adelaide. At Tolley's behest, Redman decided to make 'burgundy' for the British market at the improved price of just over two cents a litre, double the price he could obtain for the juice, if he could sell it at all. Making the wine, however, was another thing entirely. Though Tolley supplied the hogsheads, the equipment was Redman's own problem. Using a grape crusher sold to him by a teetotal family on the condition that the wine produced from it not be sold in the district (a most acceptable condition as there were few sales to be had), the Tolley barrels, heads removed, as fermenters and a tiny cheese press, Bill Redman made the first of his forty-five vintages.

Tolley continued to take the wine and the connection worked well until the early 1920s when he refused to take further supplies on the ground that the wine was too good. His English buyers would take nothing else and as he had much more to sell, he felt obliged to terminate the arrangement. Though this was a setback, Redman had satisfied himself that his Coonawarra reds were of such quality that, given time, they would make a great impact in the wine world beyond Coonawarra.

For Australian winemakers, the First World War brought with it both internal and external problems.

At first wine exports proceeded almost normally, 2.859 million litres being sent overseas for the year ended 30 June 1915. The following year actually saw an increase to 3.27 million and it was not until Germany began to make wider use of its submarine fleet later in 1916 that exports began to decline, falling to 2.71 million in 1917 and 1.65 million by mid-year 1918. This figure was virtually doubled to 3.164 million in the first few months of peace after the armistice in November 1918 and thereafter wine shipments went on at a level comparable to the prewar years. The good times, indeed times of unparalleled prosperity, were just around the corner.

Yet at home society was in turmoil. The war provoked a violent anti-German reaction, the immediate effects of which were name changes throughout the Barossa Valley. By Act of Parliament, Kaiser Stuhl became Mount Kitchener, Siegersdorf Dorrien and Gnadenfrei Marananga.

It also spurred on a 'patriotic' prohibitionist movement. As the temperance-minded 'Patriot' thundered in 1917, 'it is abundantly clear that our national drinking habits have kept Britain back from exerting her full strength in the great conflict'. It suggested that the liquor trade was selfish, unpatriotic and dangerously powerful and concluded, most nobly no doubt for its readers, 'if South Australia does its duty, South Australia will be free from that element that may very largely enslave England'.

The temperance movement, however, had reckoned without the economic importance of the wine industry and the native common sense of most Australians. Recognising the threat to the very existence of the industry, the Vinegrowers' Association of South Australia began an immediate drive for funds to meet the challenge, raising a levy of one shilling (ten cents) per acre (0.4 hectares) of vines and sixpence (five cents) per ton of grapes bought for winemaking or distilling. The press too was generally supportive of the industry and the South Australian government, aware of the threat that a teetotal state might pose to its revenues, if not to its economy as a whole, was resistant to prohibition. It finally decided that six o'clock closing of hotels, introduced as a result of a referendum in 1916, was a sufficient curb upon alcoholism. The spectre of prohibition created one lasting benefit for the wine industry. It forced the creation of the Federal Viticultural Council in 1918. The wine industry had become national.

Despite the chauvinistic indignation rampant among the general public during the war, those families of German origin, now in their second and third generation, went quietly about the business of winemaking. The acquisitions made by Seppelt have already been detailed. Now it was the turn of the Gramp family, till 1911 a relatively small winemaking concern. In that year it began to buy grapes from other Barossa growers. In 1912 the family business became a limited liability company, G. Gramp & Sons, with Hugo Gramp, the son of Gustav, as managing director. The winery at Rowland Flat, already enlarged in 1911, was further expanded as production increased in 1913, 1915 and 1917. In 1916 Gramp's, following the liquidation of the Adelaide Wine Company and perhaps taking a leaf from the Seppelt book, bought the Moorooroo cellars and vineyards, founded originally by the Jacob brothers, from the company's liquidator. The war had dampened but few spirits in the Barossa.

Not far from Rowland Flat at Angaston, Yalumba now entered its third generation of family management. Sidney Smith had died in 1908 and the succession now passed to the flamboyant Tiger Smith. But if the name 'Smith' was becoming famous in South Australian wine, the name 'Hill' was on everybody's lips, for the whole state was devoted to cricket and Clem Hill was amongst the finest batsmen playing the game at that time. With the marriage of Tiger Smith and Ida Hill, sister of the illustrious Clem, the Hill Smith family, which still owns Yalumba to this day, came into being.

The destiny of Yalumba, however, still lay with wine and it was a much more reserved Tiger Smith who led Yalumba through the uncertainties of the First World War as exports began to dry up. Though sales slowed in 1915 Tiger's lean but sound management throughout the war saw a 1918 vintage not far off a million litres and wine sales at an average of thirteen cents a litre.

Even in the dark days of the war, 'expansion' was a word never foreign to the Hardy nature. Robert Borrough Hardy, in sole charge since the death of his father in 1912, was attracted by the Riverland. Within the space of two years, 1915-16, two wineries were built, one at Waikerie, the other some sixteen kilometres away at Murray View, and a vineyard established on nearby land bought by Hardy and a partner, Samuel Sage. In 1919 the Waikerie winery was sold to become the Waikerie Co-operative. In 1920 Murray View was disposed of to Penfold's and in the same year construction of the

Cyrilton winery began, so named after Hardy's eldest son Robert Cyril, mortally wounded in battle at Bullecourt in 1917. The Hardy whirl of winery building continued and in 1920 the company moved into the Barossa, completing its Dorrien cellars in time for the 1921 vintage.

The Riverland beckoned others also. In 1910 Thomas Carlyon Angove, a graduate of Roseworthy, with his brothers Edward and Leonard, built a distillery at Renmark to make fortifying spirit from an overproduction of grapes. Even then, recurrent gluts were to present problems for some and opportunities for others. In 1912 the Angoves established another winery at Lyrup on the River Murray and Angove's were in Riverland to stay. Indeed they pioneered winemaking and distillation in the South Australian river areas. Yet years later in 1923 Carl Angove was cautionary. Though doubtful that Riverland would ever make wine equal in quality to that of other non-irrigated districts, he nontheless advised the planting of proper wine grape varieties. 'They could undoubtedly make better wine from shiraz than from the currant.' He was prophetic also. 'They must cut out the doradillo or bye and bye there would be such a supply of these grapes that the wineries would not care whether they took them or not.' His pessimistic prophecy would be fulfilled sooner than he knew.

At this time in the Riverland there were other venturesome beginnings born of the growers' desperation to dispose of surplus grapes. The first of these was the Renmark Growers Distillery, later to become the Renmano Wines Co-operative Limited, which was the first cooperative winery set up in Australia. As a consequence of the dismemberment of the Adelaide Wine Company, in 1916 a group of 130 winegrowers formed a cooperative to buy the 'surplus to requirements' distillery built by Chateau Tanunda in 1914. Buying its members' crop of 1000 tons, it put the lot through the still, starting a brandy and fortifying spirit tradition that was to last virtually until the Second World War.

In the same year, 1916, another extempore operation began in the nearby town of Berri. Equipped to distil surplus raisins and sultanas, this distillery, though crushing only one hundred tons by 1918, was formed into a cooperative in 1922, when a sizeable grape surplus was anticipated. Like Renmano, the Berri Growers Co-operative Distillery for many years made only brandy and fortifying spirit, but the day would come when it, too, would turn to fortified wine.

At Clare in the second decade of the twentieth century there were changes also. By this time the Stanley Wine Company and Buring & Sobels between them produced three-quarters of the region's wine. In 1911 the quick-tempered John Christison died, his estate's shares in Stanley being bought by J. H. Knappstein. Thus for eight years, including the turmoil of the First World War, Knappstein was in sole charge of Stanley until his death in 1919.

For Buring & Sobels, its Quelltaler (the 'h' had been dropped around the time of World War I) brand was proving most popular, being well thought of in Adelaide for both red and white table wines while in Melbourne Quelltaler hock was beginning an era of popularity that was to last another sixty years. Here death also wrought its inevitable changes, Hermann Buring dying in 1919 and Carl Sobels four years later.

In the Hunter Valley the years after Federation enfeebled the vineyards. The South Australians had come to Sydney, seen their auspicious hour and seized the market. The shield of tariff protection suddenly snatched away had left the Valley growers defenceless; the lure of coal mining in nearby Cessnock, proclaimed a town in 1908, with its long but regular hours and more importantly regular income had lured away the youthful labour upon which the local vineyards depended.

Of local winemakers, only the giant Lindeman's offered any real challenge to South Australian competition. The partnership of the Lindeman brothers had ended in 1906, Herbert retiring while his brothers Charles Frederick and Arthur Henry became manager and winemaker respectively of the new Lindeman & Company, Arthur also becoming owner of the established Cawarra vineyard on the Paterson River. With vineyards of such quality producing excellent table wine in the Hunter Valley and others at Corowa becoming equally renowned for the rich 'burgundies' and fortified wines so much sought after by the export market, Lindeman & Co. was solidly established in the New South Wales market, setting up its headquarters in Sydney's Queen Victoria Building in 1900 and moving also to expand its empire. In 1912 it acquired the Ben Ean winery at Pokolbin from the McDonald family and within the space of two more years bought 'Coolalta', 'Catawaba' and 'Kirkton'.

In buying 'Kirkton' the company gained the Kelman vineyard on the original James Busby property, although the Kelman and Lindeman families had been united by marriage some years before.

This spate of acquisitions, however, boded ill for the company and for Charles Frederick Lindeman in particular. In 1916 he suffered a stroke, retiring in 1918, to be succeeded by his son, Eric. New management was to no avail for in 1923 the company, heavily in debt, reluctantly accepted the appointment of its bank's nominee as manager. For the Hunter Valley and its table wines, gold had definitely been transmuted to lead.

But not all was gloom in New South Wales. Before the events of 1914 plunged the world into war, one more major development took place that was to shape the future course of Australian viticulture. Farmers and pastoralists in western New South Wales had long been envious of the irrigated land schemes set up on the Murray River with the assistance of the South Australian and Victorian governments. Now it was the turn of New South Wales, richer if anything in water resources than either of its sister states. The Murrumbidgee River, fed by permanent springs in the mountain country north of Cooma and flowing north, then west and south-west to join the Murray near Balranald in western New South Wales, had often flooded the towns along its banks.

What better way to mitigate this nuisance, and even better to open up fertile lands whose only disadvantage was lack of reliable rainfall, than controlled irrigation. It would work. Small private schemes had been tried successfully near Yanco in the last years of the nineteenth century. Now it was time for the broad brush of the New South Wales government. Late in 1906 the *Burrinjuck and Murrumbidgee Canals Construction Act* was passed, enabling the construction of the Burrinjuck Dam near Yass where the waters of the river were to be controlled. From there they were to flow along the bed of the stream for almost 400 kilometres to the Berembed Weir where they were to be diverted along canals to irrigate the farms. The first waters flowed along those canals in July 1912.

By October 1913 the energetic JJ McWilliam, realising the potential of the area, had taken a lease of two ten hectare blocks at Hanwood and planted 33 500 cuttings. In 1916 the first twenty tonnes of grapes from Hanwood were taken back to Junee for crushing. By the following year JJ had erected the Hanwood winery in time to receive its first serious vintage, 170 tonnes. In 1920, as the crop was ever increasing, a second winery and distillery were built at Yenda. The 1920s were set to roar for the Murrumbidgee Irrigation Area.

Elsewhere in New South Wales the final years of the old century and the first of the new saw phylloxera reach the outskirts of Sydney. In 1898 it decimated Minchinbury, which was replanted on resistant rootstock. A few years later in 1902 a young winemaker named Leo Buring, aged twenty-six and son of Herman, owner of Quelltaler, came to Minchinbury as champagne maker, producing his first vintage the following year. Minchinbury 1903, released in 1908, was the forerunner of the brand that was to provide stiff opposition for Great Western in the years to come, especially as his sparkling wines had won a series of awards both at home and overseas in the years to 1912, a fact which undoubtedly influenced Penfold's when it purchased Minchinbury in that same year. Buring pressed on at Minchinbury until 1919 when he sought independence as one of Australia's first wine consultants.

ELEVEN

The First World War— its aftermath

Apart from the increasing popularity of fortified wine first noticed at home in the 1880s and then abroad in the years immediately before and after the First World war, five events of major importance occurred during and after that war which were to enhance and bedevil the Australian wine industry for a long time. Briefly summarised they were the Anglo-Portuguese Treaty of 1916, post-war soldier settlement, the *Federal Wine Export Bounty Act 1924*, the system of imperial preference instituted by the British budget of 1925, and of course the Great Depression that began in late 1929.

Initially all was not clear. Some eminent authorities such as Cuthbert Burgoyne, who had succeeded his father Peter, seemed to misread tastes, if not policies, entirely. In 1920 in a speech to the first Australian Viticultural Congress, he confidently asserted,

> the policy in Great Britain appears to be to control strong drink and to create an increased demand for light wines and beers, not to relinquish control of the sale of spirituous liquors. If the ideal of 'Empire' is to be economically self-contained, then Australia should be the Empire's vineyard.

In the midst of the horrors of the First World War, Britain and its oldest ally, Portugal, could perhaps be forgiven for allowing a loophole to occur in the treaty of friendship, alliance and trade that was signed in 1916. By this treaty, Portugal became solely entitled to the use of the words 'port' and 'madeira' as primary descriptive terms in the British market. The treaty, fortunately for the Australian wine industry as events were to turn out, overlooked the word 'type'. Fortified wines, it will be recalled, carried a far higher rate of customs duty than table wines and though such Portuguese fortifieds were taxed at the same rate as Australian, the advantage they gained because of lower shipping costs could not be matched.

So for eight years the Anglo-Australian trade in heavy red table wines continued in much the same way as it had since the 1880s. Enter now a British market sympathetic to Australian goods since the ultimate sacrifices made by many young Australians in the war; state governments anxious to resettle those returning soldiers on irrigated farms, many of which had vineyard blocks; and a federal government bent on increasing wine exports in a buoyant post-war market and determined, as regards shipping costs, to put Australian wine on an equal footing with European; and the stage was set in 1924 for an export surge, not of table wine as Cuthbert Burgoyne had prophesied, but of Australian port-types and other fortifieds. And when as an ultimate gilding of the lily, a sympathetic British government in the following year put trading teeth into the concept of 'empire' by instituting a system of imperial preference which gave empire wines a fifty per cent margin in customs duty, there was an export boom unparalleled to that date in Australian wine history.

Although it provoked great consternation amongst sectors of the traditional British port-shipping fraternity, the people's 'port' proved extremely popular, but this very popularity brought with it unfortunate consequences. So attractive did Australian 'port' futures appear to business at large that many people without the remotest knowledge of the trade began to import Australian wine to London. Even as the market became saturated, imports grew, being placed in ever-increasing bond stores, where unwanted wines lay neglected in barrels in some cases for years, much to their detriment despite fortification. Yet the speculators' despair was a boon to Australia and South Australia particularly, which in the estimate of the South Australian delegate to the Federal Viticultural Council in 1925 had been relieved of 500 000 gallons (2.28 million litres) of wine otherwise surplus to market requirements. But the portents of disaster were plain to see. The combination of the Australian export bounty and imperial preference would hasten the planting of further vineyards whose produce, vastly in excess of local demand, could only be channelled into export. Just how much more could the London market (by far Australia's largest at that time) absorb?

The optimists (and speculators) wanted increased production, those in Australia, desirous of planting greater vineyard area; those in Britain of importing more fortified wine. The pessimists (and realists) yearned for stability, assured markets and a steady return. Under pressure from both sides, the federal government, whose export bounty was to expire in August 1927, instructed the Tariff Board to conduct an inquiry. Its controversial report, produced in March of that year, saw the Board chairman in a minority. Despite this the government accepted his advice that the bounty should continue for three more years but that it be reduced from four shillings a gallon (about nine cents a litre) to three shillings a gallon (6.6 cents a litre). Ill-advisedly the government gave six months notice of its intention to reduce the bounty.

The united dismay of winemakers and grapegrowers was short-lived, as winemakers worked frenziedly to ship as much wine to London as possible before the reduction came into effect and to take advantage of Winston Churchill's beneficent 1927 budget, whereby duties on non-imperial fortified wines were effectively increased by one-third, which meant that duties on Australian fortified wine at four shillings a gallon were only half those on Portuguese (eight shillings a gallon), a very real preference for Australian winemakers. In the words of Oscar Seppelt, 'the Australian sweet wine trade had been placed on a permanent footing'. Indeed from wine exports of 823 962 gallons (3.75 million litres) in 1924, shipments had shot up to 4 224 500 gallons (19 million litres) by 1927, a figure to be surpassed only twice more (1937 and 1938) before the Second World War and then not again until 1987.

But despite the aura of contentment that this newly found export stability should have created at home, the Barossa growers, now responsible for sixty per cent of Australia's wine, were gravely affronted when the large winemaking companies offered no higher prices for 1927 grapes than for the previous vintage. Hard-hit by increased costs of labour and production, they felt that at least a greater proportion of the bounty should be passed on to them. When the makers refused, they appealed to the federal minister, who sympathised by awarding them a substantial rise of about $2.50 a ton (by the way of comparison cabernet sauvignon grapes were bought for $16 a ton in 1925). On the whole the industry resented the intrusion of the minister in the price-fixing mechanism because of the precedent created, but as it was due to the government bounty that many grapes were sold at all, his intervention was felt to be inevitable.

For South Australia 1927 was not only a record year for export, it was a record vintage, over 72 million litres being produced. It was also a year in which, prophetically, the crop from the Riverland irrigation areas outstripped that of the Barossa for the first time and production from those soldier-settlement vineyards really began to make its mark.

Badly damaged by a late spring frost, which reduced crop levels by twenty-five per cent, the ensuing vintage (1928) was accompanied by two other nasty surprises, a further reduction in the bounty of two cents per litre (this time without notice) and a price increase for wine grapes of $1 a ton. Not unexpectedly, vignerons were outraged at these federal-government-inspired 'breaches of faith', the politicians unrepentant as imperial preference was now 'really effective at last'. But exports continued at a high level and there remained the problem of oversupply of the British market, which by May 1928 was overflowing with Australian sweet red wine; one estimate was that at this time there were 3.2 million gallons (14.5 million litres) of such wine held in various bonded warehouses throughout the country. By September, with another vintage only months away, the situation had become so critical that the prime minister, Mr Bruce, agreed to meet a delegation of grape growers and their local members of parliament. The prime minister offered no solutions, but shortly afterwards the idea of an overseas marketing authority was mooted. In March 1929 the *Wine Overseas Marketing Act* became law. By that Act, a marketing board was created consisting of a government representative, two members chosen by cooperative wineries and distilleries, two delegates from South Australia, and one each from Victoria, New South Wales and Western Australia. For a three-year period the board was to be responsible for all wine intended for export. The Act further provided for an export fund, a London agency and the licensing of all traders in wine. At the end of three years the wine industry would decide once again (it had been required to approve the scheme, before the Act came into force) whether the board would continue.

All of this took place in the first few months of 1929. By that time the first marks of depression were indelibly etched upon the Australian economy. There was already widespread unemployment and a reduced demand for consumer goods, including wine. In Britain the situation was no better. The problem of wine speculation and the consequent oversupply had proved insoluble. In 1928 exports to London fell to 1.7 million gallons (7.73 million litres), less than half that of the previous year. This dramatic though predictable reduction combined with another huge harvest in 1929 of 84.5 million litres left Australia awash with wine. Vineyard planting came to a full stop. Depressing headlines such 'Vine Planting Slumps in Nuriootpa' began to appear in industry journals (*Wine and Spirit News*, July 1929). Official notices were equally grim.

> AUSTRALIAN WINE BOARD
>
> WARNING TO GROWERS
>
> Owing to the dangerous position arising from overproduction, growers are warned against any further planting of wine grapes.
>
> *Signed: Herbert Kay*
> *Chairman*

The diabolical combination of fewer markets, reduced bounty payments and fixed grape prices was rapidly driving growers, already accustomed to an irregular income, into total poverty. As Francois de Castella, Victorian Government Viticulturalist, reported in 1929, 'Grape prices can be fixed, but winemakers cannot be forced to buy'.

There were also threats to what was left of the British market. Ways around the imperial preference were being explored by British merchants, including the sudden emergence of a British winemaking industry based upon the import of European grape must, not dutiable and therefore extremely attractive if only in price, as a cheap source of alcohol. These so-called 'British wines', according to the Federal Viticultural Council, 'acquired considerable popularity in workingmen's clubs and generally in industrial areas'. A second challenge to preference was the judicious blending of low strength foreign wines (25° proof—British import duty 6.6 cents per litre) with a smaller part of high strength foreign wine (42° proof—British duty 17.7 cents per litre) to give a wine only marginally dearer than its Australian competition.

To meet this danger in its only viable market, growers and winemakers once more appealed to the federal government to raise the bounty from 2.2 cents per litre to four cents per litre. The government reluctantly agreed, but virtually with the same hand in March 1930 (to finance the increased bounty, so it said) imposed substantial increases in the excise upon fortifying spirit.

Appalled, the bigger winemakers threatened to close their wineries, but the government remained adamant. Finally a compromise was reached; the government would continue to charge the old excise rate on all fortified wine in bond at the date of the rise, and the new rate would come into force in respect of all fortifying spirit used thereafter, in return for which the makers agreed to obtain all their grape requirements at the prices fixed by the government, thus in the government's view protecting the grape growers from winemaker exploitation. The Wine Overseas Marketing Board (or simply the Australian Wine Board as it had come be called) was also to press vigorously for the expansion of foreign markets.

The board decided to establish its London agency and Australian wine had its first official representative in London since Edward Burney Young nearly thirty years before. Its emissary this time was Henry Laffer, who opened the board's London office on 1 October 1930. His immediate mission was to stabilise and improve the

London market. To this end the board had in June of that year introduced a minimum price scheme. The price fixed was three shillings and seven pence a gallon (eight cents a litre) f.o.b. (free on board) wood included. The British equivalent, freight added, was four shillings and threepence a gallon (9.5 cents per litre). It was of course intended that the minimum price apply only to the lowest quality of wine shipped, so as to give both London merchant and Australian shipper a reasonable return on capital invested, but that was not to be the outcome.

From the start the merchants treated the scheme as a challenge to their evasiveness. The minimum price became the maximum price offered for wine of any quality, even the highest, and when, soon after, the Australian pound was devalued against the pound sterling, they demanded even a slice of the devaluation. In Laffer's own words, the Wine Board and its 'attempts to regulate and control export were looked upon as an "Aunt Sally" to be shot at and defeated'. Worse still, the weakness of the Australian shippers aided and abetted the London merchants in their evasive endeavours. The Wine Board indeed became an 'Aunt Sally', shot at by both sides and therefore rendered purposeless by surreptitious price-cutting. Laffer estimated that such practices cost the Australian wine industry over £1 million between the years 1933 and 1938. Nor was it an advantage passed on to the British wine consumer at the time. The same retail price was paid as before the price war; only the wholesale trade benefitted. So even though the minimum price scheme was abolished in 1936, the price war continued until by 1938 the price had plunged to two shillings and six pence a gallon (5.5 cents a litre). That Australian wine shipments to Britain in 1939, impelled by the immediate prospect of another world war, were exceeded only by Portugal, did not matter very much. Cheap fortified wine seemed well on the way to impoverishing our wine industry both financially and perhaps more importantly, in self-esteem.

The decade of the 1920s was most marked by the expansion of the Barossa Valley and the Riverland regions of South Australia. After all they were the areas, together with McLaren Vale and Clare, best equipped to supply the needs of the market.

At Thomas Hardy & Sons, now without the guiding hand of its founder, there was both change and continuity. In 1920 the Company moved into the Barossa Valley, building an impressive

Thomas Hardy & Sons' Tintara Winery,
McLaren Vale, c. 1920.

new winery at Vine Vale in Dorrien which in its first vintage (1921) crushed 1100 tonnes. The original Hardy home Bankside, was sold in 1924 to a man who immediately began a market garden. Thomas Hardy would have approved wholeheartedly. As well, a young man named Colin Haselgrove proposed that the Tintara winery, now proving too costly, be closed and all grapes be sent to McLaren Vale for ensuing vintages. Robert Borrough Hardy, Thomas's youngest son, retired aged sixty, management being taken over by his nephew, Tom Mayfield Hardy, and his second son, Kenneth. Yet the old family connections remained. The Stowards and Nottages still worked in the business. Colin Haselgrove left for France where he studied for a year at Montpellier in 1926, completing a two-year viticulture course in only one and spending 1927 gaining practical experience in red-winemaking in Algeria. At home, his recommended closure of the Tintara winery was taking effect, all Tintara fruit being sent to the enlarged McLaren Vale facilities for the 1927 vintage. In 1929 Haselgrove became Hardy's chief winemaker.

The following year there began a trading connection which many years later was to lead to a further expansion of the Hardy realm.

In 1924 the old established Emu brand, famous in Britain and widely known in Canada, was sold by Pownalls to W. H. Chaplin & Co. aggressive wine marketers, who soon wrested control of the British market form Burgoyne's. In 1930, to consolidate its supply of Australian wine for this market, Chaplin's purchased the Morphett Vale winery and vineyard of R. C. H. Walker, a boom-time baby of the wine bounty and imperial preference. Thus the Emu Wine Company, after fifty years of existence in England as an Australian brand, came home to roost. To its local board were appointed Walter Bagenal as managing director, Tom Mayfield Hardy as director and Colin Haselgrove as technical director to supervise production from the McLaren Vale area of the Australian port style, which remained, despite the efforts of the misguided wine speculators described above, a favourite of the English market. In that time of depression, Emu became a rock upon which the McLaren winegrowers could depend at least for their bread and butter.

As Colin Haselgrove became more and more involved with Emu, it was decided that Hardy's should appoint a chief winemaker in his place. On Haselgrove's own recommendation, Roger Warren, a Roseworthy graduate but without winemaking experience, was appointed. Under Haselgrove's tuition, Warren, fortunately endowed with an exceptional palate, more than justified the faith placed in him, becoming in due course one of Australia's most famous red-winemakers during the 1940s and 1950s, specialising in blending reds from many regions.

Gradually the South Australian wine industry recovered during the late 1930s, but it was still to endure the numbing tragedy of a major air disaster, which affected Hardy's and other companies equally grievously. The federal government had called a meeting in Canberra of wine industry leaders for late October 1938. On 25 October Tom Mayfield Hardy, Sidney Hill Smith and Hugo Gramp boarded the *Kyeema* at Parafield Airport near Adelaide for a flight to Melbourne. *Kyeema* did not arrive, having crashed in dense fog into the Dandenong Ranges near Melbourne. All on board were killed. In one tragic accident many of the third-generation leaders of the Australian wine industry were wiped out.

In the Barossa Valley, time had also taken its toll at Orlando, but not before there had been major expansion at Rowland Flat. A new winery had also been erected in 1920 with five fermenting

WHITE WINES.

	Per Doz. Quarts	Per Doz. Pints	Per Gallon
LIGHT DRY.			
No. 0 HOCK .. .. Prize White Wine.	25/-	13/6	—
REISLING .. .. The best of the Light White Wines made in the Colony.	22/6	12/-	—
DORADILLA .. .. A fine Light Wine, grown at Tintara.	18/-	10/-	—
CHABLIS .. .. Equal to imported.	12/-	7/-	—
MEDIUM, OR FULL BODIED			
OOMOO WHITE .. .. A first-class Wine, slightly sweet.	24/-	13/-	10/-
ANGASTON SHERRY .. .. Fine Wine. Guaranteed over 6 years.	22/6	12/-	10/-
OLD SHERRY (Special) .. .. Vintage, 1879.	36/-	—	—
SWEET.			
FRONTIGNAC .. .. Constantia character, very fine.	25/-	13/6	10/-
MADEIRA .. .. One of the best Sweet Wines.	25/-	13/6	10/-
MUSCAT .. .. Champion Wine (Liqueur).	18/-	10/-	8/-
SWEET WHITE .. .. Good Wine for family use.	12/-	—	5/-
OLD WHITE	8/-	—	3/3
VERMOUTH .. .. Pure Tonic Wine.	20/-	—	—
OLD BRANDY	42/-	—	—

All the Sweet Wines can be had in Half-Gallon Glass Flagons, which are charged 6d. each, and allowed for when returned.

All Wines delivered free in Adelaide and Suburbs. Reduction in taking a quantity for laying down. All returned packages and bottles taken at their fair value (less cost of carriage).

CASKS AND PACKAGES ARE CHARGED AS FOLLOWS:—

Quarter Casks	8/-	10 to 20-gallon Kegs	10/-
5-gallon Kegs	7/6	New 1-doz. Cases	2/-
Old 1-doz. Cases	1/-	Old 4-doz. Cases	2/-

Flagons ½-gallon each .. .. .. 6d.

White wine list of Thomas Hardy & Sons, c. 1920: mostly fortified in line with contemporary tastes.

tanks capable of holding 95 000 gallons (432 250 litres) of wine. A spirit bond was added in 1923 and storage space steadily increased until by 1930 storage capacity exceeded 6.3 million litres of wine, fortifying spirit and brandy. In addition the company had over

250 acres (101 hectares) of its own vineyards and bought grapes from 240 district growers. Gustav Gramp, now well into his seventies, still managed the company, ably assisted by his sons, Hugo and Fred. In 1927 Gustav died and Hugo became managing director, a position held until his death in the *Kyeema* air disaster in 1938.

As the export market boomed, winery building in the Barossa and its surrounds became infectious. Penfold's established its Eden Valley winery in 1922 and in the same year Walter Reynell & Sons erected their Lyndoch facility.

In addition the winemakers of the Valley were becoming more commercially aware. Old family partnerships now became limited liability companies, in some cases even with new equity. The old firm of W. Salter & Son was incorporated in 1920 under the managing directorate of Leslie Salter, whose old Roseworthy friend Ronald Martin, a Roseworthy gold medallist in 1902, bought a one-third share in the new company. Salter was a leading figure of the South Australian wine industry in his time, a member of the Federal Viticultural Council (1918–36) and its president for seven years, as well as being a foundation member of the Wine Overseas Marketing Board; when he retired in 1937 H. M. Martin & Son (Ronald's Company) took over the management of the business.

Meanwhile Tolley Scott & Tolley (later to be called Tollana) held its first directors' meeting in 1921, awarding its active executives, Ernest Tolley and Douglas Tolley, £500 ($1000) per year. Its famous brandy trade mark TST was registered the following year.

Yalumba benefited greatly from the export boom in fortified reds, but continued to produce dry whites and reds in limited quantities for the home market. Percival Smith retired as winery manager in 1923, causing a business reorganisation which saw Walter Grandy Smith as the initial managing director and chairman of the board of S. Smith& Sons Ltd. But Tiger Smith's favoured pursuits of hunting and overseas travel still occupied his time and during his absences his son Sidney Hill Smith ran the day-to-day affairs of the business. Yalumba shared in the sadness that followed the crash of the *Kyeema*, losing Sidney Hill Smith in the disaster. For that company it was grief redoubled, for his father, the ebullient Walter, had died earlier in the same year. To Sidney, a man of foresight as events would prove, the Valley owed a lasting debt, for it was he who encouraged the planting of rhine riesling in the Eden Valley at a time when local table wine consumption was minimal.

At Seppeltsfield also there were changes in this era. Just after the First World War ended, a new winery was established at Dorrien, adjoining a rail siding on the Nuriootpa line; the company was incorporated and in the early 1920s achieved its first million gallon (4.55 million litres) vintage. Seppeltsfield also was expanded. From a thriving wine village it became a small town, with some buildings covering an acre (0.4 hectares) or more in area, occupying in all more than 10 acres (four hectares) on both sides of the creek. Later in that decade, in 1927, the company bought a building at Nuriootpa, which it converted into a winery, and at the end of the decade bought a substantial acreage at Barooga in New South Wales. Not far from Rutherglen, it was intended at first as a rootstock nursery in case of an attack by phylloxera, still a haunting nightmare to South Australian growers, but later it was planted to varieties that suited the fashion of the time, fortified wine. For the house of Seppelt, the long second generation came to an end in 1931, with the death of Benno Seppelt, a few weeks before his eighty-fifth birthday. The last of South Australia's wine patriarchs had died and the succession passed smoothly to the board of directors under the chairmanship of Oscar Seppelt. For the board it was business as usual, though in difficult times the cloth had to be carefully tailored. At Seppeltsfield, building continued with the erection of yet another huge maturation cellar, while in Great Western the drives were extended to 4.8 kilometres to ferment and mature more sparkling wine. In Britain, export performance had increased so significantly that the company opened its own London office in 1936. When Oscar Seppelt retired in 1939, the House of Seppelt could look back on the 1930s as a decade of achievement despite the difficulties.

At the time of the Depression, the inconsistency of export markets made the sale of grapes a wildly fluctuating business for the grower. For most of the 1920s South Australian winemakers had taken every grape they could get, though there were occasional mutterings about oversupply, especially from Riverland areas. However, growers' prospects for the 1931 vintage were grim. The local wine market was in severe decline; exports were highly uncertain. The winemakers with large wine stocks on hand were understandably cautious. In late 1930, after a meeting of leading winemaking companies (Hardy,

Penfold, Orlando, Tolley and Seppelt), it was explained to growers that grape prices needed to be reduced substantially before they would take any grapes at all. The grape growers, alarmed by the proposed twenty-five per cent price reduction, at first sought political assistance. When only sympathy was forthcoming in the face of an estimated glut of 5000 tonnes, the growers resolved to form a winemaking cooperative, which was to process 1500 of those surplus tonnes at the Tolley Scott & Tolley winery in Nuriootpa. Other factors combined to reduce the anticipated surplus to less than 500 tonnes. The larger makers relented to some extent, taking more grapes than originally estimated. The Reynell winery at Lyndoch and that of Penfold in Eden Valley were leased to growers to process their own grapes and in addition the 1500 tonnes processed at Tolley's in turn required fortifying spirit, so for this purpose even more grapes were required. Nonetheless the South Australian Grapegrowers Cooperative was in the Barossa to stay, building its own winery in time for 1933 vintage. It was to be an era fraught with financial danger for the infant cooperative as it struggled to find markets, but as the export of fortified wines improved during the mid-1930s due to the export bounty imperial preference, so did the fortunes of 'Nurivin' as its bulk export wine was called.

There were other industries also generated by the Barossa grape in these difficult times. One such was the Tarac Manufacturing Company, founded in 1931 in Nuriootpa to produce tartaric acid from marc (fermented grapeskins), the residue of winemaking and later, due to a patented process, the recovery of alcohol, also from marc. The company was to prove so successful that later in the 1930s two more plants, one at Walkerville near Adelaide and the other at Berri in the Riverland, were erected.

The end of the First World War and the decade of the 1920s initiated some grape-growing families into winemaking and marked the return of others to a time-honoured family practice. One novitiate was Carl Lindner, a small grower at Tanunda in 1912, who in common with many others of his time greeted the end of the war with such optimism that he converted a small butchery into the St Hallett winery in 1918 and expanded the vineyard. Prospering due to the fortified boom of the 1920s, the Lindner family survived the ensuing slump of the 1930s.

It was the turn now of the Burge family to resume winemaking.

Its ancestor, John Burge, arrived from Wiltshire in 1855, a tailor by occupation but very much a farmer by inclination, for within three years he had bought thirty-two acres (thirteen hectares) at Lyndoch and planted a vineyard. The family produced wine on a small scale until the 1870s when grape growing apparently became more attractive, a family tradition that also beckoned John's grandson, Percy Norman Burge, for in 1922 he bought Wilsford near Lyndoch and planted a vineyard. When later in that decade prospects for grape growing appeared distinctly gloomy, he became a self-taught winemaker, making in his first vintage (1930) the fortified wines so essential to economic survival in that era.

Other families such as Henschke chose a lower profile, continuing to make mostly fortified wine, but turning chiefly to general farming pursuits in the harsh financial climate of the 1930s. The age of the small maker of quality table wine had clearly not yet arrived.

Older names, however, whose vineyards relied on the declining table wine market and were clearly unsuited to the fortified vogue, did not survive. One such was Pewsey Vale, which in 1923 passed out of the hands of the Gilbert family, though it continued production until 1930, when its new owner decided that sheep, cattle and horses would be more profitable. Thus after eighty-three years one of South Australia's most honoured table-wine vineyards ceased to exist. Phoenix-like it would rise again, but not for another generation.

In Clare the arrival of the 1920s saw a trustee company in control of Stanley Wine, now an asset of the estate of the late J. H. Knappstein. As an administration it was to prove Dickensian in its length and disastrous in its financial outcome, for in 1938, when Stanley Wine was returned to the family, three members of which (Fred, Bernie and Mick) had been actively concerned in its day-to-day running during the administration, it owed £45 000 ($90 0000), a fortune in the interwar period. Why and how the huge debt had been accumulated was never satisfactorily explained, but the family suspected serious mismanagement and were only prevented from taking legal action against the trustee because it and Stanley's bank had directors in common, the bank agreeing to continue loan accommodation on condition that the Knappstein beneficiaries gave a total release to the trustee. It seemed strange indeed that business could have run at such a tremendous loss during the export boom, when Stanley were receiving orders from the Victorian Wine

Company in London almost every month 'for 100 or 200 hogshead' of export 'burgundy' per month. One hogshead equals about 260 litres and the lowest price brought for dry wine would have been about five cents per litre; Stanley had successfully continued its traditional export trade.

Buring & Sobels, however, under the management of Rudi Buring and Talbot Sobels and without the incubus of a trustee company, shared the prosperity of the mid-1920s and, along with the rest of Clare, the steep decline of the Depression. Yet it was a resilient company with expansion always high on its list of priorities, so much so that the Quelltaler winery was extended in 1932 by the addition of an east wing for wine storage and shortly after another bulk storage cellar to house 400 000 litres of wine was erected at the western end. In addition a large new Adelaide office entitled Quelltaler House was opened in 1934. As for wine, exports of bulk dry red continued to the United Kingdom, while on the home market Quelltaler hock helped to resist the sliding popularity of table wine. In 1936 Australia was introduced to a new product, certainly fortified but with much more finesse than most of the heavy 'ports' of the period and one that emphasised lifestyle in an age when economic conditions did not favour such frivolities. Granfiesta Sherry was to establish a half century of popularity and be the basis of many a sherry party in the ensuing decades.

In this era there were openings and closings in Clare as in many other South Australian vineyard areas. St Andrews closed its winery doors in 1934 after nearly forty years of winemaking. And after many murmurings in the late nineteenth century, the cooperative movement finally reached the town in 1930 for the usual reason—unwanted grapes. As in the Barossa, most of the wine made was fortified and either sold locally, often from the back of a truck or disposed of to large companies at a very low price. No matter, survival was all that counted and the Clarevale Co-operative winery did survive.

The smaller wineries, too, shared the struggle of those boom and bust years. At the family concern, A. P. Birks, Roly Birks, began a winemaking career in 1917 that was to last sixty-four more vintages. He shared the optimism that greeted the end of war: new vineyards were planted in 1919 and 1920, the winery extended and new equipment installed. New markets were needed too when

'Wendouree' (as the estate was becoming known at this time) decided to cease producing purely for sale to Stanley Wine Co. So by offering its 'port' and full-bodied dry reds in cask sizes from hogsheads (260 litres) down to five gallon (22.8 litres) for sale throughout the mid-north and as far south as Adelaide at prices cheaper than its bigger competitors, Wendouree began to make its name.

Sevenhill College also reflected the change in tastes to fortified wines at this time, making only its mataro as dry red and its doradillo and riesling as dry white. The rest, shiraz, grenache, tokay, pedro and frontignac, according to a contemporary cellar book, being fortified with 'fifteen proof gallons of spirit to every 100 gallons of wine'. The College winemaker was then Brother George Downey, whose winemaking reputation was secured for all time by the famous 1925 Sevenhill Port, described in *Classic Wines of Australia* with typical understatement by author Max Lake, who had the privilege of tasting it, as 'fabulous'.

In the years before the First World War, the Riverland regions were extremely difficult of access, the chief means of transport being a rail link to Morgan and then a riverboat for passengers and small freight or a barge for larger objects. Even after the introduction of motor transport, as the roads were little more than bush tracks, it often took a day or more to travel to Renmark, but as the river settlements began to flourish there was agitation for a rail link, which came in 1913 with the extension of the line to Paringa across the river from Renmark. After the war, rapid expansion of the area due to soldier settlement and the growing importance of the local wine industry increased pressure on the South Australian Government for a direct link to Renmark. This came in January 1927 with the opening of a substantial railway bridge.

Indicative of the frustration engendered by the dilatory pace of Riverland transport in those days is a story attributed to Colin Haselgrove, who worked briefly for Angove's in 1924. A driver employed by the company was obliged to answer a summons for slander in Renmark Court. It appeared that while driving an eight-horse team pulling a dray loaded with full hogsheads, he had a violent argument with the ferryman and called him a bastard. As the case was about to begin, the defence counsel asked if the parties could confer in the magistrate's chambers. On resumption, defence counsel indicated that his client wished to make a statement to the Bench before pleading to the charge. 'Well, Your Honour, yes I did call him a bastard, but I didn't mean he was born one, just that he grew up one.' The parties apparently shook hands and the case was dismissed.

The easier link between Tea Tree Gully and Renmark was an obvious bonus for Angove's, both for the St Agnes winery and the Renmark winery, although each functioned with a remarkable degree of independence. But already the production potential of the Riverland area was becoming apparent. In 1919, 250 tonnes of grapes were harvested at Tea Tree Gully with another 140 tonnes being bought with a wine yield of about 53 000 gallons (241 150 litres), while at Renmark 1500 tonnes were crushed.

The Angove family had suffered two bereavements in the years before and during the war; Dr William Angove died in 1912 and his son Edward was killed in action in 1918.

In 1922, as a consequence of the death of Edward Angove, Angove's Ltd was incorporated, with T. C. (Carl) Angove as chairman and managing director. During this time, H. R. (Ron) Haselgrove (brother of Colin) was in France studying at Montpellier and gaining practical experience in the production of cognac. In 1925 he returned to work at Angove's as director of winemaking and brandy production, his role being primarily to create a more delicate style of brandy than that previously produced in Australia. Since Haselgrove's first vintage in 1925, when he made a fine base wine from doradillo grapes which was double distilled in the Cognac manner, St Agnes brandy has always been regarded as one of the finer spirits of Australian brandy making.

By 1927 Angove's had become one of the larger Australian wineries. In that year it could boast 190 acres (seventy-seven hectares) of vineyard at Tea Tree Gully, which included 101 acres (forty-one hectares) of doradillo, twenty-six acres (10.5 hectares) of cabernet sauvignon, twenty-four acres (ten hectares) of mataro and fifteen acres (six hectares) of shiraz. Its St Agnes winery could ferment over 150 000 litres in twenty-five tanks and could store nearly 530 000 litres, a quarter of that capacity being in wood. In addition, fermentation and storage capacity jointly owned by Carl Angove and Ronald Martin of Stonyfell amounted to 34 800 gallons (158 340 litres) of fermentation capacity and 131 750 gallons (599 460 litres) of storage, nearly a quarter of which was in wood consisting mostly of oak but including red gum, red pine and jarrah. At Renmark the winery could ferment 47 500 gallons (216 120 litres) and store 293 365 gallons (1.33 million litres), while Lyrup Winery could ferment 21 500 gallons (97 820 litres) and store 86 500 gallons (393 570 litres). As well as the usual wine presses, St Agnes and Renmark each had a pot still for brandy making, while Lyrup confined itself to winemaking.

In the mood of the age, Angove's was also keen to export and for this purpose Carl Angove and his frequent business partner, Ronald Martin of Stonyfell, formed a London shipping house, Dominion Wines Ltd, in October 1929. Despite the imminent Depression, during the next decade Dominion established Angove's as one of the top four Australian wine exporters to Britain.

Angove's neighbour, Douglas A. Tolley of Hope Valley, was even closer to the export pace. His purchases of Bill Redman's early Coonawarra reds for blending into export 'burgundy' have already been mentioned. He too was bent on expansion. In 1914 a fifty-six acre (22.7 hectares) orchard and vineyard block, which had been part of the old Medlands Estate belonging to the Sage family, was purchased at Siegersdorf (soon after to be renamed Dorrien). Nine years later (1923), Tolley erected a small winery there to crush and ferment its grapes and transported the new wine to Hope Valley, which in the mid-1920s had substantial storage capacity—64 500 gallons (293 470 litres)—all in wood. Nor did Douglas rush to follow fortified trends. As export markets remained firm, 'burgundy' production largely continued throughout the 1920s. Now Douglas's son Len had assumed the reins Hope Valley expanded rapidly, adding nearly sixty more acres (twenty-four hectares) of vineyard to the Hope Valley estate during that decade; chief varieties planted were, according to the fashion of those 'burgundy', sweet red, sweet white and brandy days, shiraz, grenache, pedro ximines and doradillo.

Yet the depressed 1930s struck hard at Hope Valley. Not only did Douglas Tolley die in 1932, but the stringent times reduced its workforce to just two permanent employees. Wages varied from £3 to £3-10 per week.

In far-off Coonawarra in the early 1920s, Bill Redman was lamenting the loss of a steady market. However complimentary Douglas Tolley had been in refusing further supply of his Coonawarra red, Redman knew that fine words would not satisfy his creditors. So whatever Tolley's reasons had been, Redman now approached Lieutenant-Colonel Fulton of Woodley Wines, an old established house whose Adelaide vineyards had been finally swallowed by encroaching suburbia in 1922. Yes, Fulton needed wine and his palate was obviously good enough to appreciate the potential of Redman's Coonawarra reds. Recommending that Redman make 'a light dinner claret' and insisting that the wine be matured in cask for two years, Fulton took Redman's wine. Redman took Fulton's advice.

There now began an enduring partnership, which flew in the face of prevailing fashion. Not a drop of heavy red or 'port' was made. High in acidity and comparatively low in alcohol by the standards of the times, the wine would not have been suitable anyway. It was to be table wine or the still! Arguably, this was the first conscious decision made in favour of fine Australian table wine for many years. By picking his shiraz and cabernet sauvignon grapes earlier with consequent higher acidity and lower pH, Redman not only made a more stable wine, but in the process created a 'claret' style that would ultimately become world famous. It was rewarding too, even in depressed times. At a profit of nearly $12 a tonne of grapes (still no higher than twenty years before), Redman managed to make twice as much money as many of his unfortunate neighbours, who were continuing to supply their fruit for distillation at $6 a tonne. Though marketing any table wine in Australia was extremely difficult in the 1930s due not only to depression but also to public taste, stylistically Coonawarra 'claret' brought Woodley's an overseas success, a 1933 St Adele, one of Redman's best, being chosen as top wine of show at the first empire wine competition in London in 1936, all without mention of either maker or district. Redman's success, however, must be viewed in perspective for at no time had Coonawarra been able to live off grapes alone. Some, such as Harold Richardson, a Roseworthy graduate and local orchardist, made cider as well as wine on his Pyrus property. The region staggered from crisis to crisis, glut to glut. A grape-growers' cooperative proposed by Bill Redman in 1928 failed to meet with approval. A huge glut in 1936 saw the introduction of a vine-pull scheme offering to uproot vines and start dairying. As a result two-thirds of the Coonawarra vine area disappeared. Mixed farming, involving dependence on orchards and livestock as well as grapes, was not just safer and more sensible, it was the only way. By 1940 things were much as they were at the beginning of the century, except that Coonawarra had shrunk considerably in vineyard extent. Riddoch's dream had become the growers' nightmare.

In 1923 Lindeman & Co., then by far the largest wine company in New South Wales and heavily indebted to its bank, had been placed under the management of Leo Buring. Buring, though compassionate, was hardly successful, for seven years later when he too was shown the door, the bank's debt had doubled and a receiver took his place. The receivership was to be a long one. Even with stringent economies and wholesale staff dismissals, Lindeman's languished in the red until 1947. Its difficulties were symptomatic of the Hunter Valley as a whole, which at no time during that era shared the buoyancy of the South Australian trade.

Those remaining winemakers of the Valley had become very small and were to shrink even further, struggling through the 1920s and 1930s, regretting the decline of table wine in the Sydney market and looking for the meagre pickings from unfashionable table wines to be gleaned from the London market, so long dominated by South Australia. They also looked for subsistence to the larger South Australian makers, many of whom recognised the finesse of Hunter wines as excellent blending material.

Less than 1.5 cents per litre and an eighteen-month wait for payment often drove the winemaker to the wall and if not to the still, regardless of the quality of the wine, if only to make room for the coming vintage. Some, like Audrey Wilkinson of Oakdale, seeing hope in the fortified market, tried Hunter port, hardly ever a satisfactory alternative to its southern competition. Most nonetheless persisted with some table wine at least.

One such was the young Maurice O'Shea who, in 1925, took over the reins at the New South Wales Wine Co., renaming the vineyard Mount Pleasant and the winery most appropriately L'Hermitage, as many fine reds so named would issue from the winery in the next thirty years. His French mother had seen to it that O'Shea not only spoke fluent French but was educated in France as well. So it was that he spent several years there during the First World War and thereafter at the University of Montpellier. Had he known better he might have stayed, for there was little encouragement for a young winemaker in the Hunter Valley in those years. Downy mildew and declining markets had seen to that. As a wine area, it was careering rapidly downhill. The years until the Second World War would witness a decline in its vine area from one thousand hectares to a little more than five hundred.

What the financial condition of the New South Wales Wine Co. had been on O'Shea's succession is not known. It could hardly have been healthy for within five years O'Shea was seeking to sell the business. In 1930 he negotiated with Colin Haselgrove of Hardy's. In 1933 he sold a half-share to McWilliam's, who retained him as manager-winemaker at Mount Pleasant. Thus freed of financial cares, O'Shea was to achieve what can only be described as winemaking stardom during the next quarter of a century and to acquire for Hunter Valley reds a contemporary reputation matched by no other region save the embryonic Coonawarra. But what was Mount Pleasant like in O'Shea's day?

By the standards of the time it was a smallish property, 120 acres (forty-nine hectares) in extent, but its soil—that weathered red loam, only too rare in Pokolbin—produced then (and still does) excellent fruit, eminently suitable for fine table wine. In his winery—the standard Hunter structure of sturdy posts, weatherboards and corrugated iron, painted a reflective white as a concession to Hunter Valley summer heat—he was both conservative, relying on semillon, white hermitage and shiraz as major varieties, and innovative, incorporating rare varietals such as montils, picpoul and aucerot into his whites and pinot noir into his reds.[1]

He did not restrict himself, however, to his own fruit or indeed his own wine (if the quality was good enough), thereby assisting the often perilous livelihood of other growers and vignerons in the district. He bought expertly from Tyrrell, Drayton and Elliott, the names of his wines usually revealing the source of supply. It did pay of course to recognise O'Shea's encodings. Thus the Mountain series of reds of the late 1930s and early 1940s came from Mount Pleasant's own hillside slopes, TY and Richard from Tyrrell, and Charles from Elliott. As well O'Shea was known as an excellent cook and invitations to his dinner parties were eagerly sought. In all, though his French ancestry and education had ensured that he appreciated the finer qualities of life, it offered no solutions to the grim financial realities of the Hunter Valley in the third and fourth decades of the twentieth century. Yet most importantly O'Shea kept the fading beacon of table wine alight in an age when, as in other areas, it could easily have been extinguished altogether.

And what of that newly emerging Hunter and New South Wales force, Penfold's? Restoring Dalwood to a pre-eminence it had not experienced for thirty years, it soon became firmly established in the Hunter Valley. Its emphasis was on the only product in which the Hunter excelled—table wine. Indeed some of its wines were outstanding, including a notable cabernet-verdot blend of 1930, declared by Max Lake, that man of prodigious palate, to be 'best wine I ever tasted'. Penfold's too set up its chief Sydney office in the obviously fashionable Queen Victoria Building, from where it could not only keep a weathered eye on its struggling rival, Lindeman's, but also control its Hunter vineyards and its large Minchinbury estate, which had been enlarged and then encompassed over 400 acres (162 hectares) of vines, including verdelho, riesling, traminer, pinot blanc, cabernet sauvignon, shiraz and pinot noir. The sparkling wine cellars under the control of Eduard Bernier, who had succeeded Leo Buring, had also been enlarged to store 1.5 million bottles of maturing Minchinbury 'champagne'. The Hunter Valley also saw a Penfold's expansion, the eighty acre (thirty-two hectare) 'Sparkling Vale' vineyard four kilometres north of Pokolbin being planted from 1920 onwards, while smaller vignerons there such as Bob Elliott, once the worst of the 1930s was past, also saw brighter days ahead, planting what was to become a famous white-wine vineyard on sandy-gravelly soil at Belford and acquiring another vineyard at Fordwich, originally planted by a soldier-settler after the First World War. But these were very small ripples of activity in an otherwise stagnant economic pond. A grape boom would come again to the Hunter Valley, but not for another thirty years.

Wine quality, however, remained high. Besides vigneron-merchants such as the masterly O'Shea at Mount Pleasant, there were others such as Caldwell's in Sydney. The Penfold Cabernet-Verdot 1930 has already been mentioned and I particularly recall from that era a fine Tulloch red of 1936, tasted in the late 1970s, bottled by Caldwell's, as well as some marvellous Porphyry whites of Lindeman's tasted about the same time.

In Victoria in these years, except for heavy reds and fortifieds, it was the same story. Those areas suitable only for table wine went into free fall. For the Yarra Valley in the 1920s the advent of the jersey cow was equally as devastating as phylloxera had been fifty years before in Geelong. Vineyard after vineyard was grubbed out and planted to pasture. Erstwhile busy wineries became creameries, rumination replacing fermentation. Lack of interest, not only on the part of the government but by the public as a whole, saw the uprooting of the whole Yarra vignoble.

But the public as a whole was far from diffident towards Great Western. Here, if the 1920s did not perhaps roar, they at least emitted a resounding bellow. On its acquisition in 1918, Seppelt's increased vineyard area by twenty-eight acres (eleven hectares) adding a further twenty-six (ten hectares) in the following two years, seventy acres [twenty-eight hectares] in 1922-23 and eleven (4.5 hectares) in 1928. Reginald Mowatt was winemaker from 1918 to 1932, being replaced by an almost legendary name, Colin Preece, in 1932. Due to general economic conditions Preece's early years were quiet ones, not marked by any notable expansion either in cellar or vineyard; but boom times, due to war and significant migration, would come again.

With the death of John Pinney Bear in 1889, Chateau Tahbilk, then owned by Bear's widow, entered a period of quiescence. Quality of wine, and especially of the smaller amounts of brandy, remained high, but wine production dropped to 14 000 gallons (63 700 litres) in 1918 due to mildew. It had recovered in 1923 to 35 000 gallons (159 250 litres) but it was still only an average yield of 200 gallons (910 litres) per acre (the vineyard was 175 acres in area) or in weight terms, 1.33 tonnes of grapes. The vineyard was aging, as was the proprietorship. It was time for a change. For the vineyard, then sixty years old and exhausted, Francois de Castella (son of Hubert, and the Victorian Government Viticulturalist) prescribed liberal quantities of manure and perhaps irrigation during the dry winter season. For the absentee proprietor, there could be no such cure. Bear's widow died in London aged ninety-two in 1925. In the same year the property, now up for sale, came to the notice of one Reginald Purbrick, a Conservative member of the British House of Commons, who bought it. That it may have continued in absentee ownership with its vineyard reduced and its production declining, or indeed being uprooted altogether, remained a very real possibility for several years in the late 1920s (1927 vintage for instance due to severe frosts yielded only 7000 gallons (31 850 litres) until two important events happened.

The first was a further report by de Castella, this time to the Purbricks, recommending Tahbilk's continuation as a table-wine vineyard.

> Chateau Tahbilk has in the past been a productive and profitable vineyard property and can be so again. The soil and climate are admirably suited for the vine and I do not think that any other form of cultivation could show the results the vine is capable of on the vineyard portion of the estate . . . [It] is very well suited for the production of a class of wine that is becoming less plentiful in Australia as time goes on. I refer to light table wines of Claret and Chablis or Hock types, which the vineyard has in the past produced in quantity and of a satisfactory standard. Such wines are less expensive to make than sweet wines, as no spirit is required for their fortification. The demand for them is increasing, owing to the recent abandonment of many of those vineyards in cooler districts best capable of producing them. The recent expansion in Australian wines has been in sweet wines. Light dry wines are thus becoming scarcer and more sought after, a tendency which will become more accentuated as time goes on.

The second event was the decision of Eric Purbrick, Reginald's son, not to practice at the London Bar for which he was qualified, but to manage Chateau Tahbilk, which he had seen but once before, shortly after its purchase. Trained in the law with no particular knowledge or indeed background in viticulture, he made what must have been a very difficult decision. Arriving at Chateau Tahbilk in 1931 aged twenty-eight, he found that de Castella's recommendations for some replanting, manuring, new vineyard equipment and winter irrigation were being carried out, but such recommendations did not satisfy Tahbilk's most pressing need, to sell the wine it already had. So with characteristic vigour, in the midst of the Depression, he did what vignerons all over Australia were then doing, and had been accustomed to do in such adverse times. He sought out a new clientele, motoring throughout the Goulburn Valley and as far south as Melbourne, selling his wine in bulk from the back of a small truck at 2.6 cents a litre. He had come a very long way from the Inner Temple. Eric Purbrick was to acquire his wine knowledge in the university of practical experience, by listening to the eminent wine men of his time such as Francois de Castella and Tom Seabrook, a leading wine merchant who later was to become his Melbourne agent, and from others of lesser fame perhaps, but equally experienced, men such as McDonald, his first winemaker.

In the north-east times, though not good, were perhaps not as desperate as in cooler regions. After all their fortified wines were to the popular taste, if such existed at all. Nonetheless wiser winemakers everywhere relied on mixed farming where possible, if only for subsistence in the dull grey economy of the 1930s.

By 1920 the Brown Brothers vineyard at Milawa, now grafted on to rootstock and fully restored after the ravages of the vine-louse in 1916, bore its first post-phylloxera vintage. John Charles Brown of the third generation remembered well in 1988 the grape varieties used for table wines which formed eighty per cent of wine produced at Milawa in his youth: shiraz, cabernet, graciano and mondeuse for the vigorous reds; rhine riesling, muscadelle and chasselas for the whites; as well as that pride of the Rutherglen region, brown muscat, for the fortifieds. John Brown, who took over from his father in 1934, well recalled how difficult times were. Sales in very small amounts, 100 gallons (450 litres) were excellent, 500 gallons (2275 litres) an enormous volume. Regular buyers were Seabrook's and Cohn's in Melbourne, Caldwell's in Sydney and Burgoyne's at Mount Ophir for export.

In distant north-western Victoria, Mildura endured the endemic grape gluts that devilled all irrigated areas in the 1920s. True, since the erection of the Murray River locks and the extension of the railway to the town, the river no longer dried up in times of drought as it had in 1914, and even when the water levels were low, at least the railway was available for transport of produce. Yet winemaking equipment remained primitive and much fortified wine was infected by spoilage bacteria. Overseas complaints about quality finally spurred the Mildura Winery into action. In 1935, H. R. (Ron) Haselgrove, who had supervised wine and brandy production and, importantly, quality control at Angove's, was invited to join the Mildura board of directors as technical adviser. Though he continued to be employed by Angove's, this conflict of interest was finally resolved in 1938, when Haselgrove resigned from Angove's to become sales and technical director of the newly named Mildara Wine Co. For Mildara, the appointment of Haselgrove was crucial in its search for quality, without which its export markets would not long survive. Though during the late 1930s its emphasis was almost totally upon fortified wines and brandy, the time would come when, through the Mildara brand, which was then rapidly superseding the old Mildura Winery name, the influence of Haslegrove would be felt much more widely than merely in that struggling irrigation town in distant north-west Victoria.

For Western Australia the end of the First World War witnessed the arrival of many refugees from the recently dismantled Austro-Hungarian Empire. Many of these were Serbs and Croats who, with their grasp of practical winemaking and an urge to succeed in their new land, were just the impetus needed by the Swan Valley, which had become the centre of the State's viticulture. Though production stood at only 162 000 gallons (737 100 litres) for the whole state in 1920, Western Australia had virtually doubled its production a decade later to 310 000 gallons (1.4 million litres) being, like its neighbour South Australia, heavily dependent on the export to London of heavy red and fortified wines, products naturally favoured by the Swan Valley climate.

The region's largest maker was Houghton, owned by the Ferguson family since 1859. Its winemaker in 1920 was R. G. (George) Mann, who passed his winemaking mantle to his son Jack in 1930. Jack Mann, in the fashion and necessity of the times, produced chiefly fortified wines, his liqueur muscat being renowned throughout the state. Yet, surprisingly for a winemaker who loved ripeness and strength, he also had a most delicate touch, making in the years immediately before the Second World War a soft white wine, Houghton's White Burgundy, which was to achieve a nation-wide fame in the postwar years.

What had the Great Depression and the industry's failure to popularise table wines in the years before it done to the Australian wine industry? The combined effect of negative economic factors focussed the minds of winemakers throughout the nation sharply on survival. Everywhere vineyards which could not produce wines suitable for local or export markets were grubbed out or severely pruned in area. Thus the Yarra Valley disappeared in the 1920s, and by the mid-1930s Coonawarra had been reduced from 360 to 120 hectares. The Hunter Valley also shrank in size in the years 1922 to 1936 from 1100 to 600 hectares.

But there were also positive developments—Ron Haselgrove's refinement of our brandy style at Angove's and Mildura; research such as Dr John Fornachon's investigation of fortified wine spoilage (which at least preserved Australia's export market) begun in 1934; the early studies of malolactic fermentation and pH levels by Professor Alan Hickinbotham, who was also instrumental in establishing the oenology course at Roseworthy Agricultural College in 1936; and, of only slightly less importance, refinements of white table wine style such as the early bottling of rhine rieslings introduced by Yalumba's Austrian winemaker, Rudi Kronberger in the early 1930s. Though table wine was certainly not on the tip of everyone's tongue, it had not been entirely forgotten. Indeed the era of the 1930s was the age of Hamilton's Ewell Moselle and Penfold's Minchinbury Trameah, as well as Yalumba rieslings.

[1] Many years later (in the 1970s), such few of his wines as came my way were light and delicately 'Burgundian' in style, elegant yet ripe.

TWELVE

The Second World War and its aftermath

The Second World War arrived very much by appointment; the war clouds had been gathering ever since Hitler remilitarised the Rhineland in 1936. For Australia's winemakers the last years of peace had broken all records for export. For each of the five years from 1935-6, Australia exported more than 16 million litres of wine, 1936-7 and 1937-8 in particular being very successful. Even for the year ended 30 June 1940, including as it did, the first ten months of the war, 16.458 million litres were shipped overseas. Our principal customer was of course Britain. It was a very buoyant London market that saw 'ordinary sweet red wines' sold at auction in barrel for $2.88 a litre or retail at $3 a bottle. Not that the auction fervour benefited the winemaker one whit, he went on shipping as usual at 6.66 cents a litre. The British importers became extremely wealthy, but it must be said that supplies thereafter were very limited, due not only to the threat of Nazi U-boats, but also to British shipping restrictions which allotted, understandably, a very low priority to wine imports in the darkest days of war. Indeed from 20 January 1941 the British government placed an embargo on all imports of wines or spirits unless the importer had a licence from the Ministry of Food. As a result Australian exports for the year ended 30 June 1941 fell by more than half to 7.5 million litres and would fall by more than half again to 3.7 million litres in 1943, by which time Japan had also entered the war and closed off a promising South-East Asian market for brandy and fortified wines.

Yet as the fortunes of war improved so did the export markets. By 1945 exports were back to 1941 levels and in the first full year of peace, 1946–7, exports topped twelve million litres. Little did our winemakers know, however, that it would be another forty years before this figure would be surpassed, as British importers were once more turning to Europe and South Africa. Wine stocks were beginning to build up again in London bonds stores, due this time not so much to a lack of public demand as to an acute shortage of wine bottles in a post-war economy where most glass manufacturers thought first of making standard milk bottles and only if they had surplus capacity of the many different shapes of wine bottles. Yet British tastes seemed to be swinging once more and this time away from Australian sweet fortified red. The year 1946–7 was one of disaster for wine export, only 86 000 litres shipped, the lowest quantity since 1885-6, and though the following year's shipments reached 8.5 million litres, the prewar boom years of export would not return.

At home wine consumption had vastly increased during the war years. From 14.5 million litres in 1939, Australians were consuming 37 million litres by 1944. The reasons were explicable enough. Firstly, wine was rationed and in such cases most people, even those who did not usually drink wine, wished to get their share.

Secondly, Australia was home to two armies, its own and that of the USA, and soldiers are historically renowned for their drinking capacity, especially of beer. In the absence of beer (in very short supply during the Second World War and in the immediate post-war years) fortified wine and even wine of the lighter style such as the early Leo Buring Rhinegolde, obviously made a satisfyingly adequate substitute.

Thus did table wine begin to make a minute imprint on popular contemporary tastes, but Australians continued to drink vastly greater quantities of fortified wine, though now, arguably, popular tastes were inclined to favour sweet sherry rather than the fortified sweet reds and muscats of the lower-class pubs and wine saloons. Winemakers of foresight such as Ron Haselgrove, despite having to concentrate on market essentials such as brandy and new lines of sherry such as Mildara Supreme, introduced in 1949, still felt that one day in the not too distant future Australian claret style would make an impact on the popular palate.

The changing fortunes and strict financial controls of the Second World War seemed to have little effect on the disposal and acquisitions of winery property. Penfold's were particularly active, in 1942 acquiring the Hunter Valley Distillery Vineyard at Pokolbin, the following year adding Auldana, at that time one hundred acres of vineyard and a substantial winery at Magill, and two years later buying 195 acres (seventy-nine hectares) of vineyard at Modbury north-east of Adelaide and the Kalimna winery and vineyard of D. & J. Fowler Ltd in the Barossa Valley. Their acquisitive urge at this time seemed insatiable for in 1948 two other properties were bought in the Hunter Valley, Penfold Vale, planted to fifty acres (twenty hectares) of white grapes and the 15.5 acre (6.2 hectare) Matthew's semillon vineyard. Time also wrought its changes in the control of the Penfold company; the founder's grandsons, Herbert Leslie Penfold Hyland, died in 1940 and his elder brother Frank in 1948. Now it was the turn of the fourth generation of the Penfold family to propel Penfold's into the second half of the twentieth century. Penfold's were also beginning to believe that red table wine might have a commercial future, so much so that in 1949 they despatched their senior winemaker, Max Schubert, then aged thirty-four, to study winemaking in France.

Schubert had joined the company as a fresh-faced laboratory assistant at Nuriootpa in 1931. After showing aptitude at winemaking he had been transferred to the Magill cellars so that he could study chemistry at the Adelaide School of Mines. Having obviously put these studies to good effect, in 1938 he was appointed assistant winemaker, a career interrupted by war service in North Africa,

Greece, Crete, Syria and later in New Guinea. At war's end he rejoined Penfold's, being appointed senior winemaker in 1946.

In 1950 Max was in Bordeaux. Let him relate the course of events which led to the creation of Grange Hermitage.

> It was during my initial visit to the major wine-growing areas of Europe . . . that the idea of producing an Australian red wine capable of staying alive for a minimum of twenty years and comparable with those produced in Bordeaux first entered my mind.
>
> I was fortunate enough to be taken under the wing of Monsieur Christian Cruse, one of the most respected and highly qualified wine men of the old school of France at that time and he afforded me, among other things, the opportunity of tasting and evaluating Bordeaux wines forty and fifty years old, which were still sound and possessed magnificent bouquet and flavour.
>
> They were of tremendous value from an educational point of view and imbued me with a desire to attempt to do something to lift the rather mediocre standard of Australian red wine in general at that time.
>
> The method of production seemed fairly straightforward but with several unorthodox features and I felt it would only be a matter of undertaking a complete survey of vineyards to find the correct varietal grape material.
>
> Then with a modified approach to take account of differing conditions such as climate[,] soil[,] raw materials and techniques generally, it would not be impossible to produce a wine which could stand on its own feet throughout the world and would be capable of improvement year by year for a minimum of twenty years.
>
> In other words something different and lasting.
>
> The grape material used in Bordeaux consisted of four basic varieties, namely Cabernet Sauvignon, Cabernet Franc, Merlot and Malbec and these were used in varying percentages to make the Bordeaux wines.
>
> Only Cabernet Sauvignon and Malbec were available in South Australia at the time but a survey showed that they were in such short supply as to make them impracticable commercially— after all, the development of a new commercial wine, particularly of the high-grade range, depends on the quality and availability of the raw material, the maintenance of standard and the continuity of supply.
>
> I elected to use Hermitage or Shiraz only (which was in plentiful

> supply)—knowing full well that if I was careful enough in the choice of area and vineyard and coupled that with the correct production procedure I would be able to make the type and style of wine I wanted. If necessary, I could always use a small percentage of Cabernet and Malbec from our own Kalimna vineyard as a balancing factor to lift flavour and character. As it happened, this was not necessary—at least not in the early Granges. (Penfold's Wines Pty Ltd, *Rewards of Patience*, 1990)

What type of fruit was Schubert looking for? After deciding that the first experimental Grange would be sourced from Penfold's Grange vineyard at Magill and 'a private vineyard some distance south of Adelaide', he observed that 'both vineyards produced wines of distinctive varietal flavour and character with a great depth of colour and body weight' and by blending them Schubert would ensure that 'the outstanding characteristics of both vineyards' would be enhanced 'in an improved all-round wine eminently suitable for my purpose'.

Schubert continues.

> Accordingly during the 1951 vintage, the first Grange experimental wine was made, incorporating five new untreated oak hogsheads which I observed were used to such good effect in France . . . The objective was to produce a big full-bodied wine containing maximum extraction of all the components in the grape material used.

After ensuring that the 'grape material was sound and that the acid and sugar content was in balance and consistent with the style of wine as specified', Schubert sets out his parameters for Grange fruit.

> Using the Baumé scale, this was to be not less than 11.5 degrees and not more than 12 degrees with a total acidity of not less than 6.5 and not more than 7 grams per litre. With strict attention to detail and close surveillance, this was achieved.

As for the technique and equipment used in crushing and fermentation, this was, except for a heat exchanger, much in accordance with the standards of the time. He goes on.

> the must . . . and juice were pumped into a 12 tonne open concrete fermentation tank.
>
> During this operation, the must received a dose of sulphur dioxide to neutralise the wild yeasts and also an injection of pure yeast culture previously acclimatised to the level of sulphur dioxide used.
>
> The tank was filled to the exact level required. Boards, known as heading-down boards, were placed across the surface of the must in the open tank with a narrow gap between each board. These were secured by two strong pieces of timber placed across the boards and locked in position underneath four lugs built into the upper tank walls.
>
> Fermentation began almost immediately and as carbon dioxide gas pressure developed, the juice was forced through the narrow gaps between the boards, keeping the skins and other solids completely immersed underneath the surface.
>
> Although this was all fairly basic, it was important in achieving complete extraction, during fermentation particularly, if viewed in conjunction with other procedures which followed.
>
> For instance, it was thought that in order to obtain full extraction, a much longer period of fermentation and skin contact would be required, necessitating strict fermentation control.
>
> This was to be achieved by controlling the temperature generated by the fermentation, on the basis that the lower the temperature, the slower the rate of fermentation, since there would be a considerable reduction in the heat generated by the yeast in its frantic efforts to multiply and convert the grape sugars into alcohol.
>
> Of course, vice versa, by allowing the temperature to rise, an increase in the fermentation rate would result. Temperature control was to be achieved by incorporating a heat-exchanger in the process.

Schubert set his experimental wine to ferment over twelve days, thus requiring a sugar conversion rate of about one degree a day during fermentation and this was checked not only by regular hydrometer and temperature readings but also by using a graph showing the ideal fermentation straight line (twelve degrees reducing to nil over twelve days) compared with the actual fermentation line based on daily temperatures and Baumé readings of the fermenting juice. As Schubert says, 'a glance at the graph immediately showed the degree of heating or cooling required to maintain an even daily rate of fermentation over the period stipulated' and by pumping the warm juice through his heat exchanger then returning it to his fermentation tank Schubert could reduce the temperature sufficiently to conform to the graph.

After a slow and even ferment he then decided, before the end of the twelve-day period, to take 'the beautiful rich, dark ruby red, already showing above-average body, bouquet and fruit flavour' off its skins and out of the fermenter and to transfer it to cask, thereby allowing a slight increase in temperature which would allow fermentation to be completed.

The casks chosen were the five new untreated American oak hogsheads, which accommodated about 1350 litres of the new wine and a '1000 gallon [4550 litre] well-seasoned dry red cask', which contained the rest. The experimental wine in new small oak was to be compared at all stages of its barrel development with the control wine made in the then traditional Australian style. Meanwhile the skins and fermentation residue were pressed and the pressings put into thirty gallon casks for use later as topping-up material or if necessary as a 'balancing medium' for the experimental wine before bottling. The first Grange therefore duly completed its fermentation in small oak within twelve days 'as previously determined'.

What of the development of the wines?

> Within a month, vast differences became apparent . . . the control wine showed all the characteristics of a good well-made wine cast in the orthodox mould, the experimental wine was strikingly different. The volume of bouquet, comprising raw oak mixed with natural varietal fruit, was tremendous. The overall flavour was much more intense than the control, and for a big young wine, the balance was superb.

After further maturation for twelve months during which the wines were racked periodically and small amounts of tannic acid added,

> both wines were crystal clear with superb dark full rich colour and body—but there the similarity ended.
>
> The experimental wine was bigger in all respects . . . in bouquet, flavour and balance. The raw wood was not so apparent but the fruit characteristics had become pronounced and defined, with more than a faint suggestion of cranberry. It was almost as if the new wood had

> acted as a catalyst to release previously unsuspected flavours and aromas from the Hermitage grape.

Needless to say, Schubert was delighted with the wine.

> To my mind the marriage of all components had taken place and it required only the sealing of all these wonderful characteristics into bottles for the marriage to be consummated.

Thus after barrel maturation for eighteen months and no further treatment, the wine was bottled and binned away in cellars where the temperature was more or less constant at 15°C.

For several years, vintage after Grange vintage came and went, the identical winemaking method being pursued. There was one exception. In 1953, as Schubert decided that the requisite fruit balance was there, a Grange Cabernet was made from Kalimna fruit. Finally, however, in late 1956, as the Penfold's accountants were becoming anxious about the 'large amount of money lying idle in their underground cellars at Magill', a tasting of each vintage from 1951 to 1956 was arranged by the then managing director. The wraps were off; now it was time to reveal the finished product to the Sydney '*cognoscenti*'. They were horrified. Reactions in Adelaide were no better. Comments varied from 'crushed ants' to 'aphrodisiac'. It was, as Schubert relates, 'Grange's darkest hour'.

Despite support from one director of the company, Jeffrey Penfold Hyland (second son of Leslie), and other notable senior palates of the day such as George Fairbrother and Tony Nelson of Woodley Wines and some of the younger Turks such as Douglas Lamb and Max Lake, Schubert was mortified and received a final blow when the Board directed him to cease production of Grange Hermitage just before the 1957 vintage.

Stoically Schubert steered the Nelsonian course, in part obeying the direction, in that he ceased to buy new small oak casks, but continuing to make a reduced quantity of Grange in the remaining vintages of the 1950s, maturing it in the small oak used for earlier Granges. During an agonisingly long period of three years, Grange officially did not exist. It was a 'non-wine', condemned because it was unsaleable and also because this lack of acceptance and the criticism thus generated was deemed harmful to the company's reputation as a whole.

By the turn of the decade, however, as earlier Granges matured in bottle, the tide of public disfavour began to ebb and Schubert was restored to favour in the board's eyes, being instructed before vintage 1960 to make Grange once more. At last, in Schubert's own words, 'the prejudices were overcome'. For him it had been a decade of 'discovery, faith, doubt, humiliation and triumph', in which a classic Australian dry red, now world-renowned, had been born.

Schubert's experiment, though by far the most famous in Australia's red wine history, was not the only one carried out at Penfold's during the 1950s. Across the road at Auldana, John Davoren was also exploring dry red style. His solution was diametrically opposed to Schubert's and certainly more in keeping with contemporary dry-red thought, such as it was. Wines of elegant fruit, matured in large older oak casks, were how St Henri Claret evolved, 1957 being the first vintage released. It, too, was made predominantly from shiraz, until 1960 from fruit grown at Paracombe in the foothills north-east of Adelaide with, according to the dictates of wine style, cabernet sauvignon occasionally forming part of the blend and the name itself copied from old labels found in the Auldana loft. Later St Henri would become a blend of shiraz from Kalimna and other Barossa vineyards with moderate additions from Clare and Coonawarra.

Ideas for other red blends were also conceived at Penfold's during the late 1950s, wines which would make Penfold's the masters of what would be called Australia's 'cellar style' dry reds, for that company—with extensive vineyards not only at Magill (Grange and Auldana), Modbury, the Barossa (Kalimna), McLaren Vale, the Riverland and Coonawarra but also with the technical expertise of winemakers such as Schubert and Davoren—was to set new standards of quality for South Australian dry reds during the 1960s.

Yet not only Penfold's were introducing new techniques of winemaking and wine styles, there were other companies with ears finely tuned for whisperings of innovation.

The stainless steel pressure fermentation tank is hardly a thing of beauty, but for Australian white winemakers of the early 1950s it seemed to signal joy forever. Imported by Orlando and installed just in time for the 1953 vintage, the first such tank revolutionised the making of white wine in this country. Control of fermentation drove away the 'straw oxidation' bitterness of previous white wine and suddenly there was the taste of the grape, which makers of quality white wine have treasured ever since. Yalumba quickly followed and though, as with any innovation, there were those who rejected it, preferring the old ways, white wine was never to be the same again.

Yet that tank, startling though it had been in 1953, was superseded virtually within the decade, replaced by must-chilling and slow fermentation of white wine, which, perhaps even more than the tank, preserved the delicate aromaticity of the rhine riesling grape. And the first white wine made in that tank? The Orlando Barossa Special Riesling 1953 without any doubt whatsoever is the progenitor of modern Australian rhine riesling style.

There were other events of this post-war era which would have profound significance in the immediate future of the wine industry. Not the least was another development which had occurred as a result of the war, the generalisation of the practice of wine being bottled, labelled and marketed by its producer. Of course the large national companies had done this for many years with part of their wine, but much was still shipped in bulk for bottling by the local licenced trade and all export wine continued to be so shipped. Now in the years after the Second World War, winery bottling and labelling became the rule rather than the exception as winemakers started to become aware of the need to establish a brand.

As it had in the 1930s, the federal government continued its love-hate relationship with the wine industry by abolishing the wine export bounty in 1947, rationalising its decision by pointing to improved wine prices both at home and overseas. The bounty had become a substantial fund, growing rapidly in the war years due to obviously low rates of export. Thus a substantial part of this bounty found its way into consolidated revenue, but a million dollars was spared and in 1955 used to establish the Australian Wine Research Institute, an investment of incalculable worth for the future of the nation's wine industry.

The federal government again struck in 1951, increasing the excise on fortifying spirit and thereby disheartening winemakers by making their most popular product yet more expensive, but in 1953 the tax burden was eased somewhat when an amendment to the *Income*

Tax Assessment Act (s31A) allowed winemakers to retain maturing stocks of wine at a nominal valuation per litre. Thus the overall quality of Australian wines could improve by longer maturation in cask and bottle, more funds being released in the mean time for winery expansion.

The major politico-legal event of this decade, however, was the removal of beer rationing and the liberalisation of licensing laws as the result of a long royal commission. For the wine industry the immediate effect was disastrous. Consumption of fortified wine, its chief product, immediately declined and beer became king, though the way was now open for an increasingly affluent public to visit an increasing number of continental (especially Italian) restaurants, which due to postwar immigration policies were to become more common as the decade of the 1950s progressed. No longer did the majority of Australians wish to celebrate only at home with their typical tipple of beer and scotch for the men and a little sweet sherry for the women. Gradually the restaurant became an important meeting place for them—not only with their friends but with Australian table wines. And if the wines consumed would not perhaps have delighted the table wine purist as much as, say, a Hunter Valley dry red, then the wine choice of these new restaurant patrons was not fortified either. More likely it was a bottle of that latest craze—Barossa Pearl, that slightly sweet, petillant, party wine sensation of the late 1950s which, in much the same way as Rhinegold (that slightly sweet still white sensation of the 1940s and early 1950s) had done during the Second World War, introduced countless thousands of Australians to wine at a time when wine consumption had slipped to 5.8 litres per head. Pearl wine, fermented in pressurised tanks by the Charmat process, stormed the wine market in the late 1950s and early 1960s and in the minds of many winemakers at that time subsidised the minuscule yet growing quantities of dry reds, which were just beginning to find favour with an increasing number of younger sophisticated consumers.

Thus after the Great Depression, the Second World War and its aftermath of austerity, in an era when several wine companies such as Lindeman's (1943), Penfold's (1944), Orlando (1947), Yalumba (1949), Seppelt (1951) and Hardy (1953) had passed their centennial milestones, a whole new generation of Australians influenced, though perhaps they would have vigorously denied it, by newly imported European culture, had begun to experiment with 'lifestyle'.

Like a stylus stuck in the worn groove of an ancient record, history has a habit of repeating itself. After the Second World War just as after the First, irrigation areas emerged, Loxton in South Australia and Robinvale in Victoria. It seemed the politicians had not learnt the lessons of overproduction, but in the shining light of a newly won victory, who dared blame them for their optimism?

There was cause for optimism, too, for long-neglected Coonawarra. The faithful few who knew of the district and its reds were to be rewarded in the early 1950s as new faces and more importantly new money and determination reawakened the region. Not that it ever had quite suffered the fate of Rip Van Winkle, the Redman family in conjunction with Woodley's had seen to that. In fact in 1946 Woodley's had bought the Coonawarra estate of Milne & Co., the Adelaide distillers, including the classic John Riddoch cellars, then in a dilapidated and filthy condition, and fifty-two hectares of vineyard for £9000 ($18 000). The wine of this new estate, Chateau Comaum, as it was called, was made by Bill Redman and the winery was managed by his son, Owen. Unfortunately its first vintage, 1946, was a disaster devastated by downy mildew, hitherto unknown in the district.

Woodley's, however, were not to be long-term proprietors in Coonawarra, even though they now controlled the whole of the wine made there, for Redman's continued to supply all their wine to Woodley's including the famous St Adele 1947. Red table wine sales were still slow and perhaps Woodley's were finding Coonawarra too unprofitable. Perhaps a rivalry had begun to develop. In 1948 Owen Redman resigned his managerial duties to concentrate on his own vineyard. Subsequently, Chateau Comaum was placed on the market.

Enter now, in 1951, a Jewish immigrant family, albeit in Australia for the preceding thirty-eight years. At its head, aged fifty-nine years, was Samuel Wynn who had been fascinated by the wine industry since his arrival in Melbourne as a young man of twenty-one in 1913. Though it was an era when local interest in wine was confined to an affluent few, Samuel prospered as a wine merchant and restaurateur in the 1920s. At the same time, at the behest of one Reginald Collins, he had invested heavily in his first wine-producing venture, Australian Wines Ltd, whose Romalo cellars in Magill had been set up in 1919 by a French chef and former manager of Auldana, Leon Mazure, to produce sparkling wines. By 1920 the business was struggling and Collins, a man of lavish lifestyle, took over Romalo. In 1925, when the combination of the federal wine bounty and imperial preference threw open the doors of the British market to Australian wine, Collins, with Wynn's money, built a Barossa winery near Angaston called Wynvale as a sop to his business colleague. By 1927 the trade collapsed and three years later the winery was sold to Yalumba. Collins departed the scene and Wynn was left with Australian Wines Ltd and its champagne-making operation. That Wynn survived and prospered was a tribute to his own business acumen, but nevertheless by 1935 Australian Wines Ltd was crushing 2000 tonnes of grapes. Later in the 1930s, Wynn re-entered the export trade with considerable profit, by 1939 exporting over half a million litres of wine a year to London and when the Second World War slowed exports to a trickle he could then turn to Romalo sparkling wine to help slake the considerable thirst of our American allies. In 1945, upon his discharge from the RAAF, Wynn's eldest son David assumed part of the managerial responsibility and during the next few years Samuel Wynn gradually handed over full control. The new Wynn began a policy of popularising wine by introducing the returnable half-gallon (2.25 litre) flagon and also stressing the importance of wine as an accompaniment to food.

David Wynn had heard of the Coonawarra estate before. In late 1945 it had been the subject of a report by one J. L. Williams, a Roseworthy lecturer who proposed a joint venture with him. This had not eventuated and when the property, considerably refurbished under the Redman aegis, again came on to the market in 1951, the Wynns, father and son, were definitely interested. More reports were commissioned, not very favourable, and Sammy even explored the idea of forming a consortium of wine companies for its purchase to run it as a non-profit-making venture, but others declined that opportunity. Finally the Wynns decided to go it alone and on 19 July 1951 an agreement for its sale was reached at the price of £22 000 ($44 000). From their very first day of ownership, the Wynns decided that Coonawarra deserved pride of place in Australia's wine hierarchy and that their Coonawarra Estate would not only hold premier position in wine quality, it would look the part as well. So the name Coonawarra rose to the top of the market, impinging most definitely on Australia's wine psyche, for which the Wynns must receive credit not only for the quality of some of those early wines, but in part for the quality of the label, as elegant and fresh in design today as it was over thirty-five years ago. The paradox of this situation can readily be appreciated when it is realised that, scarcely five years before the purchase, the Coonawarra name was recognised by very few and then, one senses, only reluctantly acknowledged for the first time on Woodley's labels.

So began the surge to success of Wynn's Coonawarra Estate . . . famous clarets from the beginning, magnificent cabernet from the mid-1950s on and the occasional unique wine such as Michael Hermitage 1955. Yet there were sporadic blots on the escutcheon. Coonawarra is not always a kind parent. Even today its wines are sometimes thin or acid or volatile. Then, adverse vintage conditions were much harder to combat and technical and (one suspects) organoleptic standards were lower. Wynn's Coonawarra reds were no exception to the rule, but by the criteria of the time, they were not only marvellous to look at, they were a revelation to drink.

By the mid-1950s, Coonawarra had become a buzz word among the Adelaide wine establishment. Though Redman's continued to supply Woodley and would do so until 1956, inquiries were received from Hardy's and Yalumba as well as Reynella and Leo Buring, but it was Mildara which showed the greatest persistence. Buying 2250 litres of Redman wine in 1954, that company immediately requested more. It was not to be had. So to ensure its supply, Mildara commissioned the Redmans to buy twelve hectares of terra rossa soil for $7000 on the company's behalf. Ron Haselgrove, then chairman of the Mildara board, had no doubt about the future of Coonawarra nor the wisdom of his purchase. And now, neither had the Redmans. They too, using schoolboy French, incorporated the former family partnership into Rouge Homme Wines Pty Ltd with the intention of marketing their own wines for the very first time, bottling in that same year 550 cases of red (a minute amount by modern standards) and more importantly for the future of the fledgling company selling it within six months at $4.20 a case. Bill Redman, then aged sixty-seven and the patriarch of the region, retired in the same year after fifty-three years of virtually continuous involvement with Coonawarra wine. Rouge Homme Wines was to increase production steadily until at the time of its sale to Lindeman's in 1965 it was offering 4000 cases of wine to an appreciative public. In that comparatively short period of corporate winemaking independence, Rouge Homme's winemaking standards were extremely high.[1]

After the obvious success of Wynn's and the initial Mildara purchase the first Coonawarra land rush began. Mildara again bought in 1957, this time fourteen hectares for $20 000, and Penfold's were also showing great interest in the region, acquiring Sharam's Block, partly planted with old shiraz vines, in 1960. Backed by the big battalions, Coonawarra was at last on the road to success.

At this time there was a new face, or more accurately a rather old one, in the Barossa Valley also. We had left Leo Buring being shown the Lindeman's door by the disappointed Commercial Banking Co. of Sydney in 1930, having failed to trade Lindeman's out of its huge financial morass. He remained in Sydney and in 1931 began a wine merchandising partnership with Reginald Mowatt, the former Seppelt's winemaker at Great Western. This firm was to become quite successful, popularising Rhinegold, a semi-sweet Hunter Valley semillon, in the late 1930s and especially during and after the Second World War. In 1941 it acquired the respected Melbourne-based wine merchant Matthew Lang & Co. and in 1945 moved into the Barossa, buying the Orange Grove winery of the Hoffman family, substantially extending and endowing it with French 'chic' by way of turrets. So Chateau Leonay, named after Buring's Sydney home, was born. In 1955, at the age of seventy-nine, he was joined by a then recent graduate of Roseworthy, John Vickery, whose contribution to Australian rhine riesling style during the 1960s and 1970s was outstanding. Leo Buring died in 1961 and by a paradox of fate his company was acquired a year later by none other than Lindeman's.

Just as the 1840s had brought great numbers of willing German settlers into the Barossa, so the 1940s introduced others, often, one imagines, rather unwillingly, as prisoners of war and other internees became 'guests' of His Majesty's Australian government. Most were repatriated at war's end. One internee who wished to remain was Hermann Thumm, a qualified winemaker who had been interned by the British in 1941 while setting up a winery in Persia. In 1947 he bought a ruined winery near Lyndoch that had once been owned by the defunct Adelaide Wine Company, making both white and red table wines, some with a degree of sweetness that was especially popular among his patrons. By 1960, Chateau Yaldara was well on the way to becoming one of the showplaces of the Barossa.

In the same year a rather more willing young German arrived, brought to Australia by the South Australian Winegrowers Co-Operative Ltd (Kaiser Stuhl) to assist in the production of sparkling wine. His name was Wolf Blass. Though he had trained in champagne, his contribution to Australian wine was to be much more important.

Like their colleagues in the Barossa Valley, most of the Clare winemakers had relied upon fortified wines in the 1940s but by 1953 a much lower level of exports, removal of beer rationing and the increase in the excise on fortifying spirit had all combined to present a very bleak picture to makers of fortifieds. Though sherry was a viable commodity, port was impossible to sell, as Australians turned in their thousands to cascades of unrationed beer.

So at Clare Stanley returned to making dry red and some white, being fortunate that in Lindeman's, with its extensive Sydney market, it had a major client keenly interested in its dry red style. It was fortunate too that after the war it had established considerable areas of vineyard on a sharefarming basis. So now it could revert to dry reds (and whites, for it had a considerable area of riesling) without too much pain.Even those vine types used primarily for fortification such as grenache could be grafted over to more commercially acceptable varieties. Stanley had other clients interested in its reds and whites also—familiar names such as Penfold, Seppelt and Hardy, but Lindeman's predominated and that, for Stanley in the difficult period of transition from fortified to table wine in the 1950s, was important. It was the difference between a possible demise and stability. But for how long should such an arrangement continue?

For Quelltaler, the end of the Second World War and the ensuing years brought both consolidation and bereavement. Vineyards previously leased were bought, and the second generation of the Buring and Sobels families yielded inevitably to the third. Rudi Buring died in 1950 and Talbot Sobels four years later, but in Australia's sherry age, Granfiesta importantly retained its popularity.

War's end and the continuance of the fortified boom until 1953 brought an unusual prosperity to the struggling Clarevale Co-operative. In 1946 Jim Barry, a young winemaking graduate of Roseworthy managed the winery, expanding the crush to 2200 tonnes by 1952. The following year saw the collapse of the boom and almost the end of the Co-operative when a major Sydney customer went into bankruptcy. Fortunately Clarevale managed to salvage one plank from the wreck, the bankrupt merchant's wine licence and the business. Thus the Co-op's Sydney branch was established. One of its major clients was the Taylor family, which had developed a considerable trade in Clarevale wine after the war. Their subsequent move to Clare in the late 1960s would lead to the construction of a large winery at Auburn in the southern end of the Clare Valley.

In McLaren Vale also it was a time of both expansion and consolidation. In 1938 K. T. (Ken) Hardy had become managing director and chairman of Thomas Hardy & Sons, steering the company through the war years which, for Hardy's like most other companies, were made easier by the spending power of the stream of American servicemen based in Australia and on leave from Pacific battlefronts. Later, in 1953, Hardy's celebrated their centenary. It was a time for expansion of its Cyrilton winery and vineyards at Waikerie in the Riverland. Time too for the retirement of senior directors such as Colin Haselgrove (to become managing director of Walter Reynell & Sons) and for the fourth generation of Hardys to become involved in senior management, as T. W. Hardy (1948) and David Hardy (1959), sons of Tom Mayfield Hardy killed in the *Kyeema* disaster, were appointed directors of the company. Regrettably in 1960, there was also a notable departure, Roger Warren, chief winemaker and blender of the legendary Hardy Cabernets of the 1950s, died. For Hardy's it was time to recall the Barossa's German heritage and to rename its Dorrien winery Siegersdorf. In the years to come its Siegersdorf Rhine Riesling would become one of Australia's most popular whites.

Elsewhere in McLaren Vale it was business as usual as small makers such the Kay family at Amery continued to make fortifieds and those heavy 'ferruginous' reds destined for the London trade, but even in McLaren Vale there were stirrings for change. Some small makers such as Osborn were even thinking of their own label and

Ben Chaffey at Seaview was carving a reputation for cabernet reds. But in McLaren Vale innovations sped snail-like as the tradition of fortifieds and 'ferruginous' continued.

At this time, except for the new rieslings and party 'fizz' of the Barossa, the trickle of great red from Wynn's Rouge Homme in Coonawarra and Max Schubert's revolutionary Grange, the winemaking prescription in South Australia had been unchanged for forty years, but the boom was about to arrive.

In New South Wales the Hunter Valley, its vineyard area ever shrinking (down to 440 hectares in 1947), battled on, still loyal to table wines. Yet at a time when eighty-five per cent of Australian production was fortified and only 7.5 per cent still table wine, Maurice O'Shea at Mount Pleasant achieved some of his greatest triumphs, wines such as the Mountain series (1937-44), the Henrys (1942-52), Pinot Hermitage 1952 and Richard 1954, virtually all made completely of shiraz, surely emphasising the suitability of that grape to the Hunter Valley. O'Shea died in 1956. He had, like his friend Roger Warren of Hardy's, an excellent palate and was a consummate blender of wines. Max Lake, writing a few years later after O'Shea's death, poses a pertinent question in *Hunter Wine* when he asks, 'would it be presumptuous to suggest that O'Shea follows only Busby in his influence on Australian wine in general and Hunter wine in particular?'

Death claimed other veterans of the Valley at this time. Within three years of O'Shea, both Bob Elliott and Dan Tyrrell were dead. Tyrrell, who started as a boy of fifteen, completed seventy-five vintages before his death in 1959.

For Lindeman's, the corporate death of receivership was removed in 1947, when the last of the debt due to its bankers was repaid after twenty-four years of default. The company was restructured, new shares being issued to loyal long-serving employees such as the cellar manager, Bert Bear, and the interest of the Lindeman family, no longer serving the company in any active executive capacity, reduced. Like some corporate phoenix, the company once more rose quickly to pre-eminence, exploiting the postwar boom in fortified reds and, when that bubble burst in 1952, soliciting the sweet tooth of its patrons with a white muscat-based sweet wine marketed as Montilla Sweet Sherry, much to the chagrin of rival makers, who vainly tried to explain that that was not how sweet sherry was made. So profitable and successful was it that Lindeman's was listed on the Stock Exchange in 1953. In the meantime its Ben Ean winery in the Hunter Valley could carry on with its relatively small production of Cawarra table wine (no more than ten per cent of the company's sales at the time), and even the production of an occasional new line such as Ben Ean Moselle (1956). This was another Lindeman's wine which was produced in its early days primarily from Stanley fruit. Even here, however, there were innovations, a pressure tank fermenter being installed in 1956. Lindeman's, as the company with an established reputation for quality table wine, was also beginning to notice a greater sophistication in the Sydney market, which was increasing demand for such wine. This in turn led to more buying trips to Clare and other vineyard areas in South Australia. By 1960 Lindeman's had once more become a major force in the Australian wine industry.

In Victoria the few outposts of wine struggled on, though in the Goulburn Valley the first new vineyard for many years, Osicka's near Graytown, was established in 1955. At nearby Tabilk, in 1960, the Purbricks celebrated the centenary of the chateau Tahbilk, whose Marsanne had been served during the coronation festivities seven years earlier.

Great Western continued to produce Australia's best sparkling wine and, almost as a hobby, some of Australia's best reds, complex long-living blends of cabernet sauvignon, shiraz, malbec, esparte (mataro) and meunier such as J13 and J34 of 1953 and the early precursors of Moyston Claret and Chalambar Burgundy. The genius of Colin Preece had come to fruition.

In the hot north-east of the state, the sudden demise of the fortified market saw several large vineyards grubbed out late in the 1950s—Fairfield, Graham's and Burgoyne's Mount Ophir all disappeared—and other makers such as Morris and Bailey returned to the huge dry-red styles so natural to that area, while continuing to produce smaller quantities of those regional nectars, liqueur muscat and tokay. Of the reds, so firm and unyielding was their constitution that it was said they required at least twenty years in bottle and even then were fit only for heroes. Others said they were both wine and food with a cigar thrown in for good measure.

In the north-west, Mildara, as we have seen, had turned its attention to sherries and also to table wines, enthused by the prospects of Coonawarra and by the excellence of their yellow label Cabernet Shiraz reds, which were usually blends of wine bought from the Southern Vales, Hunter Valley and Coonawarra, put together by Ron Haselgrove.

In far-off Tasmania, an intermittent flicker of interest in table wine was once again evident as a French migrant, Jean Miguet, struggled to establish a very small vineyard in the face of government indifference. The flame would not yet be all-consuming, but neither would it be again extinguished.

That wine tastes were inching towards change due to a wider European mix of the Australian population, easier economic times and an increasing Anglo-Celtic understanding of the proper use of wine, there was little doubt. Busby and Hubert de Castella would have rejoiced. Though markets had swung violently during the decade, the 1950s ended on a note of optimism. The 1960s and the red-wine boom would remove the wine industry from a long period of stagnation and provide a long-needed impetus for growth.

[1] In particular 1959 was an outstanding Rouge Homme year, marked by the superb quality of its Cabernet, which when tasted nearly twenty years later had matured into a brick red minty magnificence.

THIRTEEN

The 1960s—the red wine boom and the road to recovery

Any optimism among wine producers at the end of the 1950s was scarcely justified by wine consumption figures, or in the first years of the new decade by the economy as a whole. From 7.3 litres of wine per head of population in 1950, consumption had slumped to 5.1 litres by 1960 with no improvement at all in the following recession year.

The 1961 recession was but a slight hiccup in the upward mobility of the 'lucky country'. If the 1850s had been the age of gold, the 1960s were certainly the decade of the motor car. Full employment was the catchcry of a government that seemed imperishable. By the mid-1960s Australians had never been more prosperous. With that little extra money they could afford, after 1961, not only that car, but the occasional weekend pursuit of pleasure. For some, as yet very few, it was perhaps a visit to vineyards to taste table wines, which were increasing in popularity, as statistics were beginning to show. Compared to all fortified wine, table wine (including sparkling wine) had taken a junior role in 1959-60, sales being 13.4 million litres as opposed to 44.5 million litres. Six years later, in 1964-5, though sales of fortifieds had declined but slightly (43.42 million litres) table wines were showing a strong upward trend (22.05 million litres). In particular, dry red sales had risen from 5.96 million litres to 9.58 million litres and dry white from 3.42 million to 5.56 million.

This was an era when prime ministers drank table wine in public and publicly endorsed its quality (a far cry from later times). Indeed the 'Menzies' Claret, as it was unofficially called, proved the inspiration for a successful series of signature wines marketed by Yalumba during the 1960s and 1970s.

In a budding age of promotion and a public yearning for information about wine, the prime minister was not the only one to extol table wine in public. For the first time Australia suddenly had a regular wine press. The *Bulletin* magazine's Cellarmaster column was instituted in 1962 by a young migrant called Len Evans, at that time in his early thirties, who had already spent seven years 'careering' around Australia in occupations as diverse as dingo fencing, glass washing, script writing and beverage management. His wine writing certainly helped the wine industry domestically at that time and later; further writing and wine judging would help it internationally, as well as gaining him world wide fame as a wine expert and critic. But then he wrote his Cellarmaster columns with a verve and wit hardly ever seen in the more serious wine writing of the present time, believing, as he did, that wine should be fun and should be promoted as such. No wonder then that in 1965 he was appointed inaugural director of the Australian Wine Bureau, the first domestic promotional body for the wine industry, financially assisted by the Wine and Brandy Producers Association.

There were other publicists of the industry at this time, larger-than-life figures such as Max Lake, 'a legend in his lifetime', as he once described himself, writing such wine works as *Hunter Wine* and *Classic Wines of Australia* as well as busily planting his beloved 'Folly', the first new Hunter vineyard since the Second World War.

Indeed the public thirst for books on wine seemed unshakeable. Lifestyle and the consumer society had arrived to stay, at least for an indefinite period.

For the youth of Australia it was also a time to travel, as thousands made their way to Europe on their own versions of the eighteenth-century grand tour, often for more than a year, basing themselves in London and journeying as far and as often as time and their meagre budgets would allow. Though such travel did not breed wine connoisseurs, perhaps not connoisseurs of anything, it certainly countered the insularity of Australian life and inured young Australians to the customs of European life, amongst which was the civilised use of table wine as an everyday beverage, a practice with which their parents were as a rule totally unfamiliar.

Everywhere in the 1960s there was renewed energy as old established companies threw off the shackles of depression, the siege mentality of war and confidently prepared for expansion.

In South Australia the planning and planting had begun in the dawn of the 1960s with new and, paradoxically, old visions of quality. For Yalumba in 1961 it was all uphill from the slopes of Angaston to the more remote reaches of Pewsey Vale, which had not seen vines since 1930, when economics forced the abandonment of the last of the original Pewsey Vale vineyard planted eighty years before. The new vines, cabernet sauvignon and rhine riesling, would become as famous as their predecessors had been, and would unwittingly pioneer the move later in the decade to cool climate viticulture in the loftier areas above the Barossa Valley and the Adelaide Plain. Others noted this upward direction also. Orlando acquired Steingarten (an apt name) in 1962 and like Yalumba planted riesling. On this site German ancestry and a German varietal combined to evoke German methods—close planting on sparse country in the fashion of the Mosel. Steingarten was to be followed in 1969 by the planting of a major vineyard in the Eden Valley with thirty-four hectares of rhine riesling and seventeen of gewurzttraminer.

Lindeman's now arrived in the Barossa Valley for the first time, having bought Leo Buring Pty Ltd in 1961 quite cheaply. Two other reasons besides price were responsible for this advantageous purchase. First was the death of Leo and the fact his company relied virtually exclusively on Rinegolde which had been largely supplanted in market favour by the new tank-fermented 'pearl' wines.

Lindeman's soon ensured that a sparkling Rinegolde came into being. But more importantly for the future of quality table wine, the company encouraged John Vickery to produce from superb Eden Valley fruit a marvellous line of Leo Buring rhine rieslings, which continue to this day. There had been other Barossa developments also.

In 1956 the South Australian Grapegrowers' Co-operative Ltd, established as a means of survival by the straitened Barossa growers in 1931, appointed Ian Hickinbotham as winemaker; until that time he had served Wynn's as winemaker in Coonawarra. That cooperative, hitherto a producer and supplier of bulk wine for export (when circumstances permitted) and sale to other companies, now embarked on a change in direction. The move to the production of dry red in flagons and the new label, 'Kaiser Stuhl', introduced in 1958, were immediately successful. So too was the production of the new immensely popular pearl-wine styles for sale to other companies, a measure which provided the cash flow needed to ensure the continued production of an extensive range of wine styles, which in turn would secure a market base broad enough ultimately to ensure independence for the company and prevent reliance on one or two wines. Soon the cooperative needed new staff for its sparkling wine production, a requirement which, as we have seen, introduced a young Wolf Blass to the rapidly changing Australian wine scene. Ian Hickinbotham left Kaiser Stuhl in 1964, to be followed by Yugoslav-born George Kolarovich who in his turn was to make Kaiser Stuhl and its lightly sweet grenache-based rosé one of the marketing successes of the 1960s.

Wolf Blass also left Kaiser Stuhl in 1964, becoming a consultant winemaker to several smaller wineries in the Barossa for five years. Blass began to make his own reds in 1966, his first consisting of Langhorne Creek shiraz and Great Western malbec. Significantly it was a blended red, matured in new Nevers oak, two winemaking techniques which were to gain national fame for Blass in the ensuing decade when reds were largely out of fashion. But in the late 1960s a consultant's life was a hard one, with the result that in 1969 he began work for Tolley Scott & Tolley as technical director, retaining the right to make his own wines.

In the same year he had bought a two hectare block four kilometres east of Nuriootpa as a future winery site.

Blass's new employer, a prominent producer of brandy in the

1940s and 1950s, which had been bought by the UK company Distillers Ltd in 1961, had also sensed the market swing to table wines and began to plan for it in the mid-1960s, extensively renovating its cellars at Nuriootpa and buying new vineyard land at Woodbury in the Eden Valley and at Waikerie in the Riverland. Blass was an essential part of this strategy, producing many fine reds during his four years with the company.

There were other moves in the Eden Valley also. In 1965 Hamilton's bought the old Penfold winery at Springton and Cyril Henschke at Keyneton was rapidly building a national reputation for his superb shiraz reds, Mount Edelstone and Hill of Grace, while at Saltram a few years before a new winemaking face had arrived, Peter Lehmann taking over from Bryan Dolan in 1959 and beginning a twenty-year stint as winemaker that was to bring Saltram to the forefront in Barossa red style.

In McLaren Vale, a region accustomed to large wine exports since the 1890s, the 1960s saw such exports fall into the doldrums and a definite lack of enthusiasm in the British market. The recessive tendencies indicated by the lack of export sales worried wine exporters to such an extent that they all but ceased buying grapes at this time, with the result that in 1964 a surplus of 10 000 tonnes glutted the market. The Emu Wine Company, which had strictly controlled its fruit purchases since 1961, now acquired the Tatachilla winery—originally built by Alexander Kelly's son John in 1903 to handle the glut of that year—and promptly closed it down. Penfold's also closed its McLaren Vale winery and when Hardy's, often the saviour of the region in times of oversupply, declined to help on this occasion, the growers were left with no alternative other than the formation of a cooperative. So the Southern Vales Co-Operative Winery Ltd was formed in 1965, crushing over 2700 tonnes of grapes in its first vintage. Perhaps more importantly for the future of the area, many smaller growers, disappointed by the attitude of the larger wine companies, began to investigate the feasibility of making their own wine, especially as they were now beginning to hear of the domestic market's increasing interest in dry red. It was not that the region had ever lacked small makers, but an opportunity for independence was certainly beckoning.

One such small maker who caught the market tide at this time was D'Arry Osborn. He now seized his chance and was suitably rewarded in 1967 when his 'burgundy' (a blend of grenache and shiraz) stormed the Australian wine show circuit, winning seven trophies and twenty-five gold medals.

Another name which came to fame in the 1960s (and remains nationally prominent) was Seaview, a small producer of rhine riesling, a very much sought-after cabernet sauvignon and minute quantities of sauvignon blanc. More importantly for pockets than palates at the time, it also produced and sold bulk dry red for home bottling, a practice which was to become quite customary amongst the wine *aficionados* of the time. The red wine boom, which was soon to make such transactions a blessed memory for non-irrigation area reds, had not quite taken off.

Yet a year later (late 1967) it most certainly had. Mildara was releasing its first Coonawarra reds, including its famous 1963 cabernet sauvignon (nick-named 'peppermint Pattie'), to an enthusiastic public at $2.05 a bottle, a price previously unheard-of, except for hard-to-get Grange Hermitage. 'Pattie' was rationed too, even to those who travelled to the company's headquarters in far-away Merbein. In October 1967 I recall queuing at the winery at Merbein (Mildara had no cellar-door sales at Coonawarra then) and being most gratified to be allowed to buy a quarter of a dozen. 'Pattie', so called because of a voluminous peppermint character on nose and palate, perhaps caused by a combination of young vines, new oak maturation and fermentation finished in that same medium, was the 1960s sensation. Though 'Pattie' aged well, she was very much an individual; none of her successors ever quite exploded upon the palate with that unique peppermint impact.

Mildara rapidly built up its land-holdings at Coonawarra during the 1960s, so much so that by decade's end it was second only in vineyard size to Wynn's (342 hectares to 440 hectares).

By this time, however, another event of profound importance to the area had already occurred. Rouge Homme Wines Pty Ltd had entered the decade upon the crest of that wave of excellence created by the magnificent cabernet sauvignon of 1959. But nature at Coonawarra is a great leveller and seldom allows its vignerons to bask in an excess of glory for very long. After the peak of 1959 came the abyss of 1961 when an early summer frost destroyed all but fifteen tonnes of that 1961 vintage. Yet Rouge Homme were kept extremely busy by the management demands of the Mildara and Penfold's vineyards in the district. As well, other companies including Hardy's, an old and valued customer, and a newly revivified Lindeman's, spurred on by the energetic direction of Ray Kidd, all eagerly sought supplies of the now famous Rouge Homme red. Perhaps it all became too much for the Redman family, for the management arrangement with Mildara was terminated in 1962.

But if the stress of management eased somewhat, the demand for wholesale supply of Rouge Homme red did not. Lindeman's was especially persistent. It even offered Rouge Homme a loan so that it could expand both its vineyard and its production, while assuring the family that it would take all the wine that was produced. This offer was refused by Rouge Homme as it was trying to reduce workload, not increase it. This rebuff only renewed Lindeman's zeal. It had now become a suitor and soon made an attractive offer to buy. This time the Redman family did not refuse. So in June 1965 Lindeman's became the owners of Rouge Homme; the transaction included all buildings (the winery and two houses), plant, wine stocks bulk and bottled, thirty hectares of vineyard and, most importantly for Lindeman's, now planning for expansion, 160 unplanted hectares of the famous red bank, the terra rossa soil that set Coonawarra reds apart from the rest.

The Lindeman purchase did not spell finis for the Redman name in Coonawarra. Not only was Jock Redman, a nephew of Bill, managing Wynn's, but within weeks of the completion of the sale Owen had bought sixteen hectares of established shiraz vines from an old Redman grower, Arthur Hoffman. For the first time in nearly sixty years of family winemaking, the name 'Redman' would appear on a Coonawarra label.

For others, the Lindeman move meant changes also. Especially for Eric Brand, Bill Redman's son-in-law, hitherto as much an orchardist as a vigneron, it was a step into the relatively unknown world of winemaking—a move brilliantly achieved in the fine Coonawarra year of 1966 with a little winemaking help from a friend, Owen Redman, while Hardy's, anxious no doubt to ensure a continuity of supply of Coonawarra red now that the Rouge Homme source had ceased, gave practical assistance in the form of a crusher. 'Laira', as Eric Brand called his estate, made a brilliant start with its 1966 shiraz and a lasting impression upon a growing number of young tourists who came to the region seeking its famous wines, seemingly in vain, until they saw the wooden sign that betokened the only vineyard in the region during the period 1966 to 1969 open for sales to the public. So much for the tourist attitudes of large wine companies in Coonawarra at that time! In 1969 Owen Redman opened his Redbank Winery, having made his first three vintages (1966-8) at Laira and with Mildara (erected 1962) and Laira (1966) became the third new winery in Coonawarra that decade.

Obviously Coonawarra had now emerged from its dark age.

Of course this re-awakening of the Coonawarra region and its subsequent national fame had caused a concomitant boom in land prices, too much for some, and so certain corporate eyes began to look elsewhere for similar land but dissimilar prices.

Seppelt's, sensing the change in national mood towards table wine and aware that its then existing vineyards were more attuned to the production of brandy and fortifieds than delicate table wines, cast about for a way out of what might become an ever-diminishing market. In 1963, based on a favourable report by Karl Seppelt, a decision was taken, in hindsight quite far-reaching, to buy 356 hectares of land some eighty kilometres north-west of Coonawarra in an area whose viticultural worth had never been previously tested. True, Keppoch, as the place was called, had soils not dissimilar to those of Coonawarra; it also stood on a limestone subsoil above a watertable and shared the same modest rainfall. As an earlier government report had said, 'the deeper sites of the terra rossa soils should make first-class garden [i.e. vineyard] soils'. So in that same year an experimental vineyard was planted, followed in the next year by more substantial plantings of varieties suitable for dry red, for that was the wine type expected to boom. By 1965 nearly fifty hectares were under vine.

Other corporate eyes were also focussed firmly on Seppelt's pioneer vineyard in Padthaway-Keppoch, as the district had come to be called. In October 1968 Hardy's, acting on a 1967 report of David Hardy, also took the plunge, buying some 217 hectares for $215 000 and planting twenty-six hectares of red grapes in the ensuing year, most of which was decimated by frost a few months later. Importantly, the vines were trellised with an innovation—the mechanical harvester—in mind.

In the same year Lindeman's, though by now firmly established at Coonawarra, also made the decision to go north to Padthaway, buying the first of several properties in the area and planting in 1970 vines whose first produce when marketed a few years later as Padthaway Villages could scarcely be considered a commercial success.

Another smaller concern planting land at Padthaway during the late 1960s was the Reynella-based winery Glenloth. Its Padthaway presence was brief, for the Sydney brewer, Toohey's Ltd bought it and the McLaren Vale winery, Seaview, in 1971, acquiring Wynn's in the following year, which had coincidentally managed the Padthaway vineyard of Glenloth. The result of these tortuous corporate machinations was that the Glenloth Padthaway vineyard ultimately became known as Wynn's.

What was the *raison d'etre* of the Padthaway-Keppoch region? For Seppelt's and for Karl Seppelt, its national vineyard manager at the time, it was the inspiration to take that company away from the brandy and fortified wine market which would stagnate and ultimately decline, to an area which it confidently predicted could supply an enthusiastic market yearning for red. For Hardy's, faced with basically the same market problems as Seppelt's, the reasons were very similar—sufficient supply at an economic price. For Lindeman's, however, the rationale was different. It had already built up its market for red, especially in Sydney, and there was a need to provide enough material to service its middle market brands, which Coonawarra, Clare (it remained a steady customer of Stanley) and Pokolbin might not be able to satisfy. So that company was not necessarily wedded to the idea that Padthaway would turn out to be a new cheaper Coonawarra, an area of ultimate quality for red.

It was to be proved correct. Events from the mid-1970s onwards caused by that initially Australian phenomenon—the white wine boom—would prove beyond doubt that Padthaway is much better suited for white wines than for red and that Coonawarra remains unchallenged as the prince of Australian red wine regions.

To the north of Adelaide, Clare also was beginning to feel the effects of the red wine boom. Though for many years it had existed as a region of fortified wines and medicinal reds, it is fair to say that companies such as Quelltaler had never abandoned the table wine tradition. Thus Quelltaler had continued to make its popular lighter whites such as hock as well as being extremely successful with flor sherry styles like Granfiesta.

So with the slump of the fortified market and the restoration of the reign of beer, Clare, substantially planted with shiraz, could certainly survive if not prosper on dry red and, with increasing areas of rhine riesling, was poised to exploit any upturn in the white wine market as well.

As we have seen, the Stanley Wine Company was particularly well placed to satisfy any burgeoning market demand. From 1966 on it began to produce a straight Clare cabernet sauvignon albeit with a small percentage of malbec in the wine. That wine became the famous Leasingham Bin 49 from the following (1967) vintage. Other reds soon followed as Stanley developed its portfolio—Bin 56 Cabernet Malbec, Bin 53 Burgundy (a cabernet-grenache blend) and also some stunning rhine rieslings, Bins 5 and 7 of the late 1960s and early 1970s were particularly fine.

And as red table wines boomed, Stanley became in the eyes of most national wine companies a most desirable bride. For instance, its average grape crush of 1100 tonnes in 1962 had risen to 5000 tonnes by 1970 and it could sell all its wines. Yet in the early 1960s, with Lindeman's as its chief customer, it had seemed logical and only a matter of time before it would be taken over by a nationally resurgent Lindeman's. Yet it did not. Even an offer from the Stanley shareholders to sell their shares to Lindeman's was rejected, so Stanley, while earnestly hoping that Lindeman's would continue its patronage (it did), began to follow an independent marketing path which, with wines such as those mentioned, had succeeded admirably by 1970. A new Knappstein was introduced to the winemaking team in 1966. Tim was to make an immeasurable contribution to the quality of Stanley table wines during his ten years with the company. The rhine rieslings and the cabernets were to rise to the top rank of Australian wines, the rieslings especially rivalling those of Leo Buring in Australian wine shows. Thus by the end of the 1960s Stanley was one of the rising stars of the wine industry and a very ripe apple for picking in the takover tree.

Quelltaler, that other large Clare winery, had in its management been dominated since the 1930s by the Sobels family. By 1960 not a single Buring remained on the board, Leo having retired in

1956. From the mid-1960s it had also been plagued by 'suitors', so much so that according to one executive normal operations became impossible. The board had become effectively hamstrung by the multiplicity of offers. Eventually in 1968 Quelltaler merged with the prominent brandy producer and its chief distributor, Nathan & Wyeth of Melbourne.

In 1962, by its purchase of the Leo Buring organisation, which of course owned the Florita vineyard at Watervale, Lindeman's had entered the Clare Valley for the first time. But little was to change; even under its new proprietorship, Leo Buring continued as an independent entity and very little wine from that source saw the Lindeman label, as the Lindeman-Stanley connection continued to be beneficial for both parties. Yet one change there was and that was the creation of a wonderfully artistic synergy between Buring's winemakers, Reg Shipster and John Vickery, and the riesling vines not only of Florita but also of the Eden Valley.

Amongst the corporate manouevrings that bemused the Clare region in the 1960s, there was one new development of real substance, directly attributable to the red wine boom. Taylor's Wines Pty Ltd, though certainly new, was formed by proprietors who were no parvenus in wine, having popularised the Chateau Clare label in Sydney during the 1950s. Seventy-eight hectares of totally red vineyard (forty-nine hectares of cabernet sauvignon and twenty-nine hectares of shiraz) were planted in the south of the Clare Valley near Auburn in 1969-70. The 1970s would see the imposing Chateau Clare winery completed though changing tastes would substantially alter Taylor's 'red' designs.

There were other changes too. In 1967 the Ackland brothers planted the first vines on what was to become their Mount Horrocks vineyard while Jim Barry, by then a substantial grape grower who was also employed by Taylor's, was pondering his own wines, trial batches of which he made in the late 1960s at Birks's Wendouree winery. Elsewhere change trod at a more measured pace. The rich reds and fortifieds were still produced by Brother Hanlon at Sevenhill College, while Roly Birks at Wendouree in 1970, then in his seventy-seventh year and fifty-third vintage, was contemplating retirement; a temporary retirement only and an unhappy one.

In the Riverland at Renmark, Angove's was also contemplating its future. The year 1962 saw the acquisition of what was to become the Nanya Vineyard—over 800 hectares of land at Murtho, east of Renmark. After overcoming substantial engineering problems so as to ensure an adequate supply of water the Company had, by 1969, planted nearly a quarter of a million vines at Nanya (about one hundred hectares). Many more would follow as Nanya was completely planted. Importantly also a vine nursery was established to provide the new varietal stock then being distributed by the South Australian Department of Agriculture, some of which had not previously been available in that state due to phylloxera quarantine. Such varieties included gewurztraminer, pinot noir, sauvignon blanc, merlot, chardonnay and colombard. There was also tarrango, a vinifera hybrid developed by the CSIRO for lighter red styles. Another innovation for Angove's was the 'bag-in-the-box', the company first selling wine in that package of convenience in 1965. Unfortunately technical problems (the plastic bag was permeable to oxygen), which reduced the shelf life of the wine, caused Angove's to withdraw its 'wine cask' from the market in 1971. Others during that decade would exploit the cask to the full.

At Berri changes were also afoot. Plans evolved in 1958 called for a winery entirely devoted to table wine at the then enormous cost of $200 000. The Berri Co-operative Winery would, during the 1970s, reap the benefits of that far-sighted decision with the production of prize-winning reds including a Jimmy Watson Trophy winner in 1977.

So promising did the red table-wine market look that by the end of the 1960s virtually all the wine establishment of South Australia had plans for expanded vineyards and wineries in the Riverland region. Seppelt had planted near Qualco, Yalumba at Oxford Landing, and close by were Tolley Scott & Tolley and Orlando. As the red boom grew, the deserts were again flowering.

Apart from its North-West, Murray and North-East regions Victoria had by 1960 been reduced to virtually two viticultural outposts, the Goulburn Valley (Chateau Tahbilk, Osicka and Darveniza near Shepparton) and Great Western (Seppelt and Best). Fresh from its centenary at which the prime minister had been present, Chateau Tahbilk, ageless in the beauty of its surrounds, had become virtually a vinous shrine, but was certainly in no danger of giving up the ghost, if the quality of its reds were any true indication. It still received visits from Hardy's winemakers seeking reds for blending, while its 'Show' wines were massively constructed, its 1962 Show Cabernet Sauvignon Bin 26, built to resist an earthquake, being hardly drinkable before the early 1980s.

At Great Western the sparkling wine tradition carried on, though Colin Preece retired in 1963 due to ill-health, after over thirty years as winemaker.

Meanwhile the Seppelt quest for suitable winegrowing sites in proximity to Great Western continued. Karl Seppelt favoured Drumborg, an area south-west of Great Western, without any prior wine history but suitable because of its soils and rainfall. Its chief disadvantage was to be its extremely cool and windy spring climate, which was to cause poor berry-set in many seasons, but all this lay in the future. Seppelt's began to plant Drumborg in 1964 with such cultivars as riesling, traminer, sylvaner, pinot noir, meunier chasselas, Irvine's white (in reality ondenc, but so-called because it was not then ampelographically identified), muscadelle, chardonnay and cabernet sauvignon. By 1972 over eighty hectares had been planted.

In the North-East the makers of fortifieds turned to red and, as they had often done in adverse times, mixed farming. Yet John Charles Brown of Milawa was not dismayed. After all table wine, not fortified, had been his chief preoccupation since his first vintage in 1934. He could now turn his attention even more closely to table wine. His Milawa reds, while sturdy and full-bodied like most Australian reds of that period, had always had a greater degree of elegance than other wines of the district. So he began at that time to lay down certain bottlings of Shiraz and that blend peculiar to Brown's, Shiraz Mondeuse Cabernet, for extended cellar maturation and for subsequent sales to an increasingly appreciative cellar-door clientele which often included skiers in transit to the excitement of the Victorian Alps.

White wines were also Brown's forte. His rhine rieslings of that time were extremely delicate for the region, though they did lack the ultimate finesse of those of Eden Valley and Clare. Yet with this variety, Brown also showed great initiative. In 1962, he had noticed a strange mould affecting the Milawa riesling, which he had seen occasionally in previous vintages. This proved to be noble rot, the Rhine Riesling of 1962 being the precursor of Brown Brothers Noble Riesling, the first of which was made in 1970. The evolution of a new sweet white style, the first of its kind based on botrytis, is but one aspect of John Brown's energy. Recognising the red wine boom as an awakening of interest in most table wine styles, he began to experiment with other table wine varieties, as well as differentiating his vineyard sites as a protection against natural calamities such as frost or hail. Thus he encouraged many local farmers to grow table-wine grapes as an alternative cash crop while acquiring 'Mystic Park' in 1969, an irrigated vineyard near Swan Hill. In this way, he could assess the suitability of many different wine varieties in many different soil and climatic conditions. By 1970 not only John Brown but three of his four sons, John, Peter and Ross, were totally involved in the business.

Although the last vines disappeared from the Melbourne metropolitan area and the Yarra Valley in the late 1920s, its wine heritage was never forgotten. By the early 1950s a prominent Melbourne wine merchant, Douglas Seabrook, was experimenting with rhine riesling vines at a relative's holiday home near Dromana on the Mornington Peninsula, an extremely cool area, now very much in viticultural fashion today. In 1963 a Melbourne barrister, Reg Egan, planted the first vines on his home block at Wantirna South in Melbourne's outer eastern suburbs. The first varieties planted were, typically for the period, riesling, cabernet sauvignon and shiraz. Later as Egan attempted to assess suitability for his area, subsequent plantings read like a nurseryman's catalogue, mataro, malbec (which turned out to be dolcetto), pedro ximines, crouchen, grenache, carignan and, unusually for the times, merlot. Most of these vines proved unsuitable, as the ripening season was too short, but finally Egan made his first estate wines, a riesling-crouchen white in 1969 and a cabernet red in 1970.

In the Yarra Valley the vine returned from a forty-year exile. In 1968 St Hubert's was reborn, albeit in a converted chicken shed and from the profits made from poultry-farming by the Cester family. No matter, Hubert de Castella would have been pleased. Yarra Yering, initially to be a partnership between Egan and scientist Dr Bailey Carrodus, but soon carried on solely by Carrodus, followed the very next year, as did the born-again Yeringberg, which had continued in the hands of the de Pury family for a hundred years, albeit without vines since the 1920s. All these plantings were small but they would grow and inspire others to plant in their turn. There, also, the medical profession soon showed its customary fascination with the vine. Lilydale doctors John Middleton and Peter McMahon, partners in medicine, each acquired the property of his choice. For Middleton it was Mount Mary, set upon the classic grey clay loam of the Yarra Valley, so highly commended by Hubert de Castella. This was a fulfilment of fifteen years of experiments in viticulture and winemaking, a logical consequence of his intense passion for the vine and the expression of that experience. There in 1971 he made his first plantings, which included the classic Bordeaux varieties, the cabernets, sauvignon and franc as well as merlot and 'malbec' (a disaster as it turned out to be dolcetto); the distinguished Burgundians, pinot noir and chardonnay; and the German aromatics, rhine riesling and gewurztraminer. Thus in the early 1970s Middleton was the sole repository of winemaking experience in the Yarra Valley.

McMahon chose Seville Estate, rolling hillsides of vivid red loam with sweeping views of the Valley. There in 1972 he planted cabernet sauvignon, shiraz, riesling and chardonnay. This was the goal of many years' hard work and a commitment to an ultimate change in lifestyle.

Others in the Yarra Valley also turned to the vine. For Graeme Miller, who had bought fifty-eight hectares of dairying country in 1967, it was time to evict some of the cows and in 1971 to plant four hectares of vines with equal areas of cabernet sauvignon and shiraz. He named his new Yarra estate Chateau Yarrinya.

Yet the renaissance of cool-area vine growing in Victoria was not left to the Yarra Valley or to its relatively distant off-shoot Wantirna South. Others too remembered Victoria's vinous heritage. Close to Geelong a local veterinarian, Daryl Sefton, together with his wife Nini, planted the Idyll Vineyard in 1966 with cabernet sauvignon, shiraz and gewurztraminer, the first new vines in the region since the massive uprootings ninety years before. Nearby at Mount Anakie, Tom Maltby established cabernet sauvignon two years later.

At Bendigo, another region devastated by phylloxera all those years before, Balgownie, the creation of pharmacist Stuart Anderson in 1969, became the first wine estate in the district in three-quarters of a century. But not only were scientifically trained professionals involved. Tom Lazar, a famous Melbourne restaurateur of his day, chose the Kyneton area, in 1968 founding his vineyard in heavily wooded country never before troubled by the vine, which he appropriately named 'Virgin Hills'. Not far away the Knight family, farmers in the locality for many years, began planting in 1970, not surprisingly selling their fruit to Virgin Hills for several years. After many years southern Victoria (that cool zone south of the Great Divide) was on the march once more, and once more, given time for its vineyards to mature and proper technical skill, it would be a force for quality to be reckoned with.

Was Lake's Folly the catalyst for the wine renaissance of the Hunter Valley? It has been a popular theory, justified rather more by coincidence than fact, though certainly wine production in the Valley had reached a low ebb by 1960. Decreasing vineyard area (468 hectares in 1956), minute production (less than 1000 tonnes in that year), poor climatic conditions (record floods in 1955, widespread hail in 1960) and low public acceptance of the product (5.3 litres per head in 1960, of which fortified wine, very little of which was made in the Hunter was still the lion's share of the market) all reinforced the gloom of the Hunter industry. By 1960 only seven wineries were in active production. Lindeman, Penfold and McWilliam were the major names, though Tulloch had begun bottling under its own label and was much sought after in restaurants over thirty years ago. The others, Tyrrell, Drayton and Elliott, sold their wine to Lindeman or McWilliam, to interstate companies such as Hardy or Mildara or perhaps to Sydney merchants like Rhinecastle. It was a familiar trade, though scarcely buoyant.

It was on to this stage that Max Lake stepped with characteristic gusto and an unswerving enthusiasm for a grape variety then almost extinct (at least not separately recorded in statistics) in the Valley—cabernet sauvignon. From 1961 to 1963 he charged through the Valley, sampling soils and assessing aspects, finally choosing twenty-five hectares of red volcanic soil on the southern slope of Rosehill. Four years and eight hectares of cabernet later came the first commercial vintage in the excellent, cool but dry Hunter year of 1967, a minty cabernet of beautiful balance more than once mistaken for a Bordeaux. For the rest of the 1960s, 'Lake's luck', as he called it, held, the damp year, 1968, providing cabernet of great finesse and 1969 a bigger though balanced wine after a drought-stricken spring during which devastating bushfires swept the area.

By 1970 Lake's Folly was a 'must' in every wine buff's cellar and the consumer move to boutique wineries had begun. In the mean time, even though McWilliam's was quietly developing its own Hunter cabernet (its first experimental wine was made in 1966, the same year as Lake's first few foot-stamped litres), Max Lake had become the indisputable cabernet champion of Australia.

The rush to replant the Hunter now grew apace and not only with cabernet. Others were hot on Lake's trail. In 1964 Jim Roberts planted a whole catalogue of grape varieties a few kilometres away at Belbourie, making his first wine in 1970. In 1966 yet another doctor, Lance Allen, bought his property, Tamburlaine, planting his first vines the following year.

By now the big battalions were forming, though on what rational basis it is difficult to see even in hindsight. Tax minimisation, future capital gain, perhaps even lifestyle are the only reasons that can be advanced. Certainly the productive capacity of most of the land planted did not merit the investment, but the red wine boom had seemed to close the eyes of even the most cautious investor and rational economics played little part in the burgeoning vineyard areas of the day.

On the Broke Road in the Parish of Rothbury a syndicate of businessmen led by Sydney accountant, John Parker, bought Hungerford's Friesian stud (the dairy cow was in retreat once more) and, naming their company 'Hungerford Hill Vineyards' after the vendor, began planting in 1968. Under the management of Norman Hanckel, who had supervised the replanting of the Pewsey Vale vineyards for Yalumba earlier that decade, eighty-two hectares of vines (over ninety per cent red) were established in the first winter, a pace never before seen in the Hunter Valley. By 1970 over 235 hectares had been planted.

The year 1968 saw the formation of the Rothbury Estate syndicate under the chairmanship of Len Evans. The director in charge of its vineyard development was Murray Tyrrell, who established twenty-eight hectares of shiraz and semillon in 1968 and twenty-seven hectares chiefly of the same varieties but with the addition of small areas of chardonnay, blanquette and cabernet sauvignon in the following year. A further thirty-two hectares of semillon and shiraz with some experimental patches of pinot noir, merlot, traminer and rhine riesling completed the picture in 1970. The enthusiasm generated by the formation of the Rothbury Estate syndicate became so great that further syndicates—Brokenback, Homestead Hill and Herlstone—were created, all intending that their grapes should be vinified by Rothbury, which by 1971 had completed the erection of an impressive winery, awarded an architectural prize at the time and locally referred to as the Pokolbin Opera House. The estate's first winemaker was Gerry Sissingh, formerly of Lindeman's, a master of white winemaking, whose skill during the 1970s would provide Rothbury with a first-class reputation when the financial going became very hard indeed.

There were other syndicates; Hermitage Estate was one such, formed in 1967 and founded upon the site of Mistletoe Farm, a much older vineyard, renowned in its day as a producer both of quality and quantity. It too expanded rapidly, planting 300 hectares of vines in five years and constructing a large winery with an H-shaped tower in 1973. Just as rapidly it went into receivership shortly afterwards, finally to form part of the Wyndham Group in 1977.

Ultimately a similar destiny was in store for Saxonvale, formed as a non-listed public company in 1970. It was merged with a publicly listed company, Pokolbin Winemakers, which existed only briefly and had bought the former Happy Valley vineyards of Barrie Drayton. Saxonvale itself owned a 160 hectare block of deep red basalt country at Fordwich about thirty kilometres north-west of Pokolbin. This was a union which should have been of great benefit to both parties, were it not for the fact that Saxonvale fell into the clutches of ill-fated general merchant and liquor wholesaler Gollin & Co. just before its collapse. So too was Saxonvale condemned to spend most of the 1970s in receivership. Despite this its contribution to the quality of Hunter wine, the whites especially, was to be remarkable.

There were other large winemaking ventures in the Lower Hunter at this time which were destined to fail. One was McPhersons, whose wine production was heavily based on varietal wine and even included a Marsanne, a variety very rare in the Hunter. It lasted little more than a decade.

The example set by Lake not only enthused the larger syndicates at this time, it encouraged smaller groups and even individuals. Dr Lance Allen has been mentioned, but there was also Dr Don Francois, whose initial vineyard plantings of 2.4 hectares were intended to be sufficiently large (or small) to be manageable by one man in his spare time.

In 1969 a somewhat larger group (nineteen in all) came together to revive Oakdale, one of the Wilkinson family vineyards which had gone out of production earlier that decade, while in October of the following year, three young lawyers (Tony Albert, James Halliday and I) with little idea of the additional workload they were about to heap upon their own shoulders banded together to pay an outlandish price for a small block of overgrown cricket pitch, which they were to call Brokenwood.

Others started at this time also, some to establish wineries, some to remain growers: Barrie Drayton at Hillside; Quentin Taperell on Deasey's Road, later to be bought by Peter Marsh and renamed Marsh Estate; Don Maxwell at Maluna; Harry Tulloch at Mount View; Murray Robson also at Mount View; and another syndicate, one of whom was Bruce Tyrrell, at Terrace Vale on Deasey's Road.

To the established winemakers of the Lower Hunter, the new wine enthusiasts making their weekend trips to the Lower Hunter were something of an enigma. The larger companies such as Lindeman's and McWilliam's ignored them, preferring their Hunter wineries to remain workstations rather than tourist haunts. To the smaller family-owned concerns, the steady stream of Saturday tourists was a godsend and a valuable aid to cash flow. All now followed Tulloch's example of the 1950s and bottled under their own label. Bulk sales to the trade became rarer. After all they could now earn much more under their own label as well as spreading their own goodwill in the form of mailing lists. Soon the wine *aficionados* began to note the dates when new releases would occur and to time their Hunter trips accordingly. I suppose I was typical of the many who would in the late 1960s leave Sydney at dawn by car for the journey to Cessnock (usually two and a half hours then) calling first at Elliott's weatherboard wineshop in Cessnock to see his latest reds and then to Tulloch's to taste the whites and reds and to assess the quality of the Private Bins (it had to be in the morning as Keith Tulloch closed at one o'clock to go to bowls in the afternoon). After a quick picnic lunch (there were no restaurants at Pokolbin in those days) it was off to Drayton's at Bellevue and to Barry Drayton at Happy Valley, finally to arrive at Tyrrell's about three o'clock to taste the latest vintage from cask and to yarn with Murray Tyrrell.

By four o'clock, unless an appointment had been made to see Max Lake at the Folly (he was rarely there on weekends) to taste his Cabernets, it was back to Sydney along the dusty but picturesque Wollombi Road. By eight, dinner and a quick look at one of the newest treasures before it was packed away into the cellar. Such was a typical Hunter visit about 1968—a pilgrimage of pleasure to be prescribed at least three times a year. Later those tourist hundreds would turn into thousands and the future of the Hunter would seem assured.

In 1966 the Hunter Valley saw its first multinational purchase, Reed Paper acquiring Tulloch's, much to the sorrow of the weekend enthusiasts who doubted that the wine would ever be the same again. Yet the Tulloch family did not regret the sale, which enabled its older members to retire and the winery and equipment to be modernised by the injection of new capital. The Reed takeover, however, could be seen as one aspect of the trend by large international companies towards diversification. Australia was under the multinational microscope. It was politically stable and economically sound. More than that, it was flourishing and red wine sales were booming. Superficially, what more attractive investment could there be? But if the corporate think-tanks had examined the history of the industry, its cycles of boom and bust and low return on investment, they would surely have thought again. They did not, and more of these multinational moths would be attracted to the flame of Australian wine.

The Lake's Folly phenomenon, for such it was, appealed to Australians for another reason also. It presented the small winemaker as an underdog, a battler competing against aloof, anonymous winemaking organisations. This was winemaking with a human face. To the weekend tourist, the local wineries of large national winemakers were often closed. Surely the wine made by individuals and families on the spot was more pleasant. So perhaps these wine-buying tourists quite understandably came to the conclusion that wine bought from small family-run wineries with a small exclusive production really was better than wine produced by large city-run organisations. If 'small' is beautiful, then 'exclusiveness' may be excellence. This confidence in small wineries was surely the lasting contribution made by Lake's Folly to the Hunter boom of the 1960s.

Before the plethora of expansion that took place later in the

1960s, one company had decided to move from the Lower Hunter. Penfold's took this decision quite rationally and with detailed planning. Towards the end of the 1950s, Penfold's had realised finally that its yields from its old Dalwood vineyard near Branxton were totally uneconomic. But instead of planting the same site afresh over a period of years, the company opted for a complete transfer of its Hunter activities to a larger site (ultimately 520 hectares) near Wybong in the Upper Hunter, some eighty kilometres north-west of old Dalwood. There the company planted a whole range of vines; amongst the whites were rhine riesling, crouchen, semillon, blanquette, ugni blanc, chardonnay, chasselas and traminer; the reds included shiraz, cabernet sauvignon, malbec, mataro and pinot noir. Its winery was, for its day, the ultimate in technology and it was estimated that $2 million (a huge sum at that time) was spent in all. Penfold's called the new venture Dalwood Estate, retaining the name even though it had sold the old property to its long-time winemaker, Perce McGuigan; but the venture was ill-starred. Its planning had simply not shown enough appreciation of the problems likely to be encountered in an area that was for all intents and purposes completely new (even though there had been nineteenth-century vineyards in the general region). Dalwood Estate at Wybong was planted without any supplementary irrigation, though in fairness it must be said that this was virtually unknown in dry-land viticulture at the time and was certainly disapproved of as a quality-assisting factor. New varietal clones, about which the company knew very little, were being tried and were sometimes unsuitable. There were also infestations of weeds and insects. Yet fundamentally there was one serious flaw and that was simply the suitability of the soil for the types of vines planted. Basically the whites had been planted on soils suitable for red and vice versa. For Penfold's, Dalwood Estate never quite worked. In 1977 the Estate was sold and so, with the exception of a few Pokolbin vineyards, after 74 years Penfold's left the Hunter Valley.

At old Dalwood, later renamed 'Wyndham Estate' in honour of pioneer vigneron, George Wyndham, Penfold's disillusionment was to be the McGuigan family's gain. Perce McGuigan, who had served Penfold's as its Dalwood winemaker for twenty-eight years, bought the fifty-six hectare property for $24 000 in 1967. Soon after, the elder McGuigan sold the property to a syndicate consisting of his son Brian, then winemaker at Penfold's Dalwood Estate, Sydney stockbroker Tim Allen and businessman Digby Matheson. In accordance with the practice of that time, a broad selection of varieties were planted—semillon, chardonnay, sylvaner, traminer, rhine riesling, blanquette, sauvignon blanc, muscadelle and frontignan in whites, and shiraz, cabernet sauvignon, pinot noir, malbec and mataro in reds. Soon after Brian McGuigan resigned from Penfold's to concentrate full-time on the new venture, Wyndham Estate; during the ensuing decade it would rapidly grow into the region's largest producer.

The Penfold's move to the Upper Hunter was an inspiration for others, both large and small, both local and from afar, to look closely at the area. It had seen famous vineyards in the nineteenth century, Brecht at the original Rosemount was but one. Perhaps it would do so again.

David Hordern, a dairy farmer and grazier, was the first to follow the Penfold example, planting three hectares of shiraz in 1965. Two years later he was joined by Dr Bob Smith, who also had set up a vineyard nearby. Combining resources, the two built a winery with the convict-hewn stone of an 1840 prison transported form Bengala near Maitland many kilometres away. Thus Wybong Estate (or Horden's Wybong, as it came to be known) was born and made its first wine in 1969.

Other bigger fish were about also. In 1969, close to Jerry's Plains a large public company, W. R. Carpenter & Co. in concert with a subsidiary of Penfold's, began to establish the Arrowfield vineyard, a vast area ultimately of 485 hectares, proudly boasted as 'the largest single vineyard in Australia' of its day. This was followed by a huge bunker-like winery set into a hill. Yet Arrowfield's 'day' was past even before it began to sell the lake of red that would flow from its vineyards. The fickle tastes of the market, so often the bane of the Australian winemaker, would also plague Arrowfield in the 1970s.

Three other corporate groups also invested heavily and with high optimism in the Upper Hunter at this time.

Hollydene began life in 1968 as a venture of the Commins family. In 1969 thirty-six hectares of vines were planted to allow for mechanical harvesting with plans to triple this area by 1971 and to erect a winery by 1973. All of this came to pass but by 1976 Hollydene had been sold.

In 1970 Chateau Douglas became yet another child of the red-wine boom, unusually conceived in that it was by an association of 230 shareholders, who each held various tenancy-in-common interests in the property with a corresponding share in profit and loss.

The development of its vineyards took the usual course, losses exceeding profits, and as a result Chateau Douglas struggled through the 1970s, finally to come under the control of Tyrrell's in 1978.

Denman Estates was planned as a bulk wine producer for the trade. A large winery and extensive vineyards at Roxburgh and Mindaribba were developed but production problems, lack of promotion and failure to expand its market base were to prove insuperable difficulties for this struggling company in the mid-1970s.

The one shining success story of the Upper Hunter also began in 1969. Formed by members of the Oatley family as one aspect of a general agricultural operation, Rosemount Estate was destined not to repeat the mistakes of the unfortunate Penfold's move virtually a decade earlier. This time the vine plantings and techniques were correct and quite suited to the market conditions in which the company found itself at the time of its first commercial vintage in 1975. From 1969 to 1974, fifty hectares of rich well-drained river flat country were planted to semillon, traminer, riesling, sauvignon blanc, shiraz and cabernet sauvignon, all subject to drip irrigation. Other varieties, experimental at the time, such as chardonnay and pinot noir, were also developed. Their day would come. Based on a strong national marketing campaign and excellent wine show results, the first whites of Rosemount, especially the Rhine Riesling, struck an immediately responsive chord with the consumers of that time. By the mid-1970s Rosemount, with John Ellis as wine-maker, was riding high.

In Mudgee also the vine was undergoing a resurgence in the boom of the 1960s. From the highpoint of production in the 1880s (thirteen wineries) numbers had shrunk to just two by the 1940s, Craigmoor and Dr Fiaschi's winery, established in the first decade of the twentieth century; and then to only one by the 1960s (Craigmoor). But as in all its traditional locales interest in the vine was mounting once more in Mudgee. Alf Kurtz planted out cabernet sauvignon in 1961, building his winery in 1964, which he called, suitably enough, 'Mudgee Wines'. He also showed great foresight by labelling his wines varietally. Yet perhaps his most notable contribution to contemporary viticulture was his suspicion, correct as it proved, that a variety locally known as 'white pineau' might turn out to be chardonnay, a variety virtually unknown to Australians at the time.

If the death in 1969 of Alan 'Jack' Roth, grandson of the founder of Mudgee viticulture, Adam Roth, marked the end of a century of involvement of the Roth family with Craigmoor and Mudgee winemaking, it also in a sense spelt 'finis' to Mudgee as a struggling wine producing area. Henceforth more wine investment funds would flow into the region. The professional men and the tax advisors would see to that.

One lawyer and agriculturalist who was definitely not seeking to minimise tax was Bob Roberts. He had reached Mudgee by way of Wagga (a diploma of agriculture), Sydney (a law degree from Sydney University) and New Guinea (some years as a plantation owner). Huntington Estate was first planted in 1969. Between that year and 1972 forty-eight hectares of vineyard were established as well as a functional winery, designed and substantially built by his own hands. In the fashion of the times, the varieties planted were predominantly red with shiraz and cabernet sauvignon the major cultivars, merlot, pinot noir, semillon, chardonnay and sauvignon blanc constituting the rest of the vineyard. Roberts would also help create a first for Australia, a voluntary, self-funding appellation scheme, guaranteeing the authenticity of the local wines and administered by the Society for the Appellation of the Wines of Mudgee.

The taxes on fortifying spirit imposed by the federal government in 1953 were a heavy blow to all makers of fortified wines, not least to those in the Murrumbidgee Irrigation Area (MIA), who had relied almost exclusively on fortifieds for their livelihood since the inception of the area forty years before. Though the tax was a bitter pill, the accompanying blow of an accelerated beer market and an almost instant decline in fortified sales proved to the MIA producers that it was obviously time for a change.

McWilliam's recognised the inevitable and introduced not only new pressure fermentation tanks of the type initially imported by Orlando but also refrigeration. In addition in 1960 the company also began to plant the table wine varietals then being released by the New South Wales Department of Agriculture. The table-wine boom would have a tremendous part to play in the lower and middle sectors of the market with the consequence that the MIA's vine area would increase from 1696 hectares in 1960 to 3226 hectares in 1970.

Illustrative of the growth in popularity of table wine and of the growers' response to that trend during the 1960s is the following table showing areas of plantings of significant varieties in the MIA as at 31 December 1961 and at 31 December 1970.

	1961 (hectares)	**1970** (hectares)
cabernet sauvignon	not recorded	100.2
shiraz	275.6	754.6
grenache	257.2	248.5
semillon	265.2	660.3
trebbiano	237.6	454.6
gordo	82	199.2

Few viticultural areas in Australia have been established as a result of a government report. Though the Padthaway area in South Australia is arguably an exception to that rule the Margaret River and Lower Great Southern regions of Western Australia are certainly two others. In 1955 an eminent Californian viticulturalist, Professor Harold Olmo, was commissioned by the Western Australian government to take stock of the state's wine industry and to advise on its prospects. He recommended Mount Barker and the Frankland River area in particular. As he said in his report,

> for the production of high quality light table wines, the south coastal area along the Frankland River spanning the 30 inch to 35 inch [760mm-890mm] rainfall zone is a very promising one. Here the summer climate is cool enough to promote slow maturity of the fruit and the rainfall is high enough to produce a vigorous productive vine on the better alluvial soils.

For some years the report was pigeonholed but finally in 1962 the State Department of Agriculture resolved to act on it. In 1965 a site at Forest Hill near Mount Barker was selected and planted but the vines failed due to lack of attention. In the following year the experiment was repeated, two hectares (one each of riesling and cabernet sauvignon) being planted.

The Forest Hill experiment of the Department of Agriculture was not without impact upon the local farming community. In 1968 a local grazier, Tony Smith, was inspired to begin his own experiment, a two hectare vineyard of equal plantings of shiraz and cabernet sauvignon on his property near Mount Barker. Further plantings followed at the nearby Wyjup vineyard in 1971. Named after the local shire, the Plantagenet winery would become the region's largest wine-producer in the 1970s.

At the same time (1965) but independently of the Forest Hill experiment, Dr John Gladstones of the University of Western Australia was carrying out studies of the South-West, in particular the Margaret River region. His paper was nothing if not enthusiastic in its conclusions.

> The temperature summations, probably about 1540 day degrees immediately to the north of Margaret River, should be ideal for table wines generally. Not only should excellent quality be obtained with choice grape varieties, but the district might also be very suitable because of its equable climate for higher-yielding but still good quality varieties, such as Shiraz and Semillon.

The recommendations of this paper proved fascinating reading for Perth heart-specialist Dr Tom Cullity, who planted Vasse Felix in 1967 with cabernet sauvignon, making his first vintage in 1971. Cullity's vineyard at Willyabrup was soon followed by another, Moss Wood, the long-cherished dream of another medical man, Dr Bill Pannell, who started planting in 1970. Margaret River and the Lower Great Southern would attract more vineyard enthusiasts, some wealthy investors and comparatively few large winemaking companies. Yet they remain as areas of bountiful promise for Western Australian and national viticulture.

In Tasmania the influence of immigration was vital in the renaissance of the vine, all trace of which had been obliterated for more than a century, unless the abortive efforts of Signor Bernacchi in the 1880s are taken into account. The trials of Jean Miguet have been mentioned. Miguet did not persist, but one other did and he was Claudio Alcorso, who first planted a few vines on his Berriedale property north-west of Hobart in 1958, two years after Miguet. Despite the indifference of the Tasmanian government, yet much to the delight of the local bird population, Alcorso—refugee, textile magnate, patron of the arts and founder of Moorilla Estate—pressed on, ultimately to establish a thriving vineyard.

Other Tasmanians soon sought to emulate Miguet and Alcorso, notably Graham Wiltshire, who planted his Legana vineyard in the Tamar Valley in 1967. Wiltshire was later to play an important part in Heemskerk, another vineyard development at Pipers Brook which, with the establishment of the neighbouring Pipers Brook vineyard in 1974, would make that region the hub of Tasmanian viticulture.

In Queensland, Bassett's Romavilla vineyard maintained that state's tenuous connection with the wine grape, albeit with fortified wine predominantly. Further south in the Granite Belt around Stanthorpe, interest in the vine was also high, but for many years only as fresh fruit, although in this mainly Italian community, wine was made from table grapes for home consumption. Fruit markets however become glutted from time to time and gluts of such varieties as muscat and purple cornichon led to impromptu winemaking which proved popular amongst the local community. As a result, local wineries such as Biltmore Cellars became well known in the district. In the mid-1960s interest in true wine varieties also began to grow. Both production and quality would increase during the 1970s.

So what were our winemakers' expectations for the 1970s? By mid-year 1970 per capita wine consumption had reached 8.9 litres which, though hardly more than the 8.2 litres of 1952 (the year before the marketing of beer was liberalised), was beginning to assume a different complexion. Sherry of all types was still a favourite tipple, 32.05 million litres being consumed by Australians in the year ended June 1970. Dry red, however, was rapidly overhauling it (25.47 million), followed by a declining fortified market (17.32 million litres) and good growth in dry white (13.88 million). Sales of sparkling wines of all types amounted to 11.38 million while other table wines (rosé and sweet white sauterne-styles) stood at 5.2 million litres. Out of a total of 109.7 million litres, table wine sales at 55.9 million litres had thus reached 50.96 per cent of consumption. Therefore by mid-year 1970 it could at last be said that Australian wine consumers preferred table wine to fortified.

And as for the expectations of winemakers, they were, if the grape-use statistics of vintage 1970 compared to 1975 are any sure guide, that the wine boom, particularly in red, would continue well into the 1970s if not beyond. During 1970 vintage, for example, 27 896 tonnes of shiraz were used in winemaking. By 1975 this had increased to 72 257 tonnes. Use of premium white wine varieties such as rhine riesling was also increasing. In 1970 vintage, 3992 tonnes of this variety were crushed. By 1975 this had risen to 9976 tonnes.

The optimism of winemakers would not prove to be unfounded, but there were some nasty surprises in store for those who relied solely on red.

FOURTEEN

The 1970s—the age of white

If the most striking feature of the 1970s was the failure of the wine industry to forecast the white wine boom in the middle and later years of that decade, then the rise of chardonnay later in that decade and its triumphant march into the 1980s must have been, as Churchill said, 'a riddle wrapped in a mystery inside an enigma', striking proof if any were needed of its total inability to forecast public taste. There was little evidence of the white boom in 1970; in fact only the previous year the public were being exhorted by advertising to drink more white (if only to take the pressure off red). From a sales base of 17.5 million litres for the year ending June 1970 (hardly 1.5 litres per head of population), sales of white table wine (including white bottle-fermented sparkling wine) soared past red in 1975 to reach almost 160 million litres in mid-1980. Why?

The explanation for this change of taste is quite unremarkable. There was no single overwhelming cause for it, but as usual a multiplicity of factors, for only a few of which the industry was directly responsible. Certainly the popular belief that white wine was somehow 'lighter' and therefore 'better' for the occasional drinker was ill-informed, as was the theory that Australians were revolting against beer. More beer than ever before was being consumed in the mid-1970s. There was more truth in the contention that it was a revolt against poor red wine, for many a poor red was hastily cobbled together from the callow vineyards of the early 1970s.

On a positive note, it must be acknowledged that white wine production was undergoing great technical advances at that time. Better refrigeration, fine filtration, air-bag presses and, most of all, the simple stainless-steel tank, capable of being cooled, portable and comparatively inexpensive. Also introduced to the wine industry and quite expensive was the hermetic centrifuge, which looked like a space capsule but was capable of recovering many extra litres from white wine lees. Introduced also were the anti-oxidant gases, carbon dioxide and nitrogen, enzymes to aid in the clarification of juice, and new yeast cultures as well as ascorbic acid to prevent oxidation. All these improved the quality of white wine and helped it evolve from the pale imitation of red which it had been in the first half of the century to the attractive nectar whose aromaticity and fruit flavours made it an extremely pleasant drink at almost any time of the day. In addition the new age of convenience packaging saw the perfecting of the 'bag-in-the-box' and the almost permanent presence of a white 'cask' in every refrigerator.

Though much of the new equipment and many of the innovatory ideas that revolutionised winemaking at this time were imported, some Australians were also at the forefront of change. One such was the Griffith winemaker turned inventor, Ron Potter, who, after nine years of winemaking, set up an engineering company, A. & G. Engineering in 1963 to specialise in winery equipment. One of his earliest and most important inventions, which he patented, was the Potter Fermenter, which became standard equipment in most modern Australian wineries in the 1970s. A far cry from the open vat which had hardly changed in a century it was constructed of stainless steel with a removable drainer for juice and was also easy to clean and able to be cooled. It was an invention that made a positive contribution to the superb quality of Australian wine in the late twentieth century. Yet Potter's mind was and still is a fertile one and a later device, the Spinning Comb Column—a process whereby the aromatics are taken from grape juice, the juice fermented, the alcohol removed and the aromatics returned, has wide application not only in the alcohol-free wine industry, but in other food processes.

All these innovations also made their mark on wine style, but none upon white wine as much as fine filtration. In the decade from 1965 to 1975, all eyes were on the delicate rhine rieslings made by Leo Buring's eminent winemaker, John Vickery. His rhines from Eden Valley and Clare were unsurpassed, though occasionally the Leasingham rhines of Stanley Wine Co. came close. From 1970 rhine riesling seemed to become sweeter as the refinement of filtration in removing all yeast particles enabled more residual sugar to be left in the wine to fill out its middle palate. The rise to respectability of this style was marked by the wine show successes of Hardy's 1975 Siegersdorf Rhine Riesling, made by Brian Croser, who was shortly thereafter to leave Hardy's to continue winemaking on his own account and to help establish Australia's second winemaking school.

The effect of the white-wine boom was that cheaper white became, at some levels of society, an acceptable alternative to beer, in whose domains (the pubs and poker-machine palaces of the era) it had hitherto hardly ever been mentioned, while red, though undoubtedly popular, continued to be drunk with meals, its more suitable environment.

At that time also, though it was of course not realised, there began the rise of a white grape variety, planted in minuscule quantity only in New South Wales and not even recorded separately in official statistics—chardonnay.

There is little doubt that chardonnay (chaudeny, as Busby called it) was introduced to the Hunter Valley with the James Busby Collection in the 1830s. After that it seemed to sink into oblivion until a white wine called pinot riesling was marketed by Penfold's from its Hunter Valley vineyards in the 1960s. This wine was a blend of two white varieties, white pinot (chardonnay, as it turned out, when correctly identified later) and Hunter Valley riesling (a common misnomer for semillon). Though chardonnay reappeared in Mudgee in the late 1960s and indeed clones of the variety had been imported by the Western Australian government in 1958 and by Penfold's in South Australia in 1959, Murray Tyrrell in the Hunter Valley was first to realise the commercial implications of the variety in Australia.

From a stock of prunings taken from the old 'pinot' vines of the Hunter Valley Distillery vineyard of Penfold's, Tyrrell, a burgundy enthusiast, suspecting that the mysterious 'white pinot' variety might be chardonnay, propagated sufficient planting stock to be in small commercial production by 1971. That first chardonnay and its successor in 1972 were made in the usual manner for those days, as cool a ferment as could be achieved and matured in big old oak. They were in their day good chardonnays made in the manner of semillon, but the chardonnay revolution really began with the Tyrrell Vat 47 Chardonnay of 1973.

Encouraged by his close friends and business associates, Len Evans and Rudy Komon, Tyrrell fermented that chardonnay in new French oak, as well as maturing it in the same medium after fermentation. Not surprisingly, in wine-judging circles accustomed at that time to the elegant aromaticity of rhine riesling, it received much the same reaction as Grange Hermitage had been given nearly twenty years earlier—virtually total rejection. At the Brisbane Wine Show in its initial year it received six points out of a possible twenty, its oak component obviously being thought by judges, ignorant of Burgundian chardonnay style, to be a very major fault. No matter, Tyrrell pressed on and Vat 47 Chardonnay was eagerly snapped up by the *cognoscenti* on its release.

Of subsequent Vat 47 Chardonnays made by the same technique, many became equally famous, wine judges having finally become reconciled to the style by the mid-1970s.

Thus Tyrrell may be given the credit for the origin of modern Australian chardonnay-making techniques, but others in the Hunter Valley were soon to follow; Saxonvale in particular produced fine chardonnays from 1977 on, in both wooded and non-wooded form, being loth to follow the Tyrrell example entirely. By 1979 virtually all Hunter wineries, big and small, were offering chardonnay, the public taste for which (though not then the Australia-wide craze that it would become in the late 1980s because of an extreme shortage of chardonnay vines in other states) was certainly off to a flying start.

If the unfulfilled promise of a red boom with its concomitant waste of resources disappointed the wine industry in the early 1970s, such disappointment was certainly not shared by corporate multinationals. To them, the wine industry remained an extremely attractive and cheap one in which to 'diversify' (the accepted business wisdom of that era). They were never more interested. Reflecting the trend of the late 1960s when Reed Paper bought Tulloch, the grocery giant Reckitt & Colman acquired both Morris and Orlando in 1970. The following year, as if to match its rival Reckitt & Colman, the worldwide Heinz empire acquired yet another variety, this time the Stanley Wine Company, though it continued under the management of the Knappstein family. Also in that year (1971), that enthusiastic buyer of the 1960s, Lindeman, was itself snaffled in a stock exchange encounter by the international tobacco titan, Philip Morris, while in 1972 Davis Gelatine firmed upon the north-east Victorian, Bailey's.

Yet all this was not one-way traffic. There were Australian companies such as Thomas Hardy interested in 'buying back the farm'. In mid-1976, Thomas Hardy paid A$4.3 million for the British-owned Emu Wine Co., returning to Australian control the Emu brand and also the English rights to the old Hardy Tintara brand. More importantly perhaps it returned to Australian ownership the Houghton and Valencia vineyards in the Swan Valley of Western Australia as well as the Morphett Vale cellars.

Still the domestic takeovers continued. Indeed the old order of family ownership and control of Australia's larger wine producers was, by the mid-1970s, radically altered. What had those changes been?

As we have seen, Lindeman's, since its release from receivership in the late 1940s, was essentially removed from family control when compensatory share issues were made to outside interests denied dividends during the lengthy receivership and further issues were made to important executives of the company who had remained loyal during that period. Its subsequent public listing in 1953 and takeover by Philip Morris in 1972 completed the process. Orlando had been sold by the Gramp family to Reckitt & Colman in 1970. In that same year Seppelt was publicly listed and, though substantially owned and controlled by the Seppelt family during the 1970s, was increasingly to become the subject of corporate manoeuvres later in that and the ensuing decade.

This swing from family ownership was most dramatically illustrated in 1976 when a 'marriage' of giants occurred. Tooth & Co., then one of Australia's larger brewers, bought Penfold's, indisputably Australia's largest winemaker, from its Penfold family connections for several million dollars.

Perhaps in making its purchase Tooth was merely following the then fashionable diversification trend among breweries, for in 1972 its rival, Castlemaine Tooheys, had acquired Wynn Winemakers, itself a short-lived publicly listed company since 1970, having also the year before bought the Seaview winery from its owner Ben Chaffey.

Why were so many family-owned wineries succumbing to the lure of corporate millions? The reasons were manifold. Apart from the fact that many family-owned businesses were then in their fourth and fifth generations with the resultant spread of ownership, inter-family tension and lack of strong central direction, the most cogent reason was the failure of federal tax legislation to encourage the investment of capital necessary to bring many wineries into line with the then rapidly changing technical scene. This discouragement was obvious when tax legislation obliged private companies to distribute 'paper' profits to shareholders (who of course were then taxed on 'income' never actually received—most such 'dividends' being credited to loan accounts in the company books and only being able to be repaid when the company finally sold the entire undertaking). Thus the investment levels necessary to meet the capital requirements for an expanding business in a time of great technical change were simply not available. Public companies and multinationals, usually endowed with large amounts of capital anyway, were subject to no such restrictions. Thus did the pendulum swing from family ownership. By 1980 only two of those substantial South Australian nineteenth-century winemaking dynasties remained in family hands, Hardy and Yalumba.

But as the established family wine companies became institutionalised divisions of ever-larger corporate conglomerates, there occurred that other phenomenon of the Australian wine industry in the 1970s, the rise of the boutique winery. Not since the 1890s and before had the wine industry seen the arrival of so many 'little' people. As mentioned previously, the phenomenon had begun in the 1960s with the arrival on the scene of such new blood as Lake at his Folly and others in the Hunter Valley.

In Victoria at this time, barrister Reg Egan had begun at Wantirna, now deemed part of the Yarra Valley, as, later in the 1960s, had Cester at St Hubert's, Fergusson of Fergusson's, Carrodus at Yarra Yering and Guill de Pury at Yeringberg (a re-establishment of the family vineyard and cellars after production had ceased in the 1920s), while Bendigo had seen Stuart Anderson beginning Balgownie and Geelong the Seftons at their Idyll vineyard.

In South Australia the wave of new winemakers also broke upon some well-established beaches. As a result of the Lindeman purchase of Rouge Homme, both Eric Brand and Owen Redman made their own first Coonawarra vintages in 1966. In the Barossa, St Hallett began trading on its own account in 1967 and the Karrawirra vineyard of the Kies family made its first wines in 1969. In McLaren Vale Keith Genders began his cellar-door trade in 1968, as did the Trott cousins a year later when they re-established the old Wirra Wirra winery, Dr Hugh Lloyd at Coriole following with his first vintage in 1970. Closer to Adelaide Ursula Pridham became Australia's first woman to make wine on her own account at Marienberg in the Coromandel Valley in 1968.

In Western Australia, new boutique winemakers such as Vasse Felix (Dr Tom Cullity) and Moss Wood (Dr Bill Pannell) pioneered the Margaret River, while in the Mount Barker region, Tony Smith established Plantagenet Wines in 1968. Even in established Western Australian areas such as Wanneroo north of Perth, winemakers such as Paul Conti placed a new emphasis on table wines.

The 1970s spurred on the frenzied rush to make boutique wine. Many new wineries came into existence, some destined to become stars shining nationally, some to bump along in the rut of subsistence, more to flourish for a few vintages until they had exhausted their owners' enthusiasm or finances or both and a few (a very few) to make a small but tidy living. Generally it was stark proof of the old saying that if winemakers wanted to make a small fortune out of a winery, they should start off with a large one.

One authority[1] estimates that by the mid-1970s there were 144 new small wineries throughout Australia producing table wine, thirty-five in New South Wales, forty-three in Victoria, thirty-eight in South Australia, twenty-four in Western Australia and four in Tasmania.

Thus the Hunter Valley saw the creation of Allandale, Calais Estates (formerly called Wollundry), Peterson's and Sutherland, while Mudgee witnessed the rise of names such as Botobolar, Burnbrae, Amberton, Miramar, Thistle Hill and, biggest of all, Montrose. Elsewhere in New South Wales, old vine haunts were re-established. At Camden, Norman Hanckel planted Camden Estate not far from the original vineyard of William Macarthur, which had been destroyed by phylloxera ninety years before. At Young, on the South-West Slopes, the first vineyards of the wine area to be known as Hilltops were being developed at Barwang and Nioka Ridge. Even close to the metropolitan area of Sydney, as older vineyards such as Minchinbury began to disappear due to the sprawl of suburbia, others like the Richmond Estate of Dr Barry Bracken appeared.

Indeed, perhaps the most important wine development in New South Wales so far as national wine interests were concerned was not the boutique boom, which after all (according to industry leaders of the time) was distracting the wine buying public from the major producers, but the establishment in 1976 of a new faculty at the Riverina College of Advanced Education (now Charles Sturt University) at Wagga in southern New South Wales. This Wine Science School was set up and headed by Brian Croser, a winemaker with excellent qualifications in the theory and practice of modern Australian winemaking. Croser, who had not long before returned from post-graduate studies at the Davis campus of the University of California, had spent two years as chief winemaker at Hardy's where, with little doubt, he had been largely responsible for refashioning the Australian rhine riesling style, so stunning was his 1975 Siegersdorf Rhine Riesling. Croser, who was to remain at Wagga for two years, retained the right to work as a wine consultant and also to make his own wine, Petaluma.

Meanwhile Victoria was also continuing its winery boom. Older areas such as the Goulburn Valley, Great Western and the North-East, which had battled through eighty years of public indifference, now gained new recruits while the success of the boutique pioneers in regions for so long lost to the vine impelled others to devote their time and resources to new winery ventures in those areas.

Thus in the Goulburn Valley Chateau Tahbilk was joined in 1972 by Mitchelton, an inspiration of the late Ross Shelmerdine, a wine enthusiast whose family involvement with Mitchelton continues to the present day. Not far away in distance but light years away in concept, Dr Peter Tisdall was beginning the planting of Mt Helen high in the Strathbogie Ranges. So too in Great Western, Seppelt's and Best's saw the planting of other vineyards such as Montara and the Fratin brothers at Mt Langi Ghiran, while the neighbouring Pyrenees region had been reborn some years earlier (1960), though not for the purpose of table wine, by the planting of brandy grapes at Chateau Remy, a venture of the Melbourne wholesale house, Nathan & Wyeth. For many years they had imported Remy Martin cognac, and had decided pragmatically enough, after France had been overrun by the Germans in the Second World War, that the marketing of a good product should not be prevented by such a small thing as a world war when good Australian brandy could be substituted. Honour was satisfied, however, by Nathan & Wyeth holding all the profits of its Australian sales in trust for Remy Martin and repatriating these at the end of the war. These were to form the financial basis for the creation of Chateau Remy in 1960 and for a much closer corporate relationship which ultimately led to Nathan & Wyeth being taken over by Remy Martin. So poor were the prospects for local brandy in the 1970s that the decision was made to convert the trebbiano production into sparkling wine base. This grape was satisfactory for ordinary sparkling wines but has now been entirely superseded by chardonnay and pinot noir in the production of such wines at the estate.

The establishment of Chateau Remy proved to be a spur to other budding vignerons in the Pyrenees region. In the early 1970s a group of Ballarat investors began a large vineyard project about twenty kilometres north-west of Avoca. Soon they became aware that they had overreached themselves (a common ailment of vineyard syndicates at this time) and so decided to sell. To their good fortune, a mysterious buyer, who subsequently, proved to be American banker John Goelet, was found. The first manager of Taltarni, as the large vineyard came to be called, was David Hohnen, later to be a winemaker of great importance in the Margaret River area. Hohnen was then succeeded by Dominique Portet, son of the former régisseur of Chateau Lafite, and in 1977 the first Taltarni vintage was made.

Not far away Neil Robb, who had spent some years at Chateau

Remy, planted Redbank in 1973, and retired Melbourne stockbroker John Barry set up Mount Avoca in 1978, while Taltarni attracted two close neighbours, Warrenmang in 1974 and Dalwhinnie in 1976.

In the North-East, Brown Brothers began to expand rapidly, taking in fruit from local farmers in the King Valley as well as planting many more hectares around the home winery at Milawa. New names such as Koombahla and Meadow Creek began to appear on their labels. The Browns, far-sighted as ever, began export initiatives too and by 1980 were one of Victoria's larger and more successful producers.

The North-East saw other changes at this time. As mentioned above, Bailey's, long established but run down by 1972, was sold to Davis Gelatine, but the quality of the liqueur muscats and monolithic reds continued under Harry Tinson, company executive turned winemaker. Elsewhere little was to change, though some descendants of established district families such as Rick Morris began winemaking on their own account and one, Melba Slamen, granddaughter of Charles Hughes Morris, bought the old and considerably run-down Fairfield property where the Morris dynasty had begun over one hundred years before.

The proliferation of Victorian boutique wineries continued. It was almost as if every prosperous person of whatever profession who had ever sipped a glass of wine wanted their own vineyard. After Stuart Anderson's successful renaissance of Bendigo, other budding vignerons joined the crush. Thus the area saw the birth of Water Wheel Vineyard in 1972, Passing Clouds in 1974, Jasper Hill and Mount Ida in 1976, Chateau Le Amon in 1977, while away to the south near Ballarat Ian Home had been establishing Yellowglen between 1971 and 1975.

Geelong too was beset by the boutique bug. The pioneering work of the Seftons at Idyll and Maltby at Anakie in the 1960s was followed by Stuart Hooper who planted a few vines in the village of Bannockburn in 1973 and then a more substantial eight hectare vineyard on the rolling hills of another of his properties some kilometres away. After Bannockburn came Prince Albert, planted totally to pinot noir in 1975 on one of the ancestral sites of Geelong, originally owned by M. Pettavel, the Swiss vigneron, responsible for some of the early vineyards of the region. By 1978 the first Prince Albert Pinot Noir was on the market and it was a revelation to those Australian consumers who understood true burgundy just how close cool area Australian pinot could come to the great red variety of the Côte d'Or.

On the other side of Port Phillip Bay, the Mornington Peninsula was arousing vine interest. It had known the vine in a casual way in the late nineteenth century and more recently in the 1950s when a member of the Seppelt family had planted 1.5 hectares of vines as an experiment at Dromana. This block with its vines was subsequently bought by the brother-in-law of the late Melbourne wine merchant Doug Seabrook, who assiduously made the wine for several vintages until the mid-1960s when the property was once again sold. Though the vineyard disappeared in the devastating Dromana bushfire of 1967, that conflagration rekindled the flicker of interest that was shown in the region, for five years later in 1972, the prominent Melbourne businessman, Baillieu Myer, made an experimental planting of 400 vines on his family property, Elgee Park. Subsequently in 1975 Nat White began to establish a 2.5 hectare vineyard at Red Hill. Further plantings followed at Balnarring and Merricks. By 1980 the Mornington vignoble, though a postage stamp compared to other Australian regions, was slightly greater in area than it had been a century before.

Meanwhile, the Yarra Valley had continued its expansion. Diamond Valley, Lilydale Vineyards and Yarra Burn all came into being in 1976. Here too was another small area waiting to prove itself and prove itself it did when Chateau Yarrinya won the famous Jimmy Watson Trophy at the Melbourne Wine Show in 1978 with its cabernet sauvignon. The Yarra Valley would continue to boom well into the 1980s.

There would be new outposts of the vine established too in Gippsland where Ken Eckersley set up his Nicholson River winery in 1978 and Phillip Jones established Bass Phillip in 1979. Gippsland would prove to be a fascinating region for pinot noir and chardonnay.

Immediately to the north of Melbourne, the far-flung Macedon area also reached for the vine. Old sites such as Craiglee, which had flourished in the nineteenth century, saw the vine once more in 1976, while further to the north near Romsey the English architect turned vigneron, Gordon Cope-Williams, made the first plantings of pinot noir and chardonnay at his Rocky Hill vineyard in 1977. Then it was time for the Knight family to build its own winery in 1979. Others would follow, but the wide diversity of climate in the Macedon region would demand that the greatest care be taken by vignerons in their choice of grape varieties for any given site.

An even greater measure of care would prove to be necessary in Tasmania as would-be vignerons sought to emulate the enthusiasm of their mainland cousins in the location of new sites. Andrew Pirie, a postgraduate student in botany, became interested in viticulture and wine after a working holiday in France in the early 1970s, so interested in fact that he decided to write his doctoral thesis on prospective cool-climate viticultural areas in Australia. After an intensive study of various regions in his quest for an area which would produce 'European-style' table wine, he selected the Pipers Brook district as the most suitable area for his purpose in 1972. All that remained was to secure the necessary financial backing. He was successful and the planting of Pipers Brook Vineyard began in 1974.

Others also saw Tasmania as a most promising prospect for the production of fine table wines. The Fesq and Haselgrove families joined with Graham Wiltshire in securing land adjoining Pipers Brook Vineyard, the Heemskerk vineyard being planted in 1975.

In the south, nearer to Hobart, Moorilla pressed ahead with its Bream Creek Vineyard, while west of the city Meadowbank was founded in 1974.

Tasmania would remain a small wine producer but it was learning the important lesson of growing its grape varieties according to site, climate and exposure.

In the West, the boutique boom, inspired by government and academic reports and begun by medical practitioners, escalated. At Margaret River in 1971 yet another doctor, Kevin Cullen, and his wife Diana, began planting at Willyabrup. In 1975 the first red wine, a cabernet sauvignon, was made. Yet Margaret River was not to remain the exclusive domain of the medical profession, as the progress of the decade saw successful businessmen who also shared a love of fine table wine seize their opportunity. Thus Leeuwin Estate was created as a showcase in the manner of the better Californian wineries and this was presumably no coincidence since in its early days in 1974 the eminent Californian winemaker Robert Mondavi performed important consultative work in site selection for owner Denis Horgan.

Another vineyard venture begun in an experimental way was that of Margaret River Landholdings, which planted one hectare of cabernet sauvignon in 1970 as a diversification measure to assuage some of the pain that the cattle industry was then enduring. This company, which was to become Cape Mentelle Vineyards, continued its planting until by 1975 there were fifteen hectares of cabernet, riesling and shiraz. In 1976 its first wines were released.

By now the doctors and company directors of Margaret River had been joined in their grape growing and winemaking endeavours by old established winemakers, geologists, professional viticulturalists and schoolteachers. So it was that the old established Swan Valley winemaker, Sandalford, came to Margaret River in 1972, and newer maker Evans and Tate two years later. Geologist Ian Lewis established Cape Clairault in 1976 and Department of Agriculture specialist Tony Devitt encouraged his family to plant Ashbrook in the same year in which schoolmaster Kevin Squance set up Willespie, an educational precedent followed by retired economics teacher Erland Happ in 1978.

At the same time as the Forest Hill experimental plantings at Mount Barker, viticultural exploration was also proceeding at Frankland River. In the late 1960s vine trials had been carried out at Westfield, the Frankland River property of the Roche family, who in 1970 decided to plant a vineyard of nearly one hundred hectares with plans for the later erection of a winery. From 1972 to 1978 the fruit was sold to Sandalford and during this time the Roche family decided to remain as grape growers. By 1979 Houghton, the principal winemaker of Western Australia and by now a subsidiary of Thomas Hardy & Sons, had become the principal buyer of Westfield grapes; so important a source of quality fruit was the Netley Brook vineyard (as it was known) to become that Houghton took a five-year lease of the vineyard in 1981.

The desire to diversify their agricultural production led other graziers along the vineyard path in the Mount Barker–Frankland River region. In 1971 Mervyn and Judy Lange planted a few hectares of vines on their sheep and wheat Alkoomi property, extending the vineyard throughout the 1970s and at first having their wines contract-made at other wineries. By 1979 they had erected their own winery to produce the distinctively 'leafy' whites and reds of the region.

In 1971 Mike and Alison Goundrey planted a hectare of vines at their Sheldon Park property. Their first vintage (1975) was made at the Plantagenet winery, a converted apple-packing shed bought in 1974. Subsequent Goundrey vintages until 1979 were made at Plantagenet (1976), in the Swan Valley (1977) and on their own property (Sheldon Park) in 1978, while late in that year they bought in the nearby town of Denmark, an old butter factory which was transformed into a working winery in time for vintage 1979. The Mount Barker–Frankland River area was up and running and would gain national recognition for the quality of its rieslings and reds a decade later.

The explosion of viticultural enthusiasm that sent its shock waves through Margaret River was also felt further north along the coastal strip extending from Busselton to Perth. Here in the predominantly sandy loam country (locally called tuart sand because of the tuart gum tree which favours this sort of terrain), Dr Barry Killerby established Leschenault near Gelorup in 1973, while a year later Will Nairn planted Peel Estate (named after the original grantee of the land, a relative of Sir Robert Peel, prime minister of England). Others followed in this region, Gill Thomas, a Bunbury pharmacist, planting near Gelorup in 1976 and yet another doctor, Peter Pratten, established Capel Vale on richer loam further south towards Busselton in 1979.

In the Swan Valley the 1970s seemed to change but little. As the decade dawned the winemaking mixture was much the same—heavy reds and fortifieds made by small families of Yugoslav and Italian stock—as it had been for the previous two generations, but changes were gradually taking place. The Houghton-Valencia combine owned by the Emu Wine Company since 1950 when the Ferguson family had sold out, was still under the control of the redoubtable Jack Mann who retired after his fiftieth vintage in 1972. The Emu Wine Company also had been influenced by Dr John Gladstones's report as it related to the areas nearer Perth, and in 1968 had purchased a large tract of land at Gingin, eighty kilometres north of Perth. The Moondah Brook Estate as it was called was initially planted with 121 hectares of vines, chiefly chenin blanc (thirty hectares), cabernet sauvignon, shiraz and muscadelle (each nineteen hectares), malbec (fifteen hectares) and verdelho (twelve hectares) with the balance allotted to such 'experimental' varieties as chardonnay.

Change continued at Houghton in the 1970s, the company being bought by Thomas Hardy & Sons in 1976.

Nearby Sandalford passed out of the exclusive ownership of the Roe family in 1971 when a Western Australian merchant bank acquired an interest after the death of winemaker David Roe. Now all eyes were focussed on Margaret River where in 1972 the company had begun the first plantings of an estate which was to encompass 125 hectares by 1980. The large United Kingdom conglomerate, the Inchcape Group, acquired a substantial interest in Sandalford in 1979.

But other people interested in wine were moving into the Swan Valley, just as others in the eastern states had moved into established viticultural areas. In 1971 two business partners, John Evans and John Tate, planted a 0.8 hectare vineyard on Evans's farm at Bakers Hill and in the following year bought the run-down Gnangara Vineyard and Winery at West Swan. The old fortified varieties were grubbed out and replaced by shiraz and the winery was extensively modernised; refrigeration was installed for fermentation and storage areas were air-conditioned, but the Evans and Tate vision was broader than just the Swan. They were also attracted by Margaret River, in 1974 buying twenty-seven hectares of land which they named Redbrook Estate and planting there mostly cabernet sauvignon, merlot and shiraz being other red varieties with chardonnay and semillon being the principal whites.

Though the rush to plant vineyards and erect small wineries was most evident in the southern states of Australia, the Stanthorpe region of Queensland was also affected. By the early 1970s basic beverage production from excess table grapes was giving way to serious winemaking from specialised varieties. Such new names as Robinson Family Vineyards and Rumbalara were joining the older established producers of the district like Biltmore Cellars (later to become Mount Magnus), Bungawarra and Sundown Valley (later Ballandean Estate). Others too hurried to join the fray. The Comino family arrived in 1976 to plant land south of Severnlea, Ian Davis began Winewood in 1979 and Jim Lawrie started Stone Ridge two years later. By 1981 the Granite Belt had a small but purposeful industry dedicated to quality table wines.

Nor were the national capital and nearby regions in New South Wales to be divorced from the nation's renewed enthusiasm for small wineries and their products. As might be expected, most vignerons were drawn from the ranks of research scientists or government administrators. Dr Edgar Riek planted his first vines virtually on the shores of Lake George in 1971, to be followed by the late Sir Brian Murray in 1973 at Doonkuna to the north of Canberra. Retired research scientist Ken Helm started to plant his vineyard south of Murrumbateman in the Yass River Valley a year later, while another scientist, Dr David Carpenter, began Lark Hill in the hills above Lake George in 1978. Problems existed in abundance and not the least were summer droughts, cockatoos and spring frosts. By the late 1970s the new Canberra vignerons were coming to terms with the demands of nature, though production would remain minute well into the 1980s.

In the meantime, a whole new viticultural region was coming into being in New South Wales. On the Lachlan River, 160 kilometres north-west of Canberra, Cowra Vineyards made its first plantings in 1973 with the intention of extending its vineyard to 160 hectares. Generously flavoured and easy drinking chardonnays would make the area's reputation in the next twenty years and draw the attention of larger producers to the potential of the region.

By 1970, although South Australia had been the dominant force in the Australian wine industry for seventy-five years, even here new wine names would rapidly become fashionable. The phenomenon of the 1970s was without doubt the meteoric rise of Wolf Blass, who in 1973 left Tollana to go into full-time winemaking on his own account. Bilyara Wines and Wolf Blass quickly became household names when reds produced by that organisation won the Jimmy Watson Trophy at the Royal Melbourne Wine Show for three consecutive years (1974–6), proving Blass's mastery of blending and wood maturation. For virtually all the rest of the 1970s Blass dominated the top sector of the red-wine market without discounting price, at a time when reds were extremely difficult to sell, in a market totally dominated by white, and managed to do this with very little vineyard of his own (the original Bilyara block being only four hectares in area including the winery) until 1980 when a forty-nine hectare vineyard site was bought at Clare. The Blass phenomenon depended on the unique circumstances of the day: great skill in the blending and maturing of red wine, selection of the best red fruit then available from many areas of Australia, a declining red market (there was an overproduction of red wine grapes—this was the era of shiraz muffins) and a general acceptance by red wine loyalists that large companies were not, with very few exceptions, making good red wine. The Blass wine show juggernaut would roll on well into the 1980s, long after the producer had ceased by any measure to be a boutique winery.

There were other young winemakers in the Barossa Valley at this time who had noted Wolf Blass's success. Two such were Grant Burge and Ian Wilson, who had first met in 1972. In 1976 they formed a company which made its first wines at the Krondorf winery, then owned by Dalgety Wine Estates (an offshoot of Dalgety Australia, a large pastoral enterprise which diversified into the wine industry with no success whatsoever). In 1978 they bought the winery at an attractive price from a very willing vendor and like Blass confined themselves to the middle and upper levels of the market, again following the Blass example of owning little vineyard of their own but buying the best fruit available from quality regions of South Australia. As in Blass's case, the coveted Jimmy Watson Trophy (won in 1980) helped the Krondorf rise. Like Blass once more, the image of a boutique winery was maintained for some years despite the fact that by the early 1980s the annual Krondorf crush exceeded 2500 tonnes. Ironically the rapidly burgeoning market share of each company, both of which became listed on the stock exchange, would ultimately attract the attention of the same suitor, Mildara Wines Ltd, though the nuptials would be some years apart.

Though Blass and in turn Burge and Wilson were the phenomena of the Barossa Valley in the 1970s, they did not rely solely on its fruit, the secrets of their success being their skill in acquiring the best grapes from many areas and blending the resultant wines into extremely palatable reds and whites. One who did so rely was Peter Lehmann, who in 1979, after nineteen years as winemaker-manager of the old established Saltram winery, also decided that the time was ripe for a change. With the financial assistance of Cerebos Australia and the Anders family, he formed a company named Masterson Barossa Vignerons Pty Ltd to erect a winery in the heart of the Valley at Tanunda, believing in the intrinsic quality of Barossa grapes and his own ability to make the best possible wine from them. In doing so, he bore in mind his difficult last vintage with Saltram (then recently acquired by the international liquor conglomerate Seagram) when, in a time of local over-production, his employer instructed him to reduce local grape purchases severely. Although it was by no means an unusual practice amongst larger winemakers in times of uncertainty, he disagreed with the decision believing that his greater loyalty lay to his region. The Masterson winery opened in time for vintage 1980. For Lehmann the future years would be a struggle but he would inspire a great revival in local winemaking morale.

The cooler high country rolling south from the edges of the Barossa Valley past Mount Lofty to the hills above McLaren Vale that encouraged Joseph Gilbert to establish Pewsey Vale in 1847 and Yalumba to replant that estate in 1961 was also an inspiration later that decade to David Wynn who not only bought the country that was to become Wynn's High Eden Estate but also nearby property on which he intended to establish a family vineyard. Mountadam Estate began its plantings in 1972 and harvested its first commercial crop in 1979. In the 1980s Adam Wynn would become the third generation of his family to make an indelible mark upon the Australian wine scene.

Well satisfied with the successful rebirth of Pewsey Vale, the Hill Smiths at Yalumba once more explored the Barossa Ranges. In 1971, quite close to Pewsey Vale, they bought a pastoral property from local grazier Colin Heggie, perpetuating his name in the fifty-six hectare vineyard subsequently planted to cabernet sauvignon, merlot, pinot noir, riesling, chardonnay, sauvignon blanc and traminer. Like its elder brother, Pewsey Vale, Heggies would prove eminently suited to riesling, chardonnay and cabernet sauvignon.

There were other vignerons anxious to explore the cool high terrain to the east of Adelaide. Brian Croser, mentioned briefly in relation to the foundation of the Faculty of Wine Science at the Charles Sturt University (then the Riverina College of Advanced Education) resigned his post there in 1977 and bought a property high in the Adelaide Hills, at the same time starting the wine consultancy business Oenotech with Dr Tony Jordan. In 1976, while at Wagga, Croser had made the first Petaluma wine, a spatlese rhine riesling from Victorian fruit and in 1977 the first Petaluma chardonnay from Cowra material. In the meantime he had become acquainted with prominent wine publicist and co-founder of Rothbury Estate, Len Evans. The acquaintanceship rapidly blossomed into a close friendship and business connection and when in 1978 the dynamic Sydney businessman Peter Fox joined the pair the new Petaluma winery was erected on Croser's Adelaide Hills property at Piccadilly. From 1979 on, the Petaluma label had a permanent home for its Coonawarra reds, Clare rhine rieslings and diversely sourced chardonnays. The vineyard around the winery planted to pinot noir and chardonnay was also developed, a tangible expression of Croser's belief in the future of the region as a premium area for the production of sparkling wines.

The boutique push also continued in McLaren Vale in the 1970s, though for some winemakers it was the second time around. One such was Jim Ingoldby who had worked his family's Ryecroft Vineyard for many years until in 1970 he sold to the Reed Consolidated Group. After five years of managing the property for the multinational, he left to begin again close by at McLaren Flat. A small winery was erected and in due course a thirty-seven hectare vineyard consisting of cabernet sauvignon (fourteen hectares), shiraz (fifteen hectares) and rhine riesling (eight hectares) was established. In 1984 the Ingoldby vineyard and winery was sold to a syndicate managed by winemaker Bill Clappis.

Other small McLaren Vale makers to strike out for themselves in the 1970s were Richard Hamilton (1972), Maglieri (1972), Woodstock (1973), Noon's (1976) and Scarpàntoni and Maxwell (both in 1979).

Nor was Coonawarra omitted from the frantic rush by wine companies large and small to acquire some of the famous terra rossa.

The big four of Coonawarra (Lindeman's, Mildara, Penfold's and Wynn's) all substantially increased their plantings during the 1970s. By 1981 Wynn's had become the largest grower in the district with 440 hectares under vine followed by Mildara, Lindeman and Penfold in that order. Another player in the big league was Coonawarra Machinery Co, which would market its own Coonawarra wines under its Katnook and Riddoch Estate labels, would take control of Hungerford Hill's Coonawarra vineyard as it then existed, would later in the 1980s rival Wynn's in size and supply many wine companies in Australia with Coonawarra fruit. There seemed no end to the demand for Coonawarra terra rossa.

Marching under the boutique banner unfurled by Eric Brand six years before, Doug Bowen, a graduate of Roseworthy in 1971, planted his first vines the following year on a sixteen hectare block in the heart of the red soil country, working at Lindeman's Rouge Homme winery while the vines came into bearing and making his first vintage on his own account in 1975. Show success followed immediately and by the early 1980s over thirteen hectares of the estate had been planted predominantly to shiraz and cabernet sauvignon with smaller areas of merlot, riesling and chardonnay.

Though Doug Bowen was a young man, Sydney Hamilton already had a lifetime's winemaking experience behind him when he came to Coonawarra in 1974 at the age of seventy-seven. The following year he erected his Leconfield winery and made his first Coonawarra vintage from purchased grapes. In the late 1970s the quality of his cabernet sauvignons was quite exceptional for a winemaker of any age, let alone one aged eighty, and by 1980 the Leconfield Estate consisted of eight hectares of cabernet sauvignon and four hectares of riesling. By 1981, however, increasing age and ill-health obliged him to sell Leconfield to his nephew Richard Hamilton.

By the end of the 1970s, Petaluma also had arrived in Coonawarra. Using the resources of the Evans and Fox vineyard, Brian Croser made his first Coonawarra red in 1979, the precursor of an outstanding series of wines.

There were other small makers destined to grow in reputation in the 1980s who were beginning their careers at this time. Ian and Wendy Hollick began the establishment of their Coonawarra vineyards in 1975, making their first wine (though not at their own winery) in 1982. Vintage 1985 saw the completion of a new winery just two years after Ian had left his managerial position at Mildara Wines.

As in the rest of vineyard Australia, the Clare region expanded significantly in the 1970s. As mentioned previously Clare had attracted the attention of the multinationals, the Stanley Wine Co. being taken over by Heinz in 1971. As a consequence the shareholdings of the Knappstein family were paid out. The youthful Tim Knappstein bought forty hectares of country some three kilometres south-east of the town in 1972. There in accordance with the wisdom current at that time he planted chiefly riesling and cabernet sauvignon (a choice he certainly did not regret) with smaller areas of sauvignon blanc, traminer, chardonnay, shiraz, cabernet franc, merlot and malbec.

In 1976 he decided to leave the Stanley Wine Co., having made his own wine at other wineries in the area in 1974 and 1975. In that same year (1976), he formed Enterprise Wines, buying as a prospective winery the old Enterprise Brewery (founded at the end of the nineteenth century by John Christison, who by coincidence had been one of the founders of Stanley). With two vintages virtually ready for sale, Knappstein was off to a flying start in his new self-employment and when in 1977 he produced from his sauvignon blanc Australia's first fumé blanc, the reputation of Enterprise amongst wine connoisseurs was quickly established.

For Andrew and Jane Mitchell, the story was very different. Running parallel to the main Clare Valley about two kilometres to the west is the Skillogalee Valley, where Andrew's parents had been grape growers for some years. Andrew Mitchell, a graduate in economics from Adelaide University, had briefly worked in government service before deciding in 1975 with his wife Jane to follow a totally different career path.

Using an old stone packing shed on the Mitchell property as an extempore winery, Andrew and Jane crushed five tonnes of cabernet sauvignon to make their first red, a wine which began a worthy succession of cabernet sauvignons to be followed by rieslings of an elegance rarely surpassed in the district.

Nor was the Clare region (or perhaps more properly the Polish Hill River district to the east of the main valley) to be without its doctor turned winemaker. Dr John Wilson bought a twenty-six hectare block in the Polish Hill River district in 1974 and for several years conducted varietal trials. The resultant small quantities of several different types of grapes taught Wilson much about winemaking and the suitability of his block for exotic varieties. By 1980 Wilson had erected a winery and come to rely on the usual Clare grape varieties, cabernet, shiraz and riesling, although pinot noir and zinfandel were to remain fascinating objects of attention.

With the purchase of Clampett's vineyard to the east of the town, Petaluma also arrived in Clare in 1977, quickly setting new standards in Australian riesling as evidenced by wines such as the 1980, for example.

In contrast to some other Australian areas, the Clare region at this time seemed to attract makers both big and little often with experience in direct proportion to their size. Perhaps it was because the area had by now firmly established a reputation for quality and reliability. Thus in 1980 both Blass and Penfold's established large areas of vineyard. The region's other large producers, Stanley and Taylor's, continued their plantings. For Stanley, whose lovely rieslings of the early 1970s had helped create the white wine boom and who were now under the control of H. J. Heinz, it was also an orderly expansion. The crush of nearly 5000 tonnes in 1970 had increased by forty per cent about ten years later and the vineyard area had reached almost 300 hectares.

For Taylor's, whose original vineyard concept had been one hundred per cent red, it was back to the drawing board when national tastes changed in favour of white. From 1977 large areas of reds were either grubbed out and replanted or grafted over to white, with the result that by 1983 about forty-five per cent of the Estate had become white. Though tastes had changed, Taylor's were equal to the task.

At the same time (1970) as new vignerons were coming into the Clare fold, one, Roly Birks, was preparing to retire at the age of seventy-seven after a lifetime at Wendouree making those big solid reds. As his son was not willing to follow him into winemaking, Roly had sold the business to a Victorian company. Unfortunately, Birks decided to leave part of the purchase money as shares in the purchasing company. The company soon floundered and the shares became worthless, its receiver selling the chief vineyards and winery in 1972 to a Sydney businessman, Max Liberman, who handed the property over to his daughter, Lita Brady, and her lawyer husband, Tony, for management. In the normal course this may have spelt disaster, but wisely a young winemaker was appointed and called in Roly Birks as consultant, drawing on his lifetime of experience. By the late 1970s, in the hands of the Bradys, Wendouree was flourishing once more and making wines in its traditional style.

So throughout Australia the era of the small winemaker planting his vineyard and building an often rudimentary winery in the hope, highly optimistic in most cases, of a prosperous future had well and truly arrived. What was the response of the wine establishment to this unforeseen development?

Basically it was to move down-market, leaving the peaks of marketing mostly to the smaller established regional wineries and to the boutiques. Keen to increase market share, they rapidly took up the 'bag-in-the-box' and lowered the standards of popular bottled brands to suit the market's pocket. Per capita wine consumption increased steadily, virtually doubling in the 1970s from 8.9 litres in 1970 to 17.3 in 1980. The cause of this was the popularity of white wine, but above all cheap wine and the bag-in-the-box. Other factors were the virtual price freeze on sparkling wine due to intense competition in that sector of the market, the proliferation of liquor outlets due to the liberalisation of licensing laws and gross overproduction of multi-purpose grapes such as sultana. Raw material for bulk white wine was never cheaper.

Yet though the consumer benefitted and corporate wine turnover increased, there was little profit in all this for larger operators, squeezed as they were by intense competition in the lower and middle sectors of the wine market and by price discounting at retail level.

There were however very significant developments in wine style during the 1970s and these must be emphasised. Firstly the retention of residual sugar in rhine riesling, secondly the fermentation and maturation of chardonnay in new small oak and thirdly the re-emergence of the blending skills of our red-winemakers particularly with wines matured in new small oak. And the acceptance of these styles indicated the increasing sophistication of the Australian palate.

There were new developments in sparkling wine also. To reduce labour costs, thereby maintaining that very necessary competitive edge, the 'star transfer method of disgorgement was widely introduced into the sparkling wine industry in the mid-1970s, thereby eliminating the costly manual removal of lees from cheaper sparkling wines and enabling economies to be passed on to the consumer. Meanwhile in the quality sector of that market, moves were afoot to use chardonnay and pinot noir, though then only available in minute quantities, as 'base wine' in the manner of true champagne. This trend would become a surge in the 1980s as large companies such as Seppelt's and smaller entities like Yellowglen sought to increase consumer awareness of quality sparkling wine and to present a credible alternative to imported sparkling wines, especially champagne.

With such advances in wine styles, an ever-increasing thirst for bag-in-the-box whites in its lowest sector and the seemingly inexhaustible growth of the boutiques in its upper, the wine market, its growers and makers ended the 1970s in a crescendo of confidence. Public taste had been fickle, but it had never wavered in its loyalty to table wine. The 1980s would see the boom continue.

[1] Brian Croser, paper presented to the Wine and Food Society of Australia in Sydney, April 1988.

FIFTEEN

The 1980s—current affairs

The 1980s, while continuing the white wine boom, added a few convolutions of its own, the most notable being the tremendous growth in the popularity of chardonnay. Here again the wine-planners were caught short and it was not until well into the decade that winemakers began even to hope that one day supply might catch up with demand. The chief sufferers in all this were the proud growers of rhine riesling, most of whom were located in South Australia. From a variety which accounted for 0.05 per cent of all varieties used in winemaking in 1975, chardonnay had risen to constitute 2.4 per cent of all white grapes used for winemaking in the 1984 vintage. By comparison, rhine riesling constituted ten per cent, both varieties lagging a long way behind the common multi-purpose cask-fillers sultana (twenty-one per cent) and muscat gordo blanco (twenty per cent). Chardonnay would continue its climb and rhine riesling falter as white wine tastes and consequent grower preference swung to chardonnay in the late 1980s. By vintage 1988, chardonnay constituted 6.1 per cent of tonnage and 6.2 per cent of white wine vineyard area compared to rhine riesling's 9.1 per cent of tonnage and 9.66 per cent of area.

However, though consumer preference for white wine had been much in evidence since the mid-1970s, growers were loath to lose faith in the better red varieties. Cabernet sauvignon, which had accounted for only 966 tonnes of the Australian vintage in 1970, had risen to 25 685 tonnes ten years later and remained at 24 971 tonnes in vintage 1988, while shiraz, which had enjoyed a meteoric growth in quantity though often not in quality during the 1970s, declined only steadily during the 1980s, as evidenced by the following raw tonnage statistics:

Vintage	**1970**	**1975**	**1980**	**1988**
Tonnage	27 896	72 583	69 634	48 083

Other red varieties such as grenache also became 'surplus to requirements', in many cases much to the growers' chagrin.

Vintage	**1970**	**1975**	**1980**	**1988**
Tonnage	42 037	58 912	53 188	29 536

Growers financially able to do so adapted as quickly as possible to the new 'white' environment, grubbing out old red and fortified varieties or, where possible, grafting over shiraz, grenache and even rhine riesling (later in the 1980s) to chardonnay. For some it was time to quit and leave to others the vacillations of public taste. For those who protested loudest and longest, in 1985 the South Australian Government, long sensitive to the lobbyings of grape growers, even unloosed the public purse strings and instituted a 'vine-pull' scheme, designed to encourage inefficient growers of unfashionable grape varieties to leave the industry. Indeed during the period 1980–8 the vineyard area of Australia in bearing declined from 63 776 to 53 608 hectares, but though its extent decreased, its quality and the enthusiasm of growers in propagating newer varieties most certainly did not.

In the Hunter Valley, enthusiasm for boutique winemaking continued unabated. Even the indomitable Len Evans, refusing to be downcast by the tribulations of the large Rothbury Estate, decided to have a foot in each camp, setting up his own boutique, Evans Family in 1979, chardonnay from the four hectare Evans Family vineyard being its initial speciality.

Yet not all new vineyard development or indeed vineyard purchases in the Hunter Valley were restricted to experienced professionals such as Evans. Those words 'Hunter Valley' still bore their own magic for many budding winegrowers. So it was that pharmacist Peter Marsh bought Quentin Estate in 1978, that Neil and Carolyn Sutherland acquired an older vineyard in 1979 to set up their own winery a few years later, that yet another doctor, Newton Potter, established Allanmere in 1984 and Barry Shields retired from the law to buy the old Elliott estate of Oakvale in 1985. Bankers and wine merchants were fascinated too. Nicholas Whitlam and Andrew Simon planted their Wollombi Brook vineyard in 1982, being then little aware that they would buy such a giant as Arrowfield in Upper Hunter in 1989. Despite its uncertain vintage weather and uneconomic yields in all but its best vineyards, the Hunter would not yet lose its siren-like charms.

Charmed though the budding winemakers may have been, in the late 1970s and early 1980s, the large winemakers of the Valley, their accountants and bank managers found Hunter economics anything but attractive. Poor soils and an unreliable spring rainfall (vine irrigation in this region was only just beginning) usually led to pathetically uneconomic yields of drought-stressed fruit supplemented perhaps according to the whimsy of nature by 250 millimetres of teeming rain at the moment the meagre vintage was ready to pick. Such were the vintages of 1971, 1976 and 1978 and the poor crops of unwanted red wine led very quickly in the 1970s and early 1980s to the grubbing out of large areas of uneconomic shiraz in the Hunter Valley. After the boom, the shiraz bust had arrived and was experienced by most of the major Hunter wine companies at that time. Hungerford Hill had large areas of planted vineyard 'surplus to requirements' by 1978. Rothbury Estate began to put its less generous vineyard blocks on a 'care and maintenance basis' only and the Tulloch Pokolbin Estate began to shrink rapidly. McWilliam's, Lindeman's, Saxonvale and Arrowfield were others whose shiraz vineyards were savagely slashed in area either by top-grafting them to some other more marketable variety where this was possible or by uprooting them altogether.

Though vineyard realists in the Hunter Valley and elsewhere knew only too well that the basic economics of grape growing demanded a crop yield of at least ten tonnes per hectare and that not only good soil but also irrigation were essential ingredients for any vineyard venture, grape growing and winemaking still remained an attractive prospect, not the least for professional winemakers of some seniority who were beginning to feel the constraints imposed by large winemaking organisations and wished to become masters of their own destiny. So whereas the 1970s had seen the rise (and often the fall) of syndicates of businessmen and members of professions, the 1980s reflected the rise of the professional winemaker-proprietor.

Thus the road to winemaking independence pioneered by winemakers such as Brian McGuigan, Wolf Blass, Tim Knappstein and Brian Croser during the 1970s was essayed by many others in the years following. Long hours during the week at their regular winery employment were often followed by equally long stints on weekends and holidays tending their own vines and wines.

Thus Ian Macrae began Miramar at Mudgee in 1977. Harry Tinson started his HJT vineyard near Glenrowan in 1979 and a host of new winemakers decided that the 1980s would be their decade of independence: Geoff Merrill in McLaren Vale, Geoff Weaver at Stafford Ridge in the Adelaide Hills, Gary Farr at Clyde Park near Geelong, Chris Pfeiffer in Rutherglen, and John Cassegrain in the Hastings Valley at Port Macquarie all began to plant or plan their own wine future at the start of the 1980s.

Others soon followed in new areas and old. Clare became especially popular, Jeffrey Grossett (1981), Neil Paulett (1983), Andrew and Neil Pike (1985) and Tim Adams (1986) all starting winemaking on their own account. Other established areas such as the Barossa Valley saw the establishment of Rockford (Rocky O'Callaghan) in 1984 and Charles Melton Wines in 1986 while Ian Hollick began winemaking in Coonawarra in 1983. Other well-known winemakers chose less well-known sites: John Ellis, the prominent former winemaker of Rosemount and later of Tisdall, choosing virtually unknown country on the chilly Macedon Plateau in 1982. Some such as Andrew Garrett, virtually ran travelling wineries, renting space and facilities from other wineries and moving their wines from winery to winery as occasion demanded until they found a permanent home. It was very much the era of the young upwardly mobile winemaker.

Yet the rise of the young winemaker-proprietor by no means blunted the enthusiasm of amateurs who remained keen to begin their own life in wine, whether as a new and totally different occupation or simply as an attractive investment which they could control themselves.

As usual, most of the enthusiasts came from the more affluent professions. They could probably afford their passion. Medicine, dentistry, the law, banking, all were represented. But there were other occupations, both similar and totally dissimilar to winemaking and viticulture. Thus there were nurserymen such as Garry Crittenden, who began Dromana on the Mornington Peninsula in 1982; clothing magnates like Mark Besen, who set up Tarrawarra in the Yarra in 1983; and even press photographer turned abalone diver Geoff Bull, who founded Freycinet Vineyards near Bicheno on Tasmania's east coast in 1980. Yet fortunately for the allure of wine, there were very few accountants.

The Yarra Valley seemed most attractive to lawyers with former legal partners Louis Bialkower and James Halliday (the latter for the second time as he had been one of the mainsprings of Brokenwood in the Hunter Valley) establishing the prominent estates Yarra Ridge in 1983 and Coldstream Hills in 1985.

Yet not only lawyers were fascinated by the Yarra, it also drew the attention of one of the world's most professional winemakers, Moët et Chandon, the champagne giant. Through Moët's Californian subsidiary, Domaine Chandon, Australia was established in 1988 at Green Point close to Yeringberg. Dr Tony Jordan, instrumental in advising this important step, was also appointed managing director.

At Margaret River the medical tradition continued, Dr Mike Peterkin establishing Pierro in 1980. For Peterkin it was the culmination of a winemaking dream that haunted him while still a student, so much so that within four years of graduating in medicine, he had also completed the Roseworthy course in 1977.

For others the wine bug bit a second time. James Halliday's instance has already been mentioned, as has the case of Sidney Hamilton, but Karl Seppelt too was a willing victim. After retiring from the Seppelt company upon its takeover by South Australian Brewing, he literally headed for the Hills, setting up Grand Cru Estate at Springton in 1981.

Similarly, corporate takeover and a later dissolution of the Burge family winemaking partnership at Wilsford saw the creation of two more small Barossa wineries in the late 1980s. Grant Burge, together with Ian Wilson, had bought the ailing Krondorf winery from Dalgety in 1978, in the ensuing few years making it highly successful and in the process listing it on the stock exchange. In a lightning coup, Mildara Wines secured control of Krondorf in 1986 and though he worked for the company for some time afterwards, Grant Burge had by 1988 set up his own 'Grant Burge' brand, relying for fruit on his family's extensive vineyards in the area. Meanwhile, the elder generation of the Burge family was nearing retirement and so it was agreed that Grant should purchase the Wilsford winery while his cousin Rick, also a highly talented winemaker, would operate Burge Family Winemakers at nearby Lyndoch.

Though the minnows of the Australian wine industry continued to frolic in the shallows, it was becoming more apparent that the bigger fish controlling the more price-conscious depths of the Australian wine lake were more and more inclined to cannibalism.

In such areas where profit per bottle was often microscopic or the market share of a bigger fish in some sensitive market sector was smaller than that of some brash newcomer or a once-vigorous but now vulnerable competitor, the accepted wisdom was to increase market share by corporate takeover. Penfold's, itself moving from family control to Sydney brewer Tooth & Co. in 1976 and later to the Adsteam group, was particularly voracious in the 1980s, absorbing Kaiser Stuhl (the Barossa Co-operative) in 1982 and the Wynn's-Seaview Group in 1985. Later in the 1980s other Penfold's acquisitions would include Tollana and in 1990 the jewel in the crown, the Lindeman's group. Hardy's too were active, buying Rhinecastle (a distributor of some of its group products) and Chateau Reynella in 1982. Mildara also felt the need to expand. After digesting the old-established Hamilton's organisation in 1979, it swallowed

Yellowglen in 1984, Balgownie near Bendigo in 1985 and Krondorf the following year. In 1991 a major Mildara move saw it merge with Wolf Blass Wines, which itself had, in the late 1980s, acquired Tim Knappstein Wines in Clare and the old Quelltaler winery at Watervale from Remy Martin. In addition, the large Riverland cooperatives at Berri and Renmark merged in 1982, creating a new giant, Consolidated Co-operative Wineries Ltd.

Some Australian wine executives even contrived to 'buy back the farm'. Such was the case in 1988 when Orlando was bought from the multinational grocery concern Reckitt & Colman by some of its senior Australian management. The 'farm's' Australian ownership was short-lived however, Orlando being sold once more late in 1989 to an overseas group controlled by Pernod-Ricard.

Sometimes the battles for control reached fever-pitch and were fought out in court. The object of one such tussle was the publicly listed Seppelt company, whose shares were at the time held by Diverse Products (the local Coca-Cola bottler) and the South Australian Government Insurance Office amongst other large institutional holdings. The suitor was the then intensely acquisitive Adsteam Group (owner of Penfold's). After a protracted legal wrangle over two years (1982–4) in which the major beneficiary was the legal profession, the suit was successfully spurned, the exhausted quarry soon after falling into the arms of the local brewer, South Australian Brewing. The ultimate irony was to occur some years later (in 1990) when Adsteam (by now cash-strapped and friendless) sold its Penfold's wine group to South Australian Brewing, who by this purchase put together Australia's largest wine production and marketing group controlling about forty-five per cent of the local industry. Such were the aggressive and defensive manoeuvrings of Australian Wine Incorporated which typified the industry and its crucial domestic markets during the 1980s.

Though the struggle for domestic market share quite naturally occupied the minds of all winemakers, the market nevertheless was buoyant. Wine was seemingly becoming an essential part of the Australian lifestyle, as rising per capita consumption figures readily showed. From a national per capita consumption of 17.3 litres for the year ended 30 June 1980, intake had steadily increased to 21.3 litres by mid-1987, a jump of over twenty-three per cent in seven years.

What were Australians drinking in 1988? That year saw sales (local and export) of 370 million litres, of which a little over ten per cent (39 million litres) was exported. Of the 331 million litres of wine sold locally, 257.2 million litres was table wine, the rest being fortified and sparkling. White wine at 204 million litres was by far the most popular tipple, leaving in its wake red (44.4 million litres) and rosé (7.2 million). Australian wine taste was becoming drier too. Of those 205 million litres of white wine, 168.21 million were below 1° Baume in sweetness. In fact such white wine accounted for nearly two-thirds (65.8 per cent) of all table wine sold in Australia. And how did most of that wine reach the market? Soft packs ('wine-casks') of two-litre capacity and larger accounted for 108.5 million litres (64.5 per cent). Such wine was relatively cheap at about $1.50 a litre and when placed in soft-packs which could be readily refrigerated, became an almost indispensable part of the summer life of many Australians, accounting as it did for 32.7 per cent of the entire wine market.

How far white wine had advanced in public favour by mid-1988 is amply illustrated by the following table:

Wine type	Quantity sold (millions of litres)	per cent
White Wine < 1° Baume	168.212	50.88
White Wine > 1° Baume	35.972	10.88
Red Wine	44.431	13.43
Rosé	7.234	2.18
Sherry (all types)	15.567	4.71
Dessert (inc. port)	19.49	5.9
Sparkling	32.642	9.88
Carbonated	1.418	0.43
Flavoured	2.969	0.89
Vermouth (sweet and dry)	2.662	0.82
Total	**330.597**	**100%**

There were other commercial uses for white wine also. One which enjoyed a surge of popularity in the mid-1980s was the wine cooler (a blend of fruit juice and white wine). But fashions like dogs have their days and after rising from a low base of less than 0.5 million litres in mid-1985 to a peak of over 5.5 million litres in summer 1987, such devotion cooled noticeably in the later 1980s.

The public passion for chardonnay however grew ever more ardent. This was in turn reflected by winemaking demand, increasing grape prices and consequent grower enthusiasm. Total chardonnay area in Australia in mid-1988 was 2978 hectares, 634 of which were not then in bearing. Chardonnay had already surpassed semillon in area (2573 hectares) and was setting out strongly in pursuit of riesling (3703 hectares) which occupied first place amongst white grapes used solely for table wine.

Of red grapes, shiraz retained its premier position (4809 hectares), although cabernet sauvignon occupied 3622 hectares, and great interest was being shown in merlot (316 hectares, with 107 hectares yet to crop) and cabernet franc (195 hectares, 73 hectares still to bear). The red cultivar obviously causing most grower excitement however was pinot noir (785 hectares, with 261 hectares not then in bearing). Whether the Australian consumer would accept these 'new' varietals, especially pinot with its characteristic paleness of colour and lightness of flavour, was debatable, but the winemakers were confident that with education they would.

As Australia approached its bicentennial anniversary, perhaps the most remarkable feature of the wine industry was the sudden upsurge of exports. For most of the 1980s, Australian wine exports had limped along at a level of between 6 and 9 million litres per year. Indeed the levels had shown little change in the previous twenty years. Then for the year ended June 1986, Australian wine exports reached 10.8 million litres, a steady yet satisfactory growth of twenty-five per cent on the previous year. There was widespread astonishment when in the next year (to 30 June 1987) exports leapt almost one hundred per cent to 21.3 million litres. It was unprecedented. Not only had the helm swung from 'steady' to 'full steam ahead', but wine exports had achieved an all-time record, surpassing the quantities of fortified wine shipped nearly fifty years before in the uncertain days before the Second World War. Was this sudden boom to be a mere aberration? Certainly not, for the ensuing year (ending 30 June 1988) produced another record, this time 39.3 million litres (a leap of eighty-five per cent) at an estimated value to the economy of A$97.5 million. Within the space of two years the world had become aware of Australian wine and was beginning to seek it. Exports had come to represent over ten per cent of sales and though as a wine exporter Australia was a very small fish by world standards (representing less than one per cent of the world's wine trade), its wine industry was determined to increase its efforts.

It soon realised that any breath of scandal such as those issuing from time to time from Europe would ruin its growing reputation for quality and value-for-money. So it decided to put teeth into its wine laws which, though uniform amongst the states, had been left to individual state health authorities to enforce. It did this by introducing its Label Integrity Program (LIP).

The existing laws concerned grape variety, region of origin and vintage and, in brief, required that if the name of any wine included any allusion to grape variety, locality or year of vintage, then the wine must contain at least eighty per cent of that variety, must be at least eighty per cent from that region and ninety-five per cent of the year of vintage. From 1990 the law was amended to authorise the Australian Wine and Brandy Corporation (AWBC) to assist on the keeping of standard winery records and to audit any claims made by the winery in respect of vintage, varietal or regional content or both. This it could do by checking winery records made at four key points in the winemaking and sales process. These were to be the winery weighbridge where grapes were bought and received; the cellar where the grapes were converted into wine; the sales desk where inter-company sales and purchases took place; and the wholesale desk where finished wine left the cellar as a product with a label stating a grape variety or grape varieties, region of origin and year of vintage or alternatively with an invoice so describing such wine if it were to be sold in bulk.

The standard system of record-keeping insisted that such weighbridge records had to show year of vintage, location of vineyard (origin), grape variety, tonnage, and name of grower. In the winery itself, such records had to indicate the identity of the wine produced from those grapes identified at the weighbridge, the volume of wine made therefrom, consolidations of identical wines, blending of non-identical wines, identity of ensuing products and records of release of the finished wine. In this way the wine retained the official identity acquired at the weighbridge, which it could have lost if it were destined to be a 'generic' (such as 'chablis') or a 'style' (such as dry red). If the wine were required to be sold in bulk or in unlabelled bottles ('cleanskin') in an inter-company transaction, then the records had to specify the identity, volume and purchaser of such bulk or 'cleanskin' wine and the source, identity and volume of wines brought in from other wineries to form the whole or part of any wine with a vintage, variety or region of origin claim. Finally if the wine were destined for the retail market, when bottled, labelled and packaged, its records had to show the total production of a wine carrying vintage variety and region of origin claims, stocks of wine carrying such claims and sales of all such wines.

Thus by the use of this 'universal recording system', as it has been called by the AWBC, it was possible for an auditor to validate the legitimacy of all vintage, variety and region of origin claims made by winemakers, indeed to go further and to check the wines of any company or group of companies and the varietal wines of any region. By means of the Label Integrity Program, requested by the wine industry itself, credible 'teeth' were inserted into a law previously seen to be only a 'paper tiger'. Needless to say there were substantial penalties for infraction, not the least, in a time of increasing export sales, the cancellation of export approvals and the subsequent necessity to recall offending wines. Such were the laws intended to protect the consumers of Australian wines, both at home and overseas.

And where were those export consumers of Australian wine and what wines were they consuming in 1988? Of those exported 39.3 million litres, table wines were by far the most sought-after type, accounting for over 35 million litres. In volume terms the leading overseas buyers for the year up to 30 June 1988 were Sweden (8.4 million litres, taken mostly in bulk), United Kingdom (7.3 million litres, taken in bottle and bulk) and USA (4.4 million litres taken mostly in bottle). In monetary terms, the positions were exactly the reverse, which proved to most shippers the value of shipping in bottle, not only because of profitability, but also for brand promotion and quality control. There was another important feature of the export market beginning to emerge also and that was the making of wines especially for that market and not just the export of wines surplus to local requirement. Indeed one of these wines, Lindeman Bin 65 Chardonnay, would be sold overseas for some years before being made available to the local market. The trend amongst leading exporters was to establish their own sales offices overseas and not merely appoint distributors. What some intended to create was a truly international market for their Australian wines with Australia simply the source and not necessarily the end-point of sales. Australians therefore might need to compete in price terms against other national markets for popular Australian 'international' wines. Australian wine export had come a very long way since Gregory Blaxland's quarter cask in 1822.

Postscript: The 1990s

So Australian wine has moved into the 1990s. Its prospects are bright. There are buoyant markets overseas; the United Kingdom in particular is again enamoured of Australian wine. This time it is not heavy red and fortified, but keenly priced table wine of delicacy and style, both red and white. Export levels approach 80 million litres, almost twenty per cent of wine produced, and A$250 million in value. An export target of one billion dollars is enshrined as a holy grail for the turn of the century and the necessary investment in vineyard and winery infrastructure to achieve this object glibly spoken of as A$1.2 billion.

Australian producers have begun to invest overseas in wineries and vineyards, in France, Italy, New Zealand, the USA and even in a minute way in China. Thus Hardy has gone to the south of France and Italy, while other Australian investors have planted vineyards in areas nearby. Penfold's has seen opportunities in California, Brian Croser in Oregon, and many companies have invested in New Zealand. Australian investment and winemaking skills are beginning to go offshore while, due to an increasingly weak Australian dollar, export prices are keen and overseas liquor giants such as the French Pernod Ricard group and Japan's Suntory can still make attractive purchases of Australian wineries.

Australia is becoming part of a truly global wine village. And as if to underline its honourable intentions it has gone further by reaching agreement with the European Community to stop using European generic names on its own labels within certain time limits in exchange for the freer entry of its wines to Europe.

At home, the larger producers of the industry are undergoing a period of what is euphemistically called rationalisation as the whole nation experiences the worst economic depression in sixty years. Australia's largest family-owned wine company, Hardy's, has been forced into amalgamation with the giant Berri-Renmano group, the emerging offspring, BRL-Hardy being publicly listed. Only two other large family-owned concerns, Yalumba and McWilliam's, remain and even at Yalumba, one branch of the Hill Smith family had bought out another. Though other medium to large family-owned companies remain, such as Brown Brothers and Rosemount, the trend of the times is veering to publicly-listed corporate status, several wine companies including Rothbury Estate, Petaluma and Peter Lehmann choosing that path in the early 1990s. It has become obvious that the capital demands of the modern medium-to-large nationally oriented winery are beyond the means of any normal family group, however successful it has been in the past.

The wine industry is also facing new challenges to its image from its traditional prohibitionist opponents who, lumping wine into the category of alcohol and alcohol into the category of narcotic drugs, have sought restrictions on advertising, citing the effects of over-consumption of alcohol on the youth of the nation and on health generally. The wine industry, through its professional organisation the Australian Winemakers Federation, seems to be distancing itself from the beer and spirits groups by espousing the consumption of wine in moderation and in its proper social context, with food either at home or in a restaurant, and by promoting its beneficial effects on health when consumed moderately. It is resolutely refusing to be backed into the corner of 'guilt by association' with more casually consumed alcohols, beer and spirits.

The 1990s will oblige the wine industry to be more inventive also, as it grapples with the need to replace generic wine labels with original yet appealing names for Australian wines. Certainly many more wines will be labelled varietally, but what will a blend of five different white or red varieties be called? And how will the industry respond to the need to raise much more investment capital to meet export targets?

In the years to come, the wine industry will need to be 'strong, determined and united' in the face of irrational and non-consultative taxation demands by governments both state and federal, as it was in late 1993 in response to a Federal government budget increase of 55 per cent in sales tax (from 20 per cent to 31 per cent), when such a proposal was defeated and a more reasonable phased increase of 30 per cent (from 20 per cent to 26 per cent over two years) accepted. The 1990s will issue many challenges.

Bibliography

Aeuckens, Bishop & Ors, *Vineyard of the Empire*, Industrial Publishers, 1988.

Baker, Tony, *The Orlando Way*, G. Gramp & Sons, 1987.

Bellperroud, J. & Pettavell D. L., *The vine; with instructions for its cultivation for a period of six years, the treatment of the soil and how to make wine from Victorian grapes*, 1859, reprinted Casuarina Press, 1979.

Bishop, G. C., *Mining, Medicine and Winemaking*, Angove's, 1986.

Burdon, R. A., *A Family Tradition in Fine Winemaking*, Thomas Hardy & Sons, 1978.

Busby, J. A., *Treatise on the Culture of the Vine . . .*, 1825, reprinted The David Ell Press, 1979.

——, *A manual of plain directions for planting and cultivating yards and for making wine in New South Wales*, 1930, reprinted The David Ell Press, 1979.

——, *Journal of a Tour through some of the Vineyards of Spain and France*, 1833, reprinted The David Ell Press, 1979.

Cobley, J., *Sydney Cove 1788–1792, Australia's first five years*, 1962, reprinted Angus & Robertson, 1980.

Croser, B. J., J. K., Walker Lecture to the Wine and Food Society of Australia, 1988, unpublished.

de Castella, F., *Handbook on Viticulture for Victoria*, 1891.

de Castella, H., *John Bull's Vineyard*, 1886.

——, *Notes of an Australian Vinegrower*, tr. from French by C. B. Thornton, Mastgully Press, 1979.

Driscoll, W. P., *The Beginnings of the Wine Industry in the Hunter Valley*, Newcastle City Council, 1969.

Dunston, D., *Morris of Rutherglen*, self-published, 1989.

Evans, L. P. & Ors, *Australian Complete Book of Wine*, Paul Hamlyn, 1976.

Francis, L. R., *100 Years of Winemaking, Great Western—1865–1965*, B. Seppelt & Sons, n.d.

Grasby, W. Catton, *Coonawarra Fruit Colony*, Garden and Field, 1899, reprinted 1990.

Halliday, F. J., *Australian Wine Compendium*, Angus & Robertson, 1985.

——, Clare Valley, Vin Publications, 1985.

——, & Jarratt, R., *The Wines and History of the Hunter Valley*, McGraw-Hill, 1979.

Heddle, E. M. & Doherty, F., *Chateau Tahbilk—Story of a Vineyard*, Lothian Publishing, 1985.

Hodder, *History of South Australia*, Sampson Low, 1893.

Hopton, M., *John Reynell of Reynella*, Investigator Press, 1988.

Kelly, A. C., *The Vine in Australia*, 1861, (eds) Hall, D. & Hankel, V., reprinted The David Ell Press, 1980.

Kuehne, Arthur, *Grapes and Gold*, self-published, 1980.

Laffer, H. E., Collection of letters and pieces published in various British publications 1938-1946.

——, *The Wine Industry in Australia*, Australian Wine Board, 1949.

Lake, M., *Classic Wines of Australia*, Jacaranda Press, 1966.

——, *Hunter Wine*, Jacaranda Press, 1964.

——, *Hunter Winemakers*, Jacaranda Press, 1970.

——, *Vine and Scalpel*, Jacaranda Press, 1967.

Macarthur, Sir W. (Maro), *Letters on the culture of the vine, fermentation and the management of wine in the cellar*, 1844.

McEwin, G., *The South Australian vigneron and gardener's manual*, printed by Andrews, Thomas & Clark, 1871.

Mayne, R., (comp.), *The Great Australian Wine Book*, Reed, 1985.

——, *Lindeman*, Appollo Books, 1993.

Norrie, P., *Vineyards of Sydney*, Horwitz, Grahame, 1990.

——,*Lindeman* Apollo Books, 1993.

Ousbach, A. (ed.), *The Australian Wine Browser*, The David Ell Press, 1979.

Paterson, D., *Hunter Wine Country*, self-published, 1984.

——, *Tyrrell's, 125 years*, self-published, 1983.

Paterson, M., *Wineries and Wines of the Hunter Valley*, Wine & Spirit Buying Guide, 1978.

Penfold's Wines Pty Ltd, *Rewards of Patience*, 2nd ed., Penfold's, 1990.

Roberts, I., & Baglin, D., *Australian Wine Pilgrimage*, Horwitz Publications, 1969.

Saltram Wine Estates, Saltram, *130 Years of Fine Wine*, Saltram, 1989.

Seppelt, B. & Sons Pty Ltd, *The House of Seppelt*, 1951.

Simon, A., *Wines, Vineyards and Vignerons of Australia*, Lansdowne Press, 1966.

Ward, E., *The Vineyards and Orchards of South Australia*, 1862, reprinted Sullivan's Cove, n.d.

Wynn, A., *The Fortunes of Samuel Wynn*, Cassell Australia, 1968.

Photograph credits

Mitchell Library, State Library of New South Wales (page 5); BRL Hardy Wine Company (pages 161, 163); Australasian Pioneers' Club (page 20); La Trobe Collection, State Library of Victoria (pages 55, 143); Mortlock Library, State Library of South Australia (pages 79, 86).

Appendix 1: Profile of the Australian wine industry 1993

Vineyard Australia is vast. Not so much in terms of production, perhaps, but certainly in size. From east to west, our vineyards lie between latitude 153° east (Port Macquarie, NSW) and latitude 116° east (Margaret River, WA), a distance of 3400 kilometres. From north to south, they extend from longitude 26.5° south (Roma in central Queensland) to longitude 43° south (Hobart, Tasmania). Within that area many potential vineyard sites await development, particularly in our cooler and more elevated regions.

Following are some relevant statistics concerning Australian wine as at June 30 1993. If statistics relate to any other period, that period is stated.

Tonnes crushed in vintage 1993: 626 187
Beverage wine produced in vintage 1993 ('000L): 413 912
Distillation wine produced in the same vintage ('000L): 46 998

Stocks of Beverage Wine and Unfermented Grape Juice ('000L)

Total fortified wine	90 028
Total sparkling wine	57 009
White table wine	
not exceeding 1° baume	257 100
exceeding 1° baume	7862
Red table wine	178 619
Total beverage wine	590 618
Unfermented grape juice	9686
Total brandy in bond ('000L alcohol)	5185

Domestic Sales and Export Approvals of Australian Wine (1000 litres)

Wine Type	Domestic	Export	Total
Bottled:			
White	44 099	32 859	76 958
Red	25 268	24 715	49 983
Other:			
White	142 306	26 907	169 213
Red	29 783	11 148	40 931
Sparkling	29 952	4 335	34 287
Fortified	27 914	2 041	29 955
Other	12 309	1 168	13 477
Total	311 631	103 173	414 804

Value of Wine Exports by Market ($'000 000 f.o.b.)

Country	1992 Value	1993 Value	% Variation
United Kingdom	91.5	127.9	+39.8
Sweden	38.6	45.2	+17.1
USA	27.5	23.2	-15.6
Canada	17.2	20.4	+18.6
New Zealand	17.5	25.2	+44
Other	41.8	47.3	+13.2
Total	234.1	289.2	+23.5

The Crystal Ball: Forecast of Australian Wine Export Sales ($'000 000)

Country	1994	1995	1996	1997
United Kingdom	164.43	196.65	229.51	260.0
USA	66.67	81.35	96.02	110.7
Japan	10.33	10.7	11.08	11.47
Sweden	29.75	35.36	38.78	42.5
Europe	18.58	23.23	27.7	31.88
Other	118.41	151.69	226.85	224.49
Total	408.18	498.98	629.95	751.1

Top 20 World Wine Producers 1991 ('000 000 litres)

Italy	6080
France	4268.9
Spain	3120
USA	1550
Argentina	1450
Former USSR	1300
Germany	1017
Portugal	1003.3
South Africa	970.4
Romania	580
Former Yugoslavia	460.7
Hungary	445
Greece	402.1
Australia	394.3
Brazil	311
Austria	309
Chile	284.6
Bulgaria	219
Mexico	166.9
Switzerland	132.6
Total world production 1991	**25130.3**
(Australian production	**1.56%)**

Area under Grapevines as at June 30 1992 ('000 ha)

New South Wales	12.2
Victoria	19.4
South Australia	25.8
Western Australia	2.2
Queensland	1
Tasmania	0.2
Total	**60.9**

Areas in Bearing and Yield of Chief Wine Grape Varieties in Australia for Vintage 1992

	Area (ha)	Yield (tonnes)
Red Varieties		
Shiraz	5 088	56 476
Cabernet Sauvignon	4 535	44 906
Grenache	1 992	29 834
Pinot Noir	1 078	10 625
Mataro	610	10 031
Merlot	519	5 105
Ruby Cabernet	286	4 367
Malbec	253	3 045
Cabernet Franc	290	2 955
Frontignac	140	917
White Varieties		
Muscat Gordo Blanco	3 460†	78 295
Sultana	15 194†	54 788
Chardonnay	4 459	48 748
Riesling	3 571	39 125
Semillon	2 649	36 947
Trebbiano	1 071	20 391
Colombard	758	20 190
Doradillo	717	17 539
Sauvignon Blanc	900	11 366
Chenin Blanc	599	10 799

† Part only of area used for wine production.

State By State Top Five Red and White Varieties

New South Wales

Red	**Area (ha)**	**Yield (tonnes)**
Shiraz	1 285	14 077
Cabernet Sauvignon	611	5 563
Pinot Noir	267	2 481
Mataro	106	1 947
Grenache	85	1 547
White		
Semillon	1 704	24 706
Trebbiano	719	13 597
Chardonnay	1 400	13 433
Muscat Gordo Blanco	716†	12 744
Colombard	239	5 826

Victoria

Red		
Cabernet Sauvignon	596	5 583
Shiraz	539	4 723
Pinot Noir	238	1 722
Grenache	87	1 221
Ruby Cabernet	59	1 058
White		
Sultana	11 131†	25 057
Muscat Gordo Blanco	1 075†	23 994
Chardonnay	776	10 701
Colombard	222	6 694
Riesling	364	4 986

South Australia

Red		
Shiraz	3 137	36 910
Cabernet Sauvignon	2 986	31 696
Grenache	1 734	26 435
Mataro	471	7 743
Pinot Noir	492	6 004

White		
Muscat Gordo Blanco	1 634†	41 436
Riesling	2 798	30 852
Sultana	1 742†	24 428
Chardonnay	1 985	23 103
Doradillo	553	13 060
Western Australia		
Red		
Cabernet Sauvignon	304	1 943
Shiraz	109	632
Grenache	86	632
Pinot Noir	43	223
Merlot	28	160
White		
Chardonnay	232	1 249
Chenin Blanc	101	1 225
Riesling	190	933
Semillon	103	761
Verdelho	57	573
Queensland		
Red		
Shiraz	18	132
Muscat Hamburgh	295†	58
Cabernet Sauvignon	9	23
Other	59	21
White		
Waltham Cross	111†	86
Chardonnay	10	56
Semillon	6	35
Other	8	34
Tasmania		
Red		
Pinot Noir	37	190
Cabernet Sauvignon	28	97
Other	6	24

White		
Chardonnay	54	205
Riesling	16	79
Other	8	34

† Part only of area used for wine production.

Per Capita Consumption of Wine 1983–1992 (litres)

1982–3	19.7
1983–4	20.4
1984–5	21.3
1985–6	21.6
1986–7	21
1987–8	20.6
1988–9	19.1
1989–90	18.3
1990–1	17.7
1991–2	18.6

Summary of Gross Value of Wine Grape Production compared to Total Gross Value of Farm & Fisheries Production 1992–93 ($'000 000)

Wine grapes	226
Fruit	1 433
Grains & oilseeds	4 827
Industrial (cotton, sugar, tobacco)	1 583
Other crops (vegetables etc)	3 111
Livestock slaughterings	5 932
Livestock products (wool, milk)	5 317
Fisheries	1 359
Total farm and fisheries	**23 562**
Percentage wine grapes of total farm and fisheries	**0.959**

Appendix 2:

Directory of Australian wine producers

It is estimated that there are over 700 wineries in Australia. What follows is a cross-section of present-day Australian wineries, wine estates and even some brands lacking their own winery. It is a wide-ranging selection of wine producers from all serious wine-producing States representing all shades of winery and brand, from the minute to the positively gargantuan.

A

TIM ADAMS WINES
PO Box 219
Clare SA 5453
Ph (088) 422 429, Fax (088) 422 429
Owners: *Tim Adams and Pam Goldsack*
Chief Winemaker: *Tim Adams*
Year of foundation: *1987*
Location of principal vineyards: *Clare Valley*
Leading wines: *Semillon, Cabernet, Aberfeldy Shiraz*
Tonnes crushed on average each year: *150*
Tonnes crushed in 1993: *130*
Best recent vintages: *Red—1990, 1992, 1993, 1991, 1989; White—1993, 1990, 1992, 1991, 1989*

ALKOOMI
Wingeballup Road
Frankland WA 6396
Ph (098) 552 229, Fax (098) 552 284
Owners: *Merv and Judy Lange*
Chief Winemaker: *Kim Hart*
Year of foundation: *1976*
Location of principal vineyards: *Frankland River*
Leading wines: *Cabernet Sauvignon, Chardonnay, Rhine Riesling*
Tonnes crushed on average each year: *250*
Tonnes crushed in 1993: *225*
Best recent vintages: *Red—1990, 1988; White—1991, 1990*

ALLANDALE WINERY
Lovedale Road
Pokolbin NSW 2321
Ph (049) 904 526, Fax (049) 901 714
Owner: *Villa Villetri (Wines) Pty Ltd*
Chief Winemaker: *Bill Sneddon*
Year of foundation: *1978*
Location of principal vineyards: *Hunter Valley*
Leading wines: *Chardonnay, Matthew Shiraz*
Tonnes crushed on average each year: *150*
Tonnes crushed in 1993: *150*
Best recent vintages: *Red—1991; White—1991*

ALLANMERE WINES
Lovedale Road
Lovedale NSW 2321
Ph (049) 307 387, Fax (049) 307 387
Owners: *Dr Newton and Virginia Potter*
Chief Winemaker: *Geoff Broadfield*
Year of foundation: *1985*
Location of principal vineyards: *Lower Hunter Valley*
Leading wines: *Durham Chardonnay, Trinity Red, Trinity White*
Tonnes crushed on average each year: *55–60*
Tonnes crushed in 1993: *50*
Best recent vintages: *Red—1988, 1989, 1991; White—1990, 1993, 1991*

ALL SAINTS ESTATE
All Saints Road
Wahgunyah Vic 3687
Ph (060) 331 922, Fax (060) 333 515
Owners: *Brown Family*
Chief Winemaker: *Neil Jericho*
Year of foundation: *1864*
Location of principal vineyards: *Rutherglen*
Leading wines: *Muscat, Tokay, Tawny Port*
Tonnes crushed on average each year: *200*
Tonnes crushed in 1993: *100*
Best recent vintage: *Red and White—1992*

AMBERLEY ESTATE
Thornton Road
Yallingup WA 6280
Ph (097) 552 288, Fax (097) 552 171
Managing Director: *Albert Haak*
Chief Winemaker: *Eddie Price*
Year of foundation: *1985*
Location of principal vineyards: *Yallingup, Margaret River*
Leading wines: *Chenin, Semillon-Sauvignon Blanc, Cabernet Merlot*
Tonnes crushed on average each year: *250*
Tonnes crushed in 1993: *250*

ANGOVE'S PTY LTD
Bookmark Avenue
Renmark SA 5341
Ph (085) 851 311, Fax (085) 851 583

Owner: *Privately owned*
Year of foundation: *1886*
Location of principal vineyards: *Murray Valley, SA*
Leading wines: *Angove's, St Agnes range of brandies, Butterfly Ridge*
Tonnes crushed on average each year: *15 000*
Tonnes crushed in 1993: *13 000*
Best recent vintages: *Red—1990, 1992, 1993; White—1989, 1990, 1991, 1992*

ARROWFIELD
Jerry's Plains NSW 2330
Ph (065) 764 041, Fax (065) 764 144
Owner: *Arrowfield Wines Pty Ltd*
Chief Winemaker: *Simon Gilbert*
Year of foundation: *1969*
Location of principal vineyards: *Hunter Valley, Cowra*
Leading wines: *Arrowfield Cowra Chardonnay, Simon Whitlam Semillon Chardonnay*
Tonnes crushed on average each year: *1800*
Tonnes crushed in 1993: *1800*
Best recent vintage: *Red and White—1991*

ASHBROOK ESTATE
Harman's Road South
Willyabrup WA 6280
Ph (097) 556 262, Fax (097) 556 290
Owners: *Devitt Family*
Chief Winemakers: *Tony and Brian Devitt*
Year of foundation: *1975*
Location of principal vineyards: *Willyabrup, Margaret River*
Leading wines: *Semillon, Verdelho, Cabernet Sauvignon*
Tonnes crushed on average each year: *130*
Tonnes crushed in 1993: *60*
Best recent vintages: *Red—1990, 1991, 1992; White—1992, 1993*

B

BAILEYS OF GLENROWAN
Taminick Gap Road
Glenrowan Vic 3675
Ph (057) 662 392, Fax (057) 662 596
Owner: *Rothbury Wines Ltd*
Chief Winemaker: *Steve Goodwin*
Year of foundation: *1870*
Location of principal vineyards: *Glenrowan*
Leading wines: *Shiraz, Cabernet, Liqueur Muscat*
Tonnes crushed on average each year: *750*
Tonnes crushed in 1993: *780*
Best recent vintages: *Red—1988, 1990, 1993; White—1990, 1993*

BALDIVIS ESTATE
River Road
Baldivis WA 6171
Ph (09) 525 2066, Fax (09) 525 2411
Owner: *Kailis Consolidated Pty Ltd*
Chief Winemaker: *John Smith*
Year of foundation: *1982*
Location of principal vineyard: *Baldivis*
Leading wines: *Chardonnay, Cabernet-Merlot, Sauvignon Blanc-Semillon*
Tonnes crushed on average each year: *100*
Tonnes crushed in 1993: *58*
Best recent vintage: *Red and White—1990*

BALGOWNIE
Hermitage Road
Maiden Gully Vic 3551
Ph (054) 496 222, Fax (054) 496 506

Owner: *Mildara Blass Ltd*
Chief Winemaker: *Lindsay Ross*
Year of foundation: *1968*
Location of principal vineyards: *Bendigo*
Leading wines: *Balgownie Estate Cabernet Sauvignon, Balgownie Estate Hermitage*
Tonnes crushed on average each year: *120*
Tonnes crushed in 1993: *122*
Best recent vintages: *Red—1991, 1990, 1988; White—1990*

BALLANDEAN ESTATE
Sundown Road
Ballandean Qld 4382
Ph (076) 841 226, Fax (076) 841 288
Owners: *Angelo and Mary Puglisi*
Chief Winemakers: *Angelo Puglisi and Adam Chapman*
Year of foundation: *1968*
Location of principal vineyards: *Ballandean*
Leading wines: *Semillon-Sauvignon Blanc, Cabernet Sauvignon, Shiraz*
Tonnes crushed on average: *150*
Tonnes crushed in 1993: *130*
Best recent vintages: *Red—1989, 1992, 1993; White—1990, 1992, 1993*

BANNOCKBURN VINEYARDS
Midland Highway
Bannockburn Vic 3331
Ph (052) 811 362, Fax (052) 811 349
Owner: *Stuart Hooper*
Chief Winemaker: *Gary Farr*
Year of foundation: *1974*
Location of principal vineyards: *Bannockburn Shire*
Leading wines: *Pinot Noir, Chardonnay, Shiraz*
Tonnes crushed on average: *110*
Tonnes crushed in 1993: *110*
Best recent year: *Red—1992; White—1992*

BAROSSA VALLEY ESTATE
Heaslip Road,
Angle Vale SA 5117
Ph (08) 284 7000, Fax (08) 284 7219
Owner: *Valley Growers Co-operative Ltd*
Chief Winemaker: *Colin Glaetzer*
Year of foundation: *1985*
Location of principal vineyards: *Barossa Valley*
Leading wines: *E & E Black Pepper Shiraz, E & E Sparkling Burgundy, Ebenezer*
Tonnes crushed on average each year: *2000*
Tonnes crushed in 1993: *2100*
Best recent vintages: *Red—1990, 1991, 1992; White—1990, 1992, 1993*

O. BASEDOW WINES
Main Street
Tanunda SA 5352
Ph (085) 632 060
Owner: *Grant Burge Wines*
Chief Winemaker: *Robert Reudiger*
Year of foundation: *1896*
Location of principal vineyards: *Tanunda and Angaston*
Leading wines: *White Burgundy, Hermitage and Cabernet Sauvignon*
Tonnes crushed on average each year: *600*
Tonnes crushed in 1993: *480*
Best recent vintages: *Red—1991, 1990, 1988; White—1988, 1990, 1991*

BASS PHILLIP
Tosch's Road
Leongatha South Vic 3953
Ph (056) 643 341, Fax (056) 643 209
Owner and Chief Winemaker: *Phillip Jones*

Year of foundation: *1979*
Location of principal vineyards: *Leongatha*
Leading wines: *Pinot Noir (several grades), Chardonnay*
Tonnes crushed on average each year: *below 20*
Tonnes crushed in 1993: *15*
Best recent vintages: *Red—1989, 1991, 1992; White—1991, 1992, 1993*

BERRI ESTATES
Sturt Highway
Glossop SA 5343
Ph (085) 820 300, Fax (085) 832 224
Owner: *Berri Estates Pty Ltd*
Chief Winemaker: *Paul Kassebaum*
Year of foundation: *1922*
Location of principal vineyards: *Riverland*
Leading wines: *Berri Estates 3 and 5 litre casks*
Tonnes crushed on average each year: *45 000*
Tonnes crushed in 1993: *45 000*
Best recent vintages: *Non-vintage wine casks produced only*

BEST'S WINES PTY LTD
Concongella Vineyard
Great Western Vic 3377
and
St Andrews Vineyard
Lake Boga Vic 3584
Ph (053) 562 250, Fax (053) 562 430
Owners: *Thomson Family*
Chief Winemaker: *Viv Thomson*
Year of foundation: *1930*
Location of principal vineyards: *Great Western and Lake Boga*
Leading wines: *Great Western Shiraz, Chardonnay, Cabernet Sauvignon*
Tonnes crushed on average each year: *Great Western—200; Lake Boga—400*
Tonnes crushed in 1993: *Great Western—200; Lake Boga—350*
Best recent vintages: *(Great Western) Red—1990, 1991, 1992; White—1992, 1993, 1990*

A. P. BIRKS WENDOUREE CELLARS
Wendouree Road
Clare SA 5453
Ph (088) 422 896
Owner: *Liberman Wines Pty Ltd*
Chief Winemaker: *Tony Brady*
Year of foundation: *1895*
Location of principal vineyards: *Clare*
Leading wines: *Cabernet Sauvignon, Cabernet Malbec, Shiraz*
Tonnes crushed on average each year: *50*
Tonnes crushed in 1993: *41.5*
Best recent vintages: *Red—1988, 1990, 1992; White—1990*

BLEASDALE VINEYARDS PTY LTD
Wellington Road
Langhorne Creek SA 5255
Ph (085) 373 001, Fax (085) 373 224
Owner: *Private shareholders*
Chief Winemaker: *Michael Potts*
Year of foundation: *1850*
Location of principal vineyards: *Langhorne Creek*
Leading wines: *Cabernet-Malbec-Merlot, Verdelho, Pioneer Port*
Tonnes crushed on average each year: *800*
Tonnes crushed in 1993: *450*
Best recent vintages: *Red—1990, 1992, 1991, 1989; White—1992, 1990, 1993, 1991, 1989*

BOTOBOLAR VINEYARD PTY LTD
Botobolar Road
Mudgee NSW 2850
Ph (063) 733 840, Fax (063) 733 789

Owner: *Private shareholders*
Chief Winemaker: *Gil Wahlquist*
Year of foundation: *1971*
Location of principal vineyards: *Mudgee*
Leading wines: *St Gilbert Dry Red, Marsanne Preservative Free White*
Tonnes crushed on average each year: *120*
Tonnes crushed in 1993: *90*
Best recent vintages: *Red—1989; White—1992*

BOWEN ESTATE
Main Road
Coonawarra SA 5263
Ph (087) 372 229
Owners: *Doug and Joy Bowen*
Chief Winemaker: *Doug Bowen*
Year of foundation: *1972*
Location of principal vineyards: *Coonawarra*
Leading wines: *Chardonnay, Shiraz, Cabernet Sauvignon*
Tonnes crushed on average each year: *120*
Tonnes crushed in 1993: *100*
Best recent vintages: *Red and White—1990, 1991, 1993*

BOYNTONS OF BRIGHT
Ovens Valley Highway
Porepunkah Vic 3741
Ph (057) 562 356, Fax (057) 562 610
Owners: *Carolien and Kel Boynton*
Chief Winemaker: *Kel Boynton*
Year of foundation: *1987*
Location of principal vineyards: *Ovens Valley near Bright, NE Victoria*
Leading wines: *Cabernet Sauvignon, Shiraz*
Tonnes crushed on average each year: *100*
Tonnes crushed in 1993: *120*
Best recent vintages: *Red—1989, 1990, 1991; White—1989, 1990, 1992*

BRANDS LAIRA WINES
Main Road
Coonawarra SA 5263
Ph (087) 363 260, Fax (087) 363 208
Owner: *Brands Wines Pty Ltd*
Chief Winemaker: *Jim Brand*
Year of foundation: *1966*
Location of principal vineyards: *Coonawarra*
Leading wines: *Cabernet Sauvignon, Shiraz, Chardonnay*
Tonnes crushed on average each year: *220*
Tonnes crushed in 1993: *225*
Best recent vintages: *Red—1993, 1991, 1990; White—1990, 1992, 1991*

BROKENWOOD
McDonalds Road
Pokolbin NSW 2321
Ph (049) 987 559, Fax (049) 987 893
Owner: *Brokenwood Wines Pty Ltd*
Chief Winemaker: *Iain Riggs*
Year of foundation: *1970*
Location of principal vineyards: *Lower Hunter Valley*
Leading wines: *Graveyard Hermitage, Graveyard Chardonnay, Sauvignon Blanc—Semillon*
Tonnes crushed on average each year: *250*
Tonnes crushed in 1993: *430*

BROWN BROTHERS MILAWA VINEYARD PTY LTD
Milawa Vic 3678
Ph (057) 205 550, Fax (057) 205 511
Owners: *Brown Family*
Chief Winemaker: *Roland Wahlquist*
Year of foundation: *1889*

Location of principal vineyards: *Milawa and King Valley*
Leading wines: *A large range of varietal wines*
Tonnes crushed on average each year: *10 000*
Tonnes crushed in 1993: *9781*
Best recent vintages: *Red—1992, 1991, 1988; White—1992, 1991, 1990*

BURGE FAMILY WINEMAKERS
Barossa Highway
Lyndoch SA 5351
Ph (085) 244 644, Fax (085) 244 444
Owners: *Noel, Rick and Bronwyn Burge*
Chief Winemaker: *Rick Burge*
Year of foundation: *1928*
Location of principal vineyards: *Lyndoch*
Leading wines: *Draycott reds, Olive Hill and Jollytown whites, Wilsford ports*
Tonnes crushed on average each year: *65*
Tonnes crushed in 1993: *60*
Best recent vintages: *Red—1993, 1991, 1990, 1988, 1986; White—1992, 1991, 1990, 1988, 1986*

BURONGA HILL WINERY
Silver City Highway
Buronga NSW 2739
Ph (050) 222 344, Fax (050) 221 076
Owner: *Orlando Wyndham*
Chief Winemaker: *Sam Cross*
Year of foundation: *1984*
Tonnes crushed on average each year: *40 000*
Tonnes crushed in 1993: *35 000*

C

CAMDEN ESTATE VINEYARDS
Lot 32, Macarthur Road
Camden NSW 2570
Ph (046) 681 237, Fax (046) 681 237
Owner: *Norman Hanckel*
Chief Winemaker: *Norman Hanckel*
Year of foundation: *1974*
Location of principal vineyards: *Camden*
Leading wines: *Camden Estate Chardonnay, Sydney Chardonnay, Pinot-Chardonnay Sparkling*
Tonnes crushed on average each year: *150*
Tonnes crushed in 1993: *140*
Best recent vintages: *Red—1988; White—1988, 1989, 1991, 1993*

CAMPBELLS WINES
Murray Valley Highway
Rutherglen Vic 3685
Ph (060) 329 458, Fax (060) 329 870
Owners: *Campbell Family*
Chief Winemaker: *Colin B. Campbell*
Year of foundation: *1870*
Location of principal vineyards: *Rutherglen*
Leading wines: *Merchant Prince Muscat, Bobbie Burns Shiraz, Rutherglen Durif*
Tonnes crushed on average each year: *600*
Tonnes crushed in 1993: *500*
Best recent vintages: *Red and White—1990, 1991, 1992*

CAPE CLAIRAULT WINES
CMB Carbunup River WA 6280
Ph (097) 556 225, Fax (097) 556 229
Owners: *Ian and Ani Lewis*
Chief Winemaker: *Ian Lewis*
Year of foundation: *1976*
Location of principal vineyards: *Willyabrup*
Leading wines: *The Clairault red, Sauvignon Blanc, Semillon-Sauvignon Blanc*
Tonnes crushed on average each year: *50*

Tonnes crushed in 1993: *50*
Best recent vintages: *Red—1990, 1991, 1992; White—1990, 1992, 1991, 1993*

CAPEL VALE WINES
Stirling Estate
Capel North West Road
Capel WA 6271
Ph (097) 272 439, Fax (097) 272 164
Owner: *Dr Peter Pratten*
Chief Winemaker: *Rob Bowen*
Year of foundation: *1975*
Location of principal vineyards: *Capel and Mount Barker*
Leading wines: *Chardonnay, Rhine Riesling, Cabernet Sauvignon*
Tonnes crushed on average each year: *400*
Tonnes crushed in 1993: *420*
Best recent vintages: *Red—1992; White—1993*

CAPE MENTELLE VINEYARDS LTD
Off Wallcliffe Road
Margaret River WA 6285
Ph (097) 573 266, Fax (097) 573 233
Owners: *Veuve Clicquot Ponsardin and David Hohnen*
Chief Winemaker: *John Durham*
Year of foundation: *1976*
Location of principal vineyards: *Margaret River*
Leading wines: *Cabernet Sauvignon, Cabernet Merlot, Semillon Sauvignon*
Tonnes crushed on average each year: *650*
Tonnes crushed in 1993: *530*
Best recent vintages: *Red—1991; White—1992*

CASELLA WINES
Farm 1471 Wakely Road
Yenda NSW 2681
Ph (069) 681 346
Owner: *Filippo Casella*
Chief Winemaker: *John Casella*
Year of foundation: *1969*
Location of principal vineyards: *Yenda*
Leading wines: *Cabernet Sauvignon, Shiraz, Chardonnay*
Tonnes crushed on average each year: *1000*
Tonnes crushed in 1993: *700*
Best recent vintages: *Red and White—1993*

CASSEGRAIN VINEYARDS
Fernbank Creek Road
Port Macquarie NSW 2444
Ph (065) 837 777, Fax (065) 840 354
Owner: *Cassegrain Family*
Chief Winemaker: *John Cassegrain*
Year of foundation: *1985*
Location of principal vineyards: *Hastings Valley*
Leading wines: *Fromenteau Vineyard Chardonnay, Cassegrain Chardonnay*
Tonnes crushed on average each year: *500*
Tonnes crushed in 1993: *680*
Best recent vintages: *Red—1991, 1988; White—1991, 1993, 1989*

CATHCART RIDGE ESTATE
Moyston Road
Cathcart
Ararat Vic 3377
Ph (053) 521 997, Fax (053) 521 558
Owner: *Farnhill Family*
Chief Winemaker: *David Farnhill*
Year of foundation: *1976*
Location of principal vineyards: *Cathcart*
Leading wines: *Cabernet Merlot, Shiraz, Chardonnay*
Best recent vintages: *Red and White—1993*

CHARLES MELTON WINES
Krondorf Road
Tanunda SA 5352
Ph (085) 633 606, Fax (085) 633 422
Owner and Chief Winemaker: *Charlie Melton*
Year of foundation: *1984*
Location of principal vineyards: *Barossa Valley*
Leading wines: *Nine Popes, Shiraz, Rose of Virginia*
Tonnes crushed on average each year: *90*
Tonnes crushed in 1993: *75*
Best recent vintages: *Red—1989, 1990, 1991; White—none produced*

CHARLES STURT UNIVERSITY WINERY
McKeown Drive
Wagga Wagga NSW 2650
Ph (069) 222 435, Fax (069) 222 107
Owner: *Charles Sturt University*
Chief Winemaker: *Rodney Hooper*
Year of foundation: *1977*
Location of principal vineyards: *Wagga Wagga*
Leading wines: *Chardonnay, Cabernet Sauvignon*
Tonnes crushed on average each year: *250*
Tonnes crushed in 1993: *200*
Best recent vintages: *Red and White—1990, 1991, 1992, 1993, 1988*

CHATEAU REMY PTY LTD BLUE PYRENEES ESTATE
Vinoca Road
Avoca Vic 3467
Ph (054) 653 202, Fax (054) 653 529
Owner: *Remy Martin*
Chief Winemaker: *Vincent Gere*
Year of foundation: *1963*
Location of principal vineyards: *Avoca*
Leading wines: *Blue Pyrenees Estate, Chateau Remy Pinot-Chardonnay, Fiddlers Creek Chardonnay*
Tonnes crushed on average each year: *700*
Tonnes crushed in 1993: *450*
Best recent vintages: *Red—1990, 1988; White—1990, 1993*

CHATEAU REYNELLA
Reynell Road
Reynella SA 5161
Ph (08) 381 2266, Fax (08) 381 1968
Owner: *Chateau Reynella Wines*
Chief Winemakers: *David O'Leary and Tom Newton*
Year of foundation: *1838*
Location of principal vineyards: *Reynella*
Leading wines: *Chardonnay, Basket-Pressed Cabernet Merlot, Basket-Pressed Cabernet Sauvignon*
Best recent vintages: *Red—1991, 1993, 1990, 1992, 1988; White—1993, 1992, 1991*

CHATEAU TAHBILK
Tabilk Vic 3607
Ph (057) 942 555, Fax (057) 942 360
Owner: *Purbrick Family*
Chief Winemaker: *Alister Purbrick*
Year of foundation: *1860*
Location of principal vineyards: *Tabilk*
Leading wines: *Cabernet Sauvignon, Shiraz, Marsanne*
Tonnes crushed on average each year: *1500*
Tonnes crushed in 1993: *1400*
Best recent vintages: *Red—1990, 1991, 1992; White—1989, 1991, 1992*

CHATEAU XANADU
Terry Road
Margaret River WA 6285
Ph (097) 572 581, Fax (097) 573 389

Owners: *Drs John Lagan and Eithne Sheridan*
Chief Winemaker: *Juerg Muggli*
Location of principal vineyards: *Margaret River*
Leading wines: *Cabernet Sauvignon, Chardonnay, Secession (Semillon-Sauvignon Blanc)*
Tonnes crushed on average each year: *100*
Tonnes crushed in 1993: *110*
Best recent vintages: *Red—1990, 1991, 1992, 1993; White—1990, 1992, 1993*

CHATEAU YALDARA
Gomersal Road
Lyndoch SA 5351
Ph (085) 242 200, Fax (085) 244 678
Owner: *Hermann Thumm*
Chief Winemaker: *Hermann Thumm (Yaldara) and James Irvine (Lakewood)*
Year of foundation: *1947*
Location of principal vineyards: *Lyndoch*
Leading wines: *Lakewood Sauvignon Blanc-Semillon, Lakewood Cabernet Merlot, Lakewood Chardonnay*
Tonnes crushed on average each year: *8000*
Tonnes crushed in 1993: *5700*
Best recent vintages: *Red—1990, 1992; White—1992, 1993*

CHATSFIELD WINES
O'Neill Road
Mount Barker WA 6234
Ph (098) 511 704, Fax (098) 511 704
Owner: *Dr K. Lynch*
Chief Winemaker: *Goundrey Wines on contract*
Year of foundation: *1976*
Location of principal vineyards: *Mount Barker*
Leading wines: *Shiraz, Chardonnay, Riesling*
Tonnes crushed on average each year: *45*
Tonnes crushed in 1993: *20*
Best recent vintages: *Red—1990, 1992, 1993; White—1990, 1993*

CHITTERING ESTATE
Chittering Valley Road
Lower Chittering WA 6084
Ph (09) 242 1150, Fax (09) 444 9056
Owner: *Kailis and Schapera*
Chief Winemaker: *Francois Jacquard*
Year of foundation: *1986*
Location of principal vineyards: *Chittering Valley*
Leading wines: *Chardonnay, Cabernet Sauvignon-Merlot, Semillon-Sauvignon Blanc*
Best recent vintages: *Red—1990, 1992, 1993; White—1990, 1991, 1992, 1993*

CLYDE PARK
c/o Bannockburn Vineyards
Midland Highway
Bannockburn Vic 3331
Ph (052) 817 274
Owners: *Gary and Robyn Farr*
Chief Winemaker: *Gary Farr*
Year of foundation: *1983*
Location of principal vineyards: *Clyde Park, Moorabool Valley, Geelong*
Leading wines: *Pinot Noir, Chardonnay, Cabernet Sauvignon*
Tonnes crushed on average each year: *10*
Tonnes crushed in 1993: *10*
Best recent vintages: *Red—1986, 1988, 1989; White—1985, 1988, 1990, 1991*

COLDSTREAM HILLS
Madden Lane
Coldstream Vic 3770
Ph (059) 649 388, Fax (059) 649 389

Owner: *Coldstream Winemakers Ltd*
Principal Winemaker: *James Halliday*
Year of foundation: *1985*
Location of principal vineyards: *Coldstream*
Leading wines: *Chardonnay, Pinot Noir, Cabernet Sauvignon*
Tonnes crushed on average each year: *300*
Tonnes crushed in 1993: *311*
Best recent vintages: *Red—1992, 1991, 1990, 1988; White—1993, 1992, 1991, 1988*

PAUL CONTI WINES
529 Wanneroo Road
Wanneroo WA 6065
Ph (09) 409 9160, Fax (09) 309 1634
Owner: *Paul and Anne Conti*
Chief Winemaker: *Paul Conti*
Year of foundation: *1968*
Location of principal vineyard: *Wanneroo*
Leading wines: *Mariginiup Hermitage, Carabooda Chardonnay, Carabooda Chenin Blanc*
Tonnes crushed on average each year: *121*
Tonnes crushed in 1993: *123*
Best recent vintages: *Red—1990, 1989, 1988; White—1990, 1992, 1993*

COWRA WINES
Boorowa Road
Cowra NSW 2794
Ph (02) 905 0765, Fax (02) 905 0765
Owner: *Cowra Wines Pty Ltd*
Chief Winemakers: *(by contract) David Lowe, Jon Reynolds, Simon Gilbert*
Year of foundation: *1973*
Location of principal vineyards: *Cowra*
Leading wines: *Cowra Estate Chardonnay, Cowra Estate Cabernet Sauvignon*
Tonnes crushed on average each year: *1070*
Tonnes crushed in 1993: *1000*
Best recent vintages: *Red—1989, 1990, 1991; White—1989, 1990*

CORIOLE
Chaffey's Road
McLaren Vale SA 5171
Ph (08) 323 8305, Fax (08) 323 9136
Owner: *Mark Lloyd*
Chief Winemaker: *Stephen Hall*
Year of foundation: *1968*
Location of principal vineyards: *McLaren Vale*
Leading wines: *Lloyd Reserve Shiraz, Coriole Shiraz, Coriole Chenin Blanc*
Tonnes crushed on average each year: *200*
Tonnes crushed in 1993: *200*
Best recent vintages: *Red—1992, 1989, 1993, 1991, 1990; White—1993, 1989, 1984, 1990, 1987*

CRABTREE OF WATERVALE
North Terrace
Watervale SA 5452
Ph (088) 430 069, Fax (088) 430 144
Owners: *Robert and Elizabeth Crabtree*
Chief Winemaker: *Robert Crabtree*
Year of foundation: *1977*
Location of principal vineyards: *Watervale*
Leading wines: *Riesling, Semillon, Shiraz-Cabernet Sauvignon*
Tonnes crushed on average each year: *64*
Tonnes crushed in 1993: *38*
Best recent vintages: *Red—1991, 1990; White— 1992, 1990*

CRAIGMOOR
Craigmoor Road
Mudgee NSW 2850
Ph (063) 722 208, Fax (063) 724 464

Owner: *Orlando-Wyndham*
Chief Winemaker: *Robert Paul*
Year of foundation: *1858*
Location of principal vineyards: *Mudgee*
Leading wines: *Chardonnay, Cabernet Sauvignon, Shiraz*
Tonnes crushed on average each year: *500*
Tonnes crushed in 1993: *500*
Best recent vintages: *Red—1990, 1993, 1991; White—1991, 1989, 1993*

CRAWFORD RIVER
Condah Victoria 3303
Ph (055) 782 267
Owners: *John and Catherine Thomson*
Chief Winemaker: *John Thomson*
Year of foundation: *1975*
Location of principal vineyards: *Condah, South Western Victoria*
Leading wines: *Riesling, Cabernet, Semillon-Sauvignon Blanc*
Tonnes crushed on average each year: *60*
Tonnes crushed in 1993: *55*
Best recent vintages: *Red—1988, 1991; White—1988, 1989, 1993*

CRESTVIEW
Fraser Avenue
Happy Valley SA 5139
Ph (08) 322 3611, Fax (08) 322 3610
Owner: *Crestview Pty Ltd*
Chief Winemaker: *Robert Dundon*
Year of foundation: *1989*
Location of principal vineyards: *McLaren Vale*
Leading wines: *Beresford, Echo Point and Crystal Brook table wines*
Tonnes crushed on average each year: *2000*
Tonnes crushed in 1993: *1850*
Best recent vintages: *Red—1990, 1992; White—1993, 1991*

CULLEN WINES
Caves Road
Cowaramup WA 6254
Ph (097) 555 550, Fax (097) 555 550
Owner: *Cullen Family*
Chief Winemaker: *Vanya Cullen*
Year of foundation: *1971*
Location of principal vineyards: *Cowaramup*
Leading wines: *Cabernet Merlot, Chardonnay, Sauvignon Blanc*
Tonnes crushed on average each year: *175*
Tonnes crushed in 1993: *150*
Best recent vintages: *Red and White—1990, 1992*

D

DALFARRAS
PO Box 143
Nagambie Vic 3608
Ph (057) 942 637, Fax (057) 942 360
Owners: *Alister and Rosa Purbrick*
Chief Winemaker: *Alister Purbrick*
Year of foundation: *1991*
Location of principal vineyards: *Fruit is sourced from all premium areas*
Leading wines: *Cabernet Sauvignon, Marsanne, Chardonnay*
Best recent vintages: *Red—1990, 1991; White—1989, 1991, 1992*

DALWHINNIE
Taltarni Road
Moonambel Vic 3478
Ph (054) 672 388, Fax (054) 672 237
Owner: *E.C. Jones*
Chief Winemaker: *David Jones*
Year of foundation: *1973*
Location of principal vineyards: *Moonambel, Pyrenees, Victoria*
Leading wines: *Chardonnay, Shiraz, Cabernet Sauvignon*

Tonnes crushed on average each year: *80*
Tonnes crushed in 1993: *50*
Best recent vintages: *Red—1991, 1992, 1990, 1988; White—1992, 1990, 1991, 1993*

d'ARENBERG WINES PTY LTD
Osborn Road
McLaren Vale SA 5171
Ph (08) 323 8206, Fax (08) 323 8423
Owner: *d'Arenberg Osborn*
Chief Winemaker: *Chester Osborn*
Year of foundation: *1912 (vineyards), 1928 (winery)*
Location of principal vineyards: *McLaren Vale*
Leading wines: *d'Arry's Original Burgundy, d'Arenberg Chardonnay, Red Ochre*
Tonnes crushed on average each year: *1000*
Tonnes crushed in 1993: *672*
Best recent vintages: *Red—1990; White—1993*

DARLINGTON ESTATE
Nelson Road
Darlington WA 6070
Ph (09) 299 6268, Fax (09) 299 7107
Owners: *B.C. and F.C. Van der Meer*
Chief Winemaker: *Balt Van der Meer*
Year of foundation: *1983*
Location of principal vineyards: *Darlington and Parkerville*
Leading wines: *Cabernet Sauvignon, Shiraz, Chardonnay*
Tonnes crushed on average each year: *40*
Tonnes crushed in 1993: *35*
Best recent vintages: *Red—1988, 1989, 1991; White—1989, 1991, 1993*

DAWSON FAMILY ESTATE PTY LTD
London's Road
Lovedale NSW 2325
Ph (049) 902 904, Fax (049) 911 886
Owner: *Benjamin G. Dawson*
Chief Winemaker: *(contract) Rothbury Estate*
Year of foundation: *1975*
Location of principal vineyards: *Lovedale*
Leading wine: *Chardonnay*
Tonnes crushed on average each year: *60*
Tonnes crushed in 1993: *60*
Best recent vintage: *White—1991*

DE BORTOLI
De Bortoli Road
Bilbul NSW 2680
Ph (069) 635 382, Fax (069) 635 382
Owner: *de Bortoli Family*
Chief Winemaker: *Nick Guy*
Year of foundation: *1928*
Location of principal vineyards: *Bilbul, Nericon (Riverina)*
Leading wines: *Noble One Botrytis Semillon, Deen de Bortoli, Sacred Hill*
Tonnes crushed on average each year: *37 000*
Tonnes crushed in 1993: *37 000*
Best recent vintage: *Red and White—1992*

DE BORTOLI YARRA VALLEY
Pinnacle Lane
Dixons Creek Vic 3775
Ph (059) 652 271
Owner: *de Bortoli Family*
Chief Winemaker: *Stephen Webber*
Year of foundation: *1971 as Chateau Yarrinya, purchased in 1987*
Location of principal vineyards: *Dixons Creek, Yarra Valley*

Leading wines: *Yarra Valley Windy Peak*
Tonnes crushed on average each year: *1200*
Tonnes crushed in 1993: *1200*
Best recent vintages: *Red and White—1992, 1993*

DELATITE WINERY PTY LTD
Storey's Road
Mansfield Vic 3722
Ph (057) 752 922, Fax (057) 752 911
Owners: *R.J. and V.S. Ritchie*
Chief Winemaker: *Ros Ritchie*
Year of foundation: *1982*
Location of principal vineyards: *Mansfield*
Leading Wines: *Riesling, Devil's River (red blend), Dead Man's Hill Gewürztraminer*
Tonnes crushed on average each year: *180*
Best recent vintages: *Red—1988, 1990, 1993; White—1990, 1992*

DELAMERE
Bridport Road
Pipers Brook Tas 7254
Ph *(003) 827 190*
Owners: *Richard and Dallas Richardson*
Chief Winemaker: *Richard Richardson*
Year of foundation: *1988*
Location of principal vineyards: *Pipers Brook*
Leading wines: *Pinot Noir, Chardonnay*
Tonnes crushed on average each year: *60*
Tonnes crushed in 1993: *52*
Best recent vintages: *Red—1988, 1990, 1992; White—1990, 1992*

DENNIS OF McLAREN VALE
Kangarilla Road
McLaren Vale SA 5171
Ph: *(08) 323 8665, (08) 323 9121*
Owner: *Dennis Family*
Year of foundation: *1970*
Location of principal vineyards: *McLaren Flat*
Leading wines: *Chardonnay, Merlot-Cabernet, Shiraz*
Tonnes crushed on average each year: *140*
Tonnes crushed in 1993: *140*
Best recent vintages: *Red—1988, 1990, 1991, 1993, 1992; White—1990, 1992, 1993*

DIAMOND VALLEY VINEYARDS PTY LTD
2130 Kinglake Road
St Andrews Vic 3761
Ph (03) 710 1484, Fax (03) 710 1369
Owners: *David and Catherine Lance*
Chief Winemaker: *David Lance*
Year of foundation: *1976*
Location of principal vineyards: *St Andrews*
Leading wines: *Pinot Noir, Chardonnay, Cabernet*
Tonnes crushed on average each year: *65*
Tonnes crushed in 1993: *45*
Best recent vintages: *Red—1990, 1991, 1993; White—1990, 1992, 1993*

DOMAINE A
Tea Tree Road
Campania Tas 7026
Ph (002) 624 174, Fax (002) 624 390
Owner: *H.P. and R. Althaus*
Chief Winemaker: *Peter Althaus*
Year of foundation: *1990*
Location of principal vineyards: *Campania*
Leading wines: *Cabernet Sauvignon, Pinot Noir, Sauvignon Blanc*
Tonnes crushed on average each year: *Vineyard not yet completely in bearing*

Tonnes crushed in 1993: *12*
Best recent vintages: *Red—1991, 1992; White—1991, 1993*

DOMAINE CHANDON
Green Point
Maroondah Highway
Coldstream Vic 3770
Ph (03) 739 1110, Fax (03) 739 1095
Owner: *Moet et Chandon (France)*
Year of foundation: *1985*
Location of principal vineyards: *Yarra Valley and Tasmania*
Leading wines: *Sparkling-Brut, Blanc de Blancs, Blanc de Noirs; Still-Pinot Noir, Chardonnay*
Tonnes crushed on average each year: *average not yet applicable, crush is increasing*
Tonnes crushed in 1993: *1000*
Best recent vintages: *Sparkling—1990, 1992*

DRAYTON'S FAMILY WINES
Oakey Creek Road
Pokolbin NSW 2321
Ph (049) 987 513, Fax (049) 987 743
Owner: *Drayton Family*
Chief Winemaker: *Trevor Drayton*
Year of foundation: *1853*
Location of principal vineyards: *Pokolbin, Hunter Valley*
Tonnes crushed on average each year: *650*
Tonnes crushed in 1993: *750*
Best recent vintages: *Red—1991; White—1993*

DROMANA ESTATE
Harrison's Road
Dromana Vic 3936
Ph (059) 873 800, Fax (059) 810 714
Owner: *Garry Crittenden*
Chief Winemaker: *Garry Crittenden*
Year of foundation: *1982*
Location of principal vineyards: *Dromana*
Leading wines: *Dromana Estate Cabernet-Merlot, Schinus Chardonnay, Schinus Sauvignon Blanc*
Tonnes crushed on average each year: *150*
Tonnes crushed in 1993: *150*
Best recent vintages: *Red—1991; White—1993*

E

EAGLEHAWK ESTATE
Quelltaler Road
Watervale SA 5452
Ph (088) 430 003
Owner: *Mildara Blass Ltd*
Chief Winemaker: *Stephen John*
Year of foundation: *1865*
Location of principal vineyards: *Watervale*
Leading wines: *Eaglehawk Rhine Riesling, Chardonnay, Shiraz-Merlot-Cabernet Sauvignon*
Tonnes crushed on average each year: *3000*
Tonnes crushed in 1993: *2500*
Best recent vintages: *Red—1990, 1988; White—1990, 1991*

ELDERTON WINES
3 Tanunda Road
Nuriootpa SA 5355
Ph (085) 621 058, Fax (085) 622 844
Owners: *Lorraine and Neil Ashmead*
Wine Consultant: *James Irvine*
Year of foundation: *1985*
Location of principal vineyards: *Nuriootpa, Barossa Valley*
Leading wines: *Shiraz, Cabernet Sauignon, Rhine Riesling*
Tonnes crushed on average each year: *250*

Tonnes crushed in 1993: *160*
Best recent vintages: *Red—1990, 1991, 1992, 1993; White—1992, 1993*

EVANS & TATE
Swan Street
Henley Brook WA 6055
Ph (09) 296 4666, Fax (09) 296 1148
Owner: *Tate Family*
Winemaker: *Brian Fletcher*
Year of foundation: *1972*
Location of principal vineyards: *Margaret River, Swan Valley*
Leading wines: *Margaret River Cabernet Sauvignon, Hermitage, Classic Dry White, Gnangara Shiraz*
Tonnes crushed on average each year: *500*
Tonnes crushed in 1993: *450*
Best recent vintages: *Red—1992; White—1993*

F

FERGUSSON WINERY
Wills Road
Yarra Glen Vic 3775
Ph (059) 652 237, Fax (059) 652 389
Owner: *Peter W. Fergusson*
Chief Winemaker: *Chris Keyes*
Year of foundation: *1968*
Location of principal vineyards: *Yarra Valley*
Leading wines: *Victoria Chardonnay, Jeremy Shiraz, Benjamin Cabernet Sauvignon*
Tonnes crushed on average each year: *100*
Tonnes crushed in 1993: *75*
Best recent vintages: *Red—1990; White—1992*

FREYCINET VINEYARDS PTY LTD
Tasman Highway
Bicheno Tas 7215
Ph (002) 578 574, Fax (002) 578 454
Owners: *Geoffrey and Susan Bull*
Chief Winemaker: *Claudio Radenti*
Year of foundation: *1980*
Location of principal vineyards: *Bicheno*
Leading wines: *Chardonnay, Cabernet Sauvignon, Pinot Noir*
Tonnes crushed on average each year: *50*
Tonnes crushed in 1993: *50*
Best recent vintages: *Red—1993, 1992, 1991, 1990; White—1993, 1992, 1990*

G

GALAFREY WINES
114 York Street
Albany WA 6330
Ph (098) 416 533, Fax (098) 512 022
Owners: *Ian and Linda Tyrer*
Chief Winemaker: *Ian Tyrer*
Year of foundation: *1977*
Location of principal vineyards: *Mount Barker*
Leading wines: *Rhine Riesling, Shiraz, Cabernet Sauvignon*
Tonnes crushed on average each year: *75*
Tonnes crushed in 1993: *65*
Best recent vintages: *Red and White—1990, 1991*

GEHRIG'S WINERY
Murray Valley Highway
Barnawartha Vic 3688
Ph (060) 267 296, Fax (060) 267 424
Owners: *Bernard and Brian Gehrig*
Chief Winemaker: *Brian Gehrig*
Year of foundation: *1858*
Location of principal vineyards: *Barnawartha*
Leading wines: *Chardonnay, Shiraz, Vintage Port*
Tonnes crushed on average each year: *120*

Tonnes crushed in 1993: *60*
Best recent vintages: *Red—1991; White—1992*

GIACONDA
McClay Road
Beechworth Vic 3747
Ph (057) 270 246, Fax (057) 270 246
Owner and Chief Winemaker: *Rick Kinzbrunner*
Year of foundation: *1985*
Location of principal vineyards: *Beechworth*
Leading wines: *Chardonnay, Pinot Noir, Cabernet Sauvignon-Merlot-Cabernet Franc*
Tonnes crushed on average each year: *14*
Tonnes crushed in 1993: *12.5*
Best recent vintages: *Red and White—1992*

GOONA WARRA VINEYARD
Sunbury Road
Sunbury Vic 3429
Ph (03) 744 7211, Fax (03) 744 7648
Owners: *John and Elizabeth Barnier*
Chief Winemaker: *John Barnier*
Year of foundation: *1863, re-established in 1983*
Location of principal vineyards: *Sunbury*
Leading wines: *Chardonnay, Semillon, Cabernet Franc*
Tonnes crushed on average each year: *30*
Tonnes crushed in 1993: *25*
Best recent vintages: *Red—1991, 1992, 1993; White—1991, 1993*

GOUNDREY
Muir Highway
Mount Barker WA 6324
Ph (098) 511 777, Fax (098) 511 997
Owner: *Goundrey Wines Ltd*
Chief Winemaker: *Brenden Smith*
Year of foundation: *1971*
Location of principal vineyards: *Mount Barker*
Leading wines: *Rhine Riesling, Cabernet Sauvignon, Chardonnay*
Tonnes crushed on average each year: *500*
Tonnes crushed in 1993: *500*
Best recent vintages: *Red—1989; White—1992*

GRANT BURGE WINES
Jacob's Creek
Barossa Way
Tanunda SA 5352
Ph (085) 633 700, Fax (085) 632 807
Owners: *Grant and Helen Burge*
Chief Winemaker: *Grant Burge*
Year of foundation: *1988*
Location of principal vineyards: *Barossa Range, Jacobs Creek, Lyndoch*
Leading wines: *Meshach Shiraz, Sparkling Pinot Noir–Chardonnay, Barossa Range Chardonnay*
Tonnes crushed on average each year: *750*
Tonnes crushed in 1993: *495*
Best recent vintages: *Red—1993, 1991, 1990, 1988; White—1988, 1990, 1991*

GROSSET WINES
King Street
Auburn SA 5451
Ph (088) 492 175, Fax (085) 492 292
Owner and Chief Winemaker: *Jeffrey Grosset*
Year of foundation: *1981*
Location of principal vineyards: *Clare Valley*
Leading wines: *Polish Hill Riesling, Chardonnay, Gaia Cabernet Sauvignon and Cabernet Franc-Merlot*

Tonnes crushed on average each year: *100*
Tonnes crushed in 1993: *92*
Best recent vintages: *Red—1991; White—1993, 1990*

H

THE HANGING ROCK WINERY
Jim Road
Newham Vic 3442
Ph: (054) 270 542, Fax (054) 270 310
Principal shareholders: *John and Ann Ellis*
Chief Winemaker: *John Ellis*
Year of foundation: *1987*
Location of principal vineyards: *Macedon region, Heathcote*
Leading wines: *Macedon Sparkling, The Jim Jim Sauvignon Blanc, Heathcote Shiraz*
Tonnes crushed on average each year: *250*
Tonnes crushed in 1993: *240*
Best recent vintages: *Red—1990, 1991; White—1991, 1992*

HAPPS
Commonage Road
Dunsborough WA 6281
Ph: *(097) 553 300, Fax (097) 553 046*
Owners: *Erland and Roslyn Happ*
Chief Winemaker: *Erland Happ*
Year of foundation: *1978*
Location of principal vineyards: *Dunsborough*
Leading wines: *Merlot, Cabernet-Merlot, Chardonnay*
Tonnes crushed on average each year: *140*
Tonnes crushed in 1993: *140*
Best recent vintages: *Red—1991; White—1991, 1993*

HARDY'S WINES
Reynell Road
Reynella SA 5161
Ph (08) 381 2266, Fax (08) 381 1968
Owner: *BRL Hardy Ltd*
Chief Winemakers: *David O'Leary, Tom Newton*
Year of foundation: *1853*
Location of principal vineyards: *Reynella, Padthaway, Coonawarra, Clare*
Leading wines: *Sir James Sparkling, Nottage Hill, Eileen Hardy*
Best recent vintages: *Red—1991, 1993, 1990, 1992, 1988; White—1993, 1992, 1991*

HEEMSKERK WINES
Pipers Brook Road
Pipers Brook Tas 7254
Ph (003) 827 133, Fax (003) 827 242
Owner: *Privately owned*
Chief Winemaker: *Martine Combret*
Year of foundation: *1974*
Location of principal vineyards: *Northern Tasmania*
Leading wines: *Jansz Sparkling, Chardonnay, Pinot Noir*
Tonnes crushed on average each year: *200*
Tonnes crushed in 1993: *250*
Best recent vintages: *Red—1990; White—1988, 1991, 1993*

HEGGIES VINEYARD
Eden Valley Road
Angaston SA 5353
Ph (085) 613 200, Fax (085) 613 393
Owners: *Robert and Sam Hill Smith*
Chief Winemaker: *Simon Adams*
Year of foundation: *1971*
Location of principal vineyards: *Eden Valley*
Leading wines: *Chardonnay, Cabernets, Riesling*
Tonnes crushed on average each year: *250*
Tonnes crushed in 1993: *300*

Best recent vintages: *Red—1993, 1992, 1990; White—1992, 1990, 1993*

C.A. HENSCHKE & Co
Moculta Road
Keyneton SA 5353
Ph (085) 648 223, Fax (085) 648 294
Owner: *Henschke Family*
Chief Winemaker: *Stephen Henschke*
Year of foundation: *1868*
Location of principal vineyards: *Eden Valley, Keyneton, Lenswood*
Leading wines: *Hill of Grace Shiraz, Mount Edelstone Shiraz, Eden Valley Riesling*
Tonnes crushed on average each year: *600*
Tonnes crushed in 1993: *550*
Best recent vintages: *Red—1992, 1990, 1988; White—1992, 1990, 1989*

HICKINBOTHAM OF DROMANA
Wallaces Road
Dromana Vic 3936
Ph (059) 810 355, Fax (059) 810 355
Owner: *Hickinbotham Winemakers Pty Ltd*
Chief Winemaker: *Andrew Hickinbotham*
Year of foundation: *1988*
Location of principal vineyards: *Dromana, Mornington Peninsula*
Leading wines: *Chardonnay, Pinot Noir, Cabernet blends*
Tonnes crushed on average each year: *60*
Tonnes crushed in 1993: *60*
Best recent vintages: *Red—1989; White—1993*

HILL-SMITH ESTATE
Eden Valley Road
Angaston SA 5353
Ph (085) 613 200, Fax (085) 613 393
Owners: *Robert and Sam Hill Smith*
Chief Winemaker: *Andrew Murphy*
Year of foundation: *1972*
Location of principal vineyards: *Eden Valley*
Leading wines: *Sauvignon Blanc, Chardonnay, Cabernet Sauvignon-Shiraz*
Tonnes crushed on average each year: *120*
Tonnes crushed in 1993: *140*
Best recent vintages: *Red—1990, 1991, 1992; White—1993, 1992, 1990*

HJT VINEYARDS PTY LTD
Keenan Road
Glenrowan Vic 3676
Ph (057) 662 252
Owners: *Harry and Catherine Tinson*
Chief Winemaker: *Harry Tinson*
Year of foundation: *1979*
Location of principal vineyards: *Glenrowan*
Leading wines: *Chardonnay, Cabernet, Rhine Riesling*
Tonnes crushed on average each year: *18*
Tonnes crushed in 1993: *13*
Best recent vintages: *Red—1992, 1991; White—1991, 1990*

HOLLICK WINES PTY LTD
Racecourse Road
Penola SA 5277
Ph (087) 372 318, Fax (087) 372 952
Owners: *I.B. Hollick, W.C. Hollick, P.C. Tocaciu*
Chief Winemaker: *Pat Tocaciu*
Year of foundation: *1983*
Location of principal vineyards: *Coonawarra*
Leading wines: *Ravenswood, Coonawarra (a red blend of Cabernet Sauvignon, Merlot and Cabernet Franc), Chardonnay*
Tonnes crushed on average each year: *300*
Tonnes crushed in 1993: *300*

Best recent vintages: *Red—1990, 1991, 1992; White—1992, 1993*

HOUGHTON WINE COMPANY
Dale Road
Middle Swan WA 6056
Ph (09) 274 5100, Fax (09) 274 5372
Owner: *BRL Hardy Ltd*
Chief Winemaker: *Paul Lapsley*
Year of foundation: *1836*
Location of principal vineyards: *Swan Valley, Moondah Brook, Margaret River, Frankland River*
Leading wines: *Houghton White Burgundy, Moondah Brook Verdelho, Gold Reserve Cabernet Sauvignon.*
Tonnes crushed on average each year: *4500*
Tonnes crushed in 1993: *4300*
Best vintages in recent years: *Red—1992, 1990, 1989, 1986; White—1993, 1991, 1989, 1987*

HOWARD PARK
16 Little River Road
Denmark WA 6333
Ph (098) 481 261, Fax (098) 482 064
Owners: *John and Wendy Wade*
Chief Winemaker: *John Wade*
Year of foundation: *1986*
Location of principal vineyards: *Mount Barker*
Leading wines: *Howard Park Cabernet Sauvignon, Howard Park Riesling, Madfish Bay Dry White and Dry Red*
Tonnes crushed on average each year: *50*
Tonnes crushed in 1993: *50*
Best recent vintages: *Red—1992, 1990, 1986; White—1993, 1992, 1986*

HUGO WINES
Elliott Road
McLaren Flat SA 5171
Ph (08) 383 0098, Fax (08) 383 0446
Owner and Chief Winemaker: *John Hugo*
Year of foundation: *1982*
Location of principal vineyards: *McLaren Flat*
Leading wines: *Chardonnay, Shiraz, Cabernet Sauvignon*
Tonnes crushed on average each year: *100*
Tonnes crushed in 1993: *90*
Best recent vintages: *Red—1990; White—1988*

HUNGERFORD HILL
McDonalds Road
Pokolbin NSW 2321
Ph (049) 987 666, Fax (049) 987 682
Owner: *Southcorp Holdings*
Chief Winemaker: *Ian Walsh*
Year of foundation: *1967*
Location of principal vineyards: *Hunter Valley*
Leading wines: *Semillon-Sauvignon Blanc, Semillon-Chardonnay, Cabernet Sauvignon-Merlot*
Best recent vintages: *Red—1989, 1991; White—1990, 1992*

HUNTER ESTATE
Hermitage Road
Pokolbin NSW 2320
Ph (049) 987 521, Fax (049) 987 796
Owner: *Orlando Wyndham*
Chief Winemaker: *John Baruzzi*
Year of foundation: *1972*
Location of principal vineyards: *Hunter Valley*
Leading wines: *Bin 1 Chardonnay, Cabernet Sauvignon and Hermitage*
Tonnes crushed on average each year: *6500*
Tonnes crushed in 1993: *6000*
Best recent vintages: *Red—1991; White—1992*

HUNTINGTON ESTATE
Cassilis Road
Mudgee NSW 2850
Ph (063) 733 825, Fax (063) 733 730
Owners: *Bob and Wendy Roberts*
Chief Winemaker: *Bob Roberts*
Year of foundation: *1973*
Location of principal vineyards: *Mudgee*
Leading wines: *Cabernet Sauvignon, Shiraz, Semillon-Chardonnay*
Tonnes crushed on average each year: *300*
Tonnes crushed in 1993: *195*
Best recent vintages: *Red—1993, 1992, 1990, 1991, 1989; White—* 1993, 1992

I

IDYLL
265 Ballan Road
Moorabool Vic 3221
Ph (052) 761 280, Fax (052) 761 537
Owners: *D. & E.M. Sefton*
Chief Winemaker: *Dr Daryl Sefton*
Year of foundation: *1966*
Location of principal vineyards: *Moorabool (Geelong)*
Leading wines: *Cabernet, Shiraz, Chardonnay, Gewürztraminer*
Tonnes crushed on average each year: *70*
Best recent vintages: *Red—1989, 1990, 1991, 1992; White—1990, 1991, 1192, 1993*

INGOLDBY
Ingoldby Road
McLaren Flat SA 5171
Ph (08) 383 0005, Fax (08) 383 0467
Owner and Chief Winemaker: *Walter William Wilfred Clappis*
Year of foundation: *1973*
Location of principal vineyards: *McLaren Flat, Willunga, McLaren Vale*
Leading wines: *Cabernet Sauvignon, Shiraz, Colombard*
Tonnes crushed on average each year: *300*
Tonnes crushed in 1993: *312*
Best recent vintages: *Red—1990, 1992, 1987, 1989, 1991; White—1989, 1987, 1992, 1993, 1990*

J

JAMES HASELGROVE WINES
Foggo Road
McLaren Vale SA 5171
Ph (08) 323 8706, Fax (08) 323 8049
Owner: *Australian Premium Wines Pty Ltd*
Chief Winemaker: *Nick Haselgrove*
Location of principal vineyards: *McLaren Vale*
Leading wines: *Futures Shiraz, Cabernet Merlot, Sauvignon Blanc*
Tonnes crushed on average each year: *210*
Tonnes crushed in 1993: *160*
Best recent vintages: *Red—1990, 1991, 1992; White—1991, 1993*

JANE BROOK ESTATE WINES
229 Toodyay Road
Middle Swan WA 6056
Ph (09) 274 1432, Fax (09) 274 1211
Owner: *WCV Nominees Pty Ltd*
Chief Winemaker: *David Atkinson*
Year of foundation: *1932*
Location of principal vineyards: *Middle Swan*
Leading wines: *Mount Barker Rhine Riesling, Cabernet Merlot, Wood Aged Chenin Blanc*
Tonnes crushed on average each year: *100*
Tonnes crushed in 1993: *100*

Best recent vintages: *Red—1990; White—1993*

JIM BARRY WINES
Main North Road
Clare SA 5453
Ph (088) 422 261, Fax (088) 423 752
Owner: *Jim Barry*
Chief Winemaker: *Mark Barry*
Year of foundation: *1959*
Location of principal vineyards: *Clare Valley*
Leading wines: *The Armagh Shiraz, Jim Barry Cabernet Sauvignon, Watervale Rhine Riesling*
Tonnes crushed on average each year: *900*
Tonnes crushed in 1993: *750*
Best recent vintages: *Red—1990, 1989, 1992, 1993; White—1989, 1991, 1993*

JOHN GEHRIG WINES
Oxley Vic 3678
Ph (057) 273 395, Fax (057) 273 699
Owner and Chief Winemaker: *John Gehrig*
Year of foundation: *1976*
Location of principal vineyards: *Oxley*
Leading wines: *Pinot Noir, Brut, Rhine Riesling, Cabernet-Merlot*
Tonnes crushed on average each year: *80*
Tonnes crushed in 1993: *35*
Best recent vintages: *Red—1988, 1991; White—1990, 1988*

KATNOOK ESTATE
Penola Road
Coonawarra SA 5263
Ph (087) 372 394, Fax (087) 372 397
Owner: *Katnook Pty Ltd*
Chief Winemaker: *Wayne Stehbens*
Year of foundation: *1979*
Location of principal vineyards: *Coonawarra*
Leading wines: *Sauvignon Blanc, Chardonnay, Cabernet Sauvignon*
Best recent vintages: *Red and White—1990*

KAYS AMERY
Kays Road
McLaren Vale SA 5171
Ph (08) 323 8201, Fax (08) 323 9199
Owner: *Kay Bros Pty Ltd*
Chief Winemaker: *Colin H. Kay*
Year of foundation: *1890*
Location of principal vineyards: *McLaren Vale*
Leading wines: *Block G Shiraz, Cabernet Sauvignon, Liqueur Muscat*
Tonnes crushed on average each year: *100*
Tonnes crushed in 1993: *72*
Best recent vintages: *Red and White—1992, 1991, 1990, 1989*

KELLYBROOK WINERY
Fulford Road
Wonga Park Vic 3115
Ph (03) 722 2092, Fax (03) 722 2092
Owner and Chief Winemaker: *Darren Kelly*
Year of foundation: *1970*
Location of principal vineyards: *Wonga Park*
Leading wines: *Methode Champenoise, Chardonnay, Pinot Noir*
Tonnes crushed on average each year: *55*
Tonnes crushed in 1993: *57*
Best recent vintages: *Red—1993, 1991, 1988; White—1993, 1992, 1990*

KILLERBY VINEYARDS PTY LTD
Lakes Road
Stratham WA 6230

Ph (097) 957 222, Fax (097) 957 835
Owners: *Killerby Family*
Chief Winemaker: *Matt Aldridge*
Year of foundation: *1973*
Location of principal vineyards: *Stratham (Capel region)*
Leading wines: *Cabernet Sauvignon, Chardonnay, Shiraz*
Tonnes crushed on average each year: *120*
Tonnes crushed in 1993: *100*
Best recent vintages: *Red and White—1993, 1991, 1989*

TIM KNAPPSTEIN WINES
2 Pioneer Avenue
Clare SA 5453
Ph (088) 422 600, Fax (088) 423 831
Owner: *Petaluma Ltd*
Chief Winemaker: *Tim Knappstein*
Year of foundation: *1976*
Location of principal vineyards: *Clare Valley and Lenswood*
Leading wines: *Riesling, Fumé Blanc, Cabernet Merlot*
Tonnes crushed on average each year: *550*
Tonnes crushed in 1993: *455*
Best recent vintages: *Red—1993, 1992, 1991, 1990 1988; White—1993, 1992, 1990, 1989, 1985*

KNIGHT GRANITE HILLS
Burke and Wills Track
Baynton Vic 3444
Ph (065) 237 264, Fax (054) 237 288
Owner: *Knight Family*
Chief Winemaker: *Llew Knight*
Year of foundation: *1979*
Location of principal vineyards: *Baynton (Macedon region)*
Leading wines: *Granite Hills range of white and red table wines*
Tonnes crushed on average each year: *80*
Tonnes crushed in 1993: *55*
Best recent vintages: *Red—1988, 1991, 1992; White—1990, 1991, 1992*

KOMINOS WINES
New England Highway
Severnlea Qld 4352
Ph (076) 834 311, Fax (076) 834 311
Owners: *Stephen, Penelope and Tony Comino*
Chief Winemaker: *Tony Comino*
Year of foundation: *1984*
Location of principal vineyards: *Severnlea (Granite Belt)*
Leading wines: *Shiraz, Cabernet Sauvignon, Chardonnay*
Tonnes crushed on average each year: *60*
Tonnes crushed in 1993: *85*
Best recent vintages: *Red—1990, 1991, 1992; White—1991, 1992, 1993*

KRONDORF WINES
Krondorf Road
Tanunda SA 5352
Ph (085) 632 145
Owner: *Mildara Blass Ltd*
Chief Winemaker: *Nick Walker*
Year of foundation: *1978*
Location of principal vineyards: *Lyndoch and Eden Valley*
Leading wines: *Chardonnay, Chablis, Shiraz-Cabernet*
Tonnes crushed on average each year: *3000*
Tonnes crushed in 1993: *2700*
Best recent vintages: *Red—1990, 1991, 1992, 1988; White—1992, 1993, 1991, 1990*

L

LAKES FOLLY
Broke Road
Pokolbin NSW 2321
Ph (049) 987 507, Fax (049) 987 322
Owner: *Lake Family*
Chief Winemaker: *Stephen Lake*
Date of foundation: *1963*
Location of principal vineyards: *Pokolbin*
Leading wines: *Cabernet, Chardonnay*
Tonnes crushed on average each year: *60*
Tonnes crushed in 1993: *60*
Best recent vintages: *Red—1993, 1991, 1989; White—1993, 1992, 1989*

LAMONT WINERY
Bisdee Road
Millendon WA 6056
Ph (09) 296 4485, Fax (09) 296 1663
Owners: *N. & C. Lamont*
Chief Winemaker: *Corin Lamont*
Year of foundation: *1978*
Location of principal vineyards: *Swan Valley*
Leading wines: *White Burgundy, Navera, Cabernet*
Tonnes crushed on average each year: *85*
Tonnes crushed in 1993: *85*
Best recent vintages: *Red—1989; White—good most years*

LARK HILL WINERY
Lark Hill
Bungendore NSW 2621
Ph (06) 238 1393, Fax (06) 238 1393
Owners: *David & Sue Carpenter*
Winemaker: *Sue Carpenter*
Year of foundation: *1978*
Location of principal vineyards: *Lark Hill, Bungendore*
Leading wines: *Chardonnay, Cabernet Merlot, Rhine Riesling*
Tonnes crushed on average each year: *50*
Best recent vintages: *Red—1991, 1988, 1992, 1990, 1993; White—1993, 1991, 1992, 1988, 1990*

LEASINGHAM WINES PTY LTD
7 Dominic Street
Clare SA 5453
Ph (088) 422 555, Fax (088) 423 293
Owner: *BRL Hardy Ltd*
Chief Winemaker: *Richard Rowe*
Year of foundation: *1893 (as Stanley Winery)*
Location of principal vineyards: *Leasingham, south of Clare*
Leading wines: *Classic Clare, Cabernet Malbec Bin 56, Chardonnay Bin 37*
Best recent vintages: *Red—1991, 1993, 1990, 1992, 1988; White—1993, 1992, 1991*

LECONFIELD
Penola Road
Coonawarra SA 5263
Ph (087) 372 326, Fax (087) 372 285
Owner: *Dr Richard Hamilton*
Winemaker: *Ralph Fowler*
Year of foundation: *1974*
Location of principal vineyards: *Coonawarra*
Leading wines: *Cabernet Sauvignon, Shiraz, Riesling*
Best recent vintages: *Red—1992, 1991, 1990; White—1993, 1992, 1991*

LEEUWIN ESTATE
Stephens Road
Margaret River WA 6285
Ph (097) 576 253, Fax (097) 576 364
Owner: *Rural Developments Pty Ltd*

Chief Winemaker: *Bob Cartwright*
Year of foundation: *1974*
Location of principal vineyards: *Margaret River*
Leading wines: *Art Series Chardonnay, Art Series Cabernet Sauvignon, Art Series Rhine Riesling*
Tonnes crushed on average each year: *520*
Tonnes crushed in 1993: *500*
Best recent vintages: *Red—1992, 1989, 1991; White—1992, 1989, 1991*

LEO BURING
Tanunda Road
Nuriootpa SA 5355
Ph (085) 620 389, Fax (085) 622 494
Owner: *Southcorp Holdings*
Chief Winemaker: *Geoff Henricks*
Year of foundation: *1945*
Location of principal vineyards: *Eden Valley, Clare Valley*
Leading wines; Leonay Rhine Riesling
Best recent vintages: *Red—1991, 1990, 1988; White—1992, 1991, 1988*

LILLYDALE VINEYARDS
10 Davross Court
Seville Vic 3139
Ph (055) 642 016, Fax (055) 643 009
Owners: *Alex White, Martin Grinbergs and Judy White*
Chief Winemaker: *Alex White*
Year of foundation: *1976*
Location of principal vineyards: *Seville and Coldstream*
Leading wines: *Chardonnay, Gewürztraminer, Cabernet Sauvignon*
Tonnes crushed on average each year: *100*
Tonnes crushed in 1993: *100*
Best recent vintages: *Red—1988; White—1991*

LILLYPILLY ESTATE
Lillypilly Road
Leeton NSW 2705
Ph (069) 534 069, Fax (069) 534 980
Owner: *P & A Fiumara & Son Pty Ltd*
Chief Winemaker: *Robert Fiumara*
Year of foundation: *1982*
Location of principal vineyards: *Leeton*
Leading wines: *Noble Muscat of Alexandria, Tramillon, Red Velvet*
Tonnes crushed on average each year: *150*
Tonnes crushed in 1993: *120*
Best recent vintages: *Red—1992; White—1993*

LINDEMANS WINES PTY LTD
Edey Road
Karadoc Vic 3496
Ph (050) 240 303, Fax (050) 240 324
Owner: *Southcorp Holdings*
Chief Winemaker: *Phillip John*
Year of foundation: *1843*
Location of principal vineyards: *Padthaway and Coonawarra*
Leading wines: *Padthaway Chardonnay, St George Vineyard Cabernet Sauvignon, Limestone Ridge Vineyard Shiraz Cabernet (both Coonawarra)*
Best recent vintages: *Red—1991, 1990, 1986; White—1990, 1991, 1985*

LINDEMANS HUNTER RIVER WINERY
McDonalds Road
Pokolbin NSW 2320
Ph (049) 987 701, Fax (049) 987 682
Owner: *Southcorp Holdings*
Chief Winemaker: *Patrick Auld*
Year of foundation: *1843*
Location of principal vineyards: *Lower Hunter Valley*
Leading wines: *Hunter River Burgundy, Hunter River Chardonnay, Hunter River Chablis*

Best recent vintages: *Red—1991, 1989, 1987; White—1992, 1991*

LITTLE'S WINERY
Palmers Lane
Pokolbin NSW 2320
Ph (049) 987 626, Fax (049) 987 867
Owners: Michael and Margaret Little
Chief Winemaker: *Ian Little*
Year of foundation: *1983*
Location of principal vineyards: *Pokolbin*
Leading wines: *Chardonnay, Cabernet Sauvignon, Vintage Port*
Tonnes crushed on average each year: *75*
Tonnes crushed in 1993: *35*
Best recent vintages: *Red—1991, 1989, 1992; White—1991, 1992, 1993*

LOIRA VINEYARDS
Glendale Road
Loira Tas 7275
Ph (003) 947 488, Fax (003) 947 488
Owner: *Buchanan Wines Pty Ltd*
Chief Winemaker: *Don Buchanan*
Location of principal vineyards: *Loira, West Tamar*
Leading wines: *Buchanan Pinot Noir, Chardonnay, Riesling*
Tonnes crushed on average each year: *80*
Tonnes crushed in 1993: *45*
Best recent vintages: *Red—1991; White—1992*

LONG GULLY ESTATE
Long Gully Road
Healesville Vic 3777
Ph (03) 807 4246, Fax (03) 807 2213
Owners: Reiner and Irma Knapp
Chief Winemaker: *Peter Florance*
Year of foundation: *1982*
Location of principal vineyards: *Long Gully, Healesville*
Leading wines: *Chardonnay, Cabernet Sauvignon, Pinot Noir*
Tonnes crushed on average each year: *160*
Tonnes crushed in 1993: *150*
Best recent vintages: *Red—1990, 1991, 1992, 1993; White—1992, 1991, 1993*

M

McGUIGAN BROS
Broke & McDonalds Road
Pokolbin NSW 2320
Ph (049) 987 400, Fax (049) 987 401
Owner: *Brian McGuigan Wines Ltd*
Chief Winemaker: *Neil McGuigan*
Year of foundation: *1992*
Location of principal vineyards: *Hunter Valley, Mudgee*
Leading wines: *Black Shiraz, Bin 7000 Chardonnay, Night Harvest Graves*
Tonnes crushed on average each year: *1600*
Tonnes crushed in 1993: *1500*
Best recent vintages: *Red and White—1993*

McWILLIAM'S WINES
Yenda and Hanwood NSW 2681
Ph (069) 691 001, Fax (069) 681 312
Owner: *McWilliam's Wines Pty Ltd*
Chief Winemaker: *Jim Brayne*
Year of foundation: *1877*
Location of principal vineyards: *Riverina, Young*
Leading wines: *Hilltops Cabernet, Barwang range, Charles King range*
Best recent vintages: *Red—1991, 1992; White—1993, 1992*

McWILLIAM'S WINES ROBINVALE
22 Moore Street
Robinvale Vic 3549

Ph (050) 264 004, Fax (050) 264 479
Owner: *McWillam's Wines Pty Ltd*
Chief Winemakers; Max McWilliam and Mathew McWilliam
Year of foundation: *1963*
Location of principal vineyards: *Robinvale*
Leading wines: *Cream Sherry*
Best recent vintages: *White—1992, 1993, 1991*

MAGILERI WINERY
Douglas Gully Road
McLaren Flat SA 5171
Ph (08) 383 0177, Fax (08) 383 0136
Owner: *Steven Maglieri*
Chief Winemaker: *John Loxton*
Year of foundation: *1972*
Location of principal vineyards: *McLaren Flat*
Leading wines: *Lambrusco, Cabernet Sauvignon, Shiraz*
Tonnes crushed on average each year: *1500*
Tonnes crushed in 1993: *1300*
Best recent vintages: *Red—1988, 1990, 1992*

MAIN RIDGE ESTATE
William Road
Red Hill Vic 3937
Ph (059) 892 868, Fax (059) 892 686
Owners: *Nat and Rosalie White*
Chief Winemaker: *Nat White*
Year of foundation: *1975*
Location of principal vineyards: *Red Hill*
Leading wines: *Chardonnay, Pinot Noir, Cabernet*
Tonnes crushed on average each year: *14*
Tonnes crushed in 1993: *14*
Best recent vintages: *Red and White—1993, 1992, 1991*

MARIENBERG WINE COMPANY PTY LTD
Chalk Hill Road
McLaren Vale SA 5171
Ph (08) 323 9666, Fax (08) 323 9600
Owners: *Terry and Jill Hill*
Chief Winemaker: *Grant Burge*
Location of principal vineyards: *McLaren Vale*
Leading wines: *Chardonnay, Cabernet Sauvignon, Shiraz*
Tonnes crushed on average each year: *300*
Tonnes crushed in 1993: *260*
Best recent vintages: *Red—1991; White—1993*

MARKWOOD ESTATE
Morris Lane
Markwood Vic 3678
Ph (057) 270 361
Owner and Chief Winemaker: *Rick Morris*
Year of foundation: *1971*
Location of principal vineyards: *Markwood*
Leading wines: *Chardonnay, Cabernet Sauvignon, Vintage Port*
Tonnes crushed on average each year: *30*
Tonnes crushed in 1993: *15*
Best recent vintages: *Red—1986, 1988, 1990; White—1989, 1991, 1992*

MARSH ESTATE
Deasy's Road
Pokolbin NSW 2320
Ph (049) 987 587, Fax (049) 987 884
Owner and Chief Winemaker: *Peter Marsh*
Year of foundation: *1978*
Location of principal vineyards: *Pokolbin*

Leading wines: *Semillon, Chardonnay, Shiraz*
Tonnes crushed on average each year: *80*
Tonnes crushed in 1993: *85*
Best recent vintages: *Red—1991, 1989, 1993, 1990, 1992; White—1991, 1993, 1989, 1990, 1992*

MERRICKS ESTATE
Thompson's Lane
Merricks Vic 3916
Ph (059) 898 419, Fax (059) 629 4035
Owners: *George and Jacquellyn Kefford*
Chief Winemaker: *Alex White*
Year of foundation: *1978*
Location of principal vineyards: *Merricks*
Leading wines: *Chardonnay, Cabernet Sauvignon, Shiraz*
Tonnes crushed on average each year: *30*
Tonnes crushed in 1993: 27
Best recent vintages: *Red—1993, 1991; White—1993, 1992*

MILDARA WINES MERBEIN
Wentworth Road
Merbein Vic 3505
Ph (050) 252 303
Owner: *Mildara Blass*
Chief Winemaker: *Alan Harris*
Year of foundation: *1888*
Location of principal vineyards: *None*
Leading wines: *Fortified range, Brandy, Chardonnay*
Tonnes crushed on average each year: *7000*
Tonnes crushed in 1993: *6500*
Best recent vintages: *White—1992, 1991; Red—none made*

MILDARA COONAWARRA
Main Road
Coonawarra SA 5263
Ph (085) 363 339
Owner: *Mildara Blass*
Chief Winemaker: *Gavin Hogg*
Year of foundation: *1955*
Location of principal vineyards: *Coonawarra*
Leading wines: *Jamieson's Run, Coonawarra Cabernet Sauvignon*
Tonnes crushed on average each year: *5000*
Tonnes crushed in 1993: *4300*
Best recent vintages: *Red—1988, 1990, 1991, 1992; White—1991, 1992*

MIRAMAR WINES
Henry Lawson Drive
Mudgee NSW 2850
Ph (063) 733 874, Fax (063) 733 854
Owners: *I.B. & M.A. MacRae*
Chief Winemaker: *Ian MacRae*
Year of foundation: *1977*
Location of principal vineyards: *Mudgee*
Leading wines: *Chardonnay, Fumé Blanc, Shiraz*
Tonnes crushed on average each year: *150*
Tonnes crushed in 1993: *105*
Best recent vintages: *Red—1991; White—1990*

MIRANDA WINES PTY LTD
57 Jondaryan Avenue
Griffith NSW 2680
Ph (069) 624 033, Fax (069) 626 944
Owners: *Sam, Lou and Jim Miranda*
Chief Winemaker: *Shayne Cunningham*
Year of foundation: *1939*
Location of principal vineyards: *Riverina*
Leading wines: *Wyangan Estate Semillon Sauterne, Wyangan Estate Chardonnay*
Tonnes crushed on average each year: *12 000*
Tonnes crushed in 1993: *14 000*

Best recent vintages: *Red—1989, 1991, 1992; White—1989, 1990, 1992*

MITCHELL CELLARS
Hughes Park Road
Sevenhill via Clare SA 5453
Ph (088) 434 258, Fax (088) 434 340
Owners: *A.J. & C.J. Mitchell*
Chief Winemaker: *A.J. Mitchell*
Year of foundation: *1975*
Location of principal vineyards: *Sevenhill and Watervale*
Leading wines: *Cabernet Sauvignon, Watervale Riesling, Peppertree Vineyard Shiraz*
Tonnes crushed on average each year: *250*
Tonnes crushed in 1993: *150*
Best recent vintages: *Red and White—1990, 1992, 1993*

MITCHELTON WINES
Mitchellstown Vic 3608
Ph (057) 942 710, Fax (057) 942 615
Owners: *Mitchelton Vintners and Mitchelton Vineyard*
Chief Winemaker: *Don Lewis*
Location of principal vineyards: *Mitchellstown*
Leading wines: *Mitchelton Reserve, Preece, Thomas Mitchell*
Tonnes crushed on average each year: *3000*
Tonnes crushed in 1993: *2700*
Best recent vintages: *Red—1992, 1991, 1990; White—1992, 1992. 1991, 1990*

MONTROSE WINES
Henry Lawson Drive
Mudgee NSW 2850
Ph (063) 733 853, Fax (063) 733 795
Owner: *Orlando Wyndham*
Chief Winemaker: *Robert Paul*
Year of foundation: *1974*
Location of principal vineyards: *Mudgee*
Leading wines: *Poets Corner, Chardonnay, Cabernet-Merlot*
Tonnes crushed on average each year: *3000*
Tonnes crushed in 1993: *3000*
Best recent vintages: *Red—1990; White—1991*

MOORILLA ESTATE
655 Main Road
Berriedale Tas 7011
Ph (002) 492 4949, Fax (002) 494 093
Owner: *Moorilla Estate*
Chief Winemaker: *Julian Alcorso*
Year of foundation: *1958*
Location of principal vineyards: *Berriedale and Rosevears*
Leading wines: *Pinot Noir, Riesling, Chardonnay*
Tonnes crushed on average each year: *150*
Tonnes crushed in 1993: *165*
Best recent vintages: *Red—1990, 1992; White—1990, 1991, 1993*

MORRIS WINES
Mia Mia Vineyards
Rutherglen Vic 3685
Ph (060) 267 303,Fax (060) 267 445
Owner: *Orlando Wyndham*
Chief Winemaker: *David Morris*
Year of foundation: *1859*
Location of principal vineyards: *Rutherglen*
Leading wines: *Liqueur Muscat, Mick Morris Durif, Sparkling Shiraz Durif*
Tonnes crushed on average each year: *1000*
Tonnes crushed in 1993: *1000*
Best recent vintages: *Red—1992; White—1990*

MOSS WOOD PTY LTD
Metricup Road
Willyabrup WA 6284
Ph (097) 556 266, Fax (097) 556 303
Owners: *Keith and Clare Mugford*
Chief Winemaker: *Keith Mugford*
Year of foundation: *1969*
Location of principal vineyards: *Margaret River*
Leading wines: *Semillon, Cabernet Sauvignon, Chardonnay*
Tonnes crushed on average each year: *75*
Tonnes crushed in 1993: *75*
Best recent vintages: *Red—1991; White—1993*

MOUNTADAM
High Eden Ridge
Eden Valley SA 5235
Ph (085) 641 101, Fax (085) 362 8942
Owners: *David and Adam Wynn*
Chief Winemaker: *Adam Wynn*
Year of foundation: *1972*
Location of principal vineyards: *High Eden*
Leading wines: *Chardonnay, Pinot Noir, David Wynn Patriarch Shiraz*
Tonnes crushed on average each year: *600*
Tonnes crushed in 1993: *557*
Best recent vintages: *Red—1993, 1991, 1988; White—1993, 1991, 1989*

MOUNT ANAKIE WINERY
130 Staughton Vale Road
Anakie Vic 3221
Ph (052) 841 452, Fax (052) 841 405
Owners: *O. & B. Zambelli*
Chief Winemaker: *Otto Zambelli*
Year of foundation: *1968*
Location of principal vineyards: *Anakie*
Leading wines: *Shiraz, Semillon, Dolcetto*
Tonnes crushed on average each year: *90*
Tonnes crushed in 1993: *80*
Best recent vintages: *Red—1992; White—1990*

MOUNT AVOCA VINEYARD PTY LTD
Moates Lane
Avoca Vic 3467
Ph (054) 653 282, Fax (054) 653 544
Owners: *John and Arda Barry*
Chief Winemaker: *Rodney Morrish*
Year of foundation: *1978*
Location of principal vineyards: *Avoca*
Leading wines: *Cabernet Sauvignon, Shiraz, Chardonnay*
Tonnes crushed on average each year: *130*
Tonnes crushed in 1993: *115*
Best recent vintages: *Red—1991, 1988; White—1993, 1991*

MOUNT HURTLE WINERY
Pimpala Road
Woodcroft SA 5162
Ph (08) 381 6877, Fax (08) 322 244
Owners: *Geoff Merrill and Alister Purbrick*
Chief Winemaker: *Geoff Merrill*
Year of foundation: *1897*
Location of principal vineyards: *Reynella, McLaren Vale, Coonawarra*
Leading wines: *Geoff Merrill Cabernet Sauvignon, Geoff Merrill Semillon-Chardonnay, Mount Hurtle Sauvignon Blanc*
Tonnes crushed on average each year: *400*
Tonnes crushed in 1993: *468*
Best recent vintages: *Red—1988, 1990, 1992; White—1989, 1990, 1992, 1993*

MOUNT IDA
Northern Highway
Heathcote Vic 3523

Ph (054) 821 911
Owner: *Mildara Blass*
Chief Winemaker: *Toni Stockhausen*
Year of foundation: *1979*
Location of principal vineyards: *Heathcote*
Leading wines: *Shiraz*
Tonnes crushed on average each year: *35*
Tonnes crushed in 1993: *12*
Best recent vintages: *Red—1993, 1992, 1990 (only reds made)*

MOUNT MARY VINEYARD
Coldstream West Road
Lilydale Vic 3140
Ph (03) 739 1761, Fax (03) 739 0137
Owners: *Dr John and Marli Middleton*
Chief Winemakers: *John Middleton and Mario Marson*
Year of foundation: *1971*
Location of principal vineyards: *Lilydale*
Leading wines: *Pinot Noir, Cabernets, Chardonnay*
Tonnes crushed on average each year: *50*
Tonnes crushed in 1993: *37*
Best recent vintages: *Red—(Pinot) 1987, 1989, 1991, (Cabernets) 1986, 1988, 1990, 1991, White—(Chardonnay) 1990, 1991, 1992*

MOUNT PLEASANT WINERY POKOLBIN
Marrowbone Road
Pokolbin NSW 2320
Ph (049) 987 505, Fax (049) 987 761
Owner: *McWilliam's Wines Pty Ltd*
Chief Winemaker: *Phillip Ryan*
Year of foundation: *1920*
Location of principal vineyards: *Pokolbin*
Leading wines: *Elizabeth Semillon, Philip Shiraz, Mountain Range Chardonnay*
Best recent vintages: *Red—1991, 1993, 1990; White—1991, 1989*

N

NICHOLSON RIVER WINERY
Liddells Road
Nicholson Vic 3882
Ph (051) 568 241, Fax (051) 568 433
Owners: *K. & J. Eckersley*
Chief Winemaker: *K. Eckersley*
Year of foundation: *1978*
Location of principal vineyards: *Bairnsdale (Gippsland)*
Leading wines: *Chardonnay, Pinot Noir*
Tonnes crushed on average each year: *Vineyard not fully bearing*
Tonnes crushed in 1993: *15*
Best recent vintages: *Red—1990, 1991; White—1991, 1992*

NOON'S WINERY
Rifle Range Road
McLaren Vale SA 5171
Ph (08) 323 8290, Fax (08) 323 8290
Owner and Chief Winemaker: *David Noon*
Year of foundation: *1976*
Location of principal vineyards: *McLaren Vale and Langhorne Creek*
Leading wines: *Traditional Red Shiraz, Cabernet-Shiraz, Grenache*
Tonnes crushed on average each year: *40*
Tonnes crushed in 1993: *37*
Best recent vintages: *Red—1987, 1990, 1991 (only reds made)*

NORMANS WINES PTY LTD
Grants Gully Road
Clarendon SA 5157
Ph (08) 383, 6138, Fax (08) 383 6089
Owner: *Horlin-Smith Family*
Chief Winemaker: *Brian Light*
Year of foundation: *1851*

Location of principal vineyards: *Gawler River and Clarendon*
Leading wines: *Chardonnay, Cabernet Sauvignon, Fine Hermitage*
Tonnes crushed on average each year: *1500*
Tonnes crushed in 1993: *1300*
Best recent vintages: *Red—1992, 1991, 1990, 1988; White—1992, 1993*

O

OAKRIDGE ESTATE
Aitken Road
Seville Vic 3139
Ph (059) 643 379, Fax (059) 642 061
Owner: *Jim Zitzlaff*
Chief Winemaker: *Michael Zitzlaff*
Year of foundation: *1981*
Location of principal vineyards: *Seville, Yarra Valley*
Leading wines: *Reserve Cabernet Sauvignon, Quercus Cabernet Sauvignon-Cabernet Franc-Merlot, Quercus Chardonnay*
Tonnes crushed on average each year: *80*
Tonnes crushed in 1993: 65
Best recent vintages: *Red—1991, 1990*

OAKVALE WINERY
Broke Road
Pokolbin NSW 2320
Ph (049) 987 520, Fax (049) 987 747
Owner and Chief Winemaker: *Barry Shields*
year of foundation: *1893*
Location of principal vineyards: *Pokolbin*
Leading wines: *Chardonnay, Shiraz, Semillon*
Tonnes crushed on average each year: *50*
Best recent vintages: *Red—1991, 1993; White—1988, 1991, 1992*

OLIVE FARM WINES
77 Great Eastern Highway
South Guildford WA 6055
Ph (09) 277 2989, Fax (09) 479 4372
Owners: *Ian and Judi Yurisich*
Chief Winemaker: *Ian Yurisich*
Location of principal vineyards: *Swan Valley*
Leading wines: *Chenin Blanc, Chardonnay, Cabernet-Shiraz-Merlot*
Tonnes crushed on average each year: *120*
Tonnes crushed in 1993: *145*
Best recent vintages: *Red—1992, White—1993*

ORLANDO WINES
Barossa Valley Way
Rowland Flat SA 5352
Ph (085) 213 111, Fax (085) 213 100
Owner: *Orlando Wyndham Pty Ltd*
Chief Winemaker: *Philip Laffer*
Year of foundation: *1847*
Location of principal vineyards: *Eden Valley, Barossa Valley, Padthaway, Coonawarra*
Leading wines: *Jacobs Creek, Carrington, Jacaranda Ridge*
Tonnes crushed on average each year: *28 000*
Tonnes crushed in 1993: *21 000*
Best recent vintages: *Red—1990; White—1992*

P

PARKER WINES
McDonalds Road
Pokolbin NSW 2320
Ph (049) 987 585, Fax (049) 987 732
Owner: *Stan Parker*
Chief Winemaker: *David Lowe*
Year of foundation: *1973*
Location of principal vineyards: *Palmers Lane, Pokolbin*

Leadings wines: *Chardonnay, Shiraz, Pinot Noir*
Tonnes crushed on average each year: *300*
Tonnes crushed in 1993: *350*
Best recent vintages: *Red—1987, 1991, 1989; White—1993, 1988, 1989*

PASSING CLOUDS
Kurting Road
Kingower Vic 3517
Ph (054) 388 257, Fax (054) 388 246
Owners: *Graeme Leith and Sue Mackinnon*
Chief Winemaker: *Graeme Leith*
Year of foundation: *1974*
Location of principal vineyards: *Kingower, Central Victoria*
Leading wines: *Shiraz-Cabernet, Angel Blend Cabernet, Pinot Noir*
Tonnes crushed on average each year: *50*
Tonnes crushed in 1993: *50*
Best recent vintages: *Red—1991, 1992; White—none produced*

PATRITTI WINES
134 Clacton Road
Dover Gardens SA 5048
Ph (08) 296 8261, Fax (08) 296 5088
Owner: *G. Patritti & Co Pty Ltd*
Chief Winemaker: *Geoff Patritti*
Year of foundation: *1926*
Location of principal vineyards: *Blewitt Springs (McLaren Vale)*
Leading wines: *Shiraz-Cabernet, Rhine Riesling, Chenin Blanc Brut*
Tonnes crushed on average each year: *750*
Tonnes crushed in 1993: *650*
Best recent vintages: *Red—1991; White—1993*

PAULETT WINES
Off Polish Hill Road
Sevenhill SA 5453
Ph (088) 434 328, Fax (088) 434 202
Owners: *Neil and Alison Paulett*
Chief Winemaker: *Neil Paulett*
Year of foundation: *1982*
Location of principal vineyards: *Polish Valley*
Leading wines: *Riesling, Shiraz, Cabernet Sauvignon-Merlot*
Tonnes crushed on average each year: *85*
Tonnes crushed in 1993: *70*
Best recent vintages: *Red—1993, 1990, 1991, 1992, 1989; White—1993, 1990, 1992, 1991, 1989*

PENFOLD'S WINES PTY LTD
Tanunda Road
Nuriootpa SA 5355
Ph (085) 620 389, Fax (085) 622 494
Owner: *Southcorp Holdings*
Chief Winemaker: *John Duval*
Year of foundation: *1844*
Location of principal vineyards: *Barossa Valley, Clare*
Leading wines: *Grange Hermitage, The Magill Estate, Bin 707 Cabernet Sauvignon*
Best recent vintages: *Red—1991, 1990; White—1990, 1992*

PENLEY ESTATE
McLeans Road
Coonawarra SA 5263
Ph (08) 231 2400, (087) 363 211, Fax (08) 231 0589
Owner: *Penley Estate*
Chief Winemaker: *Kym Tolley*
Year of foundation: *1988*
Location of principal vineyards: *Coonawarra*

Leading wines: *Coonawarra Cabernet Sauvignon, Coonawarra Hyland Shiraz, Chardonnay Prestige Blend*
Tonnes crushed on average each year: *100*
Tonnes crushed in 1993: *100*
Best recent vintages: *Red and White—1990, 1991, 1992, 1993*

PEPPER TREE WINES
Hall's Road
Pokolbin NSW 2320
Ph (049) 987 539, Fax (049) 987 746
Owner: *Pepper Tree Wines Pty Ltd*
Chief Winemaker: *Chris Cameron*
Year of foundation: *1990*
Location of principal vineyards: *Pokolbin*
Leading wines: *Semillon, Chardonnay, Shiraz*
Tonnes crushed on average each year: *240*
Tonnes crushed in 1993: *235*
Best recent vintages: *Red and White—1991*

PETALUMA
Spring Gully Road
Piccadilly SA 5151
Ph (08) 339 4122, Fax (08) 339 5253
Owner: *Petaluma Ltd*
Chief Winemaker: *Brian Croser*
Year of foundation: *1976*
Location of principal vineyards: *Piccadilly Valley*
Leading wines: *Croser (sparkling), Chardonnay, Coonawarra (a Cabernet-dominant red)*
Tonnes crushed on average each year: *1500*
Tonnes crushed in 1993: *1500*
Best recent vintages: *Red and White—1990, 1992, 1993*

PETER LEHMANN WINES
Para Road
Tanunda SA 5352
Ph (085) 632 500, Fax (085) 633 402
Owner: *Peter Lehmann Wines Ltd*
Year of foundation: *1979*
Location of principal vineyards: *Barossa*
Leading wines: *Wood Matured Semillon, Shiraz, Clancy's Gold Preference*
Tonnes crushed on average each year: *10 000*
Tonnes crushed in 1993: *8000*
Best recent vintages: *Red—1991, 1992, 1993; White—1993, 1991, 1992*

PEWSEY VALE VINEYARD
Eden Valley Road
Angaston SA 5353
Ph (085) 613 200, Fax (085) 613 393
Owners: *Robert and Sam Hill Smith*
Chief Winemaker: *Alan Hoey*
Year of foundation: *1847, re-established 1961*
Location of principal vineyards: *Brownes Road, Eden Valley*
Leading wines: *Riesling, Cabernet Sauvignon, Sauvignon Blanc*
Tonnes crushed on average each year: *300*
Tonnes crushed in 1993: *230*
Best recent vintages: *Red—1993, 1990, 1992; White—1992, 1993, 1990*

PFEIFFER WINES
Distillery Road
Wahgunyah Vic 3687
Ph (060) 332 805, Fax (060) 333 158
Owners: *C.M. & R. H. Pfeiffer*
Chief Winemaker: *Christopher Pfeiffer*
Year of foundation: *1984*
Location of principal vineyards: *Wahgunyah*

Leading wines: *Chardonnay, Cabernet Sauvignon, Auslese Tokay*
Tonnes crushed on average each year: *140*
Tonnes crushed in 1993: *100*
Best recent vintages: *Red—1992, 1991, 1990, 1988; White—1992, 1990, 1989, 1988*

PIERRO MARGARET RIVER VINEYARDS
Caves Road
Willyabrup WA 6280
Ph (097) 556 220, Fax (097) 556 308
Owner and Chief Winemaker: *Dr Michael Peterkin*
Year of foundation: *1980*
Location of principal vineyards: *Margaret River*
Leading wines: *Chardonnay, Semillon-Sauvignon Blanc, Pinot Noir*
Best recent vintages: *Red—1990; White—1992*

PIKES POLISH HILL RIVER ESTATE
Polish Hill River Road
Sevenhill SA 5453
Ph (088) 434 370, Fax (088) 434 353
Owners: *Pike Family*
Chief Winemaker: *Neil Pike*
Year of foundation: *1984*
Location of principal vineyards: *Polish Hill River, Clare Valley*
Leading wines: *Riesling, Sauvignon Blanc, Shiraz*
Tonnes crushed on average each year: *200*
Tonnes crushed in 1993: *150*
Best recent vintages: *Red—1990, 1991, 1992; White—1990, 1991, 1992, 1993*

PIPERS BROOK VINEYARDS
Pipers Brook
Via Lebrina Tas 7254
Ph (003) 827 197, Fax (003) 827 226
Owners: *Pipers Brook Vineyard Ltd*
Chief Winemaker: *Andrew Pirie*
Year of foundation: *1974*
Location of principal vineyards: *Pipers Brook, Rosevears*
Leading wines: *Riesling, Chardonnay, Pellion Pinot Noir*
Tonnes crushed on average each year: *200 rising to 400 in 1994*
Tonnes crushed in 1993: *200*
Best recent vintages: *Red—1992; White—1991*

PLANTAGENET WINES
Albany Highway
Mount Barker WA
Ph (098) 512 150, Fax (098) 511 839
Owners: *Tony Smith, Rob Devenish and Michael Meredith-Hardy*
Chief Winemaker: *Gavin Berry*
Year of foundation: *1974*
Location of principal vineyards: *Denbarker, south west of Mount Barker*
Leading wines: *Riesling, Chardonnay, Shiraz*
Tonnes crushed on average each year: *600*
Tonnes crushed in 1993: *480*
Best recent vintages: *Red—1990, 1986; White—1992, 1993*

PLATT'S WINES
Mudgee Road
Gulgong NSW 2852
Ph (063) 741 700, Fax (063) 721 055
Owners: *B.J. & M.M. Platt*
Chief Winemaker: *Barry Platt*
Year of foundation: *1983*
Location of principal vineyards: *Gulgong and Mudgee*
Leading wines: *Chardonnay, Semillon, Cabernet Sauvignon*
Tonnes crushed on average each year: *65*

Tonnes crushed in 1993: *55*
Best recent vintages: *Red and White—1990, 1991*

PRIMO ESTATE
Old Port Wakefield Road
Virginia SA 5120
Ph (08) 380 9442, Fax (08) 380 9696
Owner and Chief Winemaker: *Joe Grilli*
Year of foundation: *1978*
Location of principal vineyards: *Virginia (Adelaide Plains)*
Leading wines: *Colombard, Botrytis Riesling, Joseph Cabernet Sauvignon Moda Amarone*
Tonnes crushed on average each year: *200*
Tonnes crushed in 1993: *200*
Best recent vintages: *Red—1991; White—1990*

PRINCE ALBERT VINEYARD
100 Lemins Road
Waurn Ponds Vic 3221
Ph (052) 418 091, Fax (052) 418 091
Owners: *Susan and Bruce Hyett*
Chief Winemaker: *Bruce Hyett*
Year of foundation: *1975*
Location of principal vineyards: *Waurn Ponds (Geelong)*
Leading wine: *Pinot Noir (only wine produced)*
Tonnes crushed on average each year: *11*
Tonnes crushed in 1993: 2
Best recent vintage: *Red—1992*

R

REDBANK
Sunraysia Highway
Redbank Vic 3478
Ph (054) 677 255, Fax (054) 677 248
Owners: *Neill & Sally Robb*
Chief Winemaker: *Neill Robb*
Year of foundation: *1973*
Location of principal vineyards: *Redbank, Percydale, Avoca*
Leading Wines: *Redbank Cabernet, Sally's Paddock, Long Paddock*
Tonnes crushed on average each year: *80*
Tonnes crushed in 1993: *50*
Best recent vintages: *Red—1988, 1990, 1991*

REDGATE WINES
Boodjidup Road
Margaret River WA 6285
Ph (097) 576 208, Fax (097) 576 308
Owners: *Bill and Paul Ullinger*
Chief Winemaker: *Virginia Willcock*
Year of foundation : *1977*
Location of principal vineyards: *Redgate and Broadvale (Margaret River)*
Leading wines: *Sauvignon Blanc Reserve (wooded), Cabernet Sauvignon*
Tonnes crushed on average each year: *180*
Tonnes crushed in 1993: *163*
Best recent vintages; Red—1988, 1991; White—1992, 1993

REDMAN WINERY
Main Road
Coonawarra SA 5263
Ph (087) 363 331, Fax (087) 363 013
Owners: *Redman Family*
Chief Winemaker: *Bruce Redman*
Year of foundation: *1966*
Location of principal vineyards: *Coonawarra*
Leading wines: *Cabernet Sauvignon, Shiraz Claret*
Tonnes crushed on average each year: *260*
Tonnes crushed in 1993: *210*
Best recent vintages: *Red—1992, 1990, 1988*

RENMANO WINES
Sturt Highway
Berri SA 5343
Ph (085) 820 300, Fax (085) 832 224
Owner: *Renmano Wines Pty Ltd*
Chief Winemaker: *Reg Wilkinson*
Year of foundation: *1914*
Location of principal vineyards: *Riverland*
Leading wines: *Chairman's Selection Chardonnay, Hermitage and Cabernet*
Tonnes crushed on average each year: *15 000*
Best recent vintages: *Red—1991, 1993, 1990, 1992, 1988; White—1993, 1992, 1991*

REYNOLDS YARRAMAN
Yarraman Road
Wybong NSW 2333
Ph (065) 478 127, Fax (065) 478 013
Owners: *Jon and Jane Reynolds*
Chief Winemaker: *Jon Reynolds*
Year of foundation: *1978*
Location of principal vineyards: *Upper Hunter Valley and Orange*
Leading wines: *Semillon, Chardonnay, Cabernet-Merlot*
Tonnes crushed on average each year: *250*
Tonnes crushed in 1993: *300*
Best recent vintages: *Red—1993; White—1991*

RIBBON VALE ESTATE
Caves Road
Willyabrup WA 6284
Ph (097) 556 272
Owner: *John James*
Chief Winemaker: *Mike Davies*
Year of foundation: *1977*
Location of principal vineyards: *Willyabrup*
Leading wines: *Sauvignon Blanc, Semillon, Cabernet-Merlot*
Tonnes crushed on average each year: *50*
Tonnes crushed in 1993: *50*
Best recent vintages: *Red—1990; White—1993*

RICHARD HAMILTON WINERY
Main Road
Willunga SA 5172
Ph (085) 562 288, Fax (085) 562 868
Owner: *Dr Richard Hamilton*
Chief Winemaker: *Ralph Fowler*
Year of foundation: *1972*
Location of principal vineyards: *McLaren Vale and Willunga*
Leading wines: *Chardonnay, Hut Block Cabernet Sauvignon, Old Vines Shiraz*
Best recent vintages: *Red and White—1993, 1991, 1990*

RICHMOND GROVE BAROSSA
Para Road
Tanunda SA 5352
Ph (085) 632 204, Fax (085) 632 804
Owner: *Orlando Wyndham*
Chief Winemaker: *John Vickery*
Year of foundation: *1897*
Location of principal vineyards: *Barossa Valley*
Leading wines: *Barossa Shiraz, Barossa Semillon, Eden Valley Rhine Riesling*
Tonnes crushed on average each year: *approx. 10 000*
Tonnes crushed in 1993: *Nil (winery acquired by Orlando Wyndham late in 1993)*

RICHMOND GROVE POKOLBIN
Hermitage Road
Pokolbin NSW 2320
Ph (049) 987 792, Fax (049) 987 786
Owner: *Orlando Wyndham*

Chief Winemaker: *Steve Clarkson*
Year of foundation: *1974*
Location of principal vineyards: *Hunter Valley and Cowra*
Leading wines: *French Cask Chardonnay, Cowra Chardonnay, Cabernet-Merlot*
Best recent vintages: *Red—1990, White—1992*

RIDDOCH
Penola Road
Coonawarra SA 5263
Ph (087) 372 394, Fax (087) 372 377
Owner: *Katnook Pty Ltd*
Chief Winemaker: *Wayne Stehbens*
Year of foundation: *1977*
Location of principal vineyards: *Coonawarra*
Leading wines: *Sauvignon Blanc, Chardonnay, Cabernet-Shiraz*
Best recent vintages: *Red—1990; White—1992*

ROCKFORD WINES
Krondorf Road
Tanunda SA 5352
Ph (085) 632 720, Fax (085) 633 787
Owner: *Tanunda Vintners Pty Ltd*
Chief Winemaker: *Robert O'Callaghan*
Year of foundation: *1984*
Location of principal vineyards: *Barossa Valley*
Leading wines: *Basket Press Shiraz, Black Shiraz, Local Growers Semillon*
Tonnes crushed on average each year: *300*
Tonnes crushed in 1993: *250*
Best recent vintages: *Red—1987, 1988, 1990, 1991; White—1989, 1990, 1991, 1992*

ROSEMOUNT ESTATES
Rosemount Road
Denman NSW 2328
Ph (065) 472 467
Owner: *R.I. Oatley BEM*
Chief Winemaker: *Philip Shaw*
Year of foundation: *1969*
Location of principal vineyards: *Hunter Valley, Coonawarra, Langhorne Creek, McLaren Vale*
Leading wines: *Roxburgh Chardonnay, McLaren Vale Syrah, Coonawarra Cabernet Sauvignon*
Best recent vintages: *Red—1990, 1991; White—1990, 1993*

ROSSETTO WINES
Farm 576
Beelbangera NSW 2680
Ph (069) 635 214, Fax (069) 635 542
Owners: *Garry Rossetto, Brian Rossetto, Kevin Rossetto, Bianca Rossetto*
Chief Winemaker: *Eddie Rossi*
Year of foundation: *1930*
Location of principal vineyards: *Beelbangera and Griffith*
Leading wines: *Chardonnay, Semillon, Shiraz*
Tonnes crushed on average each year: *7500*
Tonnes crushed in 1993: *10 000*
Best recent vintages: *Red—1989, 1990, 1991, 1993, 1992; White—1988, 1989, 1991, 1992, 1993*

THE ROTHBURY ESTATE
Broke Road
Pokolbin NSW 2320
Ph (049) 987 555, Fax (049) 987 870
Owner: *Rothbury Wines Ltd*
Chief Winemaker: *Peter Hall*
Year of foundation: *1968*
Location of principal vineyards: *Pokolbin, Denman, Cowra, Marlborough (New Zealand)*
Leading wines: *Chardonnay, Shiraz, Semillon*

Tonnes crushed on average each year: *3000*
Tonnes crushed in 1993: *3000*
Best recent vintages: *Red—1989, 1991, 1993; White—1989, 1992, 1993*

ROUGE HOMME WINES
Memorial Drive
Coonawarra SA 5263
Ph (087) 363 205, Fax (087) 363 250
Owner: *Southcorp Holdings*
Chief Winemaker: *Paul Gordon*
Year of foundation: *1908*
Location of principal vineyards: *Coonawarra*
Leading wines: *Coonawarra Pinot Noir, Coonawarra Chardonnay*
Best recent vintages: *Red—1990, 1991; White—1990, 1991, 1992*

ROVALLEY WINES PTY LTD
Barossa Valley Way
Rowland Flat SA 5352
Ph (085) 244 537, Fax (085) 244 066
Owners: *Sam, Lou and Jim Miranda*
Chief Winemaker: *Shayne Cunningham*
Year of foundation: *1919*
Location of principal vineyards: *Barossa Valley*
Leading wines: *Rovalley Ridge Old Vine Shiraz, Rovalley Ridge Show Reserve Shiraz-Cabernet, Rovalley Ridge Show Reserve Chardonnay*
Tonnes crushed on average each year: *4500*
Tonnes crushed in 1993: *6000*
Best recent vintages: *Red—1991, 1992; White—1992, 1993*

RYECROFT VINEYARDS PTY LTD
Ingoldby Road
McLaren Flat SA 5171
Ph (08) 383 0001, Fax (08) 383 0456
Owner: *Robert I Oatley*
Chief Winemaker: *Nick Holmes*
Year of foundation: *1988*
Location of principal vineyards: *McLaren Vale*
Leading wines: *Traditional (blended dry red), Flame Tree Contemporary Chardonnay, Flame Tree Shiraz*
Best recent vintages: *Red—1990; White—1992*

RYMILL WINERY
The Riddoch Run Vineyard
Coonawarra SA 5263
Ph (087) 365 001, Fax (087) 365 040
Owners: *R. & J. Rymill*
Chief Winemaker: *John Innes*
Year of foundation: *1972*
Location of principal vineyards: *Coonawarra*
Leading wines: *Rymill, The Riddoch Run*
Tonnes crushed on average each year: *600*
Tonnes crushed in 1993: *600*
Best recent vintages: *Red and White—1990, 1991, 1992, 1993*

S

ST HALLETT WINES
St Halletts Road
Tanunda SA 5352
Ph (085) 632 319, Fax (085) 632 901
Owner: *Private company*
Chief Winemakers: *Stuart Blackwell and Peter Gambetta*
Year of foundation: *1944*
Location of principal vineyards: *Barossa Valley*
Leading wines: *Old Block Shiraz, Cabernet-Merlot, Chardonnay*
Tonnes crushed on average each year: *700*
Tonnes crushed in 1993: *650*
Best recent vintages: *Red—1990; White—1991*

ST HUBERTS
St Huberts Road
Coldstream Vic 3770
Ph (03) 739 1421, Fax (03) 739 1015
Owner: *Rothbury Wines Ltd*
Chief Winemaker: *Greg Traught*
Year of foundation: *1966*
Location of principal vineyards: *Yarra Valley*
Leading wines: *Cabernet Sauvignon, Chardonnay, Pinot Noir*
Tonnes crushed on average each year: *300*
Tonnes crushed in 1993: *300*
Best recent vintages: *Red—1988, 1990, 1991; White—1991, 1992*

ST LEONARDS VINEYARD
St Leonards Road
Wahgunyah Vic 3687
Ph (060) 331 004, Fax (060) 333 636
Owner: *Brown Brothers Milawa Vineyard Pty Ltd*
Chief Winemaker: *Terry Barnett*
Year of foundation: *1860*
Location of principal vineyards: *St Leonards, Wahgunyah*
Leading wines: *Chardonnay, Cabernet Sauvignon, Wahgunyah Shiraz*
Best recent vintages: *Red—1992, 1991, 1990; White—1992, 1991, 1989*

SALTRAM WINE ESTATES
Salters Gully
Angaston SA 5353
Ph (085) 638 200, Fax (085) 642 209
Owner: *Rothbury Wines Ltd*
Chief Winemaker: *Nigel Dolan*
Year of foundation: *1859*
Location of principal vineyards: *Barossa, Eden Valley, Clare*
Leading wines: *Pinnacle Selection, Mamre Brook, Classic Varietals*
Best recent vintages: *Red—1993, 1990; White—1993, 1992*

SANDALFORD WINES PTY LTD
3210 West Swan Road
Caversham WA 6055
Ph (09) 274 5922, Fax (09) 274 2154
Owners: *Peter Prendiville and Paul Naughton*
Chief Winemaker: *Bill Crappsley*
Year of foundation: *1840*
Location of principal vineyards: *Swan Valley, Margaret River, Mount Barker*
Leading wines: *Margaret River Verdelho, Margaret River Cabernet Sauvignon, Sandalera*
Tonnes crushed on average each year: *1000*
Tonnes crushed in 1993: *600*
Best recent vintages: *Red—1991, 1992, 1993; White—1988, 1991, 1993*

SCARBOROUGH WINE CO
Gillards Lane
Pokolbin NSW 2320
Ph (049) 987 563, Fax (049) 987 786
Owners: *I. & M. Scarborough*
Chief Winemaker: *Ian Scarborough*
Year of foundation: *1987*
Leading wines: *Chardonnay, Pinot Noir*
Best recent vintages: *Red and White—1989, 1990, 1991, 1992, 1993*

SCARPANTONI ESTATE WINES
Scarpantoni Drive
McLaren Flat SA 5171
Ph (08) 383 0186, Fax (08) 383 490
Owners: *Domenico, Paula, Michael and Filippo Scarpantoni*
Chief Winemakers: *Michael and Filippo Scarpantoni*
Year of foundation: *1979*
Leading wines: *Cabernet-Merlot-Shiraz, Block 3 Shiraz, Chardonnay*

Tonnes crushed on average each year: *150*
Tonnes crushed in 1993: *150*
Best recent vintages: *Red—1990, 1992, 1993, 1991, 1989; White—1992, 1990, 1989, 1993, 1991*

SEAVIEW WINERY
Chaffeys Road
McLaren Vale SA 5171
Ph (08) 383 8250, Fax (08) 323 9208
Owner: *Southcorp Holdings*
Chief Winemaker: *Mike Farmilo*
Year of foundation: *1855*
Location of principal vineyards: *McLaren Vale*
Leading wines: *Champagne, Chardonnay, Cabernet Sauvignon*
Best recent vintages: *Red—1990, 1991; White—1990, 1993*

KARL SEPPELT GRAND CRU ESTATE
Ross Dewell's Road
Springton SA 5235
Ph (085) 682 378, Fax (085) 682 799
Owner: *Karl Seppelt*
Chief Winemakers: *Karl Seppelt and Petaluma Ltd*
Year of foundation: *1981*
Location of principal vineyards: *Springton*
Leading wines: *Chardonnay, Cabernet Sauvignon, Chardonnay Brut*
Tonnes crushed on average each year: *60*
Tonnes crushed in 1993: *45*
Best recent vintages: *Red—1990, 1991, 1992; White—1989, 1992*

SEPPELTS WINES
Great Western Vic 3377
Ph (053) 562 202, Fax (053) 562 300
Owners: *Southcorp Holdings*
Chief Winemaker: *Ian McKenzie*
Year of foundation: *1851*
Location of principal vineyards: *Great Western, Drumborg*
Leading wines: *Chardonnay, Hermitage, Salinger Sparkling*
Best recent vintages: *Red and White—1988, 1990, 1991, 1992*

SERENELLA ESTATE
Mudgee Road
Baerami Via Denman NSW 2333
Ph (065) 475 168, Fax (065) 475 164
Owners: *Cecchini Family*
Chief Winemaker: *Letitia (Tish) Cecchini*
Year of foundation: *1989*
Location of principal vineyards: *Baerami, Upper Hunter*
Leading wines: *Chardonnay, Shiraz, Cabernet Sauvignon*
Tonnes crushed on average each year: *100*
Tonnes crushed in 1993: *Less than 100*
Best recent vintages: *Red—1991; White—1992, 1993*

SEVENHILL CELLARS
Sevenhill via Clare SA 5453
Ph (088) 434 222, Fax (088) 434 382
Owner: *Manresa Society*
Chief Winemakers: *Bro. John May and John Monten*
Year of foundation: *1851*
Location of principal vineyards: *Sevenhill*
Leading wines: *Rhine Riesling, Shiraz, St Aloysius*
Tonnes crushed on average each year: *289*
Tonnes crushed in 1993: *175*
Best recent vintages: *Red—1989, 1991, 1993; White—1989, 1991, 1992*

SEVILLE ESTATE
Linwood Road
Seville Vic 3139

Ph (059) 644 556, Fax (059) 643 585
Owners: *P.G. & M.L. McMahon*
Chief Winemaker: *Peter McMahon*
Year of foundation: *1972*
Leading wines: *Cabernet Blend, Pinot Noir, Chardonnay*
Tonnes crushed on average each year: *25*
Tonnes crushed in 1993: 23
Best recent vintages: *Red and White—1991, 1990, 1988*

SHANTELL VINEYARD
Melba Highway
Dixons Creek Vic 3775
Ph (059) 652 264, Fax (059) 652 331
Owners: *Drs N. & T. Shanmugam*
Chief Winemaker: *N. Shanmugam*
Year of foundation: *1988*
Location of principal vineyards: *Dixons Creek*
Leading wines: *Chardonnay, Cabernet Sauvignon*
Tonnes crushed on average each year: 27
Tonnes crushed in 1993: 22
Best recent vintages: *Red and White—1990, 1988, 1992*

SHOTTESBROOKE VINEYARDS PTY LTD
Ingoldby Road
Myponga SA 5202
Ph (08) 383 0001, Fax (08) 383 0456
Owner and Chief Winemaker: *N.G. Holmes*
Year of foundation: *1981*
Location of principal vineyards: *Myponga (south of McLaren Vale)*
Leading wines: *Cabernet-Merlot-Malbec, Sauvignon Blanc*
Tonnes crushed on average each year: *60*
Tonnes crushed in 1993: *30*
Best recent vintages: *Red—1990; White—1993*

SKILLOGALEE WINES
Off Hughes Park Road
Skillogalee Valley via Clare SA 5453
Ph (088) 434 311, Fax (088) 434 343
Owners: *Dave & Diana Palmer*
Chief Winemaker: *Dave Palmer*
Year of foundation: *1970*
Location of principal vineyards: *Skillogalee*
Leading wines: *Riesling, Shiraz, The Cabernets (blend)*
Tonnes crushed on average each year: *100*
Tonnes crushed in 1993: *103*
Best recent vintages: *Red—1990, 1993; White—1991, 1993*

STAFFORD RIDGE
Stafford Road
Lenswood SA 5240
Ph (08) 272 2105, Fax (08) 271 0177
Owner and Chief Winemaker: *Geoff Weaver*
Location of principal vineyards: *Lenswood*
Leading wines: *Chardonnay, Sauvignon Blanc, Cabernet-Merlot*
Tonnes crushed on average each year: *70*
Tonnes crushed in 1993: *30*
Best recent vintages: *Red and White—1990*

THE STANLEY WINE CO
Silver City Highway
Buronga NSW 2648
Ph (050) 234 341, Fax (050) 234 344
Owner: *BRL Hardy Ltd*
Chief Winemaker: *Chris Proud*
Year of foundation: *1894*
Location of principal vineyards: *Riverland*

Leading wines: *Stanley, Buronga Ridge 2 and 4 litre casks*
Tonnes crushed on average each year: *30 000*
Tonnes crushed in 1993: *30 000*

STANTON AND KILLEEN WINES
Jacks Road
Rutherglen Vic 3685
Ph (060) 329 457, Fax (060) 328 018
Owner: *Killeen Family*
Chief Winemaker: *Chris Killeen*
Year of foundation: *1875*
Location of principal vineyards: *Rutherglen*
Leading wines: *Liqueur Muscat, Vintage Port, Moodemere Red (Durif)*
Tonnes crushed on average each year: *100*
Tonnes crushed in 1993: *95*
Best recent vintages: *Red—1992, 1990, 1987; White—1990*

STONE RIDGE VINEYARDS
Limberlost Road
Glen Aplin Qld 4381
Ph (076) 834 211
Owners and Chief Winemakers: *Jim Lawrie and Anne Kennedy*
Location of principal vineyards: *Granite Belt (Stanthorpe)*
Leading wines: *Chardonnay, Shiraz, Mount Sterling Dry Red*
Tonnes crushed on average each year: *22*
Tonnes crushed in 1993: *16.5*
Best recent vintages: *Red—1988, 1993, 1991, 1989; White—1993, 1992, 1991, 1990*

STONIERS
362 Frankston-Flinders Road
Merricks Vic 3916
Ph (059) 898 300, Fax (059) 898 709
Owner: *Stonier, Yuill & Limb Pty Ltd*
Chief Winemaker: *Tod Dexter*
Year of foundation: *1978*
Location of principal vineyards: *Mornington Peninsula*
Leading wines: *Reserve Chardonnay, Reserve Pinot Noir, Reserve Cabernet*
Tonnes crushed on average each year: *200*
Tonnes crushed in 1993: *188*
Best recent vintages: *Red and White—1988, 1990, 1991, 1992*

SUNNYCLIFF
Nangiloc Road
Iraak Vic 3496
Ph (050) 291 666, Fax (050) 243 316
Owner: *Katnook Pty Ltd*
Chief Winemaker: *Mark Zeppel*
Year of foundation: *1973*
Location of principal vineyards: *Iraak (Sunraysia)*
Leading wines: *Colombard-Chardonnay, Chardonnay, Cabernet Sauvignon*
Best recent vintages: *Red—1990; White—1993*

SUTHERLAND WINES
Deasys Road
Pokolbin NSW 2320
Ph (049) 987 650, Fax (049) 987 603
Owners: *Neil and Caroline Sutherland*
Chief Winemaker: *Neil Sutherland*
Year of foundation: *1979*
Location of principal vineyards: *Pokolbin*
Leading wines: *Semillon, Chardonnay, Shiraz*
Tonnes crushed on average each year: *100*
Tonnes crushed in 1993: *60*
Best recent vintages: *Red—1993, 1991, 1989; White—1993, 1991, 1990, 1989*

T

TALIJANCICH WINES PTY LTD
121 Hyem Road
Herne Hill WA 6056
Ph (09) 296 4289, Fax (09) 296 4289
Owners: *Mary and Peter Talijancich*
Chief Winemaker: *James Talijancich*
Year of foundation: *1932*
Location of principal vineyards: *Swan Valley*
Leading wines: *Verdelho, Liqueur Tokay, Liqueur Hermitage*
Tonnes crushed on average each year: *60*
Tonnes crushed in 1993: *55*

TALTARNI VINEYARDS
Taltarni Road
Moonambel Vic 3478
Ph (054) 672 218, Fax (054) 672 306
Owner: *Red Earth Nominees Pty Ltd*
Chief Winemaker: *Greg Gallagher*
Location of principal vineyards: *Moonambel and Lebrina (Tasmania)*
Leading wines: *Fumé Blanc, Cabernet Sauvignon, Clover Hill (Tasmanian sparkling)*
Tonnes crushed on average each year: *700*
Tonnes crushed in 1993: *658*
Best recent vintages: *Red—1991; White—1992*

TAMBURLAINE
McDonald's Road
Pokolbin NSW 2320
Ph (049) 987 570, Fax (049) 987 763
Owner: *Privately owned*
Chief Winemaker: *G.B. Silkman*
Year of foundation: *1966*
Location of principal vineyards: *Lower Hunter Valley*
Leading wines: *The Chapel Reserve Dry Red, Chardonnay, Verdelho*
Tonnes crushed on average each year: *below 200*
Tonnes crushed in 1993: *109*
Best recent vintages: *Red and White—1989, 1991, 1993*

TARRAWARRA VINEYARD PTY LTD
Healesville Road
Yarra Glen Vic 3775
Ph (059) 623 311, Fax (059) 623 887
Owner: *Besen and Wollan Families*
Chief Winemakers: *David Wollan, Martin Williams*
Year of foundation: *1983*
Location of principal vineyard: *Yarra Glen*
Leading wines: *Chardonnay, Pinot Noir, Tunnel Hill Chardonnay*
Tonnes crushed on average each year: *120*
Tonnes crushed in 1993: *100*
Best recent vintages: *Red—1992, 1990, 1991; White—1990, 1992, 1988*

TAYLORS WINES PTY LTD
Mintaro Road
Auburn SA 5451
Ph (088) 492 008, Fax (088) 492 240
Owner: *Taylor Family*
Chief Winemaker: *Andrew Tolley*
Year of foundation: *1972*
Location of principal vineyards: *Auburn*
Leading wines: *Cabernet Sauvignon, Hermitage, Chardonnay*
Tonnes crushed on average each year: *2800*
Tonnes crushed in 1993: *1500*
Best recent vintages: *Red—1989, 1992, 1990; White—1992, 1989*

TERRACE VALE WINES PTY LTD
Deasy's Road
Pokolbin NSW 2320
Ph (049) 987 517, Fax (049) 987 814

Owner: *Private company*
Chief Winemaker: *Alain Leprince*
Year of foundation: *1971*
Location of principal vineyards: *Pokolbin*
Leading wines: *Semillon, Chardonnay, Shiraz*
Tonnes crushed on average each year: *90*
Tonnes crushed in 1993: *96*
Best recent vintages: *Red and White—1989, 1991*

THISTLE HILL VINEYARD
McDonalds Road
Mudgee NSW 2850
Ph (063) 733 546, Fax (063) 733 540
Owners: *David and Lesley Robertson*
Chief Winemaker: *David Robertson*
Year of foundation: *1976*
Location of principal vineyards: *Mudgee*
Leading wines: *Cabernet Sauvignon, Chardonnay, Pinot Noir*
Tonnes crushed on average each year: *70*
Tonnes crushed in 1993: *78*
Best recent vintages: *Red—1990; White—1992*

THOMAS FERN HILL ESTATE
Ingoldby Road
McLaren Flat SA 5171
Ph (08) 383 0167, Fax (08) 383 0107
Owners: *W.S. & P.J. Thomas*
Chief Winemaker: *Wayne Thomas*
Year of foundation: *1973*
Location of principal vineyards: *McLaren Flat*
Leading wines: *Shiraz, Cabernet Sauvignon, Chardonnay*
Tonnes crushed on average each year: *100*
Tonnes crushed in 1993: *60*
Best recent vintages: *Red—1990; White—1987*

TISDALL WINES
19 Cornelia Creek Road
Echuca Vic 3564
Ph (054) 821 911, Fax (054) 822 516
Owner: *Mildara Blass*
Chief Winemaker: *Toni Stockhausen*
Year of foundation: *1979*
Location of principal vineyards: *Picola, Heathcote*
Leading wines: *Cabernet Merlot, Mount Helen Chardonnay, Mount Helen Cabernet Sauvignon-Merlot*
Tonnes crushed on average each year: *2000*
Tonnes crushed in 1993: *1200*
Best recent vintages: *Red—1992, 1990, 1988, 1986; White—1993, 1992, 1990*

TOLLANA WINES PTY LTD
Tanunda Road
Nuriootpa SA 5355
Ph (085) 620 389, Fax (085) 622 494
Owner: *Southcorp Holdings*
Chief Winemaker: *Neville Falkenberg*
Year of foundation: *1858*
Location of principal vineyards: *Eden Valley, Adelaide Hills*
Leading wines: *Cabernet Sauvignon Bin TR222, Eden Valley Rhine Riesling, Botrytis Rhine Riesling*
Best recent vintages: *Red—1991, 1993; White—1990, 1992*

TOLLEY WINES PTY LTD
30 Barracks Road
Hope Valley SA 5090
Ph (08) 264 2255, Fax (08) 263 7485
Owner: *Tolley Family*
Chief Winemaker: *Chris Tolley*
Year of foundation: *1892*

Location of principal vineyards: *Padthaway, Barossa*
Leading wines: *Pedare Chardonnay, Pedare Gewürztraminer, Pedare Cabernet Sauvignon*
Tonnes crushed on average each year: *2500*
Tonnes crushed in 1993: *2400*
Best recent vintages: *Red and White—1992*

TONKINS CURRENCY CREEK WINES PTY LTD
Winery Road
Currency Creek SA 5214
Ph (085) 554 069, Fax (085) 554 100
Owner: *W.R. & R. A Tonkin*
Chief Winemaker: *Phillip Tonkin*
Year of foundation: *1969*
Location of principal vineyards: *Currency Creek*
Leading wines: *Chardonnay, Sauvignon Blanc, Cabernet Sauvignon*
Tonnes crushed on average each year: *60 but increasing*
Tonnes crushed in 1993: *80*
Best recent vintages: *Red—1987, 1989, 1990; White—1989, 1990, 1993*

TRENTHAM ESTATE
Sturt Highway
Trentham Cliffs Vic 3458
Ph (050) 248 888, Fax (050) 248 800
Owners: *Anthony, Nola and Pat Murphy*
Chief Winemaker: *Anthony Murphy*
Year of foundation: *1988*
Location of principal vineyards: *Trentham Cliffs*
Leading wines: *Chardonnay, Merlot, Shiraz*
Tonnes crushed on average each year: *220*
Tonnes crushed in 1993: *240*
Best recent vintages: *Red and White—1992*

TULLOCH WINES
Glen Elgin Estate
Pokolbin NSW 2320
Ph (049) 987 503, Fax (049) 987 682
Owner: *Southcorp Holdings*
Chief Winemaker: *Jay Tulloch*
Year of foundation: *1893*
Location of principal vineyards: *Pokolbin*
Leading wines: *Hector of Glen Elgin (red), Verdelho, Hunter Cuvée (sparkling)*
Best recent vintages: *Red—1986, 1987, 1991; White—1986, 1987, 1990, 1992*

TYRRELL'S ASHMANS
Broke Road
Pokolbin NSW 2320
Ph (049) 987 509, Fax (049) 987 723
Owner: *Tyrrell Family*
Chief Winemaker: *Murray Tyrell*
Year of foundation: *1858*
Location of principal vineyards: *Hunter Valley*
Leading wines: *Vat 47 Chardonnay, Old Winery Chardonnay, Long Flat Red*
Tonnes crushed on average each year: *2500*
Tonnes crushed in 1993: *2000*
Best recent vintages: *Red—1991; White—1991, 1992*

V

THE VALES WINE COMPANY PTY LTD
Main Road
McLaren Vale SA 5171
Ph (08) 323 8656, Fax (08) 323 9096
Owner: *Privately Owned*
Chief Winemaker: *Michael Fragos*
Year of foundation: *1902*

Location of principal vineyards: *McLaren Vale*
Leading Wines: *Shiraz, Chardonnay, Cabernet Sauvignon*
Tonnes crushed on average each year: *2200*
Tonnes crushed in 1993: *1200*
Best recent vintages: *Red—1991; White—1992*

VERITAS WINERY
94 Langmeil Road
Tanunda SA 5352
Ph (085) 632 330
Owner: *R.H. Binder Pty Ltd*
Chief Winemaker: *Rolf Binder*
Year of foundation: *1955*
Location of principal vineyards: *Barossa Valley*
Leading wines: *Hanrsch Vineyard Shiraz, Chardonnay, Binders Bull's Blood*
Tonnes crushed on average each year: *150*
Tonnes crushed in 1993: *120*
Best recent vintages: *Red—1991, 1990, 1988; White—1992, 1990, 1991*

VICARY'S WINERY
Northern Road
Luddenham NSW 2745
Ph (047) 734 207, Fax (047) 734 411
Owner: *Ross Carbery*
Chief Winemaker: *Chris Niccol*
Year of foundation: *1923*
Location of principal vineyards: *Luddenham, Camden*
Leading wines: *Chardonnay, Traminer, Cabernet*
Tonnes crushed on average each year: *80*
Tonnes crushed in 1993: *120*
Best recent vintages: *Red—1989, 1990, 1991; White—1993, 1991, 1989*

VIRGIN HILLS
Kyneton Vic 3444
Ph (054) 239 169, Fax (054) 239 324
Owner: *Gilbert Family*
Chief Winemaker: *Mark Sheppard*
Year of foundation: *1968*
Location of principal vineyards: *Kyneton*
Leading wine: *Virgin Hills (dry red)*
Tonnes crushed on average each year: *50*
Tonnes crushed in 1993: *35*
Best recent vintages: *Red—1988, 1991, 1992*

W

WANTIRNA ESTATE VINEYARD
Bushy Park Lane
Wantirna South Vic 3152
Ph (03) 801 2367, Fax (03) 887 0225
Owners; R.F. & B.M. Egan
Chief Winemaker: *R.F. Egan*
Year of foundation: *1963*
Location of principal vineyards: *Wantirna South*
Leading wines: *Cabernet Sauvignon-Merlot, Pinot Noir, Chardonnay*
Tonnes crushed on average each year: *20*
Tonnes crushed in 1993: *15*
Best recent vintages: *Red and White: all except 1989*

WARRENMANG
Mountain Creek Road
Moonambel Vic 3478
Ph (054) 672 233, Fax (054) 672 309
Owners: *Luigi and Athalie Bazzani*
Chief Winemaker: *Roland Kaval*
Year of foundation: *1974*
Location of principal vineyards: *Moonambel*

Leading wines: *Grand Pyrenees (red blend), Bazzani Cabernet-Shiraz-Dolcetto, Bazzani Chardonnay-Chenin Blanc*
Tonnes crushed on average each year: *50*
Tonnes crushed in 1993: *57*
Best recent vintages: *Red—1991, 1992, 1993, 1990; White—1992, 1993, 1990, 1991*

WIGNALLS KING RIVER WINES
Chester Pass Road
Albany WA 6330
Ph (098) 412 848, Fax (098) 412 848
Owners: *Bill, Pat and Robert Wignall*
Chief Winemaker: *John Wade*
Year of foundation: *1982*
Location of principal vineyards: *King River, Albany*
Leading Wines: *Pinot Noir, Chardonnay, Sauvignon Blanc*
Tonnes crushed on average each year: *80*
Tonnes crushed in 1993: *80*
Best recent vintages: *Red—1992, 1991, 1990, 1988, 1987; White—1992, 1991, 1990, 1989, 1988*

THE WILSON VINEYARD
Polish Hill River
Sevenhill via Clare SA 5453
Ph (088) 434 310
Owner: *Wilson Family*
Chief Winemaker: *John Wilson*
Year of foundation: *1980*
Location of principal vineyards: *Polish Hill River*
Leading wines: *Gallery Series Riesling and Cabernet Sauvignon, Hippocrene (sparkling red)*
Tonnes crushed on average each year: *60*
Tonnes crushed in 1993: *37*
Best recent vintages: *Red—1992, 1990; White—1993, 1991, 1989*

WILLESPIE
Harmans Mill Road
Willyabrup WA 6284
Ph (097) 556 248, Fax (097) 556 210
Owners: *Kevin and Marian Squance*
Chief Winemaker: *Michael Lemmes*
Year of foundation: *1976*
Location of principal vineyards: *Willyabrup*
Leading wines: *Cabernet Sauvignon, Verdelho, Semillon-Sauvignon Blanc*
Tonnes crushed on average each year: *75*
Tonnes crushed in 1993: *59*
Best recent vintages: *Red—1987, 1990, 1991, 1988, 1989; White—1991, 1987, 1985, 1990, 1993*

WIRRA WIRRA VINEYARDS
McMurtrie Road
McLaren Vale SA 5171
Ph (08) 323 8414, Fax (08) 323 8596
Owners: *R.G. & R.T. Trott Pty Ltd*
Chief Winemaker: *Ben J. Riggs*
Year of foundation: *1969*
Location of principal vineyards: *McLaren Vale and Blewitt Springs*
Leading wines: *Church Block (red blend), Hand Picked Riesling*
Best recent vintages: *Red—1991, 1990; White—1991, 1993*

WOLF BLASS WINES
Sturt Highway
Nuriootpa SA 5355
Ph (085) 621 955
Owner: *Mildara Blass*
Chief Winemakers: *Chris Hatcher (white), John Glaetzer (red)*
Year of foundation: *1971*

Location of principal vineyards: *Barossa Valley, Eden Valley, Langhorne Creek*
Leading wines: *Black Label (red blend) Brown Label Classic Shiraz, Gold Label Rhine Riesling*
Tonnes crushed on average each year: *5000*
Tonnes crushed in 1993: *4900*
Best recent vintages: *Red—1990, 1991, 1992; White—1991, 1992*

WOODSTOCK
Douglas Gully Road
McLaren Flat SA 5171
Ph (08) 383 0156, Fax (08) 383 0437
Owners: *Collett Wines Pty Ltd*
Chief Winemaker: *Scott Collett*
Year of foundation: *1973*
Location of principal vineyards: *McLaren Flat*
Leading wines: *Cabernet Sauvignon, Shiraz, Chardonnay*
Tonnes crushed on average each year: *250*
Tonnes crushed in 1993: *190*
Best recent vintages: *Red and White—1991, 1992*

WYNDHAM ESTATE
Dalwood via Branxton NSW 2335
Ph (049) 383 444, Fax (049) 383 422
Owner: *Orlando Wyndham*
Chief Winemaker: *John Baruzzi*
Year of foundation: *1828*
Location of principal vineyards: *Hunter Valley*
Leading wines: *Chardonnay Bin 222, Cabernet Bin 444, Selected Hermitage Bin 555*
Best recent vintages: *Red and White—1990*

WYNNS COONAWARRA ESTATE
Memorial Drive
Coonawarra SA 5263
Ph (087) 363 266, Fax (087) 363 202
Owner: *Southcorp Holdings*
Chief Winemaker: *Peter Douglas*
Year of foundation: *1891*
Location of principal vineyards: *Coonawarra*
Leading wines: *John Riddoch Cabernet Sauvignon, Chardonnay, Michael Hermitage*
Best recent vintages: *Red—1990, 1991; White—1991, 1993*

Y

YALUMBA WINERY
Eden Valley Road
Angaston SA 5353
Ph (085) 613 200, Fax (085) 613 393
Owners: *Robert and Sam Hill Smith*
Chief Winemaker: *Brian Walsh*
Year of foundation: *1849*
Location of principal vineyards: *Coonawarra, Oxford Landing (Riverland)*
Leading wines: *Yalumba D (sparkling) Signature Cabernet Sauvignon and Shiraz, Menzies Coonawarra Cabernet Sauvignon*
Tonnes crushed on average each year: *15 000*
Tonnes crushed in 1993: *15 000*
Best recent vintages: *Red—1990, 1991, 1992; White—1992, 1993, 1990*

YARRA BURN WINERY
Settlement Road
Yarra Junction Vic 3797
Ph (059) 671 428, Fax (059) 671 146
Owners: *David and Christine Fyffe*
Chief Winemaker: *David Fyffe*
Location of principal vineyards: *Yarra Junction*
Leading wines: *Chardonnay, Pinot Noir, Cabernets*
Tonnes crushed on average each year: *80*

Tonnes crushed in 1993: *75*
Best recent vintages: *Red and white—1990*

YARRA RIDGE VINEYARD
Glenview Road
Yarra Glen Vic 3775
Ph (03) 415 1420, Fax (03) 415 1421
Owners: *Mildara Blass (51%) and Louis Bialkower (49%)*
Chief Winemaker: *Rob Dolan*
Year of foundation: *1983*
Location of principal vineyards: *Yarra Glen*
Leading wines: *Chardonnay, Sauvignon Blanc, Pinot noir*
Best recent vintages: *Red and White—1989, 1993*

YELLOWGLEN
Whytes Road
Smythesdale Vic 3351
Ph (053) 428 617
Owner: *Mildara Blass*
Chief Winemaker: *Jeffrey Wilkinson*
Location of principal vineyards: *Ballarat*
Leading wines: *Only Methode Champenoise sparkling wines made*
Tonnes crushed on average each year: *4000*
Tonnes crushed in 1993: *4000*
Best recent vintages: *White—1991, 1990, 1993*

YERING STATION
Melba Highway
Yering Vic 3770
Ph (03) 730 1107
Owner: *Joint Venture of Jim Domingues and Family*
Chief Winemaker: *St Hubert's (by contract)*
Year of foundation: *1838 re-established 1988*
Location of principal vineyards: *Yering (Yarra Valley)*
Leading wines: *Chardonnay, Pinot Noir and Cabernets*
Tonnes crushed on average each year: *100*
Tonnes crushed in 1993: *74*
Best recent vintages: *Red—1991, 1992; White—1991, 1992*

Z

ZEMA ESTATE
Main Road
Coonawarra SA 5263
Ph (087) 363 219, Fax (087) 363 280
Owner: *Zema Family*
Chief Winemaker: *Matt Zema*
Year of foundation: *1982*
Location of principal vineyards: *Coonawarra*
Leading wines: *Cabernet Sauvignon, Shiraz, Family Selection Cabernet Sauvignon*
Tonnes crushed on average each year: *100*
Tonnes crushed in 1993: *70*
Best recent vintages: *Red—1992, 1990, 1991*

Index

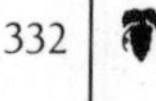